Future of Business and Finance

The Future of Business and Finance book series features professional works aimed at defining, analyzing, and charting the future trends in these fields. The focus is mainly on strategic directions, technological advances, challenges and solutions which may affect the way we do business tomorrow, including the future of sustainability and governance practices. Mainly written by practitioners, consultants and academic thinkers, the books are intended to spark and inform further discussions and developments.

Jens Kawelke · Thomas Niebisch

AI-Driven Transformation - Practical Frameworks for Real-World Impact

From Structured Requirements to Agentic Systems

Springer

Jens Kawelke
Glonn, Germany

Thomas Niebisch
Leipzig, Germany

ISSN 2662-2467 ISSN 2662-2475 (electronic)
Future of Business and Finance
ISBN 978-3-662-72548-1 ISBN 978-3-662-72549-8 (eBook)
https://doi.org/10.1007/978-3-662-72549-8

This book is a translation of the original German edition "Anforderungsmanagement in sieben Tagen," 2nd edition, by Thomas Niebisch and Jens Kawelke, published by Springer-Verlag GmbH, DE in 2024. The translation was done with the help of an artificial intelligence machine translation tool. A subsequent human revision was done primarily in terms of content, so that the book will read stylistically differently from a conventional translation. Springer Nature works continuously to further the development of tools for the production of books and on the related technologies to support the authors.

Updated and extended English-language edition based on the authors' original German textbook 'Anforderungsmanagement in sieben Tagen' (Springer Gabler, 2024).

This Springer imprint is published by the registered company Springer-Verlag GmbH, DE, part of Springer Nature.
The registered company address is: Heidelberger Platz 3, 14197 Berlin, Germany

Preface

The Journey Ahead

Artificial Intelligence, and in particular Generative AI (GenAI), has captured the imagination of professionals across industries. From spectacular headlines about new large language models to bold visions of self-directed, agentic systems, the possibilities seem endless. Yet for many organizations, these possibilities raise an uncomfortable question: *where do we actually begin?*

This book takes a pragmatic view of that question. We do not start with science fiction scenarios, nor do we assume that enterprises can—or should—leap directly into Agentic AI environments where processes are dynamically designed and changed on the fly. Such a "big bang" approach, from 0 to 100, would most likely overwhelm employees who have been used to fixed, predefined processes for years. Instead, we present a structured journey that begins with tangible, manageable steps and gradually builds toward more ambitious transformations.

Part I, *Structured and GenAI Enhanced Requirements Engineering*, stays deliberately focused. It introduces the reader to the discipline of Requirements Engineering (RE) and illustrates, through our example company, how GenAI can be applied carefully to enhance existing process steps: supporting requirement elicitation, structuring, and documentation. Here, GenAI is not portrayed as a revolution but as a supportive tool that augments proven methods. This mirrors the situation of our example company, which is only at the beginning of its GenAI transformation path. We suggest this as a sensible starting point for every organization: begin where GenAI naturally strengthens existing practices, and allow employees to gain confidence before aiming higher.

From a GenAI perspective, requirements engineering and its processes serve here as an illustrative example of how a discipline can be enhanced. From a requirements engineering perspective, GenAI provides a timely opportunity to augment established methods with new capabilities, reducing effort while improving clarity and stakeholder alignment.

Part II, *From Generative to Agentic AI: Transforming Enterprises and Software Development*, then broadens the horizon. It explores how GenAI can scale beyond isolated process steps and how Agentic AI introduces a fundamentally new paradigm—where workflows are orchestrated dynamically, where processes adapt to input data and external factors, and where entire roles begin to converge in an example business process—the software development lifecycle. This part addresses not only RE experts but professionals across business functions who want to understand how AI is transforming work, processes, and enterprises at large.

While this book is based on our German edition, the English version goes beyond a conventional translation. We have added and expanded sections to reflect the rapid advances in artificial intelligence and their far-reaching impact—not only on requirements engineering, but also on software development and, more broadly, on how organizations work and create value.

> To the point:
>
> Part One serves as a fairly complete and modern textbook on requirements engineering, enriched with practical GenAI use cases. Part Two is covering the most important aspects of Generative and Agentic AI, and illustrating how these technologies are transforming enterprises, software development, and work itself.

Taken together, both parts of the book reflect our conviction that GenAI and Agentic AI should not be seen as distant abstractions, but as practical tools that every organization can engage with today. The key is to start where you are, take structured steps, and grow capabilities at a pace that empowers rather than overwhelms.

But why does a book on Requirements Engineering and Generative AI make sense? While much of the discussion in Part I focuses on how Generative AI can transform requirements engineering practices, the relationship is not one-sided. Requirements engineering itself has a great deal to offer for the development of GenAI systems. The discipline's rigor in eliciting, specifying, and validating needs helps ensure that GenAI technologies are solutions that genuinely align with stakeholder expectations, regulatory constraints, and organizational goals. Moreover, the clarity and structure that requirements engineers bring to documenting system needs can be directly applied to practices such as prompt and agent engineering. By treating prompts, interaction patterns, and agent behaviors as requirements artifacts, engineers can reduce ambiguity, increase reproducibility, and better align GenAI outputs with intended outcomes. In this way, requirements engineering not only benefits from GenAI, but also provides essential foundations for shaping how GenAI itself is engineered and governed.

We hope that this combination of structured methods, practical examples, and forward-looking insights will equip you—whether you are just someone interested in AI, a requirements engineer, prompt or agent engineer, project manager, process owner, or business leader—to navigate the evolving world of AI with clarity and confidence.

Notes on Formatting

We value the use of the book both as a continuously readable textbook and as a reference book. For quick finding of essential content, we use the following visual and design elements:

- Using words in italics or 'single quotation marks' highlight them for emphasis.
- Essential statements and questions within the chapters are brought—as practiced above—**To the point**.
- *Glossary entries*: Terms that might be unfamiliar or specialized, especially those connected to RE and AI, are defined in the glossary.

Source literature with direct reference to a text passage we list in the appendix of each chapter.

Glonn, Germany
Leipzig, Germany
January 2026

Jens Kawelke
Thomas Niebisch

Acknowledgements

From J. Kawelke: My thanks go especially to Thomas, who had the initial idea of writing a textbook on requirements engineering. He honored me by allowing me to contribute to this project and enrich the book with GenAI perspectives. I greatly appreciate his generosity, his expertise, and his openness in shaping this work together. Collaborating with him was not only productive, but also a rewarding experience that has influenced both the content of the book and my own professional growth.

I am also deeply grateful to many of my current and former colleagues at NTT DATA, who have been invaluable sparring partners in discussions about requirements engineering, GenAI, and the broader changes AI brings to enterprises. I would particularly like to highlight Josephine Tan, who constantly challenges assumptions and drives our thinking forward. I also thank Linda Müller and Jan Pensel, who not only lent their first names and appearance to fictional personas in this book, but who continually inspire me with their energy and creativity. While I cannot name everyone from our Competence Center "NextGen AI Accelerators," I want to emphasize how much I value being part of such a motivated and innovative team.

In addition, I would like to thank Johannes Wetterich for our many conversations on the future of GenAI, as well as on UI/UX design and its close connection to requirements engineering. I am grateful to Kristjan Kristjansson for his design inspirations and even the drawing with the soup pot that found its way into this book. For the background topic of contact centers, I owe special thanks to my NTT DATA colleague Martin Troll, who enriched our knowledge with his expertise and insights.

Beyond the professional sphere, I am thankful to my family—Claudia, Josefine, and Jasmin—who patiently gave me quiet mornings and constant encouragement while I was working on this manuscript. Finally, I want to acknowledge Sascha Nehm, Heike Johannes, Enno Kätelhön, and Julian Morelli Desanzo, whose companionship and inspiration have accompanied me throughout my journey into artificial intelligence.

From T. Niebisch: After writing two books—one on requirements engineering and one on process management I was looking for a partner to give those topics a new perspective and bringing it up to date. I am particularly pleased to have found a co-author in Jens Kawelke, who has contributed with profound RE and GenAI knowledge, fresh ideas, and a lot of practical experience. We were able to incorporate our different worlds of experience into this book.

For me, this collaboration was not only about continuing a professional journey, but also about opening up entirely new perspectives. While my focus has long been on structured methods and improving established practices, Jens brought in the momentum of Generative AI—a field that is transforming not only requirements engineering, but enterprises and work itself. I see my role here not as an expert in AI, but as a partner who helped shape the foundation into which these new ideas could be integrated. Watching how GenAI reshapes professional life has been fascinating, and I am grateful to have been part of a project that combines both tradition and innovation.

Beyond the professional exchange, I am thankful for the many colleagues, clients, and partners with whom I have worked over the years. Their practical challenges and their creativity have always inspired me to think beyond the obvious and to remain open to change. This book is also a reflection of their influence, as it seeks to connect established knowledge with forward-looking opportunities.

Finally, I wish to express my gratitude to my family, who once again supported me with patience and encouragement during the months of writing. Their understanding has been invaluable, and without their support this book could not have come to life.

And now enjoy and gain maximum insight.

Competing Interests The authors have no competing interests to declare that are relevant to the content of this manuscript.

Contents

Part I

Structured and GenAI Enhanced Requirements Engineering

1 Prologue to Structured and GenAI Enhanced Requirements Engineering

Requirements and expectations confront you in many areas of life, not only related to hardware and software. They can apply to your job, your new apartment, or your future e-bike. Once you understand what distinguishes well-formulated requirements, you can use this knowledge to avoid misunderstandings and prevent bad investments.

However, this Part 1 focuses exclusively on the field of IT.

1.1 Welcome

The fact that you have picked up this work shows your interest in topics such as Requirements Engineering or Requirements Management. We welcome this interest and would like to encourage you to deepen your knowledge and your skills.

If you are already working as an experienced requirements engineer, you can compare your existing knowledge with our perspective. If your current focus is rather in a technical or management area beyond requirements engineering, we would like to pick you up from this personal starting point and show you how you can benefit from requirements engineering in your special field of expertise. The following thought experiment serves to illustrate these points.

We assume that the topic *Requirements Engineering* touches you in varying intensity again and again, whether consciously or unconsciously (Fig. 1.1). In your current role, you are regularly involved in the development or adaptation of IT solutions. However, you currently lack tried-and-tested tools to implement your IT requirements effectively, regardless of an industry, a practiced management discipline, or a preferred technology.

J. Kawelke and T. Niebisch, *AI-Driven Transformation - Practical Frameworks for Real-World Impact*, Future of Business and Finance,
https://doi.org/10.1007/978-3-662-72549-8_1

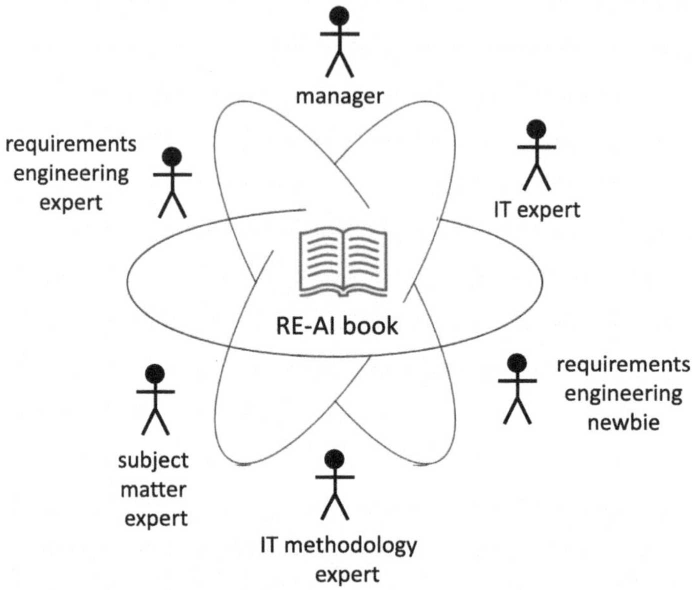

Fig. 1.1 Roles affected by requirements engineering

Let's briefly discuss the roles visualized in Fig. 1.1 and consider what your personal scenario could be and where this part of the book could offer you support:

1. If you are a *Requirements Engineering Expert* looking for new impulses, you might ask yourself:
   – In what form can AI already change your activity today?
2. As a *Subject Matter Expert* in an industrial, scientific, public law, or commercial field, you need a supportive IT solution. But in the past, you have had unsettling experiences such as:
   – IT experts implemented your requirements differently than you had imagined.
   – Communication with the IT department was difficult and misunderstood.
   – Your actual requirements were specified in more detail only in the testing phase, etc.
3. For a variety of *IT methodology experts*, a basic understanding of requirements management is helpful:
   – As a *Project Manager*, you will learn about the required roles and skills that you should demand for the IT projects that you lead.
   – As a *UI Designer*, you can put your expertise in the context with other requirements engineering aspects.
   – As a *Test Expert*, by the end of the work, you will know what quality the requirements to be tested should have.

   - As a *(Business) Process Management Expert*, you will better adapt the often-discussed Business-IT alignment, i.e., the interaction of subject matter and IT experts, to your daily work.
4. Your experience as a *Manager* or *Project Sponsor* states that previously commissioned IT projects often exceeded the cost limit without achieving the desired results. Currently, you are looking for an effective lever to improve project success. We will show it to you.
5. As an *IT Expert* you are active in one or more of the following focus topics:
   - In software development, you work as a frontend or backend developer in agile or traditional projects.
   - Innovative technologies such as Artificial Intelligence (AI), Blockchain technologies, Quantum Computing, or the Metaverse with Augmented or Virtual Reality are of interest to you.
   - Your focus is on Systems Engineering or IT Architecture. Under these circumstances, you become alert at the mention of *Requirements Engineering* and wonder how this discipline can help you to model your ideas understandably and to document them in a structured way. As an AI expert or enthusiast, you definitely want to find out how Requirements Engineering can support you in the context of AI deployment.
6. Finally: As a *Requirements Engineering Newbie* you recognize the value of this field and a perspective for your professional career.

All these mentioned roles will expand their knowledge—promised.

> **To the point**
> This is a publication for IT methodologists and others involved in IT projects who must deal with requirements (to varying degrees). It addresses both the specialists and the newcomers to requirements engineering. ◄

Unprofessional requirements engineering is often cited as the reason for failed projects. But it is too short-sighted to consider this topic as a pure *specialist* topic. We are convinced that requirements engineering can help IT projects achieve greater success if its basic knowledge is a widely spread and accepted mindset in all mentioned areas. Thus, everyone who works on an IT solution is encouraged to at least be able to articulate their own requirements in a usable way. Our driving force for this part of the book is to provide those who

- Set requirements for an IT solution,
- Collect, document, validate, and manage requirements,
- Are the recipients of the requirements,

A better insight into the topic of *Requirements Engineering*. As a reader, you will be introduced to requirements engineering as a discipline with a great methodological and communicative variety. We want to explain the world of requirements engineering to you so far that you can tackle the associated tasks more successfully and calmly.

An additional motivation that complements the mentioned incentive: One of the two authors (Jens) had the opportunity a few years ago to exchange ideas at a conference with one of the co-signers of the "Agile Manifesto" (Agile Manifesto, n.d.) and to argue with him. "There is no such thing as requirements engineering in agile projects" was the statement of the Agility expert. Jens, who has been exclusively involved in agile projects since 2008, disagrees and wants to convince you, the reader, of this.

It is widely accepted that requirements must be documented in writing. The resulting requirement specification is often the basis for the *Software Development* of custom software or standard products. But the theories of requirements engineering are equally applicable to other areas of use, e.g.,

- for the documentation of a developed system,
- for the specification of *requirements for a process,*
- in the *introduction of standard products* including configuration and customizing,
- for the creation of user manuals,
- for the *preparation of tender documents,*
- as a *basis for decision-making* such as Make-or-Buy,
- as proof of compliance with ISO standards or other standards and laws.

This part of the book particularly uses the italicized use cases. The form in which this is done will be explained to you in Sect. 1.3 "The structure of Part 1."

For didactic reasons, we would like to let you look over the shoulders of a requirements engineer and a Product Owner (PO) during their joint work. As a reader, you can choose your personal favorites from the presented models and methods that appear most helpful to you in formulating, structuring, and visualizing your own requirements for an IT solution. Refine your own sensitivity to documented requirements and derived solution approaches. Internalize the conviction, to guide your projects on the right path early on through professional requirements engineering. Remember: "*If you're running in the wrong direction, there's no point in increasing the pace*" (Birgit Breuel) (Forschelen, 2017). This realization describes precisely the importance of correct requirements for IT projects.

1.2 The Introduction of Linda and Jan

Let's construct an example together so that we can vividly illustrate the aspects of requirements engineering. As a backdrop for our explanations, we will use an insurance company. Don't worry, we don't assume any industry-specific knowledge ahead. We will reduce the processes and requirements to a manageable complexity, well aware that these only represent a part of the insurance reality.

The example insurance company primarily provides services for private customers. Its department *Contact Center* as part of the *Customer Center* has to process a variety of customer inquiries from different media (telephone, email, web form, letter). The existing processes and IT solutions are not geared toward this versatility. The affected employees often seem overwhelmed. Personnel, organizational, and processual weaknesses become apparent, so that customer inquiries are sometimes only processed with great delay.

The Customer Center aims to better meet the challenges of the market. One building block on this path is the transformation into an agile organization (Pfannstiel, 2021). The management of the Customer Center attaches special importance to the Contact Center during this transformation, as it represents a touchpoint to the customers and thus achieves a high external impact. As the next logical step, they therefore initiate a project which optimizes and professionalizes the processes of the Contact Center using modern IT solutions.

To the point
In our example, the various aspects of requirements engineering are demonstrated through the comprehensive reorganization of the process for handling customer concerns. ◄

One of the most experienced colleagues in the Contact Center is Linda. From the *Customer Center* management, she receives the task to eliminate weaknesses in the processes and—with the customer in focus—to modernize the Contact Center through a more agile way of working. Digital solutions should relieve the employees and simplify the processes. In the project, she is assigned the role of the *Product Owner.*

She is supported by a consultant from an IT company who has specialized in the role of a *requirements engineer* and has gained experience in many different projects. His name is Jan. In recent years, Jan has enhanced his expertise in requirements engineering by integrating artificial intelligence.

The two are the protagonists of the book example and work out the topics around requirements engineering in joint conversations and discussions. Let's take a look at the personas of the two.

	Linda • 45 years old, • Marital status: Married, two children (18 and 13), • Likes walking with her dog, • Education: Insurance saleswoman, • Employment status: Has been with an insurance company for 15 years, • Current position: Specialist in the contact Center; has been responsible for communication with private customers for five years.
	Jan • 36 years old, • Marital status: Single, • Hobbies: Sports (ice hockey, calisthenics), • Education: Business informatics, • Employment status: Has been with a medium-sized IT consulting company for 10 years, • Current position: Requirements engineer and UI designer, • Special skills: Use of artificial intelligence in the context of requirements engineering.

That's a brief introduction to the two actors of the book example. How they approach this task, which approach they choose, you will find out in the following section.

1.3 The Structure of Part 1

For a vivid explanation of the topic *Requirements Engineering* we still need a rough process, a roadmap for the case study. This would give the approach of the two a structure by describing the most important steps and milestones. The roadmap planning is based on the following considerations:

I. The starting points of the project are on the one hand the evaluation of received customer feedback, on the other hand the results of the internal revision. The desired goals of the project are set by the *Customer Center* management. Linda and Jan must develop solution ideas and then implement them with the available resources and financial means in the required time and necessary quality. This corresponds to a typical project approach.

II. For the implementation of this general approach, the *agile methodology* is basically suitable. It is characterized by successive iterative cycles, each of which includes conceptual, implementing, and quality assurance activities. The project therefore does not contain an extensive concept phase in which the complete IT solution is designed in all details, but after creating a rough solution model, the individual solution components are worked out and implemented successively and step by step in several cycles. The advantages of this approach for our task over a classic waterfall approach will be explained in Chapter 8.

III. Our exemplary insurance company has specific peculiarities and conditions:
   - The agile approach is not yet established in the project management methodology of the insurance company. Nor are the general basics of requirements engineering known. For both roles, the prerequisites still need to be created.
   - At present, no decision has been made on whether the IT solution will use an off-the-shelf software product (standard software) or be custom-built.
   - The company does not have the necessary developer resources in-house. To implement a custom-built IT solution, these resources must be acquired from an external IT provider and integrated into the project.

Taking into account the considerations just made, a multi-stage project implementation is suggested:

1. Project phase 1 is designed as a pre-project. This phase will analyze and structure the existing problem, define the project and system boundaries, and identify the key stakeholders. Linda and Jan will contemplate the desired future IT solution. As a result of this phase, requirements are created that are sufficiently detailed for the search for a suitable implementation partner.

   The pre-project ends with two directional decisions:
   - First, a decision is made for or against a custom or standard software based on the requirements identified.
   - This decision is followed by the selection of a suitable IT company for an implementation project. The main task of the partner is to provide the necessary project resources and to accompany the implementation project. The search takes place in form of a request for proposal (RfP).
2. Project phase 2 corresponds to the actual implementation project. After an implementation partner has been selected based on the RfP, the required IT solution is introduced in an agile project together with this partner.

Before Jan and Linda begin their work, we transfer the planned project approach into a chapter structure for this part of the publication (Fig. 1.2). The multitude of requirements engineering topics is for didactic reasons manageably portioned by distributing the content and the approach into seven weekdays:

- Following this chapter, the authors convince you in Chapter 2 of the *necessity of requirements engineering* using simple explanations and examples.

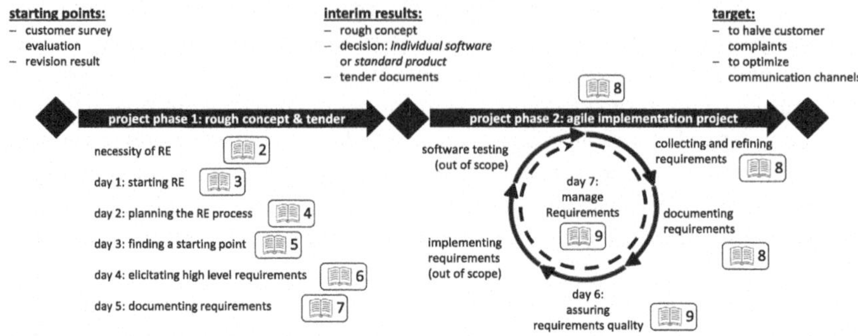

Fig. 1.2 Planned roadmap and assignment of chapters

- Jan explains his understanding of requirements engineering in Chapter 3 and provides Linda with necessary basic knowledge such as the *quality requirements for IT requirements*. Subsequently, both analyze the *initial situation* of the project based on the conducted customer survey.
- In Chapter 4, Jan and Linda will jointly dedicate themselves to the project start. Looking forward, they start with the *planning* of requirements engineering activities and agreements.
- With Chapter 5, Linda and Jan lay the foundation for a successful project. Both of them delineate the project from the environment using a *context diagram* and name the *stakeholders*, who will set requirements for a later solution.
- The *collection of requirements* from the initial planning to the final evaluation is the content of Chapter 6.
- Chapter 7 logically continues with the *documentation of requirements*. The chapter takes into account the diverse presentation options for different requirement categories and introduces suitable notations and artifacts.
- Chapter 8 provides information about the peculiarities of requirements engineering for the *agile project* approach and supplements Chapter 7 with proven notations and artifacts from the agile project world.
- Chapter 9 is dedicated to *quality assurance* and *management* of requirements.
- Following the seven days of requirements engineering, Chapter 10 provides practical tips as a summary of what has been learned.

1.4 Reading Instructions

In the process of putting our ideas into writing, we, as authors, sought ways to enhance readability and convey the content in a more memorable way. The following elements are our means of choice:

- Software is being developed for increasingly diverse environments today. One can distinguish between pure software development for the well-known mobile and stationary end-user devices on the one hand, and the development of embedded software within the scope of systems engineering on the other hand. A very good example of the latter is the motor vehicle, which is packed with software today. When we talk about IT projects in the following, we refer to the software development projects mentioned first. We will not specifically address hardware requirements.
- The developments of recent years prove that artificial intelligence offers great advantages for many activities of requirements engineering. Of course, this topic is addressed and explained. You will learn how to make the most of these advantages and what you should pay attention to.
- During the course of the project, we will present you with different artifacts (especially in Chapters 7 and 8), which are being developed for the example insurance company, based on the methods and models used. Please keep in mind that these are simply illustrative examples designed to highlight the content in question. We have deliberately refrained from complete content.
- There are several terms for the role of the Requirements Engineer that are sometimes used as synonyms even though they have slightly different meanings:
  - Requirements Manager,
  - Business Analyst,
  - Designer (often confused with UI Designer), or
  - Subject Matter Expert.

In this book we will stick to the term Requirements Engineer.

- A formality: As you could see on the first pages of the book, the word *Requirements Engineering* is quite cumbersome for permanent use. For a smooth reading, we will therefore use the abbreviation RE. If you see the abbreviation with a leading (indefinite) article—the RE or an RE—then it means *Requirements Engineering.*
- At the end of each chapter, a bullet-point overview will summarize the most important content.

To the point
This part of the book covers most of the topics related to requirements engineering, which we frequently encounter in our IT and process management projects, albeit in varying intensity. Our aim in documenting these recurring thought processes is that they may prove valuable to you in similar situations.◀

In the abundance of the topic 'Structured and GenAI enhanced Requirements Engineering,' the first part of our book is a rather slim work, which gives you a good overview of RE in your respective role. It explains to you using the example of *reorganization of the process for handling customer concerns*, how Linda and Jan define the context of the project, gather details from all requirement owners, and document and check the multitude of requirements. As a reader, you will learn how the two approach the task at hand, which activities are necessary from their point of view and which models are useful in the respective constellation.

We are optimistic that reading this, combined with plenty of project experience, will make you a master of requirement engineering.

References

Agile Manifesto. (n.d.) Retrived 03 March 2025 from https://agilemanifesto.org/iso/de/manifesto.html.

Forschelen, B. (2017). *Compendium of quotes for entrepreneurs and executives* (p. 176). Springer Gabler.

Pfannstiel, M., Siedl, W., & Steinhoff, P. (2021). *Agilität in Unternehmen.* Springer Gabler.

Understanding the Need for Professional RE

2

Let's start by illuminating the contribution that requirements engineering can make to the success of an IT project. To do this, we first look at negative project patterns and phenomena in order to find suitable solutions afterwards.

For you as a reader, this chapter has the same importance as a warm-up for an athlete, because it prepares you for the upcoming tasks and brings your most important body functions up to operating temperature. In principle, you could do without this warm-up exercise. Nevertheless, we recommend that we loosen our thoughts a little together and prepare for the upcoming chapters.

2.1 Connecting Two Sides of a Coin

IT projects often revolve around two opposing sides, much like the faces of a coin. On one side are the departments and business teams that rely on IT to manage their day-to-day operations. From their perspective, IT plays a service role that should support the business processes and function flawlessly. On the other side of the coin are the software architects and developers, who design and build the technological infrastructure that supports those business needs. They often lack knowledge of the specific business processes or user behavior and thus important knowledge for designing an optimal IT solution.

Both sides of the coin significantly impact one another. However, the link between these two sides is often too weak to be truly effective. Usually, there are department employees with an IT affinity who hold both sides together. A more professional approach would lie in the integration of a professional group that could bridge the gap between business and IT experts with a specific methodology. These bridgeheads are *requirements engineers* (see also the synonyms introduced

J. Kawelke and T. Niebisch, *AI-Driven Transformation - Practical Frameworks for Real-World Impact*, Future of Business and Finance,
https://doi.org/10.1007/978-3-662-72549-8_2

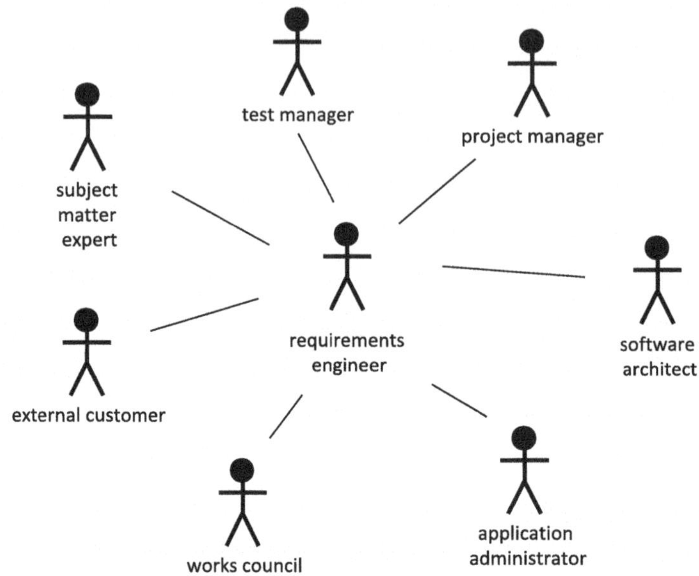

Fig. 2.1 The requirements engineer at the center of the software development lifecycle

in Sect. 1.4), who act as interpreters and mediators between business departments and IT. Their task is to collect the business requirements as complete as possible as a basis for an IT solution. They work to bridge the gap by translating the business experts' world for IT professionals and vice versa, ensuring the business side receives precisely the IT elements it needs.

But there is not only a need for interpretation between business experts and IT specialists. The requirements engineer is a communicative hub between a multitude of project participants, as Fig. 2.1 shows.

The participants shown in the figure were chosen somewhat arbitrarily and do not represent a comprehensive list. But each of the groups shown has their view of things and sets different priorities regarding an IT solution. The essence of good requirements engineering lies in:

1. Identifying all stakeholders involved in defining requirements,
2. Gathering both their explicit and implicit ideas about a solution, and.
3. Synthesizing these inputs and perspectives into a cohesive whole.

Similar to a puzzle whose pieces are scattered among several owners, these individual views must be gathered and assembled into a complete picture. Contradictory or late formulated expectations of the solution are poison for project success. In this phase of the project, skilled requirements engineers often determine whether the outcome is successful or not.

2.2 Resolving an IT Project Paradox

We often observe a contradiction in IT projects:

- On the one hand: Well-defined, accurate, and comprehensive requirements are universally recognized as the basis for successful projects. There is a wealth of methods, research, and practical reports on RE—from lightweight process models like Scrum to heavyweight process models like the V-model, including tooling, testing procedures, and traceability. The books on these subjects are extensive, and the available tools are typically quite powerful. With all these resources, one would expect it to be straightforward to describe even the most complex IT solutions.
- On the other hand: Common project issues—such as exceeding time and resource estimates or failing to meet agreed-upon customer requirements—continue to occur. Moreover, requirements are often only specified during the test phase at the end of a sprint or the project. Unfortunately, it is only at this stage that end users realize what they actually need.

Disappointment prevails wherever the reality created within a project deviates significantly from one's own expectations. It becomes clear that certain human abilities remain indispensable. The contradiction described emerges in a series of pressing questions at various levels—questions you may well recognize from your own projects:

- Language Barriers.
  - Question: Why doesn't my IT service provider understand me? I just want to implement an IT solution!
  - Communication among different expert teams can be challenging. Their high degree of specialization leads to a profusion of technical terms, and individual departments often develop their own "language worlds." As a result, a common vocabulary must first be established with IT specialists who may not be familiar with the subject.
- Methodological Weaknesses.
  - Question: Why doesn't the department clearly and systematically articulate its expectations? The requirements are incomplete or ambiguous—this must be improved!
  - Requirements engineers demonstrate the many different ways in which requirements can be formulated. Consequently, the knowledge of requirements engineers is indispensable for any company conducting IT projects. If that knowledge exists only in fragments, the quality of tender documents, specifications, epics, features, and user stories inevitably suffers.

- Project Planning Tasks.
  - Question: Which work steps are required to identify and manage the IT project's requirements? Who will do what, when, how, and with which resources?
  - The fundamental work steps should be defined in a company-specific process model for IT projects. However, mid-sized companies rarely invest in developing their own process model.
- Team Setup.
  - Question: Do I have the right people for RE on board in the project?
  - Not everyone is cut out to handle the multitude of requirements and represent them in models. A quiet developer is just as ill-suited for gathering requirements as an overly dominant subject matter expert. The right people must be found for these tasks.
- In the Middle of the Project.
  - Where do the boundaries of the system under consideration lie?
  - How do we transition from the process to the IT solution?
  - How are existing systems integrated?
  - How should we document open questions and their answers so that they remain easily retrievable?
  - What interfaces exist for testing and acceptance processes?

As long as a company or a project does not find answers to these questions, IT projects will repeatedly miss their targets. Some of these questions need to be answered fundamentally in the company, others individually in the project. In agile projects, we suggest to create a *Way of Working* document in which project procedures are defined.

As previously noted, numerous studies on the causes and effects of failed IT projects indicate that most project participants consider well-defined and clearly articulated requirements—as well as corresponding concepts or refined user stories—to be indispensable. It is widely understood that only clarifying critical requirements at a late stage leads to subsequent changes to the solution, which are significantly more expensive and more complex to implement. Errors and omissions in Requirements Engineering frustrate both customers and developers. None of these insights are new, yet the contradictions mentioned above still seem insurmountable.

RE offers numerous ways to avoid these seemingly inevitable project pitfalls. However, it's not enough to recall a few RE principles only when a project is already underway. Instead, introducing RE should be viewed as a management responsibility and firmly embedded within the organization. That means treating RE as an investment, one that merits the allocation of both time and financial resources. Paradoxically, though, solutions intended to address these very conflicts are often dismissed as too academic, too expensive, impractical, or already proven failures.

To increase the efficiency of RE in projects, at least three factors are needed:

- Management support at all levels, even outside of specific projects,
- trained RE specialists, and,
- time and budget for answering the above open questions.

To the point
The paradox of IT projects is that, while the importance of RE is widely acknowledged, many organizations hesitate to commit the necessary financial, personnel, and time resources. ◀

2.3 Requirement Defects and their Impacts

The main challenge in making a case to management is quantifying the return on investment for RE. There are now statistical data indicating how costs increase when requirement defects are discovered late, thereby strengthening the argument for RE (see Sect. 2.3.4). Before examining these statistics, we'll review the categories of requirement defects to better understand the potential issues. These defects can be:

- Ambiguous requirements (Sect. 2.3.1).
- Incomplete requirements (Sect. 2.3.2).
- Erroneous requirements (Sect. 2.3.3).

Let's delve into each category in detail.

2.3.1 The Power of the Word

Of course, you've come across this common source of frustration: ambiguous or easily misinterpreted words. Have you ever wondered how someone could misunderstand you so completely? You meant one thing—but your listener envisioned something else entirely. Take a look at some classic dish names: "hot dog," "hamburger," and "buffalo wings." None of these foods involves actual dogs, ham, or buffalo. The literal interpretation can be hilariously misleading, even though we usually know from context what they really are.

Admittedly, these are contrived examples, but they vividly illustrate the risk of misunderstandings arising from imprecise communication. Normally, we infer the intended meaning from context. But when context is missing, uncertainties lead to multiple interpretations. Avoiding them would require checking every statement against all conceivable variants, which would be fatal to efficient communication.

That's why people often dismiss such concerns with a casual "We all know what's meant." We can only hope so—and risk being disappointed later.

If a sentence allows different interpretations, those variations will be discovered. This is simply the nature of communication. Therefore, the challenge is to formulate your own requirements in an unambiguous way.

For reasons not entirely clear, the overall awareness of proper formulation often remains moderate, even after numerous training sessions. One way to gauge your colleagues' sensitivity to this issue is by conducting a simple role-play:

1. **Assign Roles:** You act as the subject matter expert, and everyone else plays competing requirements engineers.
2. **Prepare a Hidden Figure:** You have a basic geometric shape in front of you—hidden from the rest of the group—which represents your requirements.
3. **Communicate Your Requirements:** Describe the figure (i.e., your requirements) to the group. While doing so, record your explanation (or have it transcribed by AI).
4. **Sketch and Compare:** Each participant sketches what they believe the requirements look like. Simultaneously, use an AI tool capable of text-to-graphic transformation to generate its own depiction from your recorded description.

Our hypothesis: Even though everyone hears the same words at the same time, sees the same facial expressions, and works under the same constraints, each participant—and the AI—will produce a unique sketch. You may be surprised to find that even the AI's rendering deviates from your original shape. In other words, each recipient interprets and processes the same requirements differently.

Of course, if all versions still meet your underlying intent, multiple solutions might be acceptable. But in IT, differing interpretations often prove undesirable and can lead to significant issues. The challenge, then, is to formulate requirements so clearly that neither humans nor AI can misinterpret them.

What happened?

The various solutions arose because your stated requirements were likely incomplete—partially vague or open to interpretation. Meanwhile, each requirements engineer believed they had understood everything correctly. Unconsciously, they filled in missing information based on their own experiences. In doing so, each requirements engineer formed their own internal images, embellished them as best they could, and mentally produced their own "film." This internal cinema ultimately leads to discrepancies between your expectations and the final implementation. A helpful reminder for this situation is:

To the point
Saying is not the same as *Meaning* and *Hearing* is not the same as Understanding. ◄

What does this exercise tell us about our IT project? The project's outcome shouldn't depend on whether the customer happens, by chance, to formulate clear requirements or whether the consultant is simply having a "good day" and interprets them correctly. Instead, a systematic approach, solid knowledge, and reliable methods are needed to align the customer's vision with the consultant's understanding. This alignment also requires strong communication skills—after all, good requirements cannot be determined without effective dialogue.

2.3.2 No Courage for the Gap

A second category of requirement defects are incomplete requirements.

Gaps arise when requirements are overlooked or when stakeholders implicitly assume that everyone already knows certain details. Even as requirements engineers (REs), we sometimes fall into this trap—particularly when we're highly familiar with the subject area and begin to exhibit "operational blindness." This is why it's never a bad idea to involve someone new to the industry on the RE team. Such a newcomer often asks about basic or fundamental requirements that form the foundation for a shared understanding. For instance, developers might also be new to the industry, lacking key background knowledge.

Two exaggerated but telling examples—and a brief detour into systems engineering—illustrate what can happen when requirements are incomplete:

1. A smartphone's size is minimized by putting the keyboard on the back of the display, because the requirement that both must be on the same side is missing.
2. A car turns left when the steering wheel is turned to the right.

These scenarios show just how crucial it is to specify all essential requirements.

In a modification of the Kano model (Sauerwein, 2000) we can divide the sum of all requirements into

- Basic requirements,
- Performance requirements, and.
- Excitement requirements.

categories.

Basic requirements are often assumed rather than explicitly stated—for example, that a car drives, that you can make phone calls with a mobile phone, or that

Office files can be saved. The system's requirements are so obvious that only an industry newcomer might question them. Such requirements typically become a topic of discussion only when they are not met. Their implementation is taken for granted, and if they are not implemented, the product becomes unfit for use. To avoid disasters like the one in our smartphone example, basic requirements can also be determined using observation techniques. This involves literally observing the user or business department during their daily work.

Performance requirements are most likely to be communicated to us by the business department. These are usually requirements that arise from daily work and are obvious. These can be quickly collected as they are present in the stakeholders' imaginations. Implementing performance requirements generates little euphoria, as they meet the stakeholders' formulated expectations.

Excitement requirements are those that go beyond a basic expectation of a system, far exceed it, and thus generate enthusiasm in the future user of the system. By their very nature, these requirements are not identified during the collection phase. Especially in product development, i.e., for apps or systems that have to assert themselves on the market against strong competition, the identification and development of these excitement requirements is a crucial factor that determines the success or failure of the product. To give an example of excitement requirements in systems engineering, we would like to mention the return to the use of wind power for large cargo ships, which achieves a reduction in CO2 emissions. In software development, the integration of chatbots into customer communication, which took place a few years ago, was a real excitement factor. It has now become the norm. On the other hand, the application possibilities of artificial intelligence, which also gradually improve the chatbots, are causing euphoria in many industries today.

It is in human nature to get used to things if they are present long enough. Functions that once could inspire are increasingly taken for granted. Thus, over time, what were once excitement requirements become standard performance or even basic requirements.

2.3.3 The Causes of Actual Errors

The third category of requirement defects includes the actual errors within the requirements (not to be confused with bugs that arise during implementation). Errors in the requirements often propagate as software bugs.

How can actual errors in requirements arise? They all have one thing in common: they are due to unprofessional RE. For example, when the requirements engineer does not correctly analyze and question the wish of a single stakeholder. This wish becomes a requirement and later a system component, but it contradicts the goals of the system or even the company.

Another source of error arises in inconsistencies in requirements collected from the same or different stakeholders. These contradictions must be recognized and resolved by the requirements engineer.

Table 2.1 Factors for correction costs at different detection times.

specification	development	testing	or after rollout
1	5–10	10–20	20–100

Here too, artificial intelligence has now advanced to the point where it can assist in discovering inconsistencies (Sect. 9.1.1).

With number-specific requirements, it can happen that different scales or metrics serve as a basis and the numbers do not match as a result. This actually led to a complete loss of the Mars Climate Orbiter in 1999 (Mars Climate Orbiter, n.d.). The orbiter entered Mars orbit at too low an altitude due to the mixing of the international SI unit system and the so-called imperial system, causing it to burn up in the Martian atmosphere.

2.3.4 Possible Effects of Requirement Defects

Appropriate techniques help, especially during the collection and quality assurance of requirements, to avoid errors directly or at least to identify and correct them. The use of these techniques prevents a later cost explosion.

In Table 2.1, the efforts for correcting requirement defects are related to the time of detection. The effort for direct discovery by the requirements engineer is set at 1 (without unit). The other listed factors are long-term experience values that increase the correction costs by the listed factor.

The later a defect is discovered, the greater the impact on other requirements. It becomes apparent that the effort due to re-running the development process increases exponentially.

In agile projects, the factors are significantly lower than in projects that follow the V-model. However, even here, the costs for defect correction can quickly escalate into project-threatening areas. Would you like a small example calculation?

Assumptions for simplification:

- The discovery and correction of a defect through direct quality measures during the specification take 1 h.
- Five defects are discovered by the RE.
- Five defects are discovered by the developer (factor 5).
- Five defects are discovered by the test analyst (factor 10).
- Five defects are discovered by the user after rollout (factor 20).

In the example of Table 2.2, we calculate with the lower bounds of the value ranges from Table 2.1. Nevertheless, the difference in effort is remarkable when comparing very early detection (5 hours) to very late detection (100 hours). If we were to calculate with the upper bounds, which are more aligned with the heavyweight V-model, we would arrive at the astonishing discrepancy of 5 hours

Table 2.2 Comparison of correction costs at different detection times.

	Detection of a requirement defect by …			
	the RE	the developer	the test analyst	the end user
Number of defects	5	5	5	5
Factor	1	5	10	20
Correction effort	5 hrs.	25 hrs.	50 hrs.	100 hrs.

to 500 hours, or more illustratively, from less than one working day to more than 60 working days.

At the beginning of Sect. 2.3, we asked ourselves how to argue the *Return on Investment* to management. The example calculation shown should now convince every responsible person of the benefit of the investment.

To the point
Analytical techniques that enable early defect detection must be applied to avoid later cost explosions. Additionally, projects should be set up with an agile approach wherever possible. ◀

We have pointed out that professional analytical quality assurance measures are very important. However, it would be even better to avoid requirement defects already during documentation. This is referred to as constructive quality assurance (Chris Rupp & the SOPHISTs, 2020). After working through this book, you should be able to minimize requirement defects—be they misunderstandings, gaps, or errors—in your documentation.

After this short excursion into possible RE error sources, you can answer the question yourself how successfully you have already circumvented these in the past.

2.4 Accept the Challenge

The example described in the following chapters only represents one way of how RE can be practiced. In the IT world, there are a multitude of approaches. If you ask three craftsmen how they solve a certain problem—you will get at least three different answers. And all three might be correct. But if you break down their solutions into meaningful basic building blocks, it always involves a set of activities—like sawing, drilling, screwing—and the corresponding tools.

With this book, we want to introduce you to such activities and tools, offer them to you, and put them in your personal toolbox. From this, you can serve yourself depending on the project and circumstances and put together your solution path. Those who expect a user manual rather than a toolbox from this book, we will have to disappoint right at the beginning. There is no complete process that gives you the security with the magic words: *If you work through these steps in the given order, your project will automatically end successfully.* But don't worry, there are techniques that we will recommend for every project or under certain project conditions.

This book describes the toolset you need for RE in IT projects, as well as an exemplary way to apply it. Adapt this approach or look for alternatives. Even if the topic initially seems like an additional burden, it will simplify your work after a certain learning and practice phase.

To the point
There is no one-size-fits-all approach for requirement collection, documentation, validation, and management. However, there are a multitude of individual means and methods that lead to good requirements. You just need to know them, integrate them into a complete picture, and apply them. ◄

So! The warm-up of this chapter should have sufficiently stimulated your synapses. The most important people of our book project have also been mentioned. Now it can really get started!

References

Chris Rupp & the SOPHISTs. (2020). *Requirements engineering and management* (7th ed.). C. Hanser Verlag.

Mars Climate Orbiter. (n.d.) Retrived 03 March 2025 from https://en.wikipedia.org/wiki/Mars_Climate_Orbiter.

Sauerwein, E. (2000). Das Kano-Modell der Kundenzufriedenheit (The Kano Model of Customer Satisfaction). Deutscher Universitäts-Verlag.

Day 1: Starting Requirements Engineering

3

3.1 Clarify the Current Situation

In the *Contact Center* where Linda works, the communication channels for customers have been significantly expanded. Previously, communication was exclusively through *letters, phone calls, and emails.* Now, customers can receive direct assistance *via live chat*. Additionally, contact through text messages in a *web form* is possible. Furthermore, customers can search for answers to their questions in a *knowledge database*. Currently, contact options via *social media* or *chatbots* are not available.

Due to her long affiliation with the Customer Center, her expertise in the Contact Center, and her interest in project activities, Linda has repeatedly been involved in optimization projects in the past. This time, too, she was invited to a joint meeting by the management of the Customer Center. Since Linda knew that a recent revision in customer service and sales had taken place alongside a customer survey, she was curious about the topics that would be discussed in the meeting. She had guessed correctly: The core was about the results of the customer survey and the revision report.

Indeed, she found the deficiencies pointed out to her in this meeting alarming. She had not been aware of these deficits to this extent before. It was clear to her that these deficiencies had to be eliminated. She was pleasantly surprised by the request for her to take over the technical leadership. Subsequently, she kept rereading her notes:

- The revision criticized the following points:
  - Different input channels for customer communication are not consolidated; instead, they are processed separately. Corresponding processes are either undocumented or only partially documented.

J. Kawelke and T. Niebisch, *AI-Driven Transformation - Practical Frameworks for Real-World Impact*, Future of Business and Finance,
https://doi.org/10.1007/978-3-662-72549-8_3

  - Digital messages are still often printed out and filed.
  - There is no customer communication via social media or chatbots.
  - Operational and legal retention periods for documents related to customer interactions are not adhered to.
- The result of the customer survey states:
  - A large number of customers complain that the company does not respond or only responds very late to their concerns. In some cases, they threaten to terminate the contract.
  - 52% of all the surveyed customers are dissatisfied with the service.
  - Customers willing to switch would opt for another insurance company because they find the customer processes too complex and too inflexible.
  - Especially younger customers and prospects miss a contact option via social media.
  - The use of chatbots was a concern for many existing customers.
- Linda's tasks:
  - Develop a concept that consolidates different service channels and optimizes processes.
  - Introduction of an IT solution that increases the efficiency of the Contact Center processes.
  - Introduce an IT solution that increases the efficiency of various Contact Center processes.
  - Achieve a customer satisfaction of 80% within one year.

Linda had never had to master tasks of such complexity before. The Contact Center was running in organizationally calm waters and had—apart from the above-mentioned expansion of communication channels—never been the focus of major changes. Now, however, she realized that these channels had not been introduced as part of an overall concept, but that each channel corresponded to an individual solution. She saw this as the root of all evil.

The Contact Center was running smoothly in terms of organization and had, apart from the above-mentioned expansion of communication channels, never been the focus of major changes.

Linda suspected that despite her many years of experience, she could not accomplish this task on her own. Since it was obviously not to be a purely organizational-processual solution, it was necessary to request active support from the IT department in addition to their professional experience. This collaboration had been somewhat difficult in the past. There were friction losses caused by misunderstandings, inaccuracies, or significant errors.

Based on these experiences, she realized that she would need support from a qualified consultant with know-how in process management and requirements engineering, who also has good communicative and analytical skills and is ideally familiar with topics from the contact center environment.

There was no such type of consultant in her insurance company. She had no choice but to look around the external market. For this purpose, she prepared a corresponding tender and asked for support from the *Purchasing* department. They had indeed received suitable offers and passed them on to Linda. After several online interviews, Linda was sure that she had struck gold with Jan. He had the highest hourly rate of all applicants, but Linda knew from previous IT projects that requirements engineers with drive and experience can be much more efficient than inexperienced or only theoretically trained consultants. She hoped that the investment would pay off.

Jan is an employee of a well-known IT consulting firm and sees himself as an interpreter between technical and IT specialists. He does not yet have any contact center skills, but he brings many years of experience as a requirements engineer in application development and views every application as an embedded part of a technical overall process. This sounded promising to Linda, so she wanted to involve him in her project. They agreed to start in Linda's office.

3.2 Structuring Available Information

Day 1, 9:00 am: Jan visits Linda in her office. Over the past few days, Linda has gathered additional information for her task. She now wants to inform Jan about her current state of knowledge and discuss the next steps. After the usual small talk, they got straight to the point. Let's listen in:

Linda: Following the negative audit report and the sobering customer feedback, action is needed in customer service and sales. The focus is on improving service quality within the contact center. As I mentioned in the interview, I have been tasked with setting up the *Reorganization of the Contact Center* project. This initiative will consolidate the IT landscape alongside process improvements. I have already forwarded my notes from the conversation with the customer center management to you.

Jan: I have received the notes. First and foremost, I would like to personally thank you for choosing me. I am very excited about this task.

Linda: The solution to the problems will likely be an Omni-Channel system that supports the overall process. That's why you're on board. I'm confident you can evaluate such systems for our contact center. We'll choose one and implement it in the company. With a few more organizational adjustments, we will have fulfilled the customer center management's directive.

Jan: At the moment, I am skeptical about whether this approach will succeed easily or if it is even the right way to go. We need a clear understanding of:

- How the processes currently run and how they should be carried out in the future,
- What defects the current processes have,
- What additional functions we expect from the tool.

Do we already have this information and documentation? I can think of other aspects that we should clarify before deciding on a solution. Otherwise, I see the risk of choosing the wrong tool due to a lack of information.

Linda I can already contribute some information.Since the processes fall within my area of work, I have already spoken with my colleagues. First, I would like to share what I have discovered so far. Then, we can look for a solution together.
The *Contact Center* department, where I work, is responsible for first level support within the customer Center. This is managed by our agents. The contact Center itself is composed of several groups, two of which are currently coming into focus. Both groups handle incoming customer concerns from our private customers, including all postal and digital correspondence. While one group handles inquiries from prospects and the setup of new customers, the other group takes care of existing customers. The two group leaders responsible say they do not understand the mandate for reorganization, as things have been running the same way for years.
If our agents cannot resolve customer concerns independently, they forward the process to knowledgeable clerks and experts. For example, if damage cases are reported, these colleagues provide second and third level support. Their departments are also part of the customer Center. Damage cases involving amounts in the four-digit euro range are always forwarded to specially trained experts.
If customers complain, we forward the complaint to complaint management, which is responsible for resolving it. Complaint management has reported an increase in complaints recently. This seemed logical to me, as the company's business has been developing positively. This growth has increased the number of customers and, consequently, the volume of customer inquiries. Unfortunately, the customer survey revealed that the percentage of dissatisfied customers is far too high at 52%.
I also spoke with other colleagues from our department. A few clerks mentioned that the work has become more complicated. Letter contact has shrunk to a minimum, and customers now use all possible channels. In addition to telephone customer service, clerks also have to communicate directly with customers in live chat. Additionally,

- They still receive their mail assigned by the mailroom,
- They have to check the email program for incoming customer mail,
- They check additional email mailboxes for messages from the web form,
- They regularly update the knowledge database.

Currently, emails are not pre-filtered or assigned by the mailroom. This means clerks have to check all emails, ranging from spam and info inquiries to new customer applications and complaints. Since there is no pre-filtering, every clerk has to review and evaluate every open email, which can lead to oversights or duplicate processing. The group leaders have not clearly communicated this problem to me, so I need to ask them about it again. I also spoke with accounting, and it is important to them that they receive relevant documents for commercial processing immediately. Otherwise, they are not affected by the incoming mail. Personally, I would like to exclude the topic of invoice receipt, as it does not fall within our core competence.
I also spoke with colleagues from the mailroom. They confirmed that the number of letters has decreased significantly. They do not feel the impact of increased customer numbers and are worried that fewer positions will be needed, leading to potential job cuts. They are also concerned about being repurposed, as they are not subject matter experts who can process the mail content. There is a lot of uncertainty among them.

This is my current state of information. Now, we need to find a solution for this. I have an idea, but I would be interested in hearing your opinion on this situation.

Jan You have seen me speechless the entire time—This will rarely happen in the future. I am a visual type, so I had to literally create a picture of what was said. During your explanations, I tried to capture the essence in a sketch (Fig. 3.1). Please take a look to see if I succeeded. But first, a question that is still open for me: Should the mailroom also work with the Omni-Channel solution in the future, or should we leave it as it is with the classic mail distribution?

Linda Yes, I hadn't mentioned that. The number of letters is significantly decreasing. While an IT solution for digitizing the mail through central scanning and electronic distribution is technically possible, I currently estimate the real potential for improvement as not particularly high. From a cost-benefit perspective, we are initially excluding an IT solution for mail.
Otherwise, let's see:

- The departments of the Customer Center are fully represented. Accounting is not really part of the customer Center, but we have already separated their concerns. Therefore, we can leave the organigram as it is.
- It is also correct that we want to improve the business process 'handling customer concerns' in the contact Center. Looking at the sketch, I realize that the process does not exclusively run in the contact Center. The other departments will also be affected by my process changes. Therefore, I will have the authorization explicitly confirmed by the sponsor to adjust the processes of the other departments.
- When I think about our daily business, our tasks in the process 'handling customer concerns' include:
  - o Purely organizational or IT-distant activities of the individual employees, e.g., when they have to process a paper form,
  - o Activities for which they work with an IT application, such as making a Schufa inquiry, and,
  - o Activities that are fully automated by the IT solution.

According to this logic, the process activities include more than just IT activities, as you have already correctly visualized. A central task of the project is to establish a supporting IT solution for this business process. It will likely be an Omni-Channel system. Therefore, integrating the IT system into the business process is a correct approach.
In my opinion, you have accurately summarized and presented the described problem. Well done!

Note from the authors: We acknowledge that a proper Customer Center is more complex and handles significantly more business processes. However, for the purpose of conveying RE basics in this publication, this task is sufficiently challenging

Jan I'm glad I have understood the basics for now. Let's get back to your problem description. You've opened up a mixed bag of wishes, worries, and problems here. Initially, the topic sounds quite simple: Just reorganize the contact Center. But upon closer inspection, it's not that simple anymore. It seems that customer communication across the many channels is overwhelming your agents. First, I would like to work out possible connections for the information you have presented, so that it appears more manageable. Since you have already described the problems we need to solve very well, I suggest that we:

1. List and structure the communication possibilities, and,
2. Document the different roles and their relationships to the communication options.

Linda What needs to be structured about the communication options? And why do you want to document roles and their relationships?

Jan OK, one thing at a time. First, let's address point 1. I initially understood that the process runs across departments. You collaborate with the second and third level support as well as complaint management on customer concerns. This collaboration can sometimes lead to problems in daily communication, hence the need for structuring. There is direct and indirect communication. Direct communication with the customer uses telephone and live chat, also known as synchronous communication. All other communication channels are asynchronous.

Linda I thought you weren't that familiar with contact centers. How do you know these terms?

Jan Both forms of communication are important for me as a requirements engineer when communicating with stakeholders like you. If you are available, I communicate with you synchronously, e.g., via a video call. If you are not available, I write to you either in chat or in an email.

I suggest we relate the communication forms you have mentioned so far to each other as a conceptual model in the form of a UML class diagram.

Linda I've heard the abbreviation UML before, but I can't quite place it.

Jan Well, UML stands for unified Modeling language.But before we get lost in the details, let's pause the project approach for a moment and take a more basic look at the topic of models. A brief excursion into modeling will help convey my basic understanding and the most useful models and standards for our project.

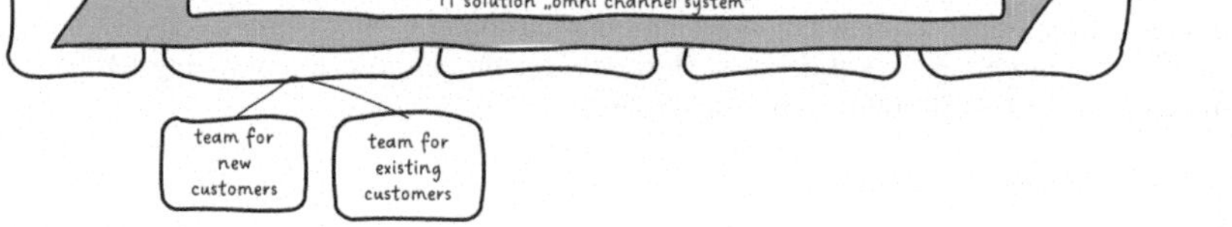

Fig. 3.1 Visualization of Linda's information

3.2.1 The Introduction to Modeling

Jan It's well-known that communication between business experts and IT specialists can be quite complicated and often fails. But that's not the only issue. Sometimes a technical matter is so complex that it needs to be visualized to maintain an overview. This is done through modeling.We use the word *models* quite loosely in everyday use—Everyone knows models. But what characterizes them?

Linda In my opinion, models always serve to better illustrate a concept or topic. If someone shows me a proper model of a complex matter, I can understand it better.

Jan And there's a reason for that. A definition that triggered an aha moment for me and sharpened my awareness of models is provided by model theory. Stachowiak (1973) characterized models roughly as follows:

- Models represent the required or desired features of an original, thereby creating an *image of reality*.
- Models dispense with unnecessary features of the original and *reduce reality* to a required or desired form.
- The high art of good modeling lies in *pragmatism*—The ability to differentiate and decide between the above two points. This distinction depends on the respective goal or target group of the model. What seems important to some may be uninteresting to others.

A model selects specific features of reality to represent. It simplifies reality by omitting certain details to better highlight others.

You may be familiar with this from building a house. I bet you had to deal with several models. The first model came from the seller, showing you how great the house will look in the end. This is important to get you to close the sale. However, it is impossible for any construction company to build the house according to this sales model. So, there is another model with the floor plan model. From this model, the expert recognizes where each wall needs to be placed. But that's not enough for the structural engineer. For him, there is a third model. Then comes the fourth model, the integration into the site plan, which positions your house on the property. Then the development plan, etc.

To the point

Modeling involves viewing the original from different perspectives, tailored to the target group. By definition, a model is incomplete compared to reality.◀

Jan Models always focus on certain aspects of the house. Depending on which aspect is currently in focus, there are different models for the real world. Yet, we are still talking about only one house. The different participants (our stakeholders), however, need different views for their work on this one house. It's the same in IT. What conclusions can we draw from this?

Linda That there is not *one* model, but we should use several. I understand.

Jan That covers the universal part of modeling.In the next step, we will transfer these insights to our project. With my sketch (Fig. 3.1), I want to clarify my personal approach to thinking and modeling in two tracks:

- On the one hand, we need a view of the *processes*. The business process 'handling customer concerns' that we aim to improve is not optimally designed. This point—Who does what in which order—Is not documented and only exists in the minds of the employees. However, we need this knowledge as a crucial basis for the second level of consideration, because ....
- This process will be supported by an *IT system, 'Omni-Channel.'* However, describing an IT system requires different perspectives, similar to the house construction example.

As we just discussed—One reality, multiple views.

Linda I hope we can rely on proven models in this context. To my knowledge, there are already standardized models. But how should one navigate their multitude?

Jan Primarily by their distribution and comprehensibility for a wide range of stakeholders. Only models that are understood guarantee the acceptance of our work results. A valuable source of standardization is the object management group (OMG). The representatives of OMG have the appropriate standard for each of our two ways of thinking:

1. I'll start with the newer standard, *business process model and notation* (BPMN). It offers the possibility to not only visualize processes but also execute them as a sequence with the appropriate software. For us, however, the graphical representation is sufficient. On one hand, I could introduce you to the essential design elements now, but I would like to postpone this theoretical part. This is because, in my opinion, we will discuss the business process 'handling customer concerns' in the workshops. Rather than explaining a lot of theory now, I prefer to link the explanations later with the practical part of our business process to be created (Sect. 6.3.2.2). This way, the theory can be presented more memorably. I had also planned for our first day to explore the meaningful and revealing connection between process management and RE (Sect. 3.3). In this, you will find, if not an explanation, at least a very superficial representation of the essential graphical elements of BPMN. As you can see, this standard will cross our path at several points in our project.
2. You've probably already noticed that I'm a big fan of the *Unified Modeling Language* (UML). Before the development of BPMN, some smart minds developed a wide range of models and diagrams that are understandable for both business experts and IT specialists. UML is a modeling language designed to reduce communication-related difficulties for people like us. Sometimes the diagrams are more business-oriented, sometimes more IT-heavy. This standard is so significant that ISO has included it under ISO/IEC 19505–1 in its repertoire.

Throughout the project, when we discuss modeling, we will primarily rely on the capabilities of BPMN and UML.

Linda I wasn't familiar with BPMN before. When we described processes in the past, they were proprietary representations or we tried our hand at EPCs (Blokdyk, 2020). However, creating process models was rare, so I have nothing against adopting a new standard. But I digress—You actually wanted to tell me about UML and class diagrams.

Jan Exactly. Alphabetically, UML includes, among others:

- Activity diagram (Sect. 8.1.4)
- Use case diagram (Sect. 5.5)
- Interaction overview diagram
- Class diagram (Sect. 3.2.1)
- Communication diagram
- Component diagram
- Composite structure diagram
- Object diagram
- Package diagram
- Sequence diagram
- Deployment diagram
- Timing diagram
- State diagram (Sect. 7.3.2).

For RE, use case, class, activity, and state diagrams are mainly suitable. If you want to learn more, you can educate yourself with numerous publications such as *learning UML 2.0* (Miles & Hamilton, 2006).

Linda But a *class diagram* sounds very technical to me. I'm worried that I might not be able to follow you right from the start.

Jan You're right, the term "class diagram" can be misleading. This type of diagram was primarily created for object-oriented software development, such as creating data models. However, it is also excellent for modeling terms and their relationships in RE, usually in conjunction with a glossary.By the way, maybe you can start maintaining such a glossary afterwards.

Linda Of course. Now let's see your class diagram.

Jan Here you go. In Fig. 3.2, you can see my suggestion. I have already added the new communication channels *Chatbot* and *social media* that were missing from your list. As discussed, I have omitted the communication channel *letter mail.*

Linda I agree with you. We should exclude analog postal communication from our problem-solving process. I find the diagram interesting. What do the arrows at each end of the relationships mean?

Jan As a requirements engineer, I have to disagree with you on the word *each* because there is only an arrow at one end of the relationships.

Linda Don't be more papal than the pope—You know what I mean.

Jan Of course, I just want to sharpen your sense of accuracy in language when it comes to requirements. In doubt, such articulations lead to misunderstandings and thus errors.
So, these arrows represent generalizations. A generalization is a summary of similar things or facts under a general term, in the direction the arrows point. For example, email is a specific tool (among several) for asynchronous communication.

Linda I see, and the chatbot is both a representative of synchronous communication, as it communicates directly with the customer, and a representative of asynchronous communication, in case one asks for a callback.

Jan Correct, and the knowledge base is a one-way street of information and therefore not a communication tool.
As promised, let me now present the most important roles and their interactions with the tools (Fig. 3.3). For this, I am not using a UML diagram, but rather a proprietary sketch, which should serve the purpose of visualizing relationships. The arrow directions represent the flow of data and communication between the different stakeholders and the tools.

Linda Wow, for the first time, you can see at a glance how many different channels the customers have available and the clerks have to monitor. For the latter, it is difficult to maintain an overview.I have seen a similar representation in an IT course, but there was only one element in the middle, and it was oval.

Jan I know which diagram you mean—The context diagram. We should look at it in detail later. But the oval in the middle is exactly what you imagine—a single Omni-Channel system that synchronizes all these tools from Fig. 3.3. My open question is whether you should introduce a standard tool to which the existing communication tools can be connected, or extend the existing tools with appropriate software. With the second alternative, you could develop your individual Omni-Channel system.

Linda You bring up an interesting thought, although I'm convinced we need to introduce a standard tool.

Jan But we don't have to decide right away whether to use a standard system or a custom tool. Let's get back to the task at hand. Our next steps would be the same for both alternatives.

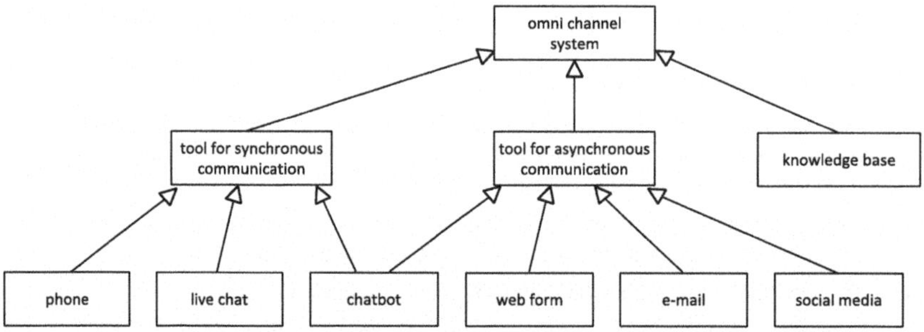

Fig. 3.2 Conceptual model of the Contact Center

3.2.2 Farewell to Illusions

Linda I suggest we conduct a workshop next to collect ideas from colleagues. It's very annoying that customers seem to complain more and more, and I would like to know why. To find out, we invite all involved colleagues and ask them for causes and solution suggestions for this issue. Afterwards, we write the requirements into a concept, choose a tool, and implement it.

Jan The plan seems initially plausible, but it could lead us into a dead end. When you say 'the requirements' and 'into a concept,' it sounds very much like a so-called waterfall project. In this type of project, the requirements for the software are documented in their entirety before a single line of source code is written or configurations have been done.

Linda That was indeed my plan until now. What's wrong with it? If we record the requirements and introduce a tool based on them, we can't proceed agilely, can we?

Jan Our initiative seems quite large, a complex IT system with many requirements. In this case, I would always recommend an agile approach. During the project, requirements can change, which in turn necessitates changes to other requirements. With agility, we can react much more flexibly to this dynamic and draw conclusions from it for already implemented functionalities.

Linda OK, OK. I'm somewhat familiar with agility. However, I can't imagine how you want to use agility in our project.

Jan I fear you have the idea that we will collect all the requirements, hand over the entire monolithic documentation to a tool provider, and a few weeks later everything will be set, right?

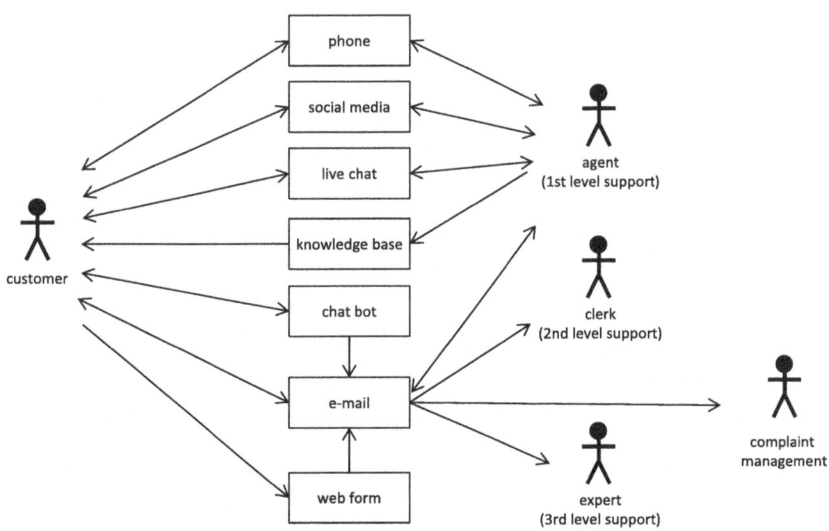

Fig. 3.3 Roles and their interactions with the tools

Linda Maybe not quite so straightforward, but in principle, yes. Do you have a better suggestion?

Jan My idea will probably surprise you, but I hope to convince you.

Linda I'm curious...

Jan There's nothing wrong with the workshop you planned initially. I actually think it's a good idea to supplement the requirements you already have in mind with additional requirements from other stakeholders. We can enrich this collection through individual interviews and rough basic requirements that I want to record using observation techniques. Additionally, we can have a group of customers fill out a questionnaire. The documentation of these requirements collected through four different techniques should only represent a *high-level concept*.

Linda And you think that the high-level concept is not enough to commission a tool provider?

Jan No, it is. I believe that it will be sufficient as a basis for a tender—Either for a product provider, i.e., a provider of standard software, or a software consulting firm, that also develops custom software.

Linda So you're still not ruling out the possibility of developing our IT solution for the contact center ourselves?

Jan As I said, I would at least keep the option open for now. You already have some individual technical components for an omni-channel system, but they are individual island solutions. These need to be centrally connected and synchronized using either a standard tool or custom software.

Linda Interesting thought, but won't it be much more expensive—Even with this starting position—To aim for custom development?

Jan We have to evaluate that. Introducing a tool makes you dependent on the tool manufacturers, who implement their own understanding of contact center processes and declare them as their standard. If the processes in your company largely coincide with those implemented in the tool, it could be cheaper. Small deviations could be compensated by configuring the tool. However, if the processes deviate more significantly, then there are two possibilities:

1. You adapt your processes to the processes of the tool provider. They like to call this 'standardizing the processes.'
2. You adapt the processes implemented in the tool through extensive customization to fit your ideas. This is essentially implementing the functionalities you need into the existing product. In the end, you pay for a special version of the tool, which incurs additional customization costs every time a new product version is rolled out.

Either way, you have to adapt one of the two—Business processes or their representation in the tool.

Linda These are not generally fixed standard processes, but only standard processes from the tool manufacturer's point of view. He has defined these for himself, which means …

Jan … that they do not necessarily have to be the best possible processes for you. Well, there are, of course, exceptions. Some tool providers offer many configuration options, so no line of code needs to be changed or rewritten. This keeps the adjustments to the company's internal processes within a financial framework.

Linda OK, in summary, we have two tasks:

1. Create a rough specification as a basis for a tender.
2. Decide whether the introduction of a standard tool or custom software development is more sensible for the contact center.

Jan Yes, more or less... But that's not all. The rough specification and the tender also serve as the basis for a rough effort estimate for the implementation project. Your sponsor will want to know the estimated costs.
And another hint: We will determine the result of the analysis in point 2 using a decision matrix.Additionally, I would like to give you some tips later on that are useful for the agile implementation project, such as...
3. The specification of user stories.
4. The formulation of acceptance criteria during the agile implementation project.
With the appropriate documentation, we would have four of many possible documentation artifacts in RE, as Fig. 3.4 is intended to illustrate.

We will focus on the four artifacts shown in Fig. 3.4 as we proceed.

- A *rough concept* as a basis for a tender: During the creation of the rough concept, we will explain general basics of RE in combination with the compact collection of requirements using the waterfall method.
- The created rough concept then serves as a basis for a *decision matrix*. With the help of this matrix, the decision is made whether the future IT system will be an established tool or developed through individual software development.
- You are aware that most software development and tool introduction projects nowadays are set up agile or at least semi-agile. Therefore, we will specifically address RE in agile projects. The most frequently used artifact in agile projects is the *User Story*. The term *Sprint Backlog Item*, or less commonly the term *Ticket*, are used synonymously.
- *Acceptance criteria* are essential for the approval of requirements. They specify the precise conditions and standards that must be fulfilled for a requirement to be deemed complete and satisfactory. These criteria act as clear benchmarks for both stakeholders and developers, ensuring a shared understanding of what constitutes successful implementation of the requirements.

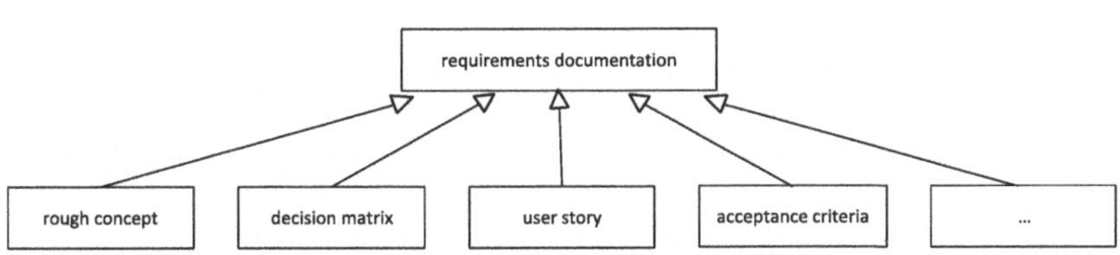

Fig. 3.4 Special manifestations of requirements documentation

Linda Ah, another class diagram with generalization relationships! It seems to be your favorite type of diagram.

Jan I also like other types of diagrams. However, like any tool, it has to fit the task. The class diagram is very suitable at the beginning of a project for correctly classifying terms.

Linda Yes, it definitely does that for me. I was not aware of the many possibilities for using a requirements specification. I thought a specification was always just the basis for software development or tool introduction. However, the fact that a tender can contain requirement documentation is completely logical.

3.3 Recognize the Relationship between Requirements and Process Management

Linda Now we should focus on preparing the workshop, right?

Jan Yes, we can certainly do that. During this process, we should also assess whether procedural adjustments are necessary for you. I believe that a new IT system alone will not suffice. In Fig. 3.1, I suggested that an IT system typically covers only part of a business process. However, we should examine the entire business process. I have two questions for you regarding this:

1. Is there a process owner for incoming customer inquiries and general communication with customers? You are only concerned with the contact Center.
2. Which stakeholders should participate in the workshop?

Linda Yes, your sketch made me realize that we should invite a representative from each department. We will document their ideas and incorporate them into our rough concept. Later, they will approve this concept, allowing us to develop the tender based on it.

Jan So far, we do not yet know the optimal process for 'handling customer concerns' in your contact Center, and therefore we do not know how an IT system could support you. At the moment, we can only make a few statements about how the contact Center process should *not* operate. Suggestions for improvement are, at best, patchy and inconsistent. What functionalities do you expect from the IT system? Suppose you introduce a tool. How do you choose the right tool with these unclear ideas?

To the point

To select the appropriate tool, you need to understand both the business process and the requirements for the supporting tool. ◄

Jan	I could think of a number of other questions. So far, we do not have a conclusive answer to any of these questions. The requirements engineer for system development would ask the same questions. My initial questions as a representative of a tool provider would be: • How is the process currently running? • Is the current process documented somewhere? • What procedural improvements are being sought? • Which steps of the customer Center process 'handling customer concerns' can the Omni-Channel system map? I could think of several other questions. So far, we do not have conclusive answers to any of these questions. A requirements engineer for system development would ask the same questions.
Linda	Now we should focus on preparing the workshop, right?
Jan	... Who would gladly take over these tasks without actually knowing your company. Additionally, you make yourselves dependent on them for the next few years by relinquishing complete responsibility. The disadvantage of using external companies is that if they leave the company one day, they also take their accumulated knowledge with them. For every process change, you will then have to consult the consultants of the tool provider.
Linda	I hope that won't happen to me with you.
Jan	I promise you that we will document the knowledge we build together in an appropriate format.

Linda already recognized from the frequently referenced sketch (Fig. 3.1) that business processes are increasingly supported and influenced by IT. The processes are becoming more and more a blend of...

- Process steps without IT,
- IT-supported process steps and.
- fully automated process steps.

Also, artificial intelligence is making its way more and more into the semi and fully automated process steps.

IT in general plays a major role in shaping process flows. Conversely, processes also require software that is appropriately tailored to them. The task of the requirements engineer is to address this interaction, structure complex issues, gather the necessary information as comprehensively as possible, and develop solutions in collaboration with IT architects, product owners, and the development team.

The support of process steps by IT occurs at various levels of complexity. It is becoming increasingly difficult to distinguish between process steps with and without IT. The following figures illustrate a simplified, abstract version of the symbiosis between processes and IT.

For their representations, we want to return to BPMN—the *Business Process Model and Notation.* BPMN offers several diagram types for different purposes, depending on whether the focus is on all individual activities and roles within the overall process or on the exchange of messages and communication relationships

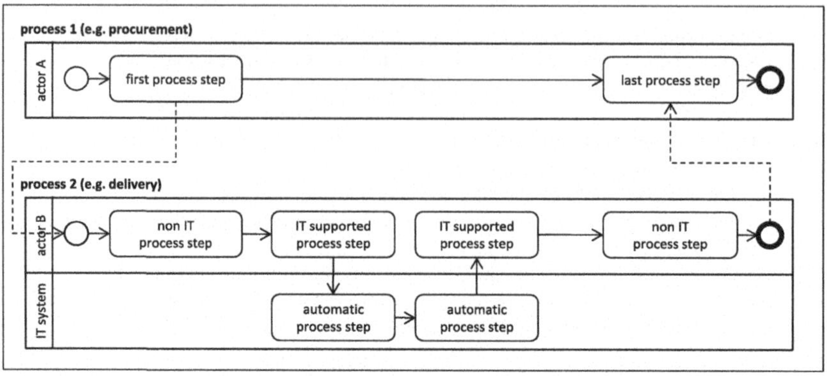

Fig. 3.5 Simple process representation

between actors. Interesting to note: Version 2.0.1 of BPMN was elevated to an international standard in ISO/IEC 19510 4 in 2013.

Returning to the explanation, let's first focus on the purely process-oriented representation from Fig. 3.5.

In Fig. 3.5, two interconnected processes are depicted. These are represented as pools in the form of rectangles and are read from left to right in the example. Process 1 (*Procurement*) interacts with Process 2 (*Delivery*). Actor A in Process 1 initiates the process (e.g., by *placing an order*) and expects feedback at the end of the process (e.g., *confirmation of the delivery of the ordered goods*). What occurs in Process 2 is not relevant from the perspective of Process 1. The reason for this lack of relevance could be that both processes occur in different companies but need to be synchronized with each other.

Actor B and an IT system are involved in Process 2. Actor B carries out activities without IT (e.g., *removing goods from the warehouse*) or with IT support (e.g., *booking out goods*); the IT system can handle individual process steps fully automatically (e.g., *reordering small quantities*).

Actor B and an IT system are involved in Process 2. Actor B performs activities either without IT (e.g., *removing goods from the warehouse*) or with IT support (e.g., *booking out goods*). The IT system can also handle individual process steps fully automatically (e.g., *reordering small quantities*).

If you apply a design trick and incorporate the (*process-supporting*) IT system into Process 2, the representation becomes significantly more complex (Fig. 3.6). The support of Process 2 (*Delivery*) by IT raises questions that extend beyond the traditional process view, such as:

- Who should work with this IT system?
- How should the user interface of the IT system be designed for the user?
- Are there other systems within the process that play a role?
- What are the interfaces to other processes and their IT applications?

- Does the process run 24 hours a day, and does the IT system need to be designed accordingly?
- What data needs to be measured and recorded?
- How are legal regulations for archiving and deleting data complied with?
- Can business rules that control the process be represented in a separate application?

At this stage, the boundaries between process management and IT merge. In the example provided, the initial focus is on the process view, which is quickly expanded to include technical and user-specific questions.

Linda and Jan decide to include the open questions about the process view as a key item in the workshop agenda.

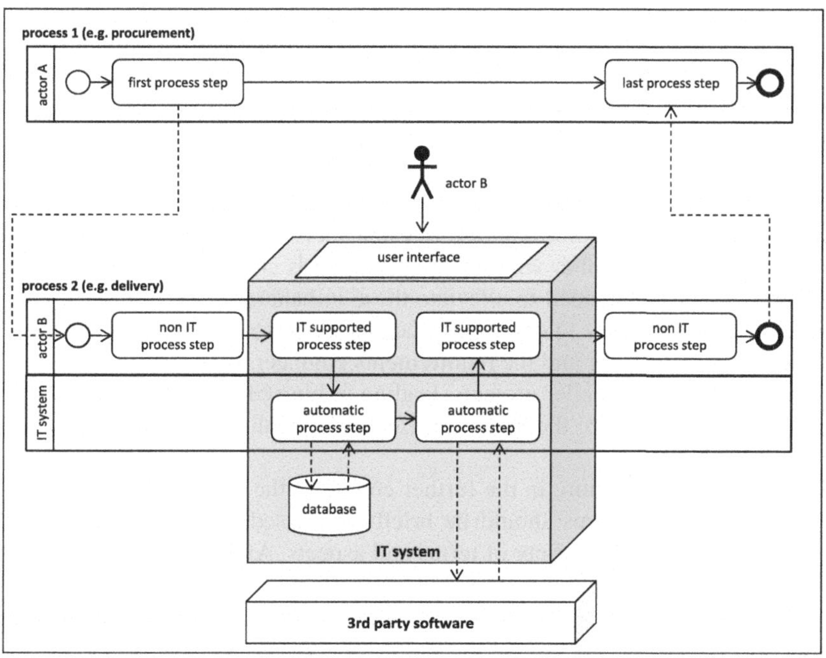

Fig. 3.6 Relationship between process and IT

3.4 Recognize the Relation between Requirements and Project Management

Linda OK. You have now structured and visualized the information so far. You have convinced me and clearly shown in Fig. 3.1 that we also need to include the process view in our work. You are probably right that merely selecting a tool is not enough. But before we get into the details, you should give me a better general understanding of RE. You mentioned some terms in our previous conversations, such as process model, work steps, and standards. I realize that I need some tutoring.

Jan Then let's untangle the jumble of terms as a first step and sort them correctly. After that, I would like to provide you with some helpful knowledge on the topics of *requirements* and *RE*. You will realize that not all requirements are the same, just as not all vehicles are the same.

'Jumble of terms' is an apt description of what sometimes prevails in projects. The reason for the confusion is simple and lies in the nature of project organization. This form of organization consists of a temporary project team, composed of members from different organizational areas or departments for each project. These members bring different working methods and varying levels of methodological knowledge. For example, the necessary modeling is highly individualized by the person currently describing the relevant facts. To complicate matters, each project participant is familiar with different standards and notations and uses them in the project. RE is intended to alleviate these imbalances.

For RE, it is necessary to distinguish between two topics and thus at least two roles: the project manager and the requirements engineer. In reality, these two roles are often combined in smaller projects, leading to blurred boundaries, internal conflicts (e.g., 'Do I prioritize the budget or rather the quality of the requirements?'), and overlooked tasks.

To provide a clear picture in the further course of the project '*Reorganize Contact Center*,' relevant terms should be briefly discussed and contextualized. It is important to organize the variety of terms and aspects. An illustration can be found in Fig. 3.7.

In this illustration, the different aspects are primarily assigned to the respective management disciplines of project management (PM) or RE. The aspects situated higher up have more of a project management character, while the lower ones have more of an RE character. Two things are noticeable at first glance:

- The topics PM and RE can be separated.
- The topics PM and RE cannot be completely separated. They need each other; there are several connections between the disciplines.

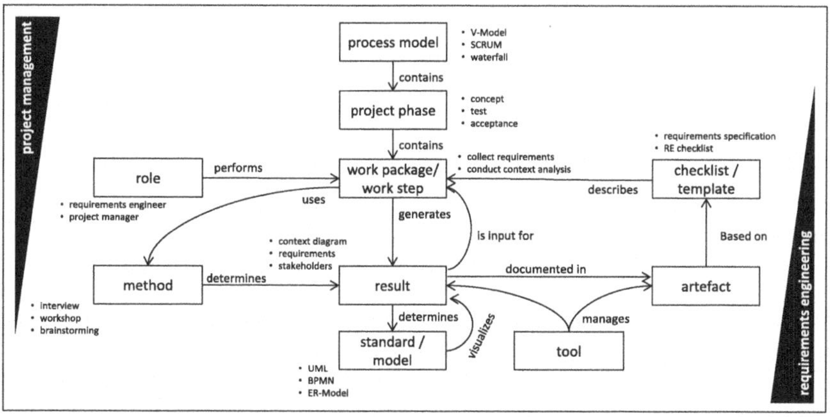

Fig. 3.7 Aspects of requirement engineering and project management

To the point
IT project management and requirements engineering are distinct IT disciplines that complement each other. ◀

But what characterizes the two major building blocks *project management* and *RE*? What distinguishes them, where are the similarities?

3.4.1 Self-Evident Aspects of Project Management

Project management is a universal discipline that enables one to plan, organize, manage, and control projects. It is independent of the type of projects and primarily deals with the project dimensions of:

- Scope.
- Time & deadlines.
- Costs & resources.

These three points are often represented in a so-called *magic project triangle* because they are always interdependent. This means that changing one parameter is not possible without adjusting another. For example, if the scope increases, it affects the costs and/or deadlines. Similarly, if deadlines are adjusted, it automatically impacts the resources or the scope to be delivered (Fig. 3.8).

In Sect. 2.3.4, we detailed the potential cost explosions that can occur when requirement defects are not detected in time. Therefore, the requirements engineer bears partial responsibility for the three dimensions in the magic triangle.

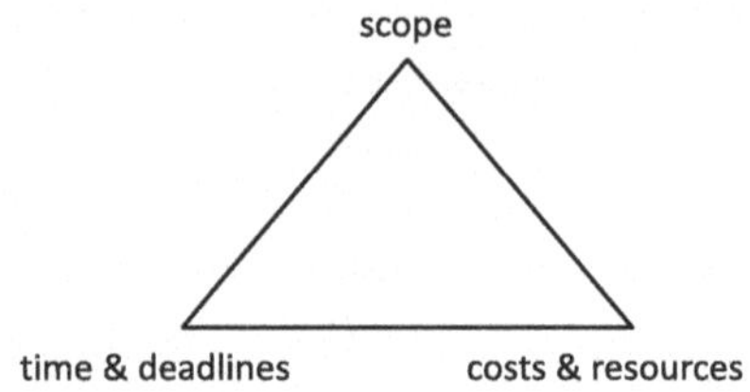

Fig. 3.8 Magic Project Triangle

There are extensive tools for controlling projects in the form of milestone plans, cost and resource plans, organigrams, project structure plans, etc.

Let's consider the project structure plan: This plan assigns larger task packages to the different project phases for everyone to see. Depending on the project (house construction, software development, or machine construction), different activities are required or even prescribed. How does the project manager know which work packages are intended for the respective project phases? Mostly from experience or with the help of prepared templates. To facilitate this, different process models have been developed for individual industries. Their purpose is to apply consistent schemes to projects of a similar type. In IT, for example, there are agile methods like *Scrum* or *Extreme Programming* and heavyweight methods like the *Waterfall model* or *V-Model*.

Most process models—whether agile or heavyweight—divide projects into phases, such as conception, realization, testing, and rollout. These phases are manageable portions of the project, aggregated from numerous work packages. Figure 3.9 shows an example of a classic project structure plan (PSP). For RE, the briefly outlined work packages are already visualized in the PSP.

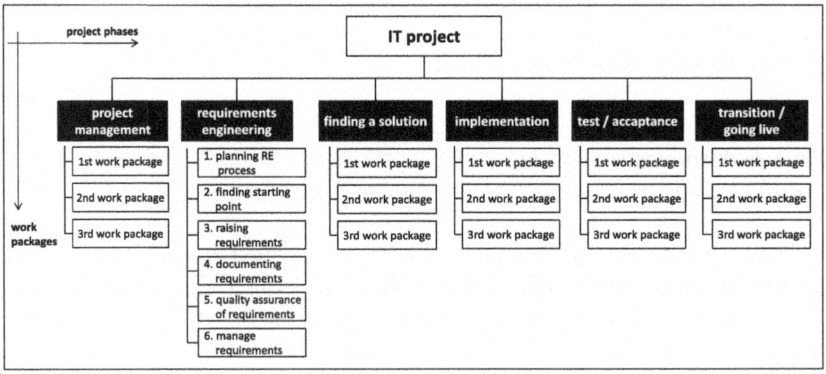

Fig. 3.9 Framework of a project structure plan

3.4.2 The Requirements Engineering Work Packages

In the literature, there are varying numbers of suggested work packages for requirements engineering (RE). The exact number is not crucial. What is important is that all necessary activities are considered in their entirety and assigned to appropriate work packages.

To the point
The project plan must specify the work packages and activities required to determine the requirements for an IT system.◄

The following proposal includes six work packages. These are the work packages that play a central role in this book, with each being dedicated a separate day in the course of the book. The exception is packages 5 and 6, which we will address together on a single day.

Work Package 1: Plan RE Process.
This work package runs parallel to project planning. The RE process plan makes general decisions, such as the content and form of documentation or the tools to be used for RE, including UI design. Concrete decisions are made in agile projects in a Way of Working document.

Work Package 2: Find Starting Point.
For a successful project, questions about the current status and the desired goal need to be clarified right at the beginning. Terms used must be recorded in a glossary, and the relationships between the terms must be modeled. Subsequently, the project content to be processed is delineated from its surrounding environment, and all important stakeholders are identified as input providers for the requirements. The initial situation of the project is transparently and comprehensibly demonstrated to all participants.

Work Package 3: Gather Requirements.
Once the boundaries have been established and the project focus has been refined, the collection of requirements begins. Requirements can come from (a) stakeholders, (b) the existing system landscape, or (c) existing documentation. However, our book limits the collection of requirements to stakeholders, i.e., point (a).

Work Package 4: Document Requirements.
Closely linked to the collection is the documentation of requirements. In the corresponding chapter, we specifically address the use of various notations, models, and artifacts to represent different requirement categories, such as processes, data elements, and interfaces.

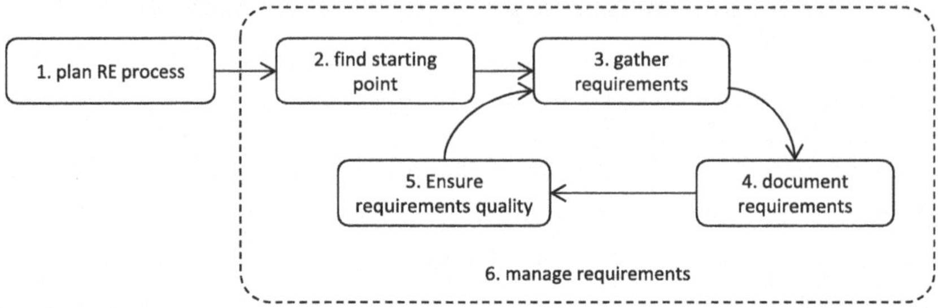

Fig. 3.10 Sequence of RE work packages during a project

Work Package 5: Ensure the Quality of Requirements.

After compiling and presenting all requirements, the requirements engineer analyzes them, e.g., for gaps and contradictions. Subsequently, the requirements in their entirety are reviewed and accepted by the stakeholders. This results in a milestone of the RE project phase, marked by approved and quality-assured requirements. In agile projects, the term milestone might be too strong, as this point must be reached repeatedly in each sprint.

Work Package 6: Managing Requirements.

Managing requirements is a fundamental work package. It may not be as visible as the others, but it ensures that all stakeholders have access to the current status of the requirements at all times and that the information is managed appropriately. Terms such as attribution, prioritization, and traceability of requirements play a major role in requirements management.

While work packages 1 and 2 are executed sequentially, work packages 3 to 5 should be addressed iteratively in both agile and heavyweight methods (Fig. 3.10). In an agile approach, the implementation of quality-assured requirements follows each completion of work package 5, whereas in heavyweight methods, all iterations are completed before realization begins.

Work package 6 runs continuously parallel to work packages 2 to 5.

We will describe the RE approach in agile methods in more detail in Chap. 8.

3.4.3 The Benefits of RE in IT Projects

After Linda and Jan decided on a procedure based on their work packages (Fig. 3.9), they turned their attention to the fundamental knowledge about requirements engineering (RE). Jan had already informed Linda that a slightly academic section was forthcoming.

To the point
Why do we need RE? After all, we all know what we want! ◄

It's about a better understanding of:

- The necessity of good requirements or the effects of poor requirements.
- The qualitative requirements for requirements.
- The style rules for formulating requirements.

The discussion begins...

Linda We have discussed the project activities, and the six work packages make sense to me. You had already mentioned that you would now share further knowledge from your experience on the subject of RE. I find this important as preparation for the workshop, because we need to convince our colleagues of the importance of professional RE. Many stakeholders are already overloaded with numerous projects and meetings. They would rather see solutions than discuss requirements in detail and ensure the quality of the documented requirements. Our task should be to convince them that professional RE is the foundation for the success of our approach. This fact is fundamentally known to everyone, but in concrete terms, most people struggle with RE.
I think you can still provide useful arguments. How do we, in your opinion, plausibly justify the necessity of professionally collected, documented, and quality-assured requirements?

Jan Well, why do we need structured and sensibly formulated requirements? Only through these can we sort out our wishes and thoughts. We can present them in a verifiable way and find consensus with other participants. This becomes very clear when we mentally simulate the scenario of having *no* well-thought-out requirements. For my example, I will switch from the IT industry to the construction industry.
Imagine it with a house: Everyone basically knows houses—Big and small, old and new. Most people live in a single or multi-family house. Nobody would think of starting the construction of a new house without an agreed plan, just because they assume that all participants already know houses. No one would start with the slogan: "We all know what houses look like. Let's start building another house." it is completely clear that you have to agree on many things—The number of apartments, the layout and equipment of the rooms, the size of the windows, the placement of the chimney, etc.
Back to IT. In IT, the reality of projects often looks different. Software is hard to visualize—Everything takes place in the mind. Relationships must be recognized and facts abstracted. The system environments are not as visibly recognizable as the walls on a construction site, which causes difficulties for many project participants. So often, they *just get started*.

Linda I know that. In my past projects, I have also frequently struggled with such uncertainties. I think that's human.

Jan Then you know very well what can go wrong. Tell me, what were, in your view, common weaknesses in the projects?

This request prompts Linda to list various observed deficiencies. Jan adds points that are problematic from an IT perspective, and together they gather the issues that bother them most in IT projects:

- The *quality of the specification* is inadequate: Often, specifications are written in a novel-like, purely natural language form. This might make them understandable for end users, but developers face difficulties. They cannot immediately distinguish between requirements, wishes, descriptions of the current state, explanations, and irrelevant content. For those who are supposed to develop the system based on these specifications, identifying the correct requirements is not an easy task. Jan adds that this also applies to tender documents, making it difficult for the consulting firm to prepare an offer.
- *Indecisive stakeholders* are another critical point. Often, they know what they *do not* want, but they do not know *what* they want. For example, a house facade would only accidentally receive the desired paint if one only knew that the color should not be black under any circumstances.
- As a third reason, they see—as already detailed in Sect.2.3 —a significant risk in linguistic misunderstandings. *Natural language* has many pitfalls. Either there are different terms for the same concept, such as running, jogging, racing, or a term has multiple meanings, such as spring or bat. This often leads to multiple interpretations, which each stakeholder makes from their own perspective.
- Important requirements are only formulated during the *test and acceptance phase*. It is only at this stage that users realize some aspects were not considered. The most frequently heard sentence is then: "I imagined it quite differently."
- These subsequently identified requirements influence the project in the form of *change requests*, which result in the revision of the project planning. As a result, costs spiral out of control, deadlines are missed, and the project duration is significantly exceeded.
- The chosen application cannot be *integrated into the existing system environment*. The components do not fit together. Unlike in football, where the round ball has to go into the square goal, in IT both components must either be 'round' or 'square.'
- The solution is *not accepted* by the users and rejected for these and other reasons.
- And the project classics: Without RE, *project tasks are forgotten* and *efforts are underestimated*. As a result, implementation times are extended and costs exceed the budget.

Linda While we have gathered all the details, I noticed that there are quite a few stumbling blocks on the way to a successful project. I had never been so aware of this before.

Jan Many of these issues will recur in projects without professional RE. If we don't want to run blindly into failure, we must deal thoroughly with RE.

Linda From a product owner's perspective, I had never considered these far-reaching consequences until today. The impact of inadequate specifications is quite striking when you think about it more closely. However, we have so far taken a very negative view. I would like to balance this by listing the essential necessities of RE for a successful project.

Jan Then let's briefly consider why we need requirements. The most obvious reason comes to mind immediately.

Linda As a guideline for the developers. How else would they know what they should develop? What other reasons do you see?

Jan Your reason is significant, but only one of several. My two favorites regarding the justification for RE are:

- The requirements are an important building block for the *cost calculation*. The better it is understood what the service to be provided should include, the better its price can be calculated.
- The described requirements should be part of the *contract*. The BGB has formulated corresponding paragraphs for work contracts or compensation for breach of duty. Even if this argument is not so important for our internal project, we should take it seriously.

Your reason is significant, but only one of several. My two favorites regarding the justification for RE are:

- Requirements are an important building block for *cost calculation*. The better the service to be provided is understood, the more accurately its price can be calculated.
- The described requirements should be part of the contract. The *common law system* in the UK has formulated corresponding principles for work contracts or compensation for breach of duty. In the USA, the *uniform commercial code (UCC)* provides guidelines for contracts, including those related to work and compensation for breach of duty. In Germany, the German civil code (BGB) has respective paragraphs.

Linda These two reasons can indeed be very existential for a company. If they are not given enough attention, it can have a significant impact on the company's finances.

Jan Other important reasons:

- The documentation of the requirements serves as a basis for communication, allowing stakeholders to exchange the current status of the requirements.
- Very crucial and often underestimated is the importance of the requirements for the test and acceptance phase. What was not precisely defined at the beginning cannot be interpreted as an error during testing if it does not meet expectations. Anyone who only specified in the requirements that they want a car cannot complain about the color or size upon delivery.

Linda That's enough for now. These are already a lot of reasons. Anyone who still does not recognize the necessity of good RE cannot be helped anymore. The arguments are very convincing. We should definitely bring up these reasons in the kick-off so that our colleagues understand the importance of the concept phase.

To the point
Professional RE removes project obstacles and simultaneously forms the foundation for other project phases.◄

3.5 Understanding the Quality Characteristics of Requirements

Linda Another point: You mentioned paying a lot of attention to the quality of the requirements. What methods do you know to assess the quality?

Jan I thought you'd never ask... This is one of the central points of RE.

Jan revisits the requirement defects introduced in Sect. 2.3 and discusses with Linda the potential impacts of defects detected too late.

Linda I have learned that many mistakes can be made when formulating requirements. These mistakes would then affect the entire project. How do I recognize poor quality requirements?

Jan Of course, there are quality requirements that you can memorize and that we will discuss shortly. But a lot is a matter of experience. Over time, you have to develop the sensitivity to recognize well-formulated and poorly formulated requirements. I'll give three general requirements as examples, which are typical in terms of their degree of precision. You tell me if you think the requirements are precise enough:

1. The car should be faster than the previous one.
2. The ATM payout should only work with a PIN.
3. The users of the tool can view and change customer data.

Are the requirements okay from your point of view?

Linda Sounds reasonable at first. I have an idea of what the requirement provider wants. But I assume you have some criticisms, otherwise you wouldn't ask the question this way.

Jan Let's see:
For 1: What exactly is the previous car? Is it your own old car or the one that just passed by? How fast was the car you are referring to? Even if we knew, how fast should the new one be? Is a minimal increase sufficient, or is a significant performance leap expected?

For 2: One can assume that the PIN is meant to be entered by the account holder. We know it no other way from personal experience. Nevertheless, it would be clearer for all parties involved if the sentence were formulated in the active voice. Then it would also be clear who the actor is and who is allowed to withdraw money.

For 3: Are these extensive rights really granted to all users? Or is it necessary to sensibly restrict them to certain user groups?
You see, there are several reasons for improvement.

Linda I personally would have accepted the original requirements. However, I would have interpreted the last example differently. Of course, it's not all users who can change customer data, but only certain groups.

Jan And why don't you just list the groups that are allowed to do this?

Linda They are known. They are the ones who are already working with the customer today.

Jan This logic is vulnerable. In the new solution, certain rights might need to be deliberately restricted or expanded. Even if not, you may know the user groups, but are you sure the developer knows them?

Linda I hadn't considered this option at all. Finish your examples now. I would be interested to know how you would have formulated the requirements.

Jan My suggestions:

- For 1: The car must be able to reach a top speed of 170 km/h.
- For 2: The customer must confirm the withdrawal at the ATM with their PIN.
- For 3: The system must offer the customer advisor the ability to create, read, and modify all customer data, but not delete it.

You are welcome to evaluate whether you prefer my requirement formulations.

Linda They are really better formulated. But what exactly do I need to pay attention to now?

Jan There are different recommendations for the properties of software requirements. The two most important quality features from my point of view are:

- *Verifiability:* The person who has to accept the requirements should not do it based on personal liking, but on defined parameters. This way, you won't end up arguing whether the requirement is met or not; see also my example with the speed of the car.
- *Unambiguity:* There should be no possibilities for interpretation at this level of requirement formulation. If two people interpret the requirement differently, then it is not well formulated. For this reason, I also advocate for noting the requirements in active form, not in passive. Not "the payout may only be possible with PIN," but "the customer must confirm with PIN."

I personally consider these properties to be the most important. Therefore, when formulating requirements, I also ask myself the following two questions:

1. Could another stakeholder understand this requirement differently (or want to)?
2. What would I base a test on, or how could the acceptance criteria be formulated?

I must be able to answer these questions myself sensibly; otherwise, the requirement is definitely not well formulated.

Linda This certainly places demands on the requirement formulator. A blanket demand like *'I would like this and that functionality'* is not sufficient.

Jan Correct. Writing requirements and thus creating the concept becomes more complex. And it gets even more challenging because there are other important quality requirements:

- *Completeness (I):* Business departments immediately think of the requirements they urgently need to be implemented. However, there are also numerous obvious basic requirements (Sect. 2.3.2). From the departments' perspective, these are self-evident things that do not need to be mentioned, as they seem to be known to all. This occurs, for example, when existing processes are only partially adapted. So, only the planned changes to the process are named, without describing the unchanged part of the process. Therefore, complete documentation of requirements becomes necessary when it is not ensured that the omitted information is truly known to everyone.
- *Completeness (II):* Furthermore, the sum of all requirements must fully describe the required functionalities and must not leave any gaps.
- *Priority* is a feature that you mentioned earlier: For various reasons, not all requirements can always be implemented immediately. Thus, it is important to be able to prioritize the multitude of requirements. A prioritization according to legal relevance would be a good idea. For example, a *must* requirement is a requirement that must be implemented, a *should* requirement should be implemented if possible, and a *will* requirement is an option for the future. However, there may also be other or additional priorities, such as legal requirements or the financial framework.
- *Consistency:* The requirements must not contradict themselves or others ('deafening silence').

There are some more *requirements for requirements.* If you want to get information beyond what we have discussed so far, I can recommend the work of *Aybüke Aurum and Claes Wohlin* (Aurum & Wohlin, 2005).

Linda Thanks for the tip—I'll take a look. Let me summarize briefly. We have discussed:

- The (requirement-specific) weaknesses in the project.
- The arguments for the necessity of good requirements engineering.
- The quality criteria that requirements must meet.

Do you have any more tips that we can use right away?

Jan Yes. I have another point from the category: It scares the English teacher, but helps the requirements engineer. If you can still remember your English lessons at school, the comments on the returned essays will have stayed in your memory. Often, it was said that you should not always use the same words or that the sentence structure was not varied enough. Unfortunately, these hints are now being followed by some inexperienced requirements engineers in specification documents where they have no place at all. It is true that formulating requirements is not comparable to writing fiction. Now, a few tricks to enhance the clarity of requirements:

- I mentioned it already—Formulate in *active voice*: A sentence formulated in the active voice contains an actor. This is the first step in developing roles and permissions. In contrast, in the passive voice, there is only an object with which something is done; the actor remains unknown.
- *Indivisibility*: A requirement should not be further subdivided. This is, of course, always challenging and only applies to the respective level of detail of the requirement description.

- Use *sentence templates*: In specification documents a lot of prose text can be hindering. It is better to write requirements according to the same sentence scheme. The use of such sentence templates may be boring to read, but it helps to reduce requirements defects. I will show you what this sentence template can look like in practice in a few days when we deal with the documentation of the requirements (Sect. 7.1).
- *Mix* natural language descriptions with graphic models. Always use the most suitable form of presentation for the requirements. For example, no architect will describe the floor plan of a house in text, and for the parameters of the heating system, they will certainly not use a pictorial representation.
- Use the same term for the same fact; do not use different terms.
- Formulate short sentences.
- Formulate legally (non-)binding requirements using the words must, should, and will, if they have been agreed upon in the project. This immediately prioritizes the requirements.
- *Question* requirements that use *universal quantifiers* like always, all, never, or similar extremes. Is this activity really always carried out, or are there exceptions? Does it affect all users, and if not, which ones?
- Mark open points.

To the point

Requirements must meet certain quality criteria. This can be achieved through various stylistic principles.◄

Linda I should have known that there was more to come. If you're interested in my opinion: I find all the diverse information you've given me very interesting. Some things I need to think through for myself. Others are crystal clear to me because I've experienced them myself. Unlike in the past, when I perceived many facts more with my gut feeling, I see myself in the future being able to question or control certain topics more consciously.

That should be enough for the first day. I understand that we can't start a workshop tomorrow. Even the invitation for it is too early. But I would like to take a step further with you—Let's start setting up our project-specific rules for RE. We'll meet tomorrow to tackle the next steps together.

I had the idea to write down the most important points. You gave me many interesting aspects and arguments. It would be a shame if I forgot them. Plus, I have a guide for the next project.

3.6 Linda's Notepad

For Linda, it was a long but informative day that brought many new insights. Her notes summarize the *basics about RE*:

Day 1: Basics about RE

The six steps of RE for a project are:

1. *Plan and control RE,*
2. *Find a starting point,*
3. *Collect requirements,*
4. *Document requirements,*
5. *Ensure the quality of requirements,*
6. *Manage requirements,*

→ *distinguish between classic and agile project approach, as these tasks are combined differently.*

- *Requirements consider not only technology, but also organization and processes.*
- *Use known standards for modeling as often as possible.*
- *Processes consist of activities without IT + activities with IT + autonomous backend processing.*
- *A conceptual model provides clarity.*
- *Effective RE has a positive effect on.*
  - *The accuracy of the calculation,*
  - *The contract components between sponsor (or client) and contractor,*
  - *The specifications for the developers,*
  - *The creation of test cases based on RE artifacts,*
  - *The acceptance of the solution by the end users and thus the success of the project,*
  - *The communication and agreement between stakeholders,*
  - *The identification of gaps and basic requirements in specifications.*
- *Consider* (quality) requirements for requirements (e.g., *unambiguous and verifiable).*

→ *ask yourself, for example, the following two questions to assess the quality of the requirements:*

1. *Could someone understand (want to understand) the requirement differently? → unambiguity.*
2. *What could the acceptance criteria or test cases matching the requirement look like? → verifiability.*

Note 'Saying does not mean meaning' and 'hearing does not mean understanding'

→ *Constantly question the formulations of requirements (e.g., form short sentences, use uniform word choice, question general statements like 'always,' 'all,' or 'never')*

References

Aurum, A., & Wohlin, C. (2005). *Engineering and managing software requirements.* Springer.

Blokdyk, G. (2020). *Event Driven Process Chain.* 5DSTARCooks.

Miles, R.,& Hamilton, K. (2006). *Learning UML 2.0* (1st ed.). O'Reilly Media.

Object Management Group. *Business Process Model and Notation.* Retrived June 06 2025 from https:// www.omg.org/spec/BPMN/ISO/19510/PDF (2013).

Stachowiak, H. (1973). *General model theory.* Springer.

Day 2: Planning RE in the Project

4

Those who start with RE initially ask themselves: Do you really need to plan RE, or can you just start with requirement collection? Sure, planning is not absolutely necessary. You could also start a journey without a plan. Those who love surprises and are attracted by randomness in observing and discovering may find planning a hindrance. But those who have a goal in mind and want to achieve it should think about the way there beforehand.

> **To the point**
> What measures and rules are necessary for a project to benefit from the use of RE?◄

4.1 Define Work Packages

In our case, planning is indispensable. Regarding RE, the responsible roles, necessary work steps, their order of execution, and much more need to be defined. Additionally, transparent rules must be agreed upon by all participants to enable effective cooperation. The established rules serve as guidelines, based on which the project process can be controlled. Such planning and control tasks are usually carried out for projects as a whole. However, there are some special considerations for RE. This chapter is dedicated exclusively to planning activities and rules from the perspective of RE.

J. Kawelke and T. Niebisch, *AI-Driven Transformation - Practical Frameworks for Real-World Impact*, Future of Business and Finance,
https://doi.org/10.1007/978-3-662-72549-8_4

Day 2 begins with Linda and Jan considering their next steps. Their goal is to create a *rough concept*, the content of which will then flow into two further artifacts:

- A *decision matrix*, which supports the decision between individual software development or an introduced standard product,
- A *tender* for the implementation project to execute the decision made.

The goal of the overall project is to eliminate the identified weak points in the Customer Center.

They decide to initially ignore the overarching project management activities related to deadlines, resources, and budget, and focus exclusively on the points they need for RE. They will then document the results of their considerations in a so-called RE plan.

Linda A Chinese proverb says that even the longest journey begins with a single step. But before we start planning, I want to address something that has been on my mind since yesterday.

Jan Go ahead, our discussions have always been refreshing so far.

Linda We have talked a lot about *the project*. But due to the separation of *rough concept creation* and the actual *implementation project*, aren't we talking about two projects?

Jan You could see it that way. However, the task is to achieve an improvement in the Customer Center. This task does not end with the rough concept, even if it forms the basis for the decision matrix and the subsequent tender. I suggest considering it as a total project with an actually implemented technical solution in terms of planning. Therefore, I would like to call this rough concept project Phase 1 for simplicity's sake, and the implementation project Phase 2. This does not mean that we have to proceed identically in both phases.

In Fig. 4.1, you can see our essential project steps outlined as a rough project plan in the form of a Gantt chart. I have also depicted the supporting resources that are absolutely necessary for individual work steps.

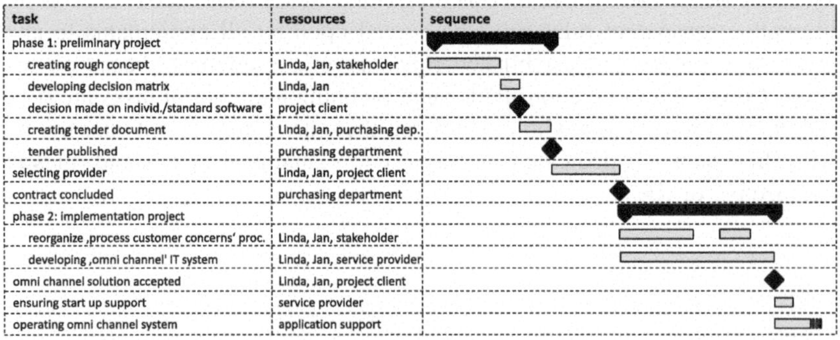

Fig. 4.1 Project plan

Jan We will collect requirements, document them in the rough concept, and ensure their quality. Our deliverables in Phase 1 are the decision matrix and the tender document, both represented as milestones in the form of a rhombus. The content of the tender document will depend not only on the rough concept but also on the decision between a *standard tool or custom software*. Therefore, we will only create the tender after the decision has been made.

The project team for Phase 1 is small, consisting of you, me, the stakeholders to be determined, and, if necessary, the project sponsor and the purchasing department. Therefore, each of us will have to take on multiple project roles. For example, you will be both the project manager and product owner. I will take on roles such as requirements engineer and quality manager. The stakeholders will provide us with the requirements. We need the project sponsor to make the final decisions—that is beyond our area of competence. The purchasing department is responsible for creating the formal tender documents and handling negotiations.

Linda Ok, I'm looking forward to shaping my roles.

Jan And just to get it out of the way: For Phase 2, I recommend that you relinquish the project manager role and focus entirely on the product owner role.

Linda I'll keep that in mind. But let's take the first step: plan RE and make agreements! Even though Phase 2 is still far away, I would be happy if we could plan for both phases in parallel. I am aware that the future contractor for the implementation phase will have their own ideas and will adjust the planning accordingly. Nevertheless, I would then be well prepared and could participate in the discussion. How do we best start—from scratch?

Jan No, luckily not. I have recapitulated some basic aspects and experiences from previous projects. I suggest that we work out the points generally required for RE planning. We won't need all of them in both phases.

Linda All right, let's hear it.

Jan I fear that my list of planning aspects might be a bit tedious. Be patient! I would start with planning contents that are sufficient for Phase 1, but of course, also play a role in Phase 2. In Phase 2, there are additional aspects to consider. There are several points that are very important to me, which initially concern the requirements themselves. For these, we should agree on common definitions:

- The number of requirements practically demands some form of structure or systematics. Therefore, we should define the initial *categories* into which we divide these requirements. One could distinguish between functional requirements, constraints, and quality requirements, as IREB—the International Requirements Engineering Board—suggests. For Phase 2, I would add solution design and operational requirements.
- Requirements can be visualized or noted in various ways using certain *notations and models*. For example, it makes sense to specify that the representation of business and system-internal processes follows the BPMN standard, rather than using UML activity diagrams or EPKs.
- The requirements must be summarized in *RE-relevant artifacts*. It must be defined which artifacts need to be created and in which format they must be accessible.
- All requirements have *attributes* that further specify them. Such an attribute could be an identifier or information about origin or urgency. Maintaining these attributes requires some effort but increases knowledge about the requirement. From a cost-benefit perspective, it is necessary to evaluate which attributes are required per requirement or requirement category.
- Are there *legally binding formulations* for the requirements (e.g., *must* a requirement be implemented or *should* it be realized if the budget allows)?

We should agree on the manifestation of these and other aspects of the requirements.

In addition to the specifications regarding the requirements, the specific *RE process* must be planned for all activities. We have already agreed on the collection, documentation, management, analysis, and quality assurance of the requirements. It needs to be planned *who* is responsible for *which* of these process steps.

The creation and maintenance of the glossary are also very important for communication. We can even include this in the tender. It will then be expanded in Phase 2.

Linda May I interrupt here, Jan? You've already talked about graphical models and now about the glossary. I assume we will delve into these topics later. But basically, I have never seen such elements in a tender. Most of the tenders we have created were mostly textual, sometimes with tabular elements.

Jan That's not unusual; I too have rarely seen tenders with graphics. Occasionally, a customer might include an architecture model, but that's about it. That's why I'm so glad I can now 'take the wheel' and create a tender as I would like it as an IT provider. This would be a tender that goes into more detail and illuminates the problem from multiple angles. As a result, a provider understands the project context well and gets a solid basis for estimating the efforts.

Linda We should have this standardized by the IPMA—the International Project Management Association. *(Linda smiles)*

Jan *(smiles back)* I couldn't agree more...
But back to the RE plan, which we need at least for Phase 1. In agile projects, where project-specific plans and procedures merge even more with RE plans, a so-called *Way of Working* document is often created, containing the details of an RE plan. We will discuss the structure of the Way of Working in detail later (Sect. 8.5)

Linda Up to this point, it sounds understandable to me. I wouldn't omit any of the points listed for Phase 1. If I remember correctly, we need specifications about requirement categories, their notation, and documentation possibilities, as well as their attribute set. Additionally, we plan the necessary tasks and assign responsibilities. We record all this in an RE plan. I am now interested in the aspects that we can push into the background in Phase 1 and that you would additionally suggest for Phase 2.

Jan Here you are:
The agreement on a *process model* for Phase 2 (e.g., Scrum or a company-specific model) is actually the responsibility of the project manager, but the requirements engineer should provide advisory input. Such process models offer a project skeleton and thus provide rules, templates, and requirements for the project in general and RE in particular. The advantage of process models is that they do not start project planning completely from scratch but build on an existing foundation. Phase 1 has low complexity in planning. Therefore, we do not agree on a specific process model.

Linda But your earlier explanations about the procedure in Phase 1, including the sketch (Fig. 1.2), are also a process model, aren't they?

Jan Hmm... actually, you're right. Even if it's a rather simple one. Well, there we have another IPMA standard for 'dummies.' *(Jan can't help but laugh)*

Linda *(laughs along)* OK, finally a point for me. What decisions should we make for phase 2?

Jan First, I see topics related to the management of requirements: The choice of tools for capturing and managing requirements is one point. Apart from facilitating the parallel capture of requirements by several requirements engineers, suitable specialized requirements management tools also support

- The traceability of requirements
- The prioritization of requirements
- The management of requirement versions
- The creation of different views on requirements
- The management of requirement changes
- The management of configurations, etc.

But since there is no such tool in your company, we must decide whether to introduce a specialized tool or rely on office and agile project management tools.

Linda But these management functions are still quite foreign to me...

Jan Don't worry, we will deal with this in more detail at the appropriate time. I am happy to list further aspects that we need to consider in Phase 2:

- If we do not introduce a specialized requirements management tool, we must decide which of the above *management functions* we mandate even without a tool and how we implement these functions.
- Requirements will be subject to changes repeatedly. The *Change Request process* (CR process) for adding or changing requirements should be defined. In Phase 1, the requirements will change frequently, but this does not affect further project phases. The CR process becomes appropriate when we start the realization phase and the changes to requirements have serious time and commercial implications.
- In every project, it is advantageous to coordinate the type of *communication* with the stakeholders:
  - How are the stakeholders kept up to date?
  - How are the review and acceptance of requirements carried out?

We will design this communication with your colleagues as needed.

- And last but not least, monitoring the requirements and evaluating the different attributes should be considered.

Linda In total, there are quite a few aspects to consider for the individual planning of RE. This planning is more challenging than I originally thought. I need to think through and question the listed points individually.

Jan Assume that not all points are necessary in every project. However, it is better to consciously exclude them than to unintentionally forget them. Such forgotten regulations will sooner or later take their toll on the project.

Linda I agree with that. My understanding of planning also primarily sees it as mental work. I mentally deal with *what* I want to achieve and *how*. And if I want to create something complex, then I should invest some thought into it.

I only see one danger in such planning topics: the lack of acceptance. The management of the Customer Center will ask me what we actually do all day. And when I then tell them that we are establishing and discussing rules for the rough concept phase, I can hear that they want to see quick results.

Jan The actual need for clarification and planning is not as extensive as it initially appears. We have already excluded many things for Phase 1 and are not considering them further. So the effort for planning is not as high as originally feared. Moreover, you can provide a counterexample: Whoever starts a marathon quickly certainly delivers fast intermediate times, but in the end, they run out of steam. The same is true for IT projects. What good is a quickly created rough concept and a quickly reached first milestone if many uncertainties come to light in Phase 2 and legal disputes with the tool provider or the IT consulting company ensue.

Linda A very vivid example that I will remember. Applied to our project world, it means: Those who do not invest time and intellectual capital in planning at the beginning will not present the best result in the end.

Jan At least they should expect some surprises.

Linda In our initial coordination meeting, we were able to align our ideas on how we want to proceed in Phase 1 and what needs to be considered. Or more accurately: your views have convinced me. I have other appointments to attend after this conversation. Can we please continue the discussion of the topic in the afternoon and document the results? I would then add the outcome to the project documents.

Jan Yes, gladly. So far, I have only addressed the points that we should consider, now we have to make decisions on each of these points and record them in RE plan. I will preformulate a proposal that we will then discuss and adopt together.

Linda That sounds good. I'm curious.

Linda and Jan are both very satisfied with their conversation. Jan feels that he has already earned Linda's trust as an external employee, and Linda enjoys gaining new insights. Incidentally, Linda finds it charming that Jan is offering to develop a proposal for an RE plan that documents the discussed steps and decisions for the RE phase.

4.2 Creating a RE Plan

The goal of the RE plan is to make transparent agreements with all RE stakeholders and to document guidelines. Stakeholders include the requirements engineers themselves, as well as later users, customers, and other project members such as developers and testers. The RE plan provides a framework and orientation for all activities associated with RE.

There are no standards or fixed contents for an RE plan. Anything worth agreeing on can be included. However, one should consider the project framework conditions, as these have a major influence on the RE plan. The following questions could be asked:

- How much RE understanding do the stakeholders have?
- What is the availability of the stakeholders?
- How experienced are the requirements engineers?
- What stability of requirements can be expected?
- What are the deliverables of the project?
- If it is about system development:
- How complex is the system?
- Is it a custom software development or is a product being developed that has to assert itself on the market against competition?

The following is the RE plan as Jan has developed it for both phases of the Customer Center project. He decides on a simple tabular structure. The first column contains all aspects that could be relevant for the two project phases. Columns 2 and 3 detail these aspects with concrete decisions. Jan still lacks a lot of information for Phase 2, but based on his experience, he fills most of the gaps with his suggestions. To achieve a better understanding among all participants, he groups several similar aspects into categories:

1. Decisions from a project management perspective (Sect. 4.2.1),
2. Decisions on survey and management processes (Sect. 4.2.2),

As a reader, you are welcome to use this RE plan as a template for your own planning or create your own template. It is important to coordinate within the project, as has happened in the following examples.

Table 4.1 RE from a project management perspective

Aspects	Phase 1	Phase 2
IT process model in the project	Specific, as discussed	Scrum
RE deliverables	– Rough concept – Decision matrix – Tender	– Product Backlog with Epics, Features, and User Stories – Sprint Backlog – Acceptance criteria in Gherkin format for each User Story
RE specific roles	– Product Owner – Requirements Engineer	– Product Owner (PO) – Lead Requirements Engineer (Lead RE) – Requirements engineer

4.2.1 Provisions from a Project Management Perspective

Table 4.1 illuminates an intersection of RE and project management. Decisions are made and communicated at a high level of consideration.

4.2.2 Provisions for Collection and Management Processes

In Table 4.2, necessary activities, rules, and methods are established, which aim to collect and manage requirements.

Table 4.2 Collection and management processes for requirements

Aspects	Phase 1	Phase 2
RE work packages + responsibilities	– Find starting point (Jan) – Collect requirements (Jan, Linda) – Document requirements (Jan) – Quality assurance of requirements (Jan, Linda) – Manage requirements (Jan)	– Sharpen starting point (Lead RE) – Collect requirements (PO) – Document requirements (Lead RE) – Quality assurance of requirements (PO) – Manage requirements (Lead RE)
Collection methods	Workshop, questionnaire, interview, observation	Interview, workshop, observation, system archaeology, brainstorming, prototyping, reuse

(continued)

Table 4.2 (continued)

Aspects	Phase 1	Phase 2
Details on requirement changes	Changes occur continuously during collection, documentation, and quality assurance of requirements.	Process: – Recording of change requests from stakeholders by Lead RE – Impact analysis by IT architect, Product Owner, and Lead RE – Fill out change request (format tbd) by Lead RE – Decision on change in the Change Control Board – Implementation of the change Change Control Board (composition): Sponsor, Product Owner, Change Manager, IT Architect, Lead RE, Project Manager, Lead QA
Agreements regarding stakeholder communication	Clarification of open questions with stakeholders is done directly in the workshop, the questionnaires, and in the interviews.	Agreements on the following questions at the start of the project: – How are stakeholders kept up to date? – Frequency of meetings; who are the participants? – Central storage of the current status of requirements? Who can view this? – Are there different views per stakeholder group?
Validation method during the 'Quality Assurance' work package	Inspection of the rough concept after completion	Before each implementation sprint: – Walkthrough with PO and relevant stakeholders – Refinement with the development team
RE tool support	– Office products, – Mindmap tool, – Modeling tool, – AI-based chatbot.	– see Phase 1 – Introduction of a requirements management (RM) tool must be analyzed.
Monitoring and reporting of requirements	Not relevant	Dependent on the introduction of RM tool

4.2.3 Decisions on Requirements Management

Table 4.3 mainly contains the agreed models for representing requirements and their properties.

Note from the authors: Linda and Jan will supplement the established RE plan in Sect. 5.2.1 with decisions on the glossary.

Table 4.3 Management information for requirements

Aspects	Phase 1	Phase 2
Categorization of requirements	Requirements for the business process Requirements for the system – Functional requirements – Quality requirements – Constraints	Requirements for the sub-processes Requirements for the system – Functional requirements – Quality requirements – Constraints – Solution design – Operational requirements
Standards and models		
– Context analysis	– Context diagram	– Context diagram
– Concept and information model	– UML class diagram	– UML class diagram
– High-Level functionalities	– Use Case diagram	– Use Case diagram
– Process description	– BPMN process diagram	– BPMN process diagram
– Data and data structures	– n.a.	– UML class diagram – UML state diagram – Transition table
– Architecture	– n.a.	– Architecture diagram
– Interfaces	– BPMN choreography diagram	– BPMN Choreography Diagram
– Requirements for the interface	– n.a.	– Mockup, – Prototypes as click dummies
– Natural language requirements	– Avoidance of linguistic effects – Use sentence template if possible	– Avoidance of linguistic effects – Use of sentence templates, User Stories, Gherkin
Attribution of requirements	Atomic requirements and requirement artifacts possess the following attributes: – *Must* -Attributes: ID, Description, Status, and Priority – *Should* -Attribute: Note, Source	Atomic requirements and requirement artifacts possess the following attributes: – *Must* -Attributes: ID, Author, Change date, Effort, Sprint, Description, Status, and Priority – *Should* -Attributes: Note, Source

(continued)

Table 4.3 (continued)

Aspects	Phase 1	Phase 2
Prioritization of requirements based on legal relevance (prioritization levels for requirements depending on risk, cost, quick wins, mutual dependencies)	– Priority *Must*: Must be implemented in phase 2. – Priority *Should*: Can be implemented in phase 2. – Priority *Will*: Is a requirement for a future expansion stage; this option must not be blocked.	– Priority *Must*: Must be implemented in the project. – Priority *Should*: Can be implemented in the project. – Priority *Will*: Is a requirement for a future expansion stage; this option must not be blocked.
Status values of a requirement	See following state diagrams	See following state diagrams
Traceability	Linking between requirements	– Horizontally (e.g., Feature and System Test) – Vertically (e.g., User Story and Realization of the User Story) – Linking between requirements (e.g., User Story and Acceptance Criteria)
Templates	No	Requirement specification template in Confluence

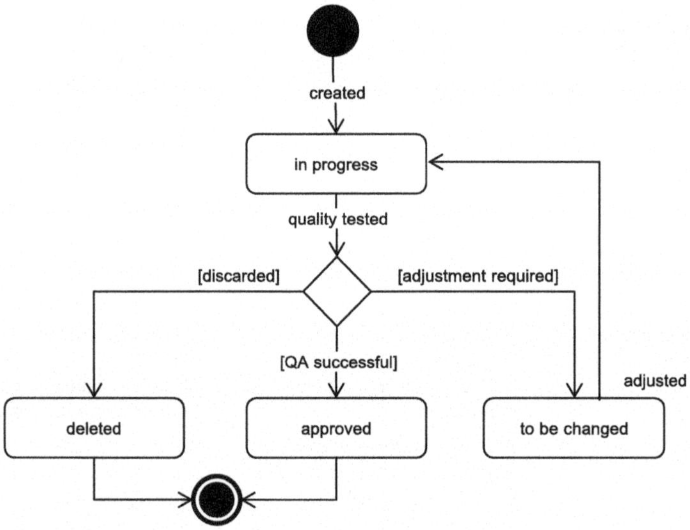

Fig. 4.2 State diagram: States of a requirement in the rough concept

After Jan made the proposal for the RE plan, the conversation continued as follows:

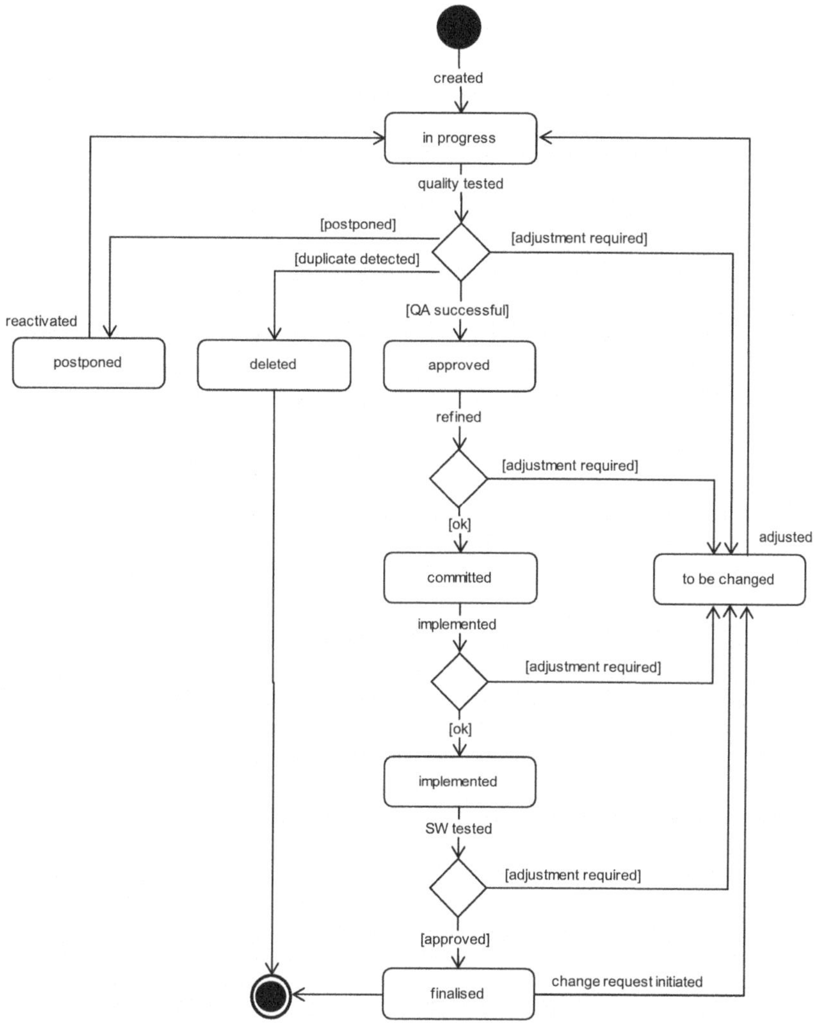

Fig. 4.3 State diagram: States of a requirement in the agile project

Linda Jan, you wanted to impress me again with diagrams I don't understand and terms I've never heard before.

Jan Don't worry, Linda. That's just the first impression. With a few explanations, you'll understand all the details for Phase 1. We'll go into detail on Phase 2 later. Shall we start with the diagram (Fig. 4.2)?

Linda Yes, please. That looks different from the UML class diagram.

Jan Right, but here we also see a UML diagram, specifically a state diagram. This is used to model states or status values of a specific object, in our case the object 'Requirement.' There is a starting status, in our case 'In Progress,' and there can be multiple final status values, such as 'Deleted' and 'Approved.' The texts on the arrows between the status values indicate the necessary triggers for the status changes.

Linda And what do the square brackets stand for then?

Jan These are the conditions for the status change. They are used when the same trigger activity can lead to different subsequent status values.

Linda OK, so if a requirement is in the 'In Progress' status, you present it to me for QA and I discover a problem, I set the status to 'To be changed.' Then you know that this requirement needs to be revised.

Jan Exactly. Hopefully, you've also left me a comment so I know what the problem is. *(smiles)*

Linda *(raises eyebrows and smiles)* Of course. You're very knowledgeable, but I don't expect you to be a mind reader.
The state diagram for phase 2 (Fig. 4.3) is a bit more extensive. However, looking at it now, it mostly makes sense to me.

Jan Mostly?

Linda Well, why did you call the last status 'Finalised' and not 'Tested.'

Jan Good question. As I mentioned, the states refer to a specific object, which in this case is the requirement. The requirement is implemented with the source code, but the testing is done at the end for the source code, i.e., the software. Therefore, 'Tested' would be a status of the software. The quality assurance of the requirement is already acknowledged with the status 'Approved.'

Linda Thanks, that sounds logical. Could you please explain one of the last points in the RE plan—the traceability and linking of requirements?

Jan This is a very interesting topic in requirements management—RM. We will deal with RM more closely on day 7 (Sect. 9.3). For now, about traceability: Through traceability, requirements are—for example—assigned or linked to other requirements. If a requirement changes, we can immediately see which other requirements this change could affect. Alternatively, a link is made to upstream or downstream artifacts. For example, if in phase 2 all requirements are linked with the respective implemented system features, you can determine whether each requirement has actually been implemented. Conversely, if there are system features to which no requirement is linked, then the developer has expanded the scope without asking and built a so-called gold-plated solution. In most cases, this leads to an unplanned cost increase.

Linda Really interesting, but certainly complex to implement.

Jan That's true. Traceability can best be implemented with a specialized RM tool.

Linda OK, we'll have to discuss that later. However, I'm still very interested in the use of Artificial Intelligence in requirements engineering (RE). You proposed an AI-based chatbot in the RE plan.

4.3 Using Artificial Intelligence in RE

Jan Yes, let's go into detail about AI. The ideas of artificial intelligence have been around since the mid-twentieth century, but the technical prerequisites for efficient use were not yet in place. In the 2010s of the twenty-first century, the necessary technological advances were made. Siri and Alexa are well-known representatives of this technology. But AI really took the world by storm, and thus also the world of RE, around the year 2023—with generative and conversational AI, the Large Language Models, and the chatbots.
Yes, let's delve into AI. The concepts of artificial intelligence have existed since the mid-twentieth century, but the technical prerequisites for efficient use were not yet in place. In the 2010s, the necessary technological advances were made. Siri and Alexa are well-known examples of this technology. However, AI truly revolutionized the world, including the field of RE, around the year 2023—with generative AI (GenAI), conversational AI, Large Language Models, and chatbots.

Linda Yes, I've already experimented with chatbots, but mostly for personal use or creating presentation content. The idea that GenAI can support RE has also crossed my mind, but I haven't applied it much yet. I'm excited to see how you plan to use GenAI efficiently for us.

Jan I want to mention one thing: The use of AI can save a lot of time. You can't trust all results 100%—we also talk about hallucinations here—but AI can take a lot of work off your hands, freeing up time for creative work. Even the hallucinations have been significantly reduced by the latest large language models.

Linda But if I enter our sensitive data into a chatbot, then these data are used to train the next language model, and the whole world sees our data.

Jan There are applications that use one of the well-known large language models (LLM) as an AI base, but disconnect it from the rest of the world. An application server then combines the knowledge of the LLM with the company's database, which the user doesn't notice via their user interface. Like this, our input is disclosed to the world. In Fig. 4.4, I have simplified the GenAI architecture of this example. In this context, I will later introduce the term 'Retrieval Augmented Generation' to you.

Linda OK, that makes sense. From your entry 'AI chatbot' in the RE plan, I gather that you are not planning to use such a specific GenAI application for Phase 1.

Jan Correct. I believe we can use a 'normal' chatbot to assist in creating the artifacts for Phase 1, as we do not yet need sensitive company data as input. It's important to give the right prompts to the chatbot to get helpful results. Prompt Engineering has already established itself as an important aspect for requirement gathering and documentation.

Linda What's behind the idea of a prompt?

Jan Sorry, my mistake. A *prompt* in the context of AI is a phrase with which you give the AI a task and from which you receive a result from the AI. The entire concept around the interpretation and processing of these prompts is called *prompt engineering*.

Linda Well, I'm curious to see how we will use the chatbot. But what about the use of AI in phase 2?

Jan Let's pause for a moment to avoid misunderstanding: We're not talking about the AI that could be used in an Omni-Channel solution in the broadest sense. Our focus is on RE and specifically on how we can use GenAI for RE.
Initially, a chatbot could be used, or we could consider introducing the AI application described above. Also, modern RM tools have upgraded with AI, initially for quality assurance of requirements, but now also for the collection and documentation of requirements including the creation of diagrams from text descriptions.
But that is not the end of the possibilities for GenAI architectures. *Agentic AI* is already revolutionizing the world. Environments like Microsoft Copilot Studio offer architectures with significantly more flexibility. They allow the design of project-specific AI agents without the need for programming skills. Multiple AI agents are taking over more and more of our jobs. So, we will not only have project-specific AI agents but also task-specific agents that communicate with each other.
Before the start of phase 2, we should analyze exactly what the market offers and what makes sense for you.

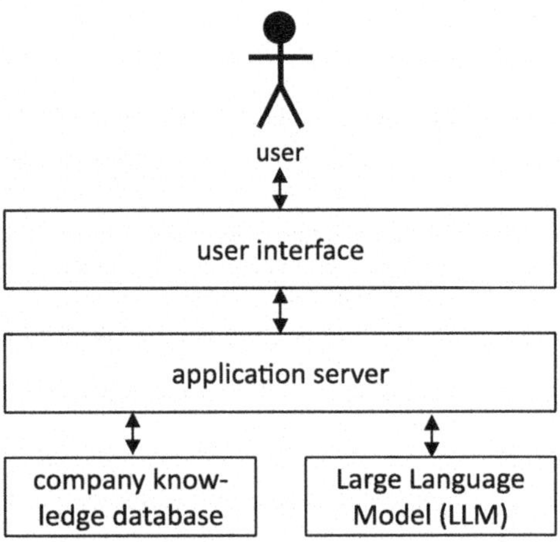

Fig. 4.4 Possible AI application that combines base models with company knowledge

We will repeatedly address the use of AI in the explanation of the creation of various RE artifacts in the following chapters. Additionally, Part II provides a detailed summary on this topic with much more depth.

4.4 Categorizing Requirements

Linda I have another question regarding the requirement categories. For Phase 1, I understand the distinction between requirements for the business process and requirements for the IT system, as the new Customer Center process for 'handling customer concerns' and the new application, the 'Omni-Channel System,' are the main topics of interest. In Phase 2, we should have fundamentally refined the overall business process. Adjustments to the process or its components should only be made if they are necessitated by the IT system being developed. However, I am unclear about the further breakdown of system requirements. Until now, I was only aware of functional and non-functional requirements, but the non-functional requirements have not been mentioned so far.

Jan Nowadays, people rarely discuss non-functional requirements. Instead, they categorize them into *quality requirements* and *constraints*. Quality requirements specify details such as performance, data security, scalability, usability, and testability.

Linda Oh yes, we just talked about data security in the context of AI.

Jan Exactly. Constraints encompass various aspects such as technology specifications, interface requirements, implementation costs, compliance requirements, specifications related to Web 2.0 or Web 3.0, and evaluation. We need to determine which specific quality requirements and constraints to consider in Phase 1.

Linda While we're at it, let's also gather a few examples of functional requirements.

Jan The entirety of an IT system's functionalities is depicted in use cases, specifically at a coarse level. We should define these in Phase 1. Describing each individual use case, often in procedural form using activity diagrams (Sect. 8.1.4), is a task for Phase 2. When we refer to processes in Phase 2, we mean the activity sequences depicted in or supported by the IT system, which we simply call sub-processes for simplicity.
All other functional requirements, such as permissions, business rules, data, and data ranges, are ultimately details of use cases. However, some details may apply to multiple use cases, resulting in n:m relationships.

Linda All clear, thank you. In phase 2, you added further sub-categories: solution design and operational requirements. I assume that user interface requirements are included in the solution design, correct?

Jan Exactly, a designer might refer to it as UI design, but it's essentially the same thing. There are many different forms of UI design, which I would be happy to explain further later (Sect. 8.1.3). In fact, AI can also provide support in this area. User experience design (UX design) is related to UI design, which is why I would place both in the same requirement category.
However, I would add another element to the solution design, which the requirements engineer is not primarily responsible for: the technical design, typically handled by the IT architect. Operational requirements have their own quality aspects and a specific constraint, namely details about software distribution. Additionally, I include documentation for user training and system description under operational requirements, which the requirements engineer is usually responsible for creating.

Linda I have noted everything and would like to summarize the system requirements, along with their categories and examples, in a mind map (Fig. 4.5).

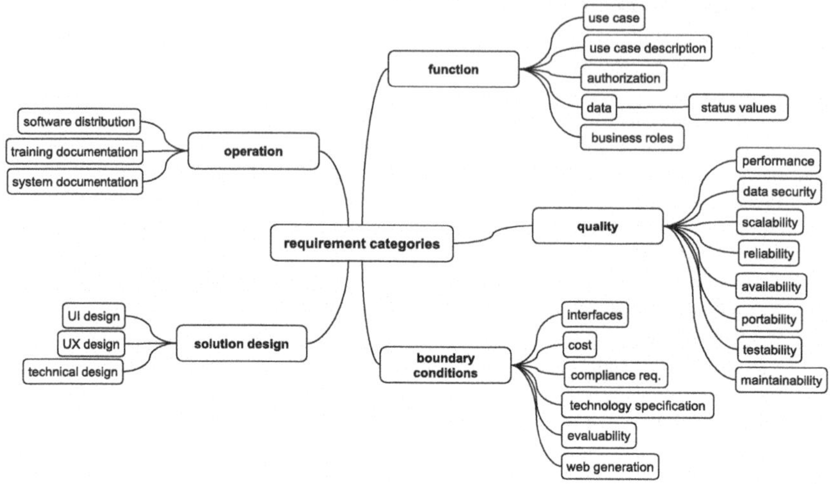

Fig. 4.5 Requirement categories and characteristics

4.5 Linda's Notepad

The second day, with its numerous planning topics, has significant potential for deterrence. However, without this planning, unresolved and unspoken issues may arise at the most unfavorable times during the RE phase, as they do in other phases. Similar to the first meeting, Linda also took notes during this step of the RE process.

Day 2: Planning RE in the project

Work steps:

1. *Define project deliverables such as rough concept or tender.*
2. *Request resources for RE.*
3. *Plan, coordinate, and fix the RE phase in the RE plan.*
   - *Determine the process model,*
   - *Define necessary activities,*
   - *Categorize requirements (functional, quality requirements, constraints)*
   - *Agree on standards and models to be used, e.g.,*
   - *Context diagram for system boundaries,*
   - *BPMN for processes,*
   - *UML state diagram for status values,*
   - *Define attributes of requirements, e.g., name, ID, priority, author, source of the requirement, legal obligation*
   - *Clarify type of documentation or determine tool question*
   - *Check requirement for traceability of requirements*

- *Define CR process*

→ NOTE: Better to consciously deselect work steps than to forget them unconsciously.

4. *Make provisions for the glossary (storage location, responsibilities, etc.).*

TIP: If there is neither a process model nor a RE tool, these special topics should be handled in separate projects.

Result of my day: We have planned RE for the project and made many associated decisions.

Day 3: Finding a Starting Point 5

Linda hopes that on the third day, after the previous theory- and planning-intensive days, she can finally discuss her actual task more concretely. First, however, they review the detailed RE plan together, which kept Linda busy after yesterday's session. Such a plan was unusual in Linda's past projects; she never had to consider its content and agreements in such detail before. Previously, stakeholders were asked about their requirements, and their statements were noted. Missing requirements were attributed to the respondents themselves. The current preparation, however, seems much more professional to Linda. She hopes this will avoid some of the friction that repeatedly occurred in the past. The disadvantage she currently sees is a lack of understanding of certain points. Some of Jan's decisions remain a mystery to Linda, such as the reason for different requirement categories. Jan assures her that these ambiguities are not problematic at the moment and will be explained in due course.

The time they spend on this review passes as quickly as the first two days. Linda is increasingly impressed by Jan's background knowledge and methodology and is eager to continue their work. Consequently, they move on to the next step of RE, which establishes their starting point for the project and defines its content and boundaries. Jan explains to Linda that it is necessary to answer questions like these for this location determination:

- What are the goals of the overall project and of phase 1?
- Which individuals or groups should or must be considered in phase 1 of the project? Who can provide important information and name requirements?
- What are the most important terms in the project environment and how are they related to each other?

J. Kawelke and T. Niebisch, *AI-Driven Transformation - Practical Frameworks for Real-World Impact*, Future of Business and Finance,
https://doi.org/10.1007/978-3-662-72549-8_5

- What content is part of the system and where are the system boundaries?
- What are the main functionalities of the IT system to be introduced?
- Which supporting tools should be used for RE?

Linda and Jan had already addressed some of these questions while creating the RE plan (Sect. 4.2).

Also in purely agile IT projects, the content presented in this chapter should always be developed during the initial sprints, before writing the first line of source code.

Let's return to the two main characters and their search for a suitable starting point for the overall project in general and Phase 1 in particular.

5.1 Formulating Goals and Non-Goals

Jan Before defining the goals for the overall project and Phase 1, I consider the motivations of each stakeholder involved. Understanding these motivations helps us better classify apparent overreactions and manage resistance. I ask myself: *Who* wants to achieve *what*?

Linda I wonder that too. I consider the answer extremely important for understanding all affected colleagues and integrating their interests into the project. Therefore, I would not only want to explore the motivations of the executive level. In my conversations with colleagues, I have also noticed their concerns and needs, which we should take seriously and consider.

Jan If I may add: Ultimately, we want the solution to be widely accepted. We are most likely to achieve this by involving those affected in the solution-finding process.

Linda In preparation for today, I have compiled the key motives of the project participants known to me. These should guide us in the project. To address your question: Who wants to achieve what?

- The *management of the Customer Center* aims to prevent image loss and business damage, while also addressing violations of legal retention periods.
- The *head of the Contact Center* aims to enhance her area of responsibility while simultaneously fulfilling the mandate of senior management.
- The *mailroom employees* are significantly concerned about their professional future. They understand that they cannot reverse the current trend of digital customer mail entries via various channels. They are deeply concerned about maintaining their jobs or securing a satisfactory future.
- In contrast to the team leads, who see no particular reason for the project, the agents and clerks are dissatisfied with the current process flow and consider the current IT solution for the contact center to be patchwork. They would like to improve the current workflows and work with a unified IT system.

Even as I describe the last point, I realize that I need to take action. The noticeable discrepancy between the team leads and clerks is concerning. I have also observed that our attrition rate has increased over the last two years.

After discussing the stakeholders' motivations, Linda and Jan look forward to formulating the goals. They adhere to the principle that only those who know the goal they want to achieve will find the right path.

To the point
Only those who know the goal can take the right path. Clarify who is pursuing which goals. ◄

This goal-finding process typically occurs within the framework of a project with the support of the requirements engineer. In Phase 1, Linda acts as both product owner and project manager, allowing her to work on this specific topic with Jan. In Phase 2, she will likely focus on her role as product owner. Let's see how Linda and Jan approach this topic.

Linda — Normally, the sponsor should already be clear about his goals and formulate them. This is only partially the case with us. But through the task, I already recognize what our sponsor wants to achieve. I have already pre-formulated the goals.

Jan — I wouldn't presume to set their goals on their behalf. What if they have goals in mind that we are unaware of? There is a risk that we might completely *miss the target* with our concept.

Linda — If you understood it that way, I misspoke. I have only pre-formulated the goals and will still coordinate them with the sponsors. However, they expect me to present concrete proposals to achieve a faster result.

Jan — Shall we look at your proposal together?

Linda — Yes, of course. My proposal includes several goals and sub-goals. All these goals must be achieved in their entirety; if any goal is missed, the project will not be successful. From one of my training sessions, I learned that goals can be represented in a tree structure. I have chosen this type of representation and depicted the goals using an *AND-OR tree* (Fig. 5.1). We can use our mind map tool for this. In my goal tree, the decision points are only *AND nodes*. For alternative goals, where only a subset of the goals needs to be met, *OR nodes* would be possible. However, this does not apply to our project. We can gladly add supplementary goals.

Jan — I like your goal tree. However, we can't leave the goals at such a high level. There are recommendations for formulating goals, one of which is to use the SMART criteria. This means goals should be:

- ***S*** pecific: Pertaining to the specific project.
- ***M*** easurable: Measurable by means of defined key figures with regard to the goal.
- ***A*** ccepted: The goals are supported by influential stakeholders.
- ***R*** ealistic: They are achievable for the project.
- ***T*** imed: A deadline for the achievement of this goal exists.

Linda — Very smart of you. This mnemonic was taught to me in the same seminar as the use of the goal tree.

Jan — Don't tell me you've already thought about this too?

Linda Of course. I took the endpoints from our goal tree and described each of these sub-goals in more detail according to SMART. You can find the results in Table 5.1.
Additionally, there are topics I want to delimit. Besides the goals, I have listed the non-goals in Table 5.2.

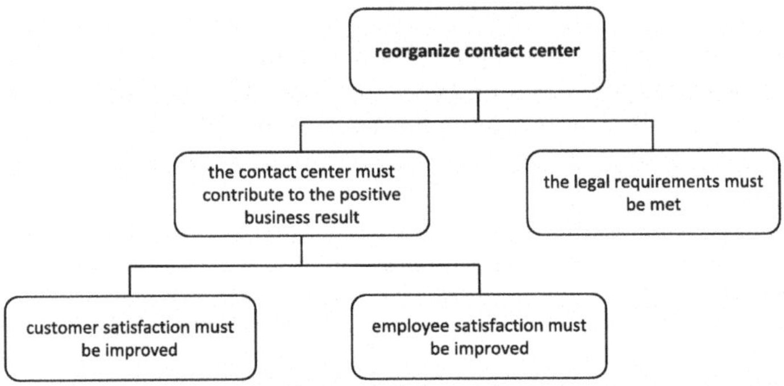

Fig. 5.1 AND-OR goal tree, exclusively with AND nodes

Table 5.1 Goals of a project

	G1: Improve customer satisfaction	G2: Improve employee satisfaction	G3: Meet legal requirements
S pecific and **M** easurable:	The number of customer complaints must decrease by 40% compared to today and the customer satisfaction survey must yield a satisfaction value of 80%.	Employee turnover must be reduced to below 10%.	All legal requirements relevant to the Contact Center must be met 100% at all times.
A ccepted:	By Customer Center management and sales	By Customer Center management and employees	By Customer Center management and audit
R ealistic:	Yes	Yes	Yes
T imed:	Will be measured 6 months after the end of phase 2 through a customer survey.	Will be measured 6 months after the end of phase 2 through an employee survey.	With the acceptance of phase 2.

Table 5.2 Non-goals of a project

Non-goal (NG)	Note
NG1: The solution should lead to staff reductions.	Should be agreed between the works council and Customer Center management.
NG2: The efficiency of the contact center employees is measurable.	Efficiency measurement of individual employees is not permissible for labor law reasons.

Jan is impressed by Linda's work. He did not expect this level of detail. If it starts like this, then nothing can really go wrong. However, there is still something on his mind.

Jan Linda, as impressive as the goal tree and SMART table look, I would still recommend formulating an overall goal for the project in one sentence. This often helps stakeholders, external consultants, and the project team better orient themselves. So, I would start at a higher level. By the way, I often generalize and abstract requirements in my projects, starting from concrete examples. From the fine to the coarse, so to speak. However, the more common approach is to go from the coarse to the fine.

Linda OK, then let's go from the fine to the coarse here. Make a suggestion.

Jan How about this: "The goal of the project is to improve customer and employee satisfaction to predefined KPIs through appropriate measures within the Contact Center and to meet the legal requirements associated with the Contact Center process."

Linda Hmm, whether this is now easier to understand than our SMART table, I doubt.

Jan I thought you never contradict *(winks)*... It is indeed the case that different formats of requirements can have a different effect on the reader. You can present the same facts this way or that, without there being a right or wrong. Can we agree that we disagree here?

Linda Of course. The formulated goals are valid for the overall project and thus also for Phase 2. For our Phase 1, I actually think that a single sentence as a goal formulation is sufficient.

Jan Well, let's hear it.

Linda Here you are: "The goal of Phase 1 is to make a decision about a technical solution based on a rough concept and to prepare a tender for the selection of an implementation partner."

To the point
The goal of Phase 1 is to make a decision about a technical solution based on a rough concept and to prepare a tender for the selection of an implementation partner. ◄

Jan Great, I would agree to that. Shall we think a bit more about this technical solution?

Linda I am sure that a purely technical solution will not fully meet all goals, just as a purely organizational solution wouldn't. You recognized this early on with your sketch (Fig. 3.1).

Jan Thank you. Although it is often advised against developing solutions too early, I believe that thinking ahead at a rough level cannot hurt. For the graphical representation of goal achievement, we can use an AND-OR tree again, this time including OR nodes (Fig. 5.2). The nodes under Technical Improvements represent OR nodes, while the angle shapes in all other connections are AND nodes.

Linda This will already indicate to our sponsor that considerable costs could be incurred for the solution, both through the purchase or development of a tool, as well as its implementation in the company. Not to mention the costs associated with organizational changes.

Jan Do you think it's right to talk about money with those responsible now?

Linda Absolutely. I'm not a typical salesperson who first highlights all the advantages, makes the other person's mouth water, and then presents the bill. In my world, it should be clear from the beginning that big wishes can indeed require a big wallet.

Jan I like your openness. Then I hope that our client can follow this approach and will agree in terms of content.

Despite good preparation, Linda is a bit nervous. She has an appointment with the Customer Center management in the early afternoon. When the time comes, she explains her proposals for the goals and non-goals of the project. Initially, her sponsor is somewhat irritated: Why should they set the goals for the reorganization of the Contact Center? They had given a task from which, in their opinion, everything was clear. However, after Linda expresses concerns from the workforce regarding job reductions and their consequences for the working atmosphere, and calculates that a combination of organizational and technical solutions will likely exceed the client's estimated effort, they become alert. A discussion ensues, in which Linda explains that the current coordination of goals provides greater planning security for all participants. With the visibility of a common goal, they can work toward it together.

Regardless of the proposed project approach, personnel discussions with the mailroom should be initiated to address existing fears and the perceived lack of perspectives. These discussions would be directly organized and conducted by the Customer Center management.

At the end of the discussion, the Customer Center management adopts the proposed goals and non-goals. They express gratitude for Linda's preparatory work and assure their availability for further discussions. For the two excluded

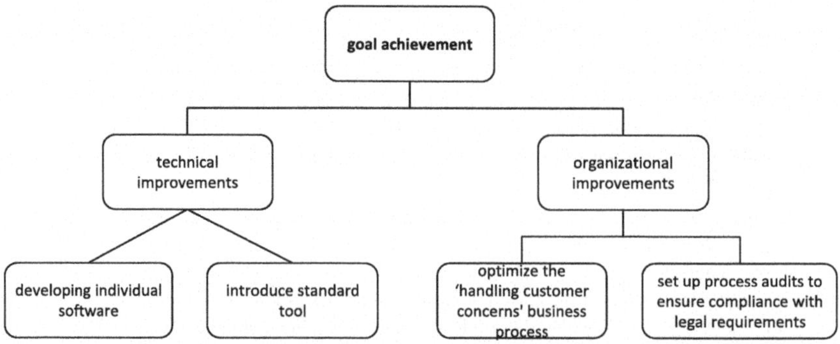

Fig. 5.2 AND-OR goal tree, with AND and OR nodes

topics (personnel discussions and measurability of employees), they will initiate appropriate measures.

5.2 Design Glossary and Conceptual Model

5.2.1 Basics and Manual Creation

Linda returns from her appointment full of enthusiasm. The first milestone has been reached, and a shared goal with the client has been established. After telling Jan about her success, they take the next step and begin working on the upcoming topics.

Linda	When we discussed the most important planning aspects to clarify, you mentioned the glossary. I had promised to create one, but I must admit I haven't started yet. Do you really think a glossary is necessary? After all, you're currently the only one who hasn't worked in this field before.
Jan	That's true. But not everyone associates the same meaning with the same words. Some terms are ambiguous, some seem simple, and others appear complex and need explanation. For example, I've noted Hamlet's famous line on this sticky note: $2b \vee [\neg(2b)]$!
Linda	I don't recognize that one. That's not a saying—it's just scribbles!
Jan	No, you do know the saying—just in a different form. "$2b \vee [\neg(2b)]$" is simply a pseudo-mathematical notation (which you're welcome to verify) for "to be or not to be." A well-known phrase, just expressed in an unfamiliar way. That's how quickly communication can break down. Let me briefly explain what I mean: When we discussed the quality requirements for requirements, we also talked about the specialization of departments. They have their own terminology and sets of abbreviations, and they assume a certain level of prior knowledge. Outsiders to these professional domains often respond with confusion or misunderstanding. Right now, I'm the only one outside that world, but in phase 2 of the project, several team members will likely be in the same position. We should prevent misunderstandings by using the glossary to eliminate such sources of error. My example was simply meant to raise your awareness.
Linda	Well, I hadn't thought of it that way. Let's go ahead and create the glossary.
Jan	Before we dive into the specifics, we should define how the glossary will be managed. The following questions need to be addressed: • Do we need separate glossaries for phases 1 and 2? • Where will the glossary be stored? • What sorting criteria will be used? • Who will be responsible for managing the glossary? • Who will have permission to add, modify, or delete entries • How will project participants be informed about changes?

Linda and Jan update the RE plan (Sect. 4.2) with the details outlined in Table 5.3.

Table 5.3 Supplement to RE plan with specifications for the glossary

Specifications regarding the glossary	
Scope of the glossary	Creation in phase 1, expansion in phase 2
Storage of the glossary	In the documentation channel of the project team platform
Sorting	Alphabetically by terms
Owner of the glossary	Linda
Rights for glossary changes	All project participants. However, each change must be documented with a timestamp and name.
Informing the team about changes	Via the chat of the aforementioned platform.

Jan Great—now we just need to define the columns, that is, the administrative details of the glossary, and then we can start populating it.

Linda I suggest the following columns: Term, Abbreviation, Description, Timestamp, and Author.

Jan A good start. Sometimes, different terms are used to describe the same concept. We should include these as synonyms. This shows that we're aware of the variations but choose to use a primary term to maintain a consistent language. Secondly, I would also suggest including the source of each description. It's important to know whether a definition comes from Wikipedia, another online source like an AI chatbot, or is based on the author's own experience.
And last but not least, I would suggest distinguishing between technical terms and project-specific terms. Perhaps we can indicate this using an abbreviation.

Linda OK, so we have these column headers:

Term, Abbreviation, Synonym, Technical (T)/Project-specific (P), Description, Source, Author, Timestamp

Which terms should we start with? If a preliminary study had already been conducted, we could simply extract the technical nouns from it—using AI, of course (winks)—and that would give us a solid foundation. Since we don't have that, we'll have to start from scratch.
To begin with, I'd like to contribute a few technical terms that could be relevant to our project. We already discussed some of these during our first day together:

- Contact Center
- Omni-Channel System
- Knowledge Database
- Chatbot
- Live Chat
- Customer
- Private Customer
- Corporate Customer
- Contact Center Employee
- Web Form

Jan Well then, all that's left for me is to add some project-specific terms, such as:

- Requirements Engineering (abbreviated as RE)
- Sponsor
- Contractor
- Tender
- Data and Data Structures
- Rough Concept (synonym: Specification Sheet)
- Custom Software Development
- Product
- Interface
- User Story (synonyms: Sprint Backlog Item, Ticket)
- Way of Working

Together, Linda and Jan populate the glossary table with these terms. Afterwards, Linda recalls a point mentioned in the RE plan.

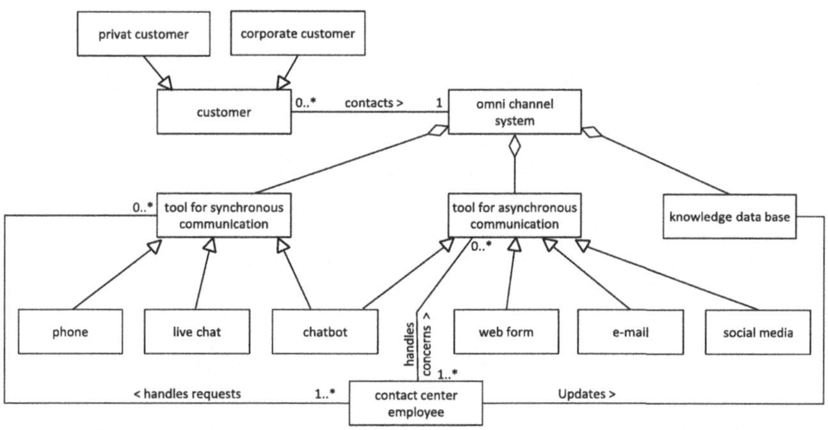

Fig. 5.3 Conceptual model in the form of a class diagram

Linda Excellent. I think we've laid a solid foundation for the glossary. Two days ago, you hinted that your favorite class diagram could be used in conjunction with a glossary. I believe you meant relating the glossary terms to one another.

Jan Exactly. In our case, it might make sense to focus solely on the technical terms and create a conceptual model just for them. Then, we can simply extend our class diagram for the contact center (Fig. 3.2) by adding relevant terms from your list (see Fig. 5.3).

Linda OK, now I understand this type of diagram much better. I recognize the generalization from private customer and corporate customer to customer, or the implicit inheritance when looking in the opposite direction. However, there seem to be a few diagram elements that you haven't explained yet. I understand the connection from customer to the Omni-Channel system because it's labeled, so customer contacts omni-channel system. But what do the numbers at the ends mean?

Jan These are known as multiplicities. In our case, you interpret them as follows: A customer contacts exactly one Omni-Channel system, and an Omni-Channel system can be contacted by zero or more customers. When reading in either direction, you start with "a," "an," or "one" in front of the first term and then apply the defined multiplicity to the second term.
For example, consider the association between a contact center employee and a tool for asynchronous communication. This means: *A* contact center employee handles customer concerns using *zero to an indefinite number* of tools for asynchronous communication. Conversely, customer concerns in *a* tool for asynchronous communication are handled by *one to an indefinite number* of contact center employees.

Linda Yes, that sounds logical. The only thing left is the explanation of the diamonds in relation to the term Omni-Channel System. In the original diagram from our first day, you also assigned generalizations there.

Jan You don't miss a thing, Linda. I actually changed this relationship from a generalization to a part-whole relationship, known as aggregation. In our case, it means that the Omni-Channel System consists of tools for synchronous and asynchronous communication, as well as a knowledge database. This approach makes more sense than presenting the tools and the database as specific instances of the system.

Linda All right, let's proceed with this version of the diagram. As we add more terms to the glossary, we'll also try to represent them in the class diagram.

Jan Perfect, but there's one thing I still need to confess to you.

5.2.2 Glossary Creation with AI Support

Jan *(smiles)* You should see yourself in the mirror. But don't worry—my confession is about artificial intelligence again. We could have saved a lot of time by transferring our work on the glossary and the conceptual model to GenAI.

Linda Oh, would that actually work?

Jan Yes, there are actually several possibilities. For instance, you could provide a chatbot with some technical background information and ask it to compile relevant terms into a glossary. If you're not satisfied with the first draft, you can request revisions through *prompts* until you achieve a satisfactory result, which you might then adjust manually.

Linda Have you tried it yourself?

Jan Yes, I wouldn't make this up. For creating the glossary, I prepared specifically today and got a decent result on the first try:
"I want to create a glossary table with seven terms related to Contact Center in an insurance company. The table should include the following columns: Term, Synonym, Description." And this was the response from ChatGPT with language model GPT o4-mini:
"Here's a glossary table with seven key Contact Center terms for an insurance company context" (Table 5.4).

That's an impressive result for a first attempt, right?

Linda Interesting. What's the other possibility you hinted at?

Jan You could provide the AI with more extensive and specific input by supplying one or more documents with technical background information. For example, this could include the documentation of your current systems.

Linda And from that, the AI system extracts the relevant terms?

Jan Exactly. And if you want to rely exclusively on a specific digital lexicon for the descriptions, you can include it. This approach requires a bit more preparation, but likely results in fewer manual corrections.
The downside of this alternative is that when using a public chatbot your input documents will be stored in the chatbot cloud, and can be used to train the next language model. If you plan to use this frequently, it's worth considering the encapsulated AI application we discussed yesterday…

Linda … to ensure our data is more secure.
But can a conceptional model actually be generated automatically from the glossary?

Jan Yes, that's possible. If the chatbot cannot generate diagrams, you can proceed in two steps: in the first step, you generate plantUML code with the chatbot and in the second step, you copy the generated code into a modeling tool that converts this code into a diagram. Or you use a specialized AI system that is trained to create diagrams from text.

Linda plantUML code… do I have to be a developer to understand that?

Jan No, no. Even though it is very easy to read, you just have to copy it from A to B. Let me show you a very simple example using the terms that we generated with AI. This is the prompt I created continuing in the same chat that created the glossary: *You are a requirements engineer. For the terms of the glossary create plantUML code for a conceptual model in the form of a UML class diagram. Apart from standard associations the relations can include aggregations, compositions, or generalizations.*
And this is the plantUML code that ChatGPT (LLM o4-mini) created:

```
@startuml

' Classes
class ContactCenter
class IVR
class ACD
class CRM
class KPI
class FCR
class SLA

' Generalization: FCR is a specialized KPI
FCR --|> KPI

' Composition: A Contact Center is composed of its
IVR and ACD subsystems
ContactCenter *-- IVR    : composed of
ContactCenter *-- ACD    : composed of

' Aggregation: Contact Center makes use of a CRM
system (shared, not owned)
ContactCenter o-- CRM    : uses

' Composition: An SLA defines one or more KPI
targets
SLA *-- KPI              : defines

' Dependencies: Contact Center adheres to SLAs and
is monitored by KPIs
ContactCenter ..> SLA    : adheres to
ContactCenter ..> KPI    : monitored by

@enduml
```

I've now copied this code into my Notepad++ too—just for display purposes—which has a PlantUML plugin and can render the class diagram (Fig. 5.4):

Linda is once again impressed and realizes she should consider introducing AI into requirements engineering. She's thinking about presenting the idea to the responsible executives to initiate a dedicated project. She's already looking forward to exploring which other RE tasks AI could support.

Table 5.4 AI response regarding glossary

Term	Synonym	Description
Contact Center	Call Center	A centralized department that handles all inbound and outbound customer interactions (calls, chats, emails) for policy inquiries, claims support, and service
Interactive Voice Response (IVR)	Automated Phone Menu	A telephony system that uses pre-recorded messages and keypad entry (or speech recognition) to route callers to the right agent or self-service option
Automatic Call Distribution (ACD)	Call Routing System	Software that intelligently queues and assigns incoming calls to available agents based on skills, priority, and wait time
Customer Relationship Management (CRM)	Customer 360	A platform that stores all customer data—policies, claims history, contact logs—to give agents full context during interactions
First Call Resolution (FCR)	First Contact Resolution	A performance metric measuring the percentage of contacts resolved on the first interaction, crucial for customer satisfaction and cost control
Service Level Agreement (SLA)	Service Level Commitment	The target response/answer metrics (e.g., 80% of calls answered within 20 seconds) that the Contact Center commits to meet
Key Performance Indicator (KPI)	Performance Metric	Quantifiable measures—such as average handling time (AHT), abandonment rate, or net promoter score (NPS)—used to evaluate Contact Center effectiveness

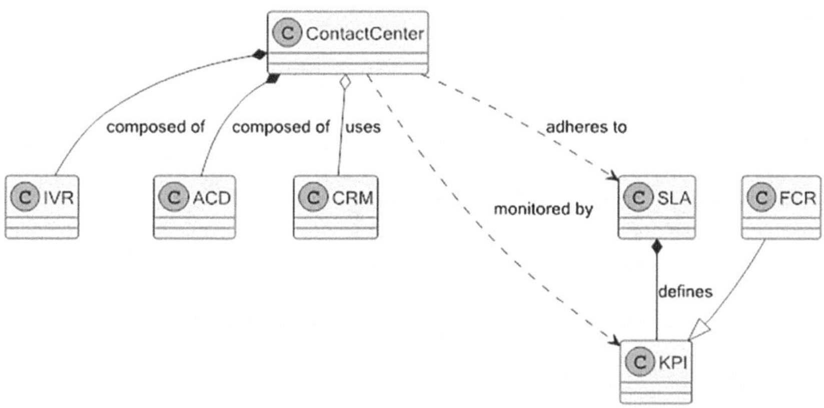

Fig. 5.4 Conceptual Model class diagram, created by the PlantUML Plugin in Notepad++

5.3 Identify and Analyze Stakeholders

With the stakeholder analysis, Linda and Jan are also indirectly approaching the system concept. In this context, *system* does not necessarily refer to an IT system. As already mentioned in Sect. 3.3, requirements engineering defines a system as a combination of interrelated elements. These elements can be technical, organizational, legal, or commercial in nature. Since Linda and Jan aim to optimize the entire business process within the contact center, they generalize both the business process and the IT system under the broader term "system." This overall system is named *Contact Center*, while the IT system corresponds to the *Omni-Channel System* (see Fig. 5.5).

Let's now turn to the people for whom the overall system is relevant.

To the point
Turning those affected into participants: In search of requirement owners. ◄

There's a well-known graphic that has circulated in the IT world in various forms since the 1970s. It captures the frustration of everyone who has ever suffered through poorly managed IT projects (see Fig. 5.6). The image vividly and clearly illustrates the issue of *stakeholders* and their lack of involvement.

Fig. 5.5 System concept in our context

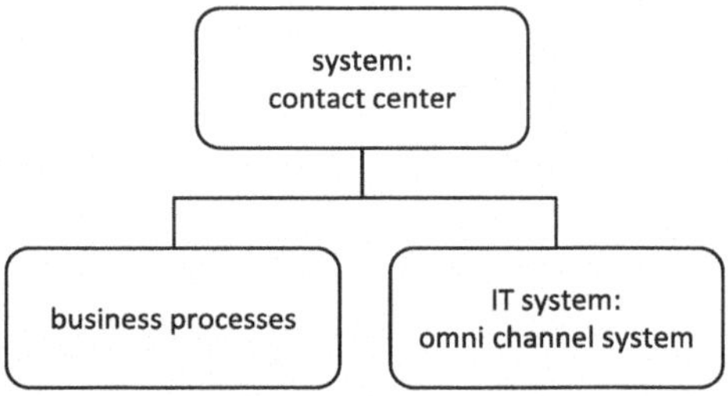

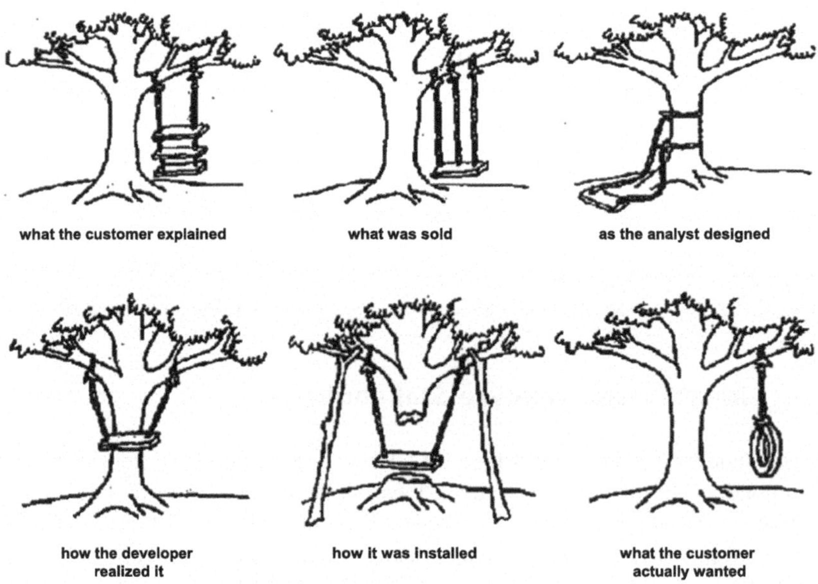

Fig. 5.6 Perceived project reality (Eigner, M., Roubanov, D., Zafirov, R. (2014). *Model-based virtual product development*. Springer Vieweg)

All of the marked project participants—assuming they were actually involved—were indeed part of the project, but their ideas and requirements were not aligned. Even the customer miscommunicated their expectations. The result can be catastrophic.

To the point

1. Could this have been avoided? Of course!
2. How? Through a stakeholder analysis!
3. What does this achieve? All stakeholders are identified as requirement owners and made visible to the project. ◄

But what exactly are stakeholders? In the context of a project, stakeholders are all individuals or groups who have an interest in the project, are affected by it in some way, or define requirements for the solution. These can include both active and passive stakeholders.

- Active stakeholders are those who work on the project (e.g., team members) or are directly impacted by it (e.g., customers, suppliers, company management).
- Passive stakeholders are only indirectly affected by the project's implementation or outcomes, but they still define requirements (e.g., legislators, works council).

Let's take a look at how Linda and Jan approach the topic.

Jan We're slowly approaching your favorite topic—the workshop. And naturally, the next question arises: Who should we invite? From this point on, it's important to make a clear distinction: On one hand, we're looking at the processes within the Contact Center that we want or need to adapt; on the other hand, we're focusing on the Omni-Channel System.

Linda Right—we tend to focus too quickly on the Omni-Channel System alone. But we also want to consider this IT system as part of the overall process and aim to optimize the affected sub-processes as well.

Jan Can you think of anyone we should consider exclusively for the process—someone who isn't relevant to the IT system?

Linda Hmm... maybe the mailroom. We initially defined their activities, but I'm still not entirely sure about that.

Jan No problem—let's include them for now. The people who are directly and actively involved in the system are easy to identify. But our task is to identify *all* key participants who could contribute requirements.

Linda On the first day, you told me that the term stakeholder refers to all participants involved in some way. Am I correct in assuming that the actors who are actively involved in our system represent only a subset of all stakeholders?

Jan Exactly. Only the full set of stakeholders—whether actively involved or not—provides us with the complete range of stakeholder requirements for the system. That's why we still need to identify the passive actors.

Linda I don't quite understand. How can someone who isn't directly affected by the system still set requirements for it?

Jan Think, for example, of legislators who mandate data retention periods. That probably answers your question.

Linda Is she considered a stakeholder too?

Jan Why not? In principle, requirements for a system can arise from a variety of sources, such as:

- The experiences, wishes, and ideas of individuals that you want to implement
- Contractual or legal conditions that impose certain constraints
- Strategic or business considerations
- The existing IT landscape or IT strategy, which introduces specific requirements

There are countless reasons for requirements—and just as many types of stakeholders. Just remember the old truism:

To the point
Forgotten stakeholders can cause your project to fail! ◄

Jan So, it's better to ask repeatedly who might still be overlooked. A prime example of this principle is our stakeholder—the *legislator*.

Linda You're right. I actually learned that lesson the hard way. One of my less successful projects was shut down by the works council due to concerns about employee-related monitoring capabilities. No one had mentioned this restriction to me beforehand. If I had involved the works council early on, we could have easily avoided that obstacle. That's why I'm especially curious to see how you'll proceed.

Jan A small selection of commonly relevant stakeholders is shown in Fig. 5.7.

Linda It's interesting that you've already included the developers and quality assurance. They don't even know how lucky they are—and we can't ask them at the moment.

Jan Right. So let's first focus on the stakeholders who are relevant for our Phase 1 and whom we can actually reach. I've copied your target tree for our topic and derived a *stakeholder tree* from it, listing potential stakeholders on its leaves (see Fig. 5.8). Our goal should be to reach a consensus on the involvement of all participants in the end.

Linda I find this representation easy to understand. For the customers, internal users, and administrators, we should define specific characteristics. However, I noticed that both of us—and our roles—are missing from the tree!

Jan You're right. In your two roles, I would place you as a product owner on the passive side, while as an expert, you belong to the group of internal users. I would classify myself as a passive stakeholder in the role of requirements engineer. But please explain which stakeholder groups you'd like to subdivide in more detail.

Linda Let's start with our internal users in the insurance company. We can divide them into the following groups:
- Agents
- Clerks
- Experts
- Supervisors
- Executives.

Agents work on the front line in the contact center—the 1st level. Clerks, on the other hand, are typically assigned to the so-called mid-office or 2nd level. They can handle certain cases, perform technical evaluations, and provide statements about insurance benefits. The experts, in turn…

Jan … belong to the back office, or 3rd level.

Linda Exactly. These include, for example, appraisers who evaluate large claims. Supervisors, on the other hand, monitor our Key Performance Indicators (KPIs) and Service Level Agreements (SLAs). Group leaders and site managers fall under the category of executives. This subgroup also includes functional leaders responsible for areas such as new business development.
Now for the subdivision of administrators. We have:
- Technical administrators
- Functional administrators

While technical administrators are responsible for the operation of our systems, functional administrators configure the systems within the given parameters.

Jan I have not expected there to be so many different internal stakeholders. Is the customer side just as complex?

Linda Not quite. Initially, we talked about private and corporate customers, but more accurately, we distinguish between:
- Policyholders
- Brokers, whether exclusive or independent
- Independent financial advisors

Jan Great. With this wide range of roles, our stakeholder list is going to be quite extensive. You can now start assigning goals to the stakeholder roles you're already familiar with. I'd refer to these roles as *stakeholder groups*. We can add more detailed information for each group later on.

Linda Well, let's ask the AI then. If necessary, I'll manually add or adjust the goals to fit our circumstances.

Jan Good idea. I have to admit, I really enjoy our collaboration. I'm impressed by how quickly you apply what you've learned.

The prompt that the two of them use is this:

Fig. 5.7 Possible stakeholders

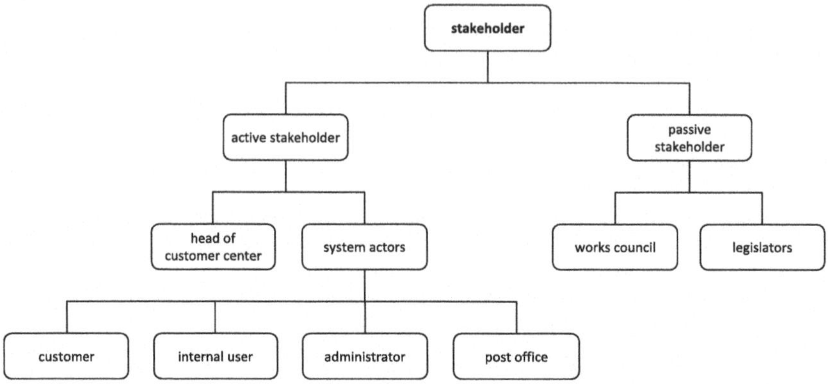

Fig. 5.8 Stakeholder tree

> *Can you name the 10 most important stakeholders of an omni-channel system and list their goals when implementing the system in an insurance company in a table?*

Since the AI chatbot only generally listed 'employees' with the goal 'more efficient workflows' in relation to customer service, Linda asks out of curiosity:

> *Do you know different goals for agents, clerks, and experts?*

The chatbot responds:

- *Agents: Improved working conditions, higher motivation and satisfaction, better training, and continuing education*
- *Clerks: More efficient workflows, faster processing times*
- *Experts: Improved quality of customer interactions, higher customer satisfaction*

Linda isn't completely satisfied and adds her own goals based on her experience. She also revises or expands the AI's output for other stakeholder groups. In particular, she can fully define the goals for her own roles as a subject matter expert and product owner. Still, the AI provided some valuable input that helps Linda and Jan quickly compile their stakeholder list (see Table 5.5). Any goals that seem incomplete to her are initially marked with a question mark.

Table 5.5 Stakeholder list, AI output manually expanded

Stakeholder group	Goals
Customer Center Management	• Contact Center must contribute to positive business results, • Reduction of complaints.
Policyholder	• competent contact person, • quick response to the concern, • availability of different synchronous and asynchronous communication channels ?
Broker	• see policyholder, • want to have own account with access to the data of their own customers.
Independent Financial Advisor	• see policyholder • want to have own account with access to the data of their own customers.
Agent	• easy and quick access to customer data and their history, • cross-channel ticket system, ?
Clerk	• Correct distribution of tasks, • Visibility of all current customer data on the screen, if customer communication is synchronous and forwarded by the agent, ?
Expert	?
Supervisor	?
Manager	• The values and culture of the company are reflected in the *User Experience* (UX) of the Omni-Channel system. • Input for feedback to the agents and clerks must be provided. • Routing in escalation cases, • Online training for agents and clerks must be available, • Monitoring at customer segment and insurance product level.
Technical Administrator	• 24/7 availability of the Omni-Channel system, • Monitoring system for displaying the status of all communication channels, ?
Functional Administrator	?
Product Owner	• Achieve all project goals in time and budget.
Mailroom	• professional perspective.
Audit	• Reduction in the number of complaints, • Compliance with retention periods and record keeping, • Customer data protection, • Identification and authentication of customers, ?

(continued)

Table 5.5 (continued)

Stakeholder group	Goals
Legislator	• Compliance with retention periods and record keeping, • Customer data protection, ?
Works Council	• Compliance with employee rights and ergonomic guidelines, ?
Requirements Engineer	• Documentation of requirements without defects.

Jan — Well, that's a good start. We'll need to fill in the question marks during the workshop. In addition, we should add three more columns to the stakeholder list:
- Representative (Name)
- Requirements Collection Method
- Availability

Linda — This is certainly necessary as preparation for our workshop. Are there any specific guidelines or best practices regarding what information should be included in a stakeholder list?

Jan — This is dependent on the project conditions. Often these columns are suggested:
Name,
Role in the project
Interests in the project
Influence on the project
Contact information
Priority
Availability
If we want to make the stakeholder list accessible to all project participants, we should handle columns 3 and 4 with care. For our first phase, I suggest we stick with the two columns *Stakeholder Group* and *Goals*, and add the following columns: *Name*, *Collection Method*, and *Availability*.

Linda — OK, we'll look at the collection methods tomorrow when the topic of requirements gathering is on the agenda.

Jan — That's what I thought.

Linda — I really appreciate the systematic approach to identifying stakeholders. At this point, I can already see the value of having taken the time for a thorough analysis. If we had overlooked a stakeholder group, that omission could have led to multiple negative consequences.

Jan — I'm glad you see us on the right track.

Jan gives Linda a few tips for Phase 2. In this phase, more stakeholders should be involved, and additional information should be recorded in the stakeholder list.

As already indicated in Fig. 5.7, the project participants for Phase 2 are added later—especially developers, testers, trainers, and application support (often referred to as *Operations*). In addition, Jan suggests assigning the role of a hacker to a suitable developer from the IT department. This person should later attempt to disrupt the system in a realistic way, thereby helping to define additional quality requirements.

5.4 Analyze Context and Define System Boundaries

Linda and Jan want to maintain their momentum and continue working after a short break.

Jan: Congratulations! We've now defined the goals, identified and modeled the key terms, and created the stakeholder list for the first project phase.

Linda: Yes, but what comes next? You mentioned system components and system boundaries. What do you generally mean by that—and specifically in the context of our project? How can we identify and represent them?

Jan: Let's first refresh our shared understanding of what we both mean by *system* (see Fig. 5.4). If we already had different views on this, we wouldn't be able to agree on the *system boundaries*.
To me, a *system* is generally a construct made up of several interrelated elements. These elements can be technical, legal, organizational, or commercial in nature. The stakeholders mentioned earlier, the affected processes, hardware and software, associated interfaces, or required resources could all be part of a system. In other words, the system we are defining is more than just an IT solution. In our case, we determined that the *Contact Center* system consists of both the business process and the supporting IT solution—namely, the Omni-Channel System.

After Linda confirmed this recap, the next step is to identify the system boundaries. These boundaries separate the actual system from everything that no longer belongs to it. However, the elements outside the system must still have a relationship to it. That's why this surrounding area is referred to as the *system context*.

First, you start by taking an external view of the system boundary and ask yourself (see Fig. 5.9):

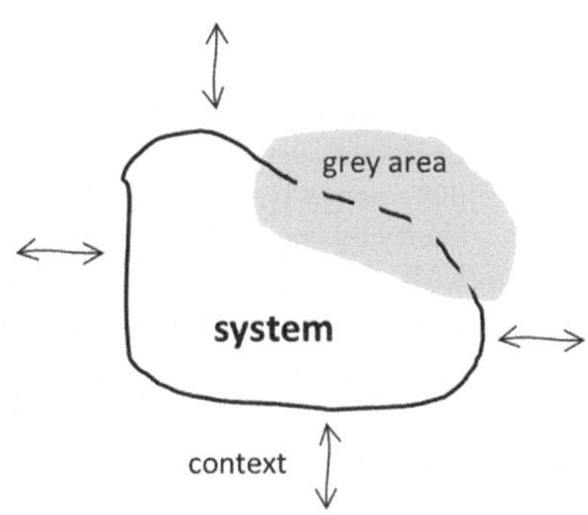

Fig. 5.9 Illustration of system boundaries, context, and grey area

- What lies outside the system but still affects it (e.g., systems and processes to be integrated)?
- What does this context expect from the system?
- What gateways and interfaces are established for the system's interaction with its environment?

This process, which considers the system to be created in the context of its relevant environment, is called *context analysis*.

As shown in Fig. 5.9, there's another aspect of context analysis that hasn't been mentioned yet: the *grey area*. This grey area arises from the difficulty of clearly defining the system boundary at this stage. For example, it may still be unclear whether certain IT systems or processes belong to the actual system or lie outside of it. Such grey areas tend to be larger in the early stages, as concrete information is often lacking. As the project progresses and more knowledge is gained, these grey areas can usually be resolved. An important tip: try to identify and become aware of these grey areas as early as possible.

To the point
Grey areas in system demarcation can become project risks and therefore need to be clarified over the course of the project. ◄

As Linda and Jan initially observed, some stakeholders are better at expressing what they don't want than what they do. This kind of exclusion logic is also a source of grey areas. However, through the upcoming systematic requirements gathering, these stakeholders will engage more deeply with the subject matter, helping to resolve those grey areas.

First, Jan responds to Linda's questions.

Jan You're raising an important point that's often overlooked: system boundaries. It's far easier to represent them than to identify them in the first place. Defining these boundaries often sparks discussions that shouldn't be avoided. A system development project that begins with uncertainty about its context and scope is already burdened from the start—and I want to spare us that.

Linda I've also noticed that the word *system* is a very flexible and interpretive term. Everyone seems to understand something different by it—sometimes defining it more narrowly, sometimes more broadly. I think it's extremely important to clarify this point. You've often explained the possibilities of UML to me. Can a UML diagram also be used to represent context analysis?

Jan For example, a UML use case diagram could be used to represent the system boundary. However, since a use case diagram already depicts the full range of functionalities of the IT system, it's too early to use it at this stage.

Linda Because we don't want to think too early and too detailed about solutions?

Jan Exactly. You always start with the pure requirements and only gradually introduce the solution concept. As the project progresses, the focus shifts: the implementation of requirements into a solution increases, while fewer new requirements are added. I've tried to illustrate this in Fig. 5.10.

Linda Aren't you oversimplifying things? If we work in an agile way during Phase 2, we'll need to refine the requirements anew for each sprint. That won't decrease over the course of the project.

Jan Correctly observed. In agile projects, the curves aren't as linear over the entire project duration. However, if you look at each sprint individually, the effort distribution looks similar again. At the beginning of a sprint, requirements are refined—usually during the previous sprint. Then the technical implementation is discussed. During this phase, the proportion of effort spent on specifying requirements decreases, while the focus on the solution increases.
But we're getting off track… Your original question was about which type of diagram is best suited for representing the context. I prefer to start with a context diagram. Even though it doesn't originate from the UML family, its syntax and semantics are still well-defined.

Linda Right, you already mentioned the context diagram during our first meeting.

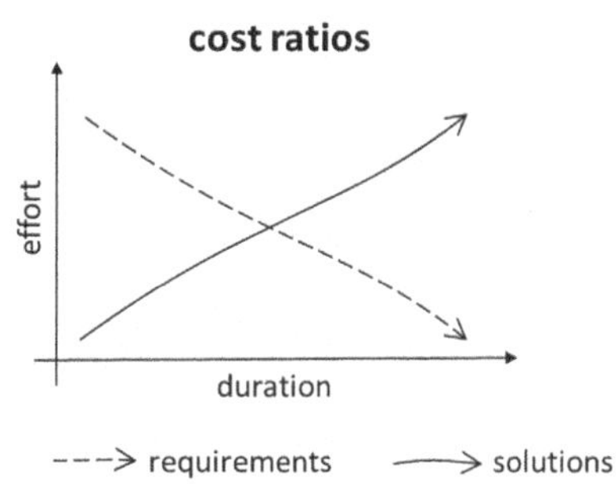

Fig. 5.10 Efforts for requirements and solutions

If an element that we initially assumed to be part of the system's context turns out to have no direct connection to the system, then by definition, it does not belong to the context and is not relevant for specifying system requirements. Nevertheless, such elements are sometimes included in the context diagram to explicitly visualize the absence of a relationship. To distinguish these, a *context boundary* is used.

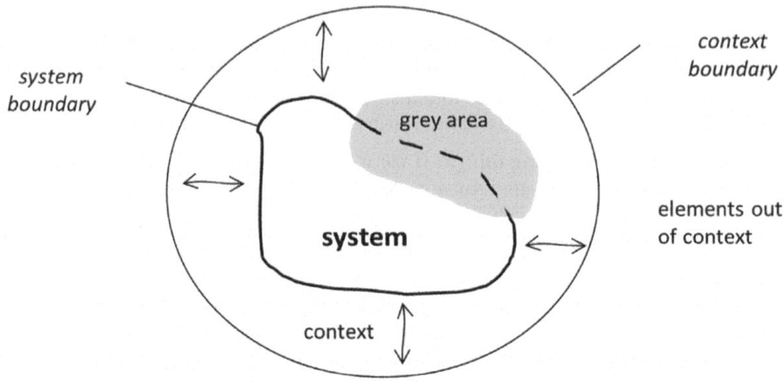

Fig. 5.11 General context diagram

Jan — So, in Fig. 5.11, I've sketched out a general context diagram. You can see the system itself with its boundary, and then the context around it, including its own boundary. I've also included that grey zone we talked about earlier—the one where it's not always clear where the system ends and the context begins.

Linda — So, I get the general idea, but what exactly do the arrows mean?

Jan — They can actually mean a few different things, depending on the context. For example:

- They might show data being exchanged between external IT systems and the system itself.
- Or they could represent how active stakeholders—like users or operators—interact with the system.
- Sometimes, they indicate how the system's business processes connect with other business processes outside the system.
- And in some cases, they show requirements coming from other elements in the context—like legal regulations from passive stakeholders such as lawmakers. In that case, the arrow would only point toward the system, since it's a one-way influence, not a two-way interaction.

Linda — Ah, I see—so the context isn't just about drawing a line between the system and its environment. It's actually more about identifying all the elements that could influence or contribute requirements to the system. I hadn't realized that before.

To the point

Requirements for a system can be derived from its context. The context exists outside the system boundary but remains within the context boundary.◂

Linda So basically, we just need to include the stakeholders from the stakeholder list and all the connected technical systems in the context, right?

Jan In principle, yes. But I'd like to make a small adjustment—I want to pull out the general term *legislator* from the stakeholder list and instead break it down into more specific topics. That way, we can later make clearer distinctions between different types of rules and laws, like compliance requirements, and data protection regulations.
So, for our case, we'd divide the context elements into these four types:

- (Adjacent) IT systems
- Stakeholders
- (Adjacent) business processes
- Legal regulations

Let's start with the first one. Do you have an overview of which *IT systems* are currently involved in the contact center process but won't be part of the future omni-channel system?

Linda Hmm… a few come to mind:

- The contract management system for our insurance policies
- Employee data from the HR system
- Backend systems that hold things like damage classifications
- And the entire communication infrastructure

Jan Good point—and the AI also suggested a couple more systems we might want to consider:

- A data warehouse that supports reporting and monitoring
- External services like regional weather data, Schufa checks, and partner workshops

I'm sure we'd come up with even more systems if we gave it a bit more thought. But at this stage, I don't think it makes sense to get too caught up in the details of each individual IT system. That's why I'd suggest we group them under broader, more generic terms—like *communication infrastructure*, *internal backend systems*, and *third-party systems*. We can then assign the specific systems to these categories as we go. I'm pretty sure we haven't captured everything yet, but this gives us a solid structure to build on.

Linda This structure gives us a solid foundation for collecting the relevant IT systems. During the workshop, we'll ask our colleagues about any additional systems they're aware of, so that by the end, we'll have a complete list.
Alright, let's head over to the flipchart and sketch out our context diagram.

As discussed, they proceed accordingly. Using a flipchart, they begin to sketch out their context diagram by hand. During a coffee break, while reflecting on their interim results (see Fig. 5.12), they realize that not all elements can be clearly represented in the diagram. In some cases, the graphic simply lacks the space to convey all necessary information.

To address this, they decide to use a table as an alternative to the graphical representation. While this approach sacrifices some of the intuitive clarity of visual relationships, it allows for a more complete and flexible documentation of the context. Their context table consists of five columns. The column headers are listed in Table 5.6, along with a brief explanation of the purpose of each column:

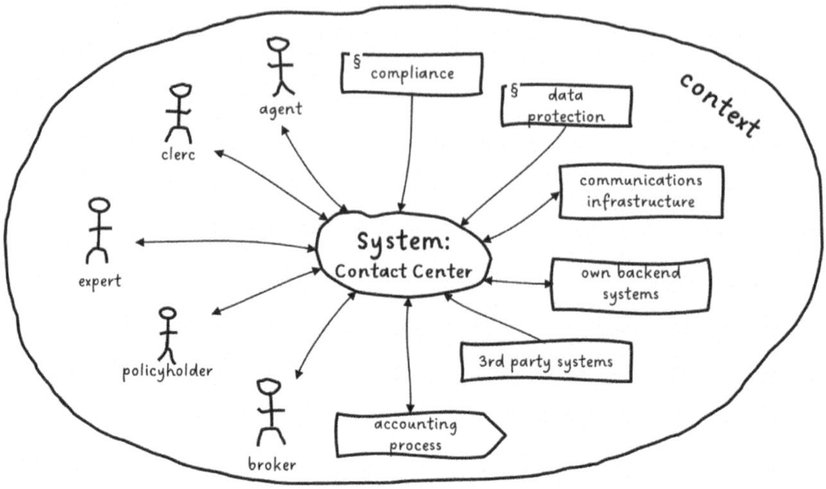

Fig. 5.12 Context diagram for the contact center

- *Context Element:* Refers to the specific elements that impose requirements on the overall system.
- *Context Type:* Jan and Linda refer back to their previously defined four categories of context elements: stakeholder, business process, IT system, and legal regulation.
- *In:* This column captures both requirements directed at the system (R) and data flows into the system (D).
- *Out:* This column primarily describes data flows leaving the system or requirements related to interfaces with other systems.
- *Remark:* Provides space for additional notes or considerations.

At this stage, the contents of the *In* and *Out* columns remain at a relatively high level of abstraction.

Linda and Jan transfer the contents of the context diagram into the context table, enriching it with information that could not be accommodated in the diagram. Table 5.6 presents an example of their work in progress to illustrate the approach. The two complete the table independently, without further observation.

5.5 Create Initial Use Case Diagram

With the previous section, we conclude the system-level perspective—understood as the combination of business processes and IT systems—and now focus exclusively on the functionalities of the IT system to be introduced. The context analysis from the preceding section provides an ideal foundation for this transition.

Tab. 5.6 System context table

Context element	Context type	In	Out	Remark
Agent	Stakeholder	Access to customer data and their history (R), details of customer request (D)	Customer data, history of communication (D)	Further requirements must be developed in the workshop.
Policyholder	Stakeholder	Synchronous and asynchronous communication channels must be available (R), professional and quick processing of requests (R), request (D)	Response (D)	
Accounting process	Process	Interface (R)	Payment data (D)	Payouts (commission, claim, etc.), raise requirements from a functional and technical perspective
Contract management	System	Interface (R), Contract data (D)	Contract additions (D)	Decision open whether the interface will be provided by the contract management or the Omni-Channel system.
Data protection	Legal regulation	Identification and authentication of customers, data protection (R)		Data must not be stored in a cloud outside the EU.

Following the creation of the context table and a subsequent break, Jan is ready to approach the next step with renewed energy.

Jan — Linda, have you noticed something? Most of the entries in the *In* and *Out* columns of the context table actually point directly to functionalities of your future omni-channel system.
Take this example: if we connect the requirement *Access to customer data and their history* from the *In* column with the data flow *Customer data, history of communication* from the *Out* column, we basically end up with a use case like *Display customer data.*

Linda — Right, but this first use case feels more like a container—it still needs to be filled with all the expectations that haven't been explicitly stated yet. For instance, the system should automatically recognize the policyholder when they get in touch, and then display their master data and the full communication history right on the agent's screen.

Jan That's totally normal. Usually, behind every use case like this, there's an underlying process that needs to be described—and we'll develop that step by step, starting from a high-level overview and then working our way into the details.
But in a workshop setting, there's always the risk of diving into those details too quickly. So our main goal for now should be to get a complete overview—to identify all the relevant use cases first. Once we've captured them all, we can visualize them in a Use Case diagram. And that diagram will give us the overall picture of the system's functionality that we're aiming for.

Linda I'm starting to understand. Are there any other guidelines we should keep in mind?

Jan Just one more formal point about naming. Just to take a quick detour—in task analysis within process management, there's this principle called *object and action*. It basically says that a task should be named so that both the object—with which something is done—and the action—what's being done – are clearly recognizable.
I'd really like us to apply that same principle to naming our use cases. So instead of calling it something vague like *Customer data* or *Customer data display*, we should go with something like *Display customer data*. That way, it's immediately clear what the system is supposed to do.

Linda Aha, now I get what you mean. That actually clears up a few things for me:
- A Use Case name should always include just a noun and a verb.
- All the Use Cases together are shown in the Use Case diagram.
- And that diagram gives us the big-picture view of the functionalities we want in the new omni-channel system.

Jan Yes, ma'am… Let's move on to how to read a Use Case diagram. In Fig. 5.13, I've sketched out all the key elements for you. There are five main ones: Use Case, Actor, external IT system, system boundary, and system name.

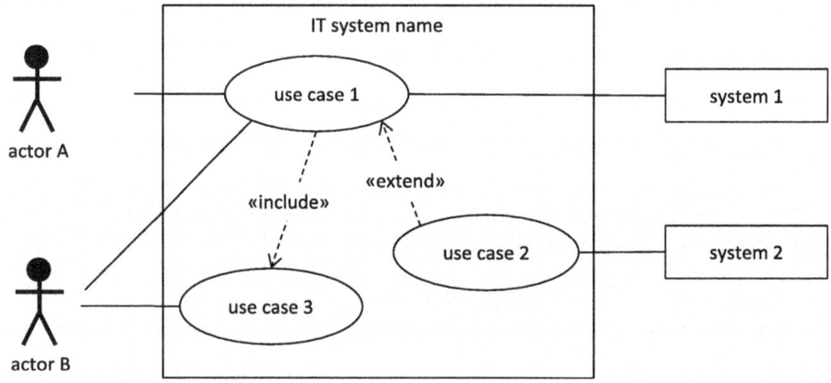

Fig. 5.13 General use case diagram

Linda This kind of reminds me of the context diagram—only here, the system boundary is drawn as a rectangle.

Jan But that's not the only difference. In our case, the system no longer refers to the entire setup that includes both business processes and supporting software. It now focuses solely on the latter one—the IT system. As a result, we're not representing the full context anymore, but only the elements that directly interact with the IT system—the actors, shown as stick figures, and the external IT systems, shown as rectangles.

Linda So, from your example, I gather that Actor A interacts with the system only through Use Case 1, while Actor B is involved in both Use Cases 1 and 3. And if I'm understanding it correctly, the connections between Systems 1 and 2 and Use Cases 1 and 2 represent the interfaces between those systems.

Jan That's exactly right.

Linda I'm still not quite sure I understand the *include* and *extend* relationships. Especially the direction of the arrows—that part's confusing to me.

Jan The direction of the arrow shows how you should read the relationship. For an *include* relationship, it means: Use Case 1 *includes* Use Case 3. So whenever Use Case 1 is executed, Use Case 3 is always used as well. It's a mandatory relationship.
Here's an example: when you shop online, Use Case 1 might be 'Buy product,' and Use Case 3 could be 'Select product.' You can't buy something without selecting it first—so 'Select product' is always included in 'Buy product.'

Linda Your example really helped—it makes the theory so much easier to grasp. Let me try to explain the *extend* relationship correctly. So, if Use Case 2 *extends* Use Case 1, that means it's optional. Use Case 1 can run on its own, but under certain conditions, it might also need Use Case 2.
If we stick with the online shopping example, Use Case 2 could be *Configure product*. Not every product needs configuration, so it's only relevant in specific cases—it extends the main process, but isn't always required.

Jan Well, what am I even here for? Sounds like you've already got it all figured out!

Linda Thanks! But I do have a question about your example. Why did you draw a connection from Actor B to Use Case 3, if Use Case 3 is always executed as part of Use Case 1?

Jan That's because Actor B can also perform Use Case 3 independently of Use Case 1. If we go back to the online shopping example, it's like being able to select a product without actually buying it. So even though 'Select product' is included in 'Buy product,' it can still be used on its own.

Linda That sounds familiar. Let's move on to our omni-channel system. It would be helpful to include all the use cases we already know in the use case diagram, and then identify any gaps together with the workshop participants.

Jan That's one option. Another would be to first illustrate the current state of your fragmented system. This helps participants connect the use cases to their day-to-day work. After that, they can start thinking about their own ideal scenarios.

Linda Let's go with that approach. Where are the pens and the flipchart?

To the point
Describing the Current State: Understanding Our Starting Point◀

Half an hour later, Linda and Jan had sketched the current system state on the flipchart (see Fig. 5.14). The process was challenging, but ultimately insightful.

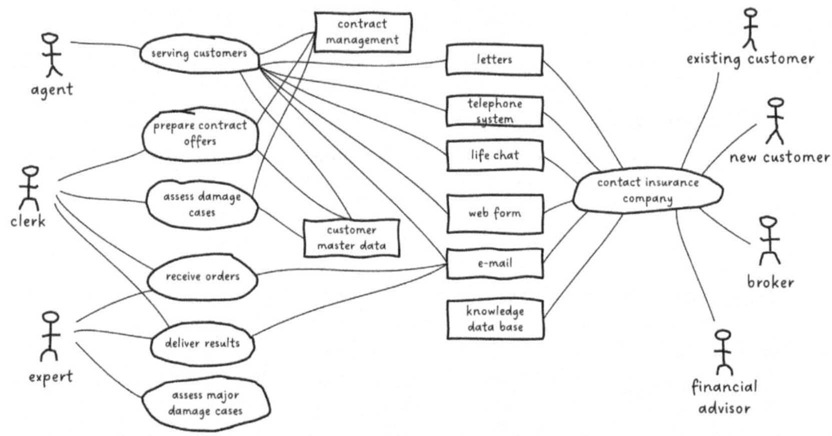

Fig. 5.14 Use cases in the current state

Jan asked numerous questions about the current procedures in the Contact Center, which Linda was able to answer with ease. When he began sketching on the flipchart, Linda was genuinely impressed.

Linda But this doesn't look like the use case diagram format you just showed me. Where's the system boundary?

Jan Exactly, Linda, that's the key point: you don't have a unified system yet. That's why I didn't draw a traditional use case diagram. Instead, I created a diagram that shows use cases, actors, and systems. Right now, all the communication tools used to interact with customers operate independently and are disconnected from contract management and customer master data. An omni-channel system would integrate all these elements. Even scanned letters would then be accessible across all channels.

Linda That makes sense. It also explains the tangled web of connections between employees and the individual tools. When an agent speaks with a customer on the phone, they have to ask for the name and date of birth. Only then can they search for the relevant information in the customer master data or contract management system to get a clear picture of the customer and their situation.

Jan Exactly. With an omni-channel system, an agent would immediately see all relevant details on the screen—regardless of the channel the customer used to get in touch.

Linda I'm really glad we started by illustrating the current state on the flipchart. To some extent, the diagram already highlights what's missing in our current setup. Comparing the use cases with the previously identified requirements and data flows from the context table is especially revealing.

Jan Sometimes it helps to take a step back. In the next step, let's represent the initial target state in a proper use case diagram to serve as a foundation for the workshop.

To the point
Designing a vision of the target state: Where do we want to go?◄

Thanks to the solid groundwork laid with the context table (Table 5.6), Linda and Jan are able to sketch an initial—albeit incomplete—representation of the target state by hand. It remains incomplete because, as indicated in the table, there are still gaps that can only be addressed through future requirements elicitation with stakeholders. Refer to Fig. 5.15 for a visual representation of the current vision for the future IT system 'Omni-Channel.'

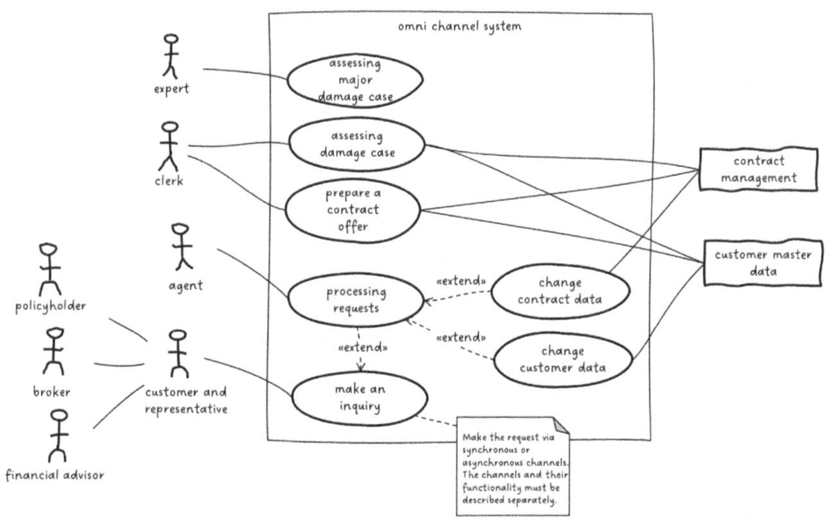

Fig. 5.15 Use Case diagram with incomplete target state

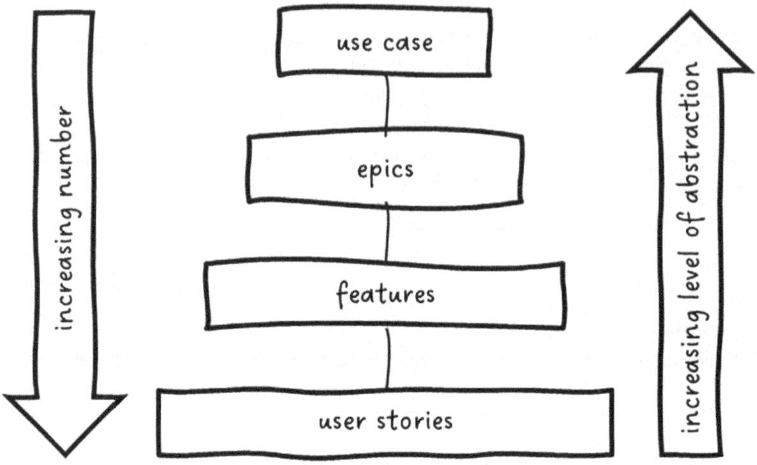

Fig. 5.16 Exemplary hierarchy of requirement levels

Linda I find it remarkable how you always manage to keep things at a high level, leaving room for many details to be filled in later. I would have gone much deeper, for example, by listing all the communication channels we want to integrate into the omni-channel system.

Jan It's important not to dive too deeply into the use case diagram right away. Doing so can quickly lead to a loss of perspective on the overall functionality. Use cases should be defined at a level of granularity that keeps the total number manageable—ideally no more than 7 to 10. We've noted your point about the communication channels as a comment within the diagram.

Linda I didn't know that—you can actually include natural language notes directly within a diagram?

Jan Exactly. It's only through the combination of diagrams and natural language documentation that a complete specification can ultimately be achieved.

Linda In phase 2, we'll add the UI and technical design!

Jan *(winks at her)* You will definitely make sure of that. And since you just mentioned phase 2—once we move into agile implementation, the use cases provide a solid foundation for defining epics. These epics can then be broken down into features, which will definitely include your specific communication channels. For the implementation packages in each sprint, the features are further divided into user stories—or, if you prefer, sprint backlog items.
Take a look at Fig. 5.16 to see how I understand the relationships between these elements.

Linda OK, nice. I just wanted to comment on the actors in our use case diagram. You suggested grouping policyholders, brokers, and financial advisors under a general actor called *Customers and Representatives*. But in contrast, you kept our internal users as separate, individual actors.

Jan That was more of a technical workaround to keep the number of use cases manageable. The main use case for *Customers and Representatives* could be effectively summarized as 'Make an inquiry,' whereas the tasks performed by our internal users—such as agents, clerks, and experts—differ too much to be grouped under a single actor.

Linda All clear. From my perspective, we've laid a strong foundation for our requirements collection methods and especially for the upcoming workshop.

5.6 Linda's Notepad

After successfully developing the initial specification artifacts, Linda takes a moment to reflect and records the key insights from her perspective for Day 3:

Day 3: Finding a starting point

Key work steps and insights:

1. *Define Supporting Requirements Management Tools*
   → Note: AI can significantly reduce time and costs.
2. *Define Goals and Non-Goals (SMART Criteria)*
   - *Use AND-OR trees and formulate each goal in a single, clear sentence.*
3. *Create Glossary and Conceptual Model*
   - *Use nouns from the preliminary study as a starting point for the glossary.*
   - *In RE, class diagrams represent concepts, not software classes.*
   - *Tip: Let AI handle the bulk of this task.*
4. *Identify Stakeholders and Create a Stakeholder List*
   - *Include both internal and external stakeholders.*
   - *Distinguish between active and passive stakeholders.*
   - *AI can assist in identifying and categorizing stakeholders.*
   - *Note: Overlooking stakeholders can jeopardize the entire project.*
5. *Perform Context Analysis*
   - *Develop a context diagram showing system and context boundaries.*
   - *If the diagram becomes too complex, use a context table instead.*
6. *Develop Use Case Diagrams*
   - *Base them on the context diagram and context table.*
   - *Visualize both the current state and a preliminary target state.*

Result of my day : From my perspective, we now have a clearly defined starting point in terms of goals, terminology, stakeholders, systems, and functionalities.

Day 4: Gathering Requirements 6

Day 4 will be particularly dynamic, shaped by a variety of elicitation methods and intensive communication with stakeholders. Both the preparation and execution of this day are critical for capturing the requirements and expectations related to the solution.

When we speak of the *solution*, we are referring not only to the implementation of an omni-channel system, but also to its integration into the broader end-to-end process of 'handling customer concerns' (see Fig. 3.1).

The contributions and feedback from stakeholders—their acceptance or resistance to the topic and the proposed approach, as well as the quantity and quality of the requirements they share—will significantly influence the development of the high-level concept. This, in turn, forms the foundation for the tender documents required for the implementation project.

Linda and Jan are well aware of the delicate balance they must strike today. As a result, their emotional state fluctuates between skepticism and curiosity, tension and anticipation. The uncertainty surrounding how the day will unfold places them in a situation not unlike that of a hiker standing at a crossroads—faced with the need to choose a direction without knowing where each path leads.

At their crossroads lie a variety of elicitation methods, modeling techniques, and standards. From these, they must select the most appropriate tools to uncover the stakeholders' true needs. Among several viable paths, they must identify the one that leads to the most meaningful and actionable requirements. It is a challenging task—one with significant implications for the success of the project.

Day 4 stands out for several reasons:

J. Kawelke and T. Niebisch, *AI-Driven Transformation - Practical Frameworks for Real-World Impact*, Future of Business and Finance,
https://doi.org/10.1007/978-3-662-72549-8_6

- While the previous work packages could realistically be completed within a single working day, Day 4 represents a virtual day. The requirements gathering phase it introduces typically spans several calendar days in practice.
- The activities planned for this "day" demand more than just technical and methodological expertise. Successful requirements elicitation also requires craftsmanship, empathy, and sensitivity—qualities essential for engaging meaningfully with stakeholders.
- Although we are still in Phase 1, which is guided by the principles of the V-model, the techniques applied here are equally relevant and effective in agile project environments. This highlights the versatility and cross-method applicability of sound requirements engineering practices.

Eliciting requirements from diverse stakeholders demands not only substantial experience but also well-developed interpersonal and communication skills.

To the point
The objective is to gain clarity: *Who* expects *what* from the solution? ◄

What sounds simple in theory often proves to be highly complex in practice. To begin, let us revisit the primary sources from which requirements can be derived:

- *Stakeholders* remain the most critical source of requirements in many projects. Their expectations, needs, and constraints form the foundation of the solution design.
- In the context of *system replacement projects*, a significant number of requirements can be identified through the analysis of the *existing IT system* and its *surrounding systems*. For each existing function or interface, it must be carefully evaluated whether it should be retained, modified, or omitted in the new system.
- Beyond the sources outlined in the context diagram, additional requirements may be derived from *existing documentation, e.g.,* of the legacy system. However, this approach can be time-consuming and carries the risk of incorporating outdated or obsolete requirements, especially if the documentation no longer reflects the current state of the system.

This chapter focuses exclusively on the first aspect: the elicitation and collection of requirements from stakeholders.

Let us now return to Linda and Jan and their tasks on this fourth day.

Jan	Let's make a note: requirements can be derived from people, existing systems, and documentation. In our project, the primary opportunity lies in gathering requirements directly from stakeholders. Given the current circumstances in your company, the other two sources are more theoretical than practical
Linda	That simplifies the elicitation process for us. So, what do we have at our disposal? • We've defined the boundaries of the proposed overall system using a context diagram • We've identified initial functionalities of the IT system through the use case diagram • And from the stakeholder analysis, we know whom we can—and must—consult The logical next step is to review these findings with the stakeholders, validate them, and enrich them with their specific requirements
Jan	Let's pause for a moment and reflect. Essentially, our day of *requirements collection* can be divided into three phases: preparation, execution, and follow-up (see Fig. 6.1). I'd like to further break down the preparation phase into two parts: *organizational* and *content* • Organizational preparation focuses on the *how* of the elicitation process—this includes selecting the appropriate elicitation methods, determining the venue, and sending out invitations • Content preparation addresses the *what*—this involves reviewing existing knowledge and preparing the content of the questions. If we've already gathered information from sources such as organizational guidelines or internal documentation, we should incorporate that here Let's take it step by step

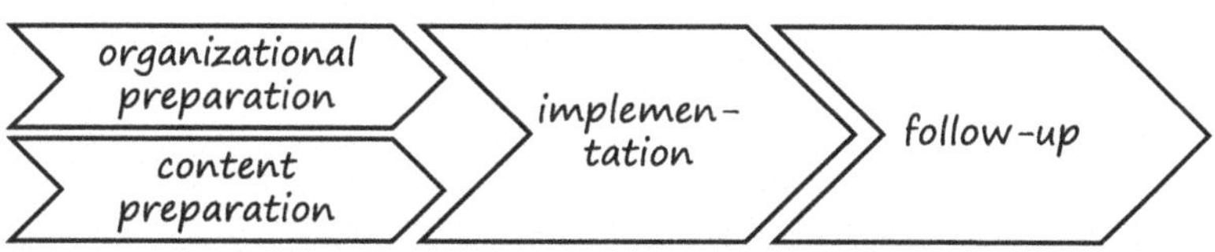

Fig. 6.1 Phases of the requirements collection

6.1 Prepare Collection Organizationally

Linda: In our stakeholder analysis, we identified a wide range of stakeholders. Now the question is: which elicitation methods should we use to explore their requirements? I reviewed some materials from my previous training sessions and found several methods we could consider:
- Workshops and brainstorming sessions
- Questionnaires and interviews
- Crowd-based elicitation, such as ongoing data collection and collaborative input
- Field observation (from a distance) and apprenticing (through hands-on experience)
- Document analysis and reuse of existing documentation from legacy systems

We now need to decide which of these methods are the most efficient and appropriate for our specific context

Jan: Which of these methods do you think would be most suitable for our situation? Do you have a preference for any particular approach?

Linda: Yes, I actually have some favorites. But from the beginning. Up to this point, you have always shone with so much knowledge, now I also want to be a bit smart: The word *method* comes from the Greek Μεθοδος and means as much as the way. The method is therefore the way to achieve the desired goal
In our case, the method is the path to be taken to best determine the requirements of the stakeholders

Jan: I completely agree. Just like standing at a crossroads, we now have to choose a direction—in our case, the appropriate method. It's about selecting the path that will lead us most effectively to the stakeholders' true requirements

Linda: With that in mind, I initially referred to our stakeholder list and grouped the stakeholders into three distinct survey groups. For each group, I propose a different elicitation method from our list:
1. Interviews

We should conduct individual interviews with the following stakeholders:
- The management of the Customer Center *(already completed)*
- The internal audit department, representing legal and regulatory requirements
- The works council, representing employee interests

2. Workshop

A joint workshop is most appropriate for the operational departments. This includes:
- Agents, clerks, and experts
- Mailroom staff
- System administrators and supervisors
- Departmental and team managers

The workshop will allow us to structure and discuss the processes of the Contact Center collaboratively. This setting will help surface the diverse perspectives of the stakeholders and guide us toward requirements that are broadly accepted
I'm still uncertain about my own role in the workshop. As the Product Owner, I'm responsible for the overall outcome, but I would also like to take on the role of moderator

3. Questionnaire

For the largest stakeholder group—our customers—I suggest using a questionnaire. Since all participants will respond to the same set of questions, we can perform a statistical analysis of the results
At this point, I would recommend refraining from using additional elicitation methods

Jan	Your suggestions regarding the elicitation methods and the corresponding stakeholder groups sound excellent. Let's proceed with that approach. I can take on the role of workshop moderator as a neutral consultant, which will allow you to focus entirely on contributing content and guiding the discussion from your perspective as Product Owner However, I would propose adding a fourth elicitation method in preparation for the workshop: *field observation*. I plan to observe selected agents, clerks, and experts in their daily work prior to the workshop. This will give me a clearer understanding of the current processes and provide a stronger foundation for steering the workshop effectively and documenting the resulting requirements If we agree on this plan, I'll move forward with the organizational preparations: • Schedule the workshop date • Prepare and send invitations to the relevant stakeholders Many of your colleagues work remotely and are accustomed to online meetings. However, I recommend that they attend this workshop in person. I'll arrange for a suitably large, well-equipped room to support the session Once these organizational tasks are complete, we'll reconvene to focus on the content-related preparation for the workshop, interviews, questionnaire, and field observation. If you'd like, you can already begin thinking about the content and key questions in the meantime

In the period that follows, Jan dedicates himself exclusively to the organizational preparation of the four selected elicitation methods:

- *Field Observation:* This method serves solely to support Jan in gaining a comprehensive understanding of the current end-to-end process prior to the workshop. He considers it valuable to observe activities across all three service levels in order to assess how these levels are currently structured and operate in practice. At Jan's request, Linda provides him with contacts for one representative from each level: an agent, a clerk, and an expert responsible for handling major damage cases.
- *Interviews:* Jan schedules individual appointments with both the works council and the internal audit department. In his invitations, he outlines the focus areas of the interviews and communicates his expectations for each stakeholder group's input. To ensure flexibility and convenience, Jan decides to conduct these interviews online.
- *Questionnaire:* The main challenge with the questionnaire lies not in its content, but in selecting a representative group of participants. Jan is aware that the insights gained from such a survey are only meaningful if the participant group is highly heterogeneous. To ensure a well-rounded picture of customer opinion, participants should vary in characteristics such as age, gender, education, income, and geographic region. In addition to carefully selecting participants, motivating them to take part is often difficult. Jan considers this challenge and develops an idea that gains the support of the insurance company. He receives a dedicated budget to organize a *prize competition* as an incentive for participation.

  Jan recruits participants through social networks, contacts within his own organization, and specialized survey communities. Ultimately, he assembles a group of 150 participants for the survey. With this solid foundation, he is now ready to begin the content preparation of the questionnaire (see Sect. 6.2.3).

- *Workshop*: Jan begins by organizing a venue that can comfortably accommodate all workshop participants. He opts to rent a conference room at an off-site location near the company. His intention is to create a setting where the equipment and ambiance positively influence the participants' engagement and spark curiosity about the topic.

  Additionally, by choosing an external venue, Jan aims to ensure that participants can fully focus on the workshop, free from the distractions of their daily work environment.

With the invitations sent to the stakeholders, Jan completes the organizational preparations. He and Linda can now turn their attention to the content-related preparations.

6.2 Prepare Content Collection

Linda constantly comes up with new aspects and questions, eager to find answers quickly. These topics swirl around in her mind in a completely unordered fashion. When she envisions the redesigned process, she often drifts into details. At times, she thinks about parameters for measuring the processing time of a request. Other times, she mentally creates value lists for the agents and clerks. When she puts herself in the position of the end user, she frequently ponders the visual design of the application.

Linda realizes that she needs an outline for preparing the interviews and workshops, designing the questionnaire, and later analyzing and documenting the results. But what could the basic structure look like?

Jan needs to step in and offer some guidance.

6.2.1 Select Requirement Categories for the Survey

Linda: Since I've been trying to focus on preparing for the requirements survey, many questions have been buzzing in my head. The more I think about it, the more questions for the stakeholders come to mind. All of these need to be answered by our colleagues:

- Which agent and which clerk handle which customer number ranges?
- How is it ensured that every asynchronous request is processed promptly? What does "promptly" mean in this context?
- Which interfaces to other systems are relevant for the rough concept?
- Will we introduce a standard product, or is custom software development more suitable?

I have many other similar questions. Additionally, I'm completely unsure how detailed we should make the tender and which aspects, in terms of their granularity, should be assigned to project phase 2

Jan	Even if it seems overwhelming right now, it's fortunately not as difficult as you fear. My approach is to note all the requirements that are communicated to us. These requirements might sometimes be too detailed for the tender, but they will be recorded in our repository and won't be lost. Later, during the follow-up, we can assign each requirement to the appropriate project phase As for the procedure, let's start by revisiting your excellent mind map of the requirement categories. We can mark the elements that we consider relevant for the rough concept and the tender. This will help us narrow down the scope of the requirement categories and allow us to focus on the rest
Linda	A pragmatic approach. If I understand you correctly, you're suggesting that we select the elements from each requirement category for Phase 1, while still keeping the other categories in mind
Jan	As you've already guessed from the number of your own questions, we should expect a flood of information when collecting requirements. If we have a plan in advance about which requirement categories to focus on during the workshop, we can guide the discussion more effectively

Linda and Jan review the mind map representation once more and discuss which variations they want to prioritize. The result is an updated mind map with the relevant categories marked in grey (see Fig. 6.2). These grey-marked requirement categories and their variations will form the content focus for the preparation of the four elicitation methods.

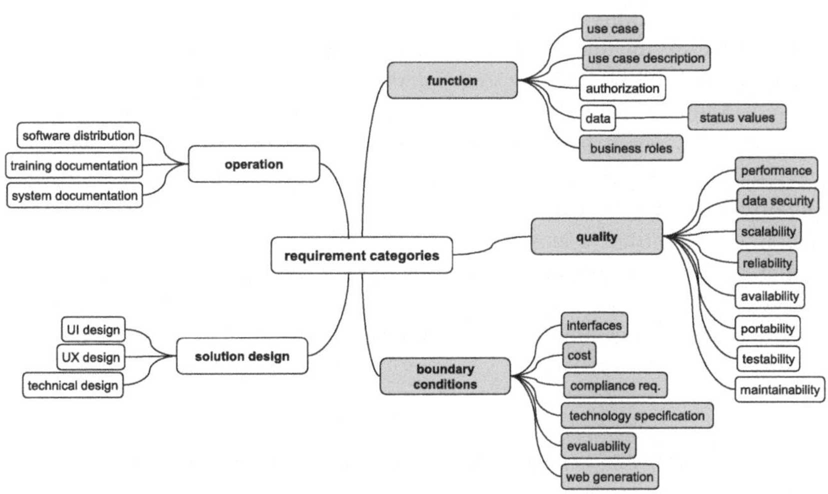

Fig. 6.2 Requirement categories and variations for Phase 1

6.2.2 Prepare Field Observation

Jan sequentially contacts his three points of contact from the 1st, 2nd, and 3rd level supports. In these brief conversations, he explains his goal: to better understand and classify the requirements of the workshop participants through field observation. He alleviates their concerns about work oversight by emphasizing that the acceptance of the omni-channel system by all participants is a critical success factor. He can only achieve this acceptance by engaging with their concrete work and understanding the resulting requirements.

After Jan coordinates the appointments with his three points of contact, he decides not to prepare further in terms of content. At the agreed times, he will simply observe their work with curiosity and ask clarifying questions if necessary. His goal is not to optimize the current process but to gain a fundamental understanding of the existing business process in preparation for the workshop. He intends to focus on the subtleties of their activities, knowing that these details might no longer stand out to the professionals themselves. In past projects, these subtleties have often helped him stimulate new solution paths with seemingly naive questions. Jan is confident that this approach will be successful once again.

6.2.3 Preparing a Questionnaire with the Help of GenAI

The questionnaire is a classic method of organizational development. It remains valuable today, especially when the number of stakeholders to be surveyed is very high, when preserving the anonymity of respondents is important, or when the effort required for individual or group interviews exceeds their benefit.

When designing a questionnaire, you can grant respondents varying degrees of freedom. Options range from closed yes–no questions to pre-formulated answer choices (multiple-choice) and completely open-ended text responses. However, it's important to note that a high degree of freedom can complicate structured, statistical, and quantitative analysis.

During the creation of the questionnaire, *Generative Artificial Intelligence* can provide valuable insights and suggest questions or question blocks. Jan takes advantage of this convenience by consulting his company-specific chatbot. He asks:

> *I want to prepare a questionnaire for policyholders to determine their requirements for a future contact center. Can you suggest 5 closed and 5 open questions? The closed questions should contain answer options that are more specific than just yes and no.*

The chatbot's answer is:

> *Absolutely! Considering your goal to precisely understand policyholders' preferences for a future contact center, I'll craft 5 closed questions with detailed answer options and 5 open questions to gather richer insights, all aligned with requirements engineering best practices.*

Closed Questions (with specific answer options):

1. *How often do you anticipate needing to contact the support center?*
   - *Multipletimes a week*
   - *Once a week*
   - *A few times a month*
   - *Once a month or less*
   - *Only during emergencies or critical issues*
2. *What is your preferred method of communication with the contact center?*
   - *Phone calls during standard business hours*
   - *Email for non-urgent issues*
   - *Live chat through website or mobile app*
   - *Social media messaging (e.g., Facebook Messenger, Twitter DMs)*
   - *Video conferencing for complex queries*
3. *What level of response time do you consider acceptable for support requests?*
   - *Immediate reply within 5 min*
   - *Response within 15 min*
   - *Response within 1 h*
   - *Response within 4 h*
   - *Same-day resolution, even if delayed*
4. *Which types of issues do you expect the support center to prioritize?*
   - *Technical problems related to policies or services*
   - *Billing and payment inquiries*
   - *Policy change requests or updates*
   - *Complaints and dispute resolution*
   - *General information and guidance*
5. *How should the contact center communicate updates or follow-ups?*
   - *Automated alerts via SMS or email at key stages*
   - *Call back from a support agent at a scheduled time*
   - *Online portal updates or live chat messages*
   - *No follow-up unless explicitly requested*
   - *Combination of automated updates and personal follow-up*

Open Questions (to benefit from detailed, qualitative responses):

1. *What specific features or tools would enhance your experience when contacting the support center?*
2. *Can you share an example of a positive support experience that exceeded your expectations? What made it stand out?*
3. *What challenges have you faced with current contact centers that you hope to see improved?*
4. *In your opinion, what are the most important factors that would make the contact center more user-friendly and efficient?*
5. *Are there any additional services, features, or support channels you would like us to consider for the future contact center?*

Would you like me to customize the questions further based on your target demographic or specific policy types?

Jan is impressed by the response. He recalls that a few years ago, getting an acceptable result from a chatbot for similar questions required a lengthy prompt chain.

However, language models have improved significantly since then. The suggestions provided are an excellent basis for creating the questionnaire. As he continues to integrate the chatbot's input, he also considers the defined requirement categories. Nevertheless, Jan still has some rework to do before the final version is completed.

6.2.4 Preparing Interviews, Partly with GenAI

The preparation effort for interviews can be less compared to that of the questionnaire, provided the degree of structuring is not too detailed. A moderate degree of structuring means less effort in preparation and greater flexibility during the interview. You only set up a rough roadmap and do not work out all questions in detail. This approach requires a high level of concentration and experience from the requirements engineer to extract meaningful information from such interviews. The follow-up and analysis of the collected requirements usually require more effort than the evaluation of structured questionnaires or very finely planned interviews.

Preparing for the interviews forces Jan to shift his perspective—from the customer's point of view to that of the audit and works council. He understands that both stakeholder groups perform different tasks within the company and therefore prioritize their requirements for a solution differently. However, there is one area where their requirements for the IT system undoubtedly overlap: data protection.

After a thorough analysis and with the help of a GenAI chatbot, Jan has identified the following topic blocks:

1. Interviews with the Audit
    - Corruption prevention when introducing the tool
    - Currently applicable guidelines and regulations relevant to the project
    - Data protection regarding customer and employee data
2. Interview Guide for the Works Council
    - Regulatory minimum requirements for the business organization of insurance companies
    - Effects of an omni-channel system on employees and their working conditions
    - Training and integration of employees
    - Avoidance of employee surveillance and protection of data from internal users

Jan does not want to break down this guide into specific questions but prefers to remain flexible in responding to the interviewees' answers. He believes that this semi-structured approach will yield the best possible results.

However, in order to be best prepared for the interviews, he uses his chatbot to do a dry-run of the interview by creating the following prompt for the Works Council interview:

Imagine you are a requirements engineer. You simulate human behavior in the chatbot and ask questions to a member of the Works Council who is supposed to provide you with council-related requirements for a business organization and a software system. This Works Council member is a real person who is speaking to you live via the prompt. I will refer to him or her as the 'stakeholder' from now on.

These are the topics you should ask questions about:

- *Regulatory minimum requirements for the business organization of insurance companies*
- *Effects of an omni-channel system on employees and their working conditions*
- *Training and integration of employees*
- *Avoidance of employee surveillance and protection of data from internal users*

After analyzing this prompt, simply say, "Hello, I'm your requirements engineer." Then wait for the stakeholder's response to your greeting. If the stakeholder starts with small talk, respond politely.

At no time should you simulate the stakeholder's reactions, answers, or questions; simply wait for the stakeholder's input via the prompt. After greetings and small talk, list the topics and ask which topic you can question the stakeholder about. Wait for the response. After their response, think of three questions for the topic, but only ask your first question.

Always ask exactly one question, then wait for the stakeholder's response; never hand over entire blocks of questions. If the stakeholder's answer is unclear, ask an additional question to clarify any confusion.

If the stakeholder rambles or becomes unprofessional, respond politely but try to bring the stakeholder back to the topic.

After the third main question, summarize the answers and let the stakeholder confirm them. Then ask if they want to talk about the next topic. If yes, then list the remaining three topics and let the stakeholder choose the next topic. And so on.

Before leaving, summarize the stakeholder's requirements and have them confirm their accuracy.

Dear reader, please try out this prompt and see for yourself how natural it feels.

Linda	Jan, I tried out your interview prompt and it works. I imagined I was a Works Council member talking to a requirements engineer and was able to have a professional conversation with the chatbot
Jan	It's amazing, isn't it? But would you prefer being interviewed by the chatbot or by a requirements engineer like me?
Linda	I thought we were using it only as preparation for the actual interview. Do you really think stakeholders can get used to being interviewed by a GenAI chatbot?
Jan	To be honest, I'm not sure yet. As of today, I would say no. However, the technology is becoming more sophisticated and capable of handling nuanced conversations. It can be a convenient and efficient way to gather initial insights, especially for routine or preliminary questions. Of course, for more complex or sensitive topics, a human touch is still irreplaceable. On the other hand, I can imagine that most bots will have 3D presentations of human beings. With these avatars, it will feel even more natural to talk to them in the future, especially when they resemble the interviewer
Linda	Interesting view. Let's talk again in 5 years...

6.2.5 Preparing the Workshop

Linda and Jan reach the point that Linda had mentioned several times—it's time to prepare for the workshop. On one hand, Linda hadn't anticipated the journey to be so complex. On the other hand, there were no aspects she could confidently say could be omitted.

Their first preparation task is setting up an agenda for the workshop. They have planned a full-day workshop and expect about 6–7 h of effective work. The first draft of their agenda (see Fig. 6.3) is based on this time span.

Linda was amazed. Although they would conduct a 6 ½ hour workshop, it was clear that this time would not be sufficient to discuss all requirement categories. Further workshops will be necessary to determine additional requirements based on the results of the first workshop, such as those related to interfaces, user guidance, or scalability. However, they decide to postpone the preparation of these subsequent workshops for now.

Once the agenda for the first workshop is finalized, they begin preparing the individual points in terms of content. The first four points of the agenda are clear. They had already discussed their contents extensively over the past few days, covering the purpose and characteristics of requirements, their features, and the delimitation of the system context. For point 5, the process recording, they combine their ideas and formulate initial thoughts to stimulate discussion during the workshop and provide a clear direction.

Agenda for the first workshop "Reorganization of the process 'handling customer concerns'"

1. Introduction and agreement of rules (20 minutes)
2. Topic Introduction (55 minutes)
   - Introduce the project (assignment, goals, project organization),
   - Explain the procedure,
   - Define key terms (requirements, process understanding, stakeholders, etc.),
   - Present the contents of the RE plan.
3. Explaining requirement categories (15 minutes)

   --- BREAK ---
4. Carry out context analysis / check system and context boundaries (60 minutes)

   --- BREAK ---
5. Defining the target business process (big picture) (90 minutes)

   --- BREAK ---
6. Analyzing and completing use cases for the contact center (120 minutes)

   --- BREAK ---
7. Final round: what happens next? (30 minutes)

Fig. 6.3 Agenda for the first workshop

Linda I see a potential risk for the workshop based on my experience. The danger lies in quickly diving into detailed discussions. It's a common phenomenon where, despite the absence of a clear overall process idea, participants start debating properties, permissions, or nuances in the processing. This can dissipate a lot of energy

Jan I fear this effect of slipping into a detailed discussion just as much as you do. To avoid this, I have noted down a few typical questions that focus on the processes and should guide us through the workshop:

- From a bird's eye view, the questions arise about the overall picture: Are the 'In' and 'Out' elements—i.e., the requirements and data flows—in their context table (Tab. 5.6) complete or are some still missing? What use cases arise for the system from these elements?
- What does the business process 'handling customer concerns' look like today? What works particularly well and which parts of the current process should be improved?
- How do the sub-processes of asynchronous communication work in particular?
- What business rules apply to this asynchronous communication?
- One level deeper, we need to question each use case:
  - What prerequisites need to be met for each use case to be carried out?
  - What trigger starts each use case? With what expected result does a use case end, both in the positive and in the negative case?

In total, I hope that these guiding questions will fuel the discussion in the workshop and lead to a lot of insights

Jan's questions are provided as examples. Workshops of this kind should be prepared more intensively (Robertson & Robertson, 2024). Ideally, there would already be a preliminary visualization of the processes as they currently exist (current processes) or as desired (target processes). For a preparatory process design, it is essential to select suitable colleagues and rely on existing documentation.

Linda But we should also ask questions related to legal or operational regulations, not just about the process itself. For example:

- Where is data from communication with the chatbot stored?
- How long must paper documents be kept after electronic archiving before they can be destroyed?
- Who is responsible for the destruction of paper documents after scanning, and how does this destruction process work?
- How long must electronic documents be retained? I believe it's ten years, but are there different regulations?
- Regarding working hours: We currently have standard office core hours, which don't require 24/7 availability. Therefore, we might not need to implement a fail-safe IT system unless the criticality demands it. But perhaps I'm mistaken?

Jan Yes, we should definitely ask these questions as well. I believe the preparation for the first workshop is sufficient at this level of detail. The principle is clear, and we have noted the most important guiding questions. We are ready for the workshop

Linda and Jan believe they are on the right track due to the thorough preparation of all four elicitation methods.

6.3 Conduct and Evaluate Survey

6.3.1 The Findings of the Field Observation

After Jan reviewed the daily operations across all three support levels, he gained a much clearer understanding of the current processes. He went a step further and conducted initial analyses on these processes.

It's no surprise to him that this project was initiated—the weaknesses highlighted by the audit are evident. Customer concerns are sometimes addressed multiple times without making substantial progress. Jan recognizes several issues:

- Customer concerns are sometimes taken up by a second agent who is unaware that a colleague is already handling the case.
- Duplicate work occurs because the processing status cannot be documented.
- Processing errors arise due to media breaks.
- The same customer concerns, which the customer has brought to the insurance company twice via different channels (e.g., chat and email), are processed twice.
- Clerks and experts start processing cases without essential prerequisites being met, leading to process loops and multiple handling.

The lack of efficiency in case processing is not due to the employees and their commitment, Jan has already ruled that out. According to his first impression, a central and controlling component is missing, which:

- Displays all other open concerns of a customer for the same contract number
- Allows the current status of case processing to be recognized
- Displays essential information for case processing
- Completes simple standard concerns fully automatically
- Monitors processing times and sends information at certain times or triggers escalations

He discusses this assumption with Linda, and they both decide to present this solution approach to the workshop participants.

6.3.2 The Results of the Workshop

The schedule for the requirements survey in Phase 1 stipulates that the workshop with the stakeholders will take place before the interviews are conducted. Although our two protagonists feel well prepared, they cannot deny their stage fright. A considerable amount of uncertainty about the prospects of success creeps into their minds. What if they are not understood at all, or if they cannot engage the group effectively in terms of content and methodology?

6.3.2.1 First Steps

The highly anticipated day has arrived. All participants arrive on time, curious about what will happen. So far, no one has shown such interest in their work that a workshop was held outside the company. Most participants appreciate that their managers have cleared their schedules for this workshop and relieved them of their daily tasks.

After the welcome, Linda and Jan present the agenda and guide the day. The first three agenda items go smoothly, allowing them to take a break as planned. Following this, the moderators present the context diagram (Fig. 5.11) and explain the syntax and semantics of the symbols used. Initially, the participants are somewhat skeptical about the method that defines the project through drawn boxes, ellipses, and stick figures. However, after a short time and a few clarifying questions, they recognize the practical use of the simple symbolism. Everyone then focuses on the content of the context diagram and the associated context table. The first step, defining the *Inside* and *Outside* in relation to the project with the help of the context analysis, is successful as hoped.

6.3.2.2 The Business Process 'Handling Customer Concerns'

The next step is to get down to business. The workshop task is to visualize the business process 'Handling Customer Concerns' using a BPMN process diagram. They create the business process under the following predetermined premises:

- **Omitting the explicit collection of the current process:** Since the omni-channel system is a novel solution intended to unify existing isolated solutions, dedicated documentation of the current processes is not necessary. Jan has already gained a preliminary understanding during his field observation.
- **Maintaining the current handling of customer concerns by 1st, 2nd, and 3rd level support:** Stakeholders are asked to keep their basic activities within the current processes in mind and, if necessary, integrate them into the target process.
- **Central control:** Jan's field observation suggests that central control could be beneficial. Therefore, he asks stakeholders to formulate their expectations for a central and fully automated control and processing of customer concerns by an omni-channel system.
- **Rough process flow:** It is widely accepted that having a rough idea of the process flow is advantageous for further requirements determination. The basic business process is needed in its target form as a big picture. However, immediately modeling the desired process flow carries risks. To mitigate these, the process is developed step by step using a structured and proven approach.

Jan begins to explain the last point. In his experience, one should not start immediately with developing the concrete sequence. He provides the following arguments for his thesis:

- **Different starting and ending points:** Stakeholders unconsciously have different starting and ending points of the process in mind. They are involved in the process at different times and for varying durations, which necessitates standardizing their ideas of the beginning and end of the process.
- **Implicit conditions and prerequisites:** Certain conditions and prerequisites for the process are only assumed by individuals. These flow implicitly into their process descriptions without being known or visible to other stakeholders.
- **Getting lost in details:** Stakeholders typically get lost in process details and special scenarios as soon as the discussion begins.

The nodding agreement of some participants confirms Jan's argument. Apparently, they had already had similar experiences in other workshops. Jan wants to avoid the beginner's mistake of starting process modeling too quickly. One possibility he sees is in the preliminary discussion of a process overview. Similar to a ball sport, the field to be played is first defined by the stakeholders. In our case, this is done not with a tape measure, but with a so-called *Process Profile* (Niebisch, 2022) (see Fig. 6.4).

The process profile documents the common understanding of all stakeholders, which they were able to agree on in a first step, regarding the beginning, end, and the essential activities and characteristics of the process. Thus, it forms the framework for the upcoming modeling.

Subsequently, the space between the start and end events must be filled by the stakeholders with process activities, rules, and decisions, taking into account all other information. However, the second step, the classic process survey, also has its risks. The greatest risk lies in overburdening the moderator or the modeler. Often, they stand at a flipchart or operate a BPM tool and try to model ad hoc what the workshop participants shout out to them. Events of this kind often run chaotically and are exhausting. But there is a way out of this difficulty.

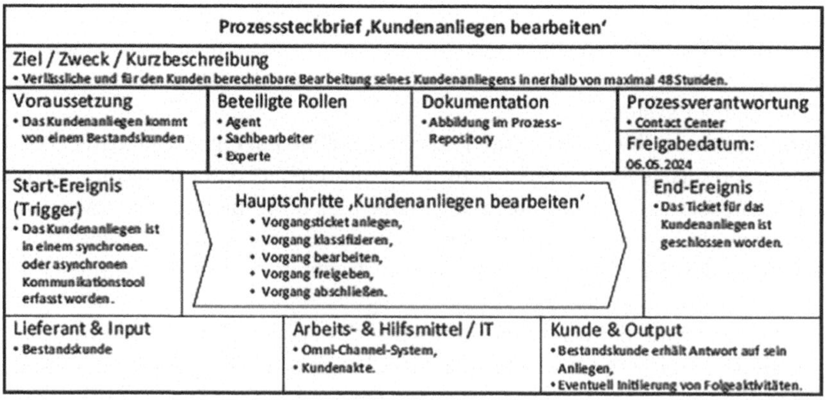

Fig. 6.4 Process Profile 'Handling Customer Concerns'

To address this, Jan has researched a special survey method. He knows that using a computer-aided process modeling tool for the initial survey can be confusing, and a discussion at the whiteboard or flipchart quickly reaches its limits. Therefore, he decided to use t.BPM (Plattner et al., 2016) to capture processes. The t.BPM method (Lübbe, 2011) thrives on all workshop participants being actively involved in the process creation.

First, the participants move the existing tables together to form a large surface and lay long paper wallpapers on it, similar to a wallpapering table. These form the basis for the process visualization. Several sets of BPMN symbols, made in advance from solid and rewritable material, are provided. With these sets, the BPMN symbols are available to all workshop participants for their active participation in a form that resembles a mix of pin cards and breakfast boards—writable, stable, and tangible. The task of the participants is to note each process activity on a separate symbol, fix it on the paper wallpaper lying on the table, and connect it through logical relationships with the other symbols to form a process.

The concrete process survey in the workshop is very dynamic. Under Jan's direction, the business process 'Handling Customer Concerns' with its activities and dependencies is discussed and visualized. The participants model the process with different scenarios. Due to the active participation based on the t.BPM methodology, every participant feels involved in the creation of process models. Details can be discussed in smaller groups. Jan consistently manages to move stuck conversations and detailed discussions forward on another level. As a result, for the first time, the company has a concrete description of the desired business process in connection with the contact center. This fact alone finds broad approval among the participants.

At the end of the 90 min, the target process is described at a level of abstraction that is comprehensible even to outsiders. The request for a task block for automatic transaction processing was met. Additionally, the three support levels each received an area for documenting their own activities. Although some points remain open, this first common draft is quite useful. Linda records the results by photographing the process graphics. Subsequently, Jan transfers the workshop results into a suitable tool (see Fig. 6.5).

At this point in the workshop, it is time to give our two protagonists—and the participants—the promised break. We will use this opportunity to provide readers who are less familiar with BPMN (Business Process Model and Notation) with a brief syntactic and semantic explanation. The goal is not to offer a full BPMN training, but rather to explain the symbols used in the context of the business process shown in Fig. 6.5, enabling readers to interpret and understand the diagram.

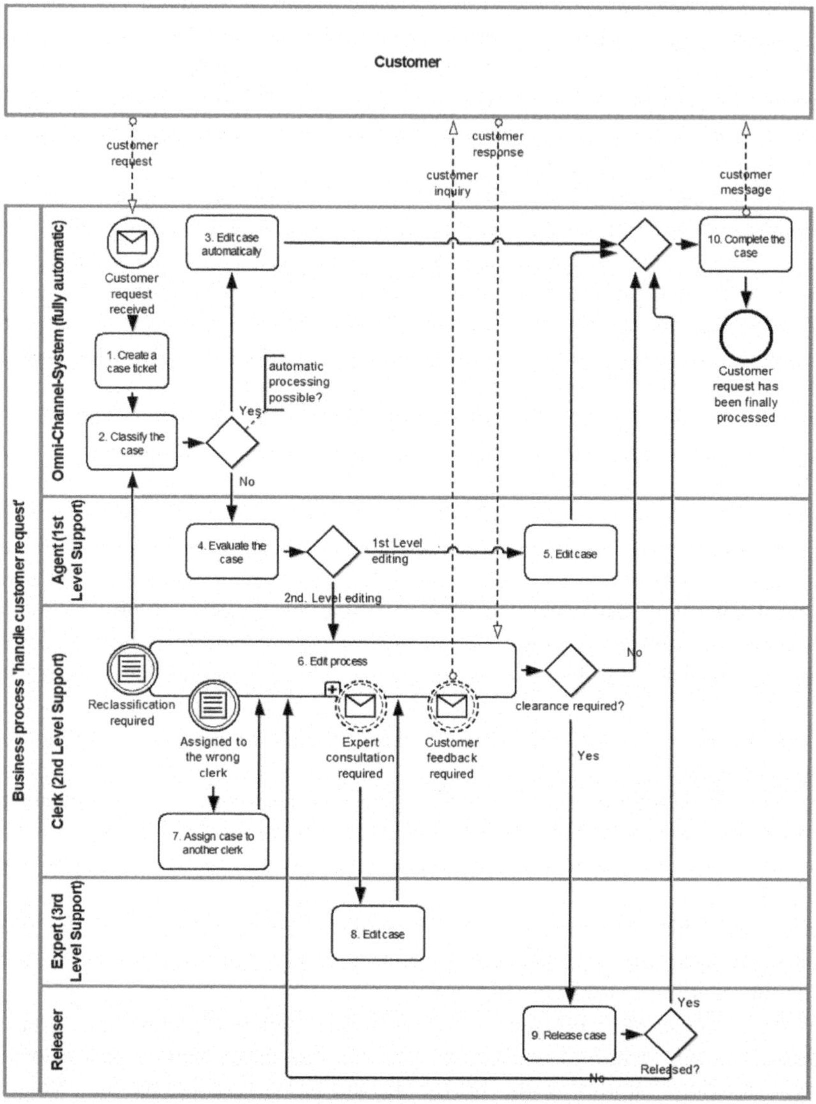

Fig. 6.5 Business process 'handling customer concerns'

- Let's begin with the overall structure. You will notice two differently sized rectangles connected by dashed arrows. These rectangles are called *pools*. Each pool represents an independent process. The dashed arrows between them are *message flows*, which indicate points of synchronization between the processes. The upper rectangle, labeled 'Customer or Representative,' is a *collapsed pool*, meaning its internal process is not shown—because it is not the focus of this model. The lower rectangle, labeled "'Business Process' Handling Customer Concerns," is an *expanded pool*, which we will examine in detail.
- Inside the expanded pool, there are five horizontal rectangles known as *lanes*. Just like in a swimming pool, each lane represents a track in which one or more *activities* are carried out. The *actor* responsible for the activities in each lane is indicated on the left edge. The four lower lanes represent human actors: the three support levels and one approver. The top lane represents the Omni-Channel system itself. At first glance, placing a yet-to-be-developed IT system alongside human actors may seem contradictory. However, from a technical and logical perspective, this representation is intentional. It allows the desired fully automated processing steps of the IT system to be aligned with the user activities, making the interaction between human and system components more transparent.

Looking inside each lane, we observe several geometric symbols that form the core elements of BPMN notation:

- Rounded rectangles represent activities—tasks or actions carried out by the actor responsible for the lane.
- Circles denote events, which are slightly more complex to interpret. BPMN distinguishes between:
  - Start events,
  - intermediate events, and
  - end events.

  Their names reflect their role in the process. Start and end events are represented by a single thin or thick border, respectively. Intermediate events are marked by a double border. Intermediate events can occur either:
  - In the middle of a process (not used in our model), or
  - Attached to the boundary of an activity, indicating that they are tied to that specific task. These are called *attached intermediate events*.

  Among the attached intermediate events, you'll notice two visual styles:
  - Solid borders indicate *interrupting intermediate events*, which stop the associated activity when triggered.

  - Dashed borders indicate *non-interrupting intermediate events*, which do not stop the activity but instead trigger additional actions.

  The meaning of these events will become clearer in the following paragraphs as we describe the process flow.
- Important note: As discussed in earlier chapters, precise and unambiguous expression is essential in requirements engineering. This also applies to naming events and activities:
  - An activity implies a duration (e.g., "the process is being handled").
  - An event has already occurred and is therefore instantaneous (e.g., "the process has been handled").
  - Remember: Activities are time-bound; events are timeless.
- Diamonds represent *gateways*, which control the flow of the process based on conditions or decisions. BPMN provides several types of gateways. In our model, we use only the exclusive OR (XOR) gateway, which ensures that exactly one of the outgoing paths is taken—no more, no less.
- Solid arrows represent the sequence flow, indicating the logical order of activities. These differ from the dashed arrows used for message flows, which represent communication between independent processes.

Now that we have explained the syntax and semantics of the core elements of the BPMN diagram, let us take a closer look at the specific target business process 'Handling Customer Concerns':

- The process begins when the Omni-Channel system is informed of a customer concern via one of the communication channels. This trigger is represented by the start event 'Customer request received.'
- The system then creates a technical process instance in the form of a ticket and classifies the concern using a configurable set of rules (see Sect. 7.3.3 for details).
- Based on the classification, the Omni-Channel system decides whether the concern can be handled fully automatically or needs to be forwarded to an agent for manual processing.
- Further human-controlled processing takes place across the three service levels, with or without IT support, up to the point of automatic or manual approval.
- Activity 6: 'Edit Process' serves as an example of how a business process model can reflect the flexibility of real-world operations. This activity abstracts from the specific steps a clerk might take—such as filling out a paper form, making a phone call, checking a credit score, or initiating a transfer. These are bundled into the single activity 'Edit Process.'

  Attached to this activity are four intermediate events, each representing a different scenario. Their meanings, moving counterclockwise, are as follows:

- Interrupting Intermediate Event: 'Reclassification required'

  Triggered when the clerk identifies a misclassification or enriches the data such that the Omni-Channel system can reclassify the concern. The activity ends for the clerk, and the process continues with automatic reclassification.
- Interrupting Intermediate Event: 'Assigned to the wrong clerk'

  Triggered when the clerk determines that another colleague should handle the case. The current processing is interrupted, and the task is reassigned—though it continues within the same role, hence the sequence flow returns to the same activity.
- Non-Interrupting Intermediate Event: 'Expert consultation required'

  Triggered when the clerk requires input from an expert. The clerk temporarily pauses their work, but remains responsible for the case. This pause justifies the use of a non-interrupting event, as the activity is not terminated.
- Non-Interrupting Intermediate Event: 'Customer feedback required'

  Similar to the previous case, this event is triggered when the clerk needs additional information from the customer. The transaction is paused until a response is received. This interaction is represented by message flows (dashed arrows) in the diagram.

This excerpt from business process management highlights the importance of establishing a shared procedural understanding before engaging in detailed requirements elicitation. If significant clarification is needed at this level, space should be created for open discussion. However, it is essential to avoid slipping into excessive detail too early, as this can divert attention from the actual project objectives.

Later, Linda and Jan will take a closer look at the top swim lane, which represents the technical process of the Omni-Channel system. In Sect. 7.3.1, they will present a proposal outlining their vision for fully automated processing at the procedural level. However, before addressing this, they will focus on the system use cases embedded within the business process during the workshop.

6.3.2.3 The Use Case Diagram 'Omni-Channel System'

The creation of the process profile and the modeling of the target business process before the break were both impressive and surprisingly challenging for the workshop participants. Although most of them have worked in the insurance industry for many years and perform these tasks daily, they were surprised by how difficult it was to describe their day-to-day work in a structured manner.

This makes them all the more eager for the next agenda item following the break—one that many consider the most exciting: the functionalities and corresponding use cases of the future Omni-Channel system. This system is intended to become an integral part of the new overall Contact Center process.

Jan presents the initial use case diagram, which he developed together with Linda, and opens the discussion. The presentation is conducted using a modeling tool, projected onto a large screen for all to see. To ensure version control and traceability, Jan uses a document management system with check-in and check-out functionalities. This allows him to maintain a clear record of all changes and ensures that he can always refer back to the original version of the use case diagram.

Even with the use case diagram, the participants find it challenging to avoid slipping into detailed discussions, often debating the specific process steps within individual use cases. Jan repeatedly steps in to slow down the conversation and reminds his colleagues that such details belong to the implementation project in Phase 2.

In the end, it becomes clear that Linda and Jan were already quite close to the final result. The main advancement achieved during the workshop is the integration of the anticipated use cases into a coherent causal structure. The updated use case diagram is presented in Fig. 6.6.

Note As previously mentioned, this example is also designed to meet didactic requirements such as *comprehensibility* and *traceability*. This means that not all information that might occur or be conceivable in practice is visualized. Figure 6.6 therefore shows only a clear and focused set of actors, use cases, and systems. For instance, the IT systems depicted are a symbolic selection. Readers who refer to

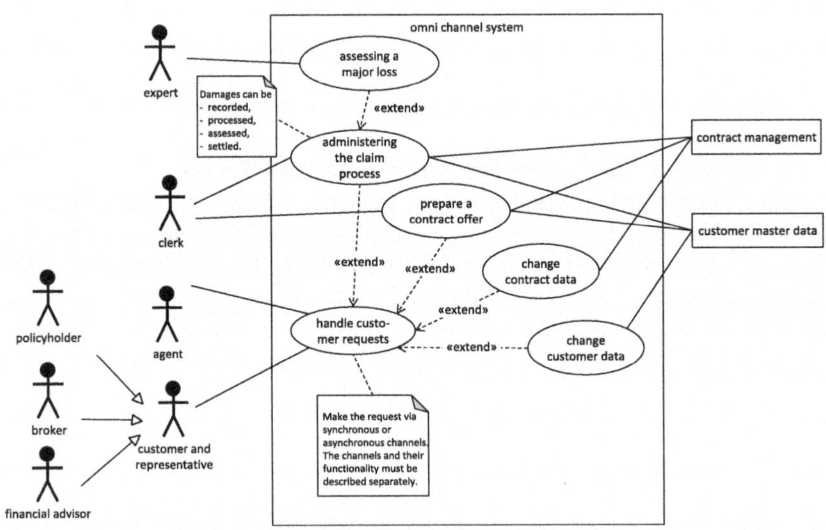

Fig. 6.6 UC diagram after the workshop

the more comprehensive system landscape in the architecture model in Sect. 7.3.5 will recognize that this simplified representation is sufficient for conveying the basic understanding.

Time flies. Everyone is surprised to find that, despite the generous time allocated for the workshop, not all questions could be addressed. Some participants are assigned follow-up tasks to bring their input to subsequent meetings. Incidentally, all participants come to the shared realization that requirements gathering in the form of a workshop can hardly be effectively conducted online.

After the workshop concludes and the participants are dismissed, Jan and Linda take time to evaluate the event.

Jan	Are you satisfied?
Linda	Absolutely. An event like this was new to me, but I'm pleasantly surprised. I was amazed at how quickly the BPMN standard for process modeling was understood and accepted, especially with good moderation. I'm sure the t.BPM methodology played a big role in that Still, I was a bit surprised by the discussions around the process flows. I always assumed the processes were clear to everyone, but that clearly wasn't the case, at least not until today. And I have to admit, without your moderation, the session could easily have descended into chaos. As we feared, everyone came in with their own detailed topics and was eager to bring them up
Jan	I think it's great that the participants, despite their initial skepticism, really engaged with the workshop. That will help build trust in us and in our approach going forward. I'm hopeful that, in the end, we'll achieve a very high quality of requirements
Linda	Me too. And going forward, I think we should apply the same division of roles we just tested in the workshop to the interviews as well. We'll conduct them together and document the results collaboratively

Linda and Jan realize that they will need to rework the results after the requirements elicitation. They notice that some points are important to one stakeholder but irrelevant to another. In some cases, requirements even contradict each other. They understand that, in a later analysis phase, certain requirements will need to be deferred or inconsistencies resolved in order to achieve a consistent and coherent set of requirements.

For now, however, their focus is on visualizing and documenting the requirements gathered so far. How they plan to do this will be explained the following day.

One final task remains for Linda and Jan today: obtaining confirmation of the workshop results from the participants. This step is essential to establish a shared commitment between the stakeholders and the requirements they have defined. It ensures that participants will generally adhere to the agreed-upon requirements throughout the project and will only propose changes with proper justification.

Without this commitment, there is a risk that stakeholders may repeatedly revisit the requirements, requesting changes or additions that could delay project progress. To prevent this, Linda sends out the workshop protocol to all participants and follows up persistently until each one has confirmed the contents and agreements in writing.

6.3.3 Conducting the Interviews

The online interviews with the works council and the audit department, conducted after the workshops, yield a multitude of additional requirements.

At the beginning of each interview, Jan makes a conscious effort to create a relaxed and pleasant atmosphere. His goal is to dispel any reservations and encourage open, willing participation—especially since Linda, a familiar colleague, is also present.

Jan begins by introducing himself and explaining the purpose of the interviews. In addition to the information already provided in the invitation, his clear and respectful explanation reinforces the importance of the participants' contributions. He emphasizes that there are no right or wrong answers and that every opinion is valued.

The questionnaire serves more as a guide than a strict script. Jan is careful not to lead the participants or influence their responses. He uses open-ended questions, only subtly hinting at his own ideas, and focuses instead on understanding the perspectives and information needs of the interviewees.

To maintain a sense of trust and comfort, Jan deliberately avoids audio recording the conversations. He does not want to unsettle the stakeholders. Instead, Linda takes detailed notes during the interviews and later sends them out as conversation protocols. They agree that, in case of additions or misunderstandings, they will follow up with the interviewees to clarify or expand on the information provided.

6.3.4 The Return of the Questionnaire

Linda and Jan were thrilled. The response rate to the questionnaire was 82%—out of the 150 invited participants, 123 completed the survey. This strong level of participation provided them with a solid and meaningful dataset to work with.

Linda Our incentivization really paid off!

Jan Yes, I'm surprised too. Now it's time to analyze the responses

Linda I think we should handle the closed multiple-choice questions and the open-ended ones differently. I'm quite familiar with statistical survey analysis, so I'd like to take care of the closed questions. Could you extract and analyze the requirements from the open-ended responses?

Jan No problem. Can you tell me a bit about the statistical methods? I'm not really an expert in that area

Linda	In my opinion, analyzing the frequency distribution is sufficient for our purposes. I've already prepared and evaluated the responses to one of our most important questions: "What would be your preferred channel when contacting our company?" (see Fig. 6.7)
Jan	Interesting that the chatbot has already become so established. Back in the 2010s, that would have been unthinkable. I'm guessing most of the responses favoring the chatbot came from younger participants under 40, and the three letters were probably from participants over 60, right?
Linda	Jan, no prejudices, please! But actually, my next step would be to break down the bar chart by age, gender, education, income, and region
Jan	OK, let's get to work.

Linda and Jan are busy evaluating the responses and assigning them to different requirement categories. Some insights will be useful later for prioritizing requirements in Phase 2, while others are already clear and need to be documented in a structured format.

By the end of the requirements gathering process, Linda and Jan have compiled a comprehensive set of requirements that provides a solid foundation for developing the initial concept and preparing the tender documents.

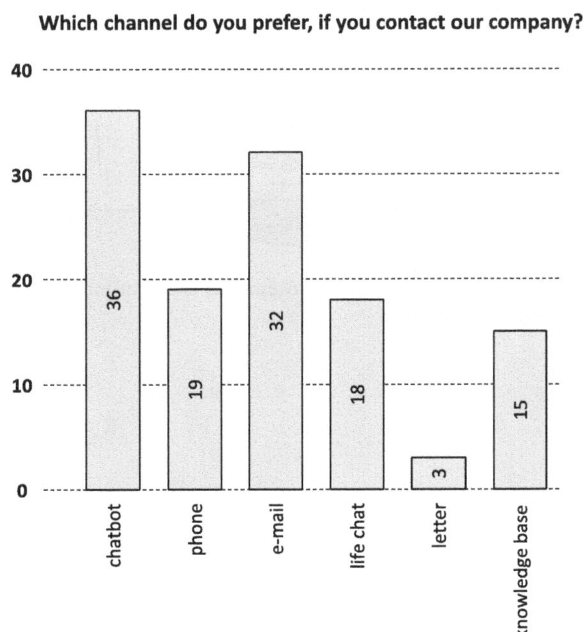

Fig. 6.7 Frequency distribution of response options

6.4 Looking at the Next Day

Jan With the different collection methods, we've already gathered a lot of information. In some areas, we'll still need to refine things, since some requirements are either missing or not at the right level of detail. Many of these gaps will only become visible during the analysis. I'd rather not search for them randomly, though—I want to use the structure we've defined with our requirement categories and their characteristics

One of the main tasks in today's workshop was modeling the business process *Handling Customer Concerns*. It includes both human activities—with and without IT support—as well as purely technical processes in the omni-channel system (see Fig. 6.5). So how can this process model help us going forward? Personally, I find that this kind of visualization helps me organize, group, and check the quality of the requirements we've collected. It lets me link them to the business process, close gaps, or spot inconsistencies. On the simplified process diagram in Fig. 6.8, I'll sketch out where I see these connections

Tomorrow, we'll continue from here and dive into our next topic: 'documenting requirements.'

At the end of the day, Jan presents seven key conclusions he has drawn from the process model (Fig. 6.8) regarding additional requirement categories:

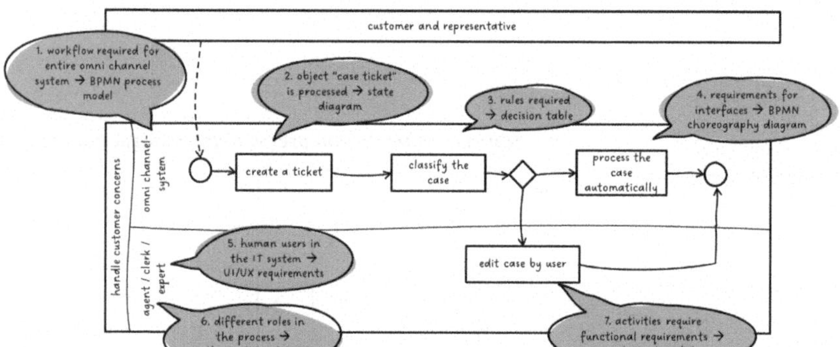

Fig. 6.8 Sketched business process 'handling customer concerns' incl. conclusions on other requirement categories

Jan

1. For our IT system 'Omni-Channel,' we do not need the complete business process with all manual activities. We only document the requirements within the framework of the rough concept from a technical point of view. A crucial point here is the use case description for the central control and monitoring of a single process, which is processed in the Omni-Channel system. We also use the *BPMN process diagram* (Sect. 7.3.1) for modeling this control workflow, similar to process modeling
2. A central object of the use case is a case ticket, which takes on different status values during its processing. We represent these status values with the *UML state diagram* (Sect. 7.3.2)
3. For the automatic classification of the case ticket, a *rule set* is required, which we document using a decision table (Sect. 7.3.3)
4. Both at the beginning and within the process, the Omni-Channel system repeatedly accesses 3rd party systems or is addressed by them. We will represent the requirements for technical interfaces with the *BPMN choreography diagram* and an *architecture model* (Sect. 7.3.5). The architecture model provides more of a static view by showing the basic structure of all technical systems, while the choreography diagram provides a dynamic view of the interaction of the IT systems
5. Our users of the IT system have requirements for usability, the interface, and other user-related behaviors. However, we only determine these in Phase 2 in the form of *mockups* or *prototypes* (Sect. 8.1.3)
6. Our users of the system assume different roles. Their *access, reading, or modification rights* within the system are only determined when processing a sprint backlog item (Sect. 8.2)
7. And last but not least, the users have functional requirements for the IT system, which we capture using a *sentence template* (Sect. 7.3.4)

We had already briefly outlined and documented all these different models and methods in the RE plan. Now, they should hopefully become a bit clearer for you. Tomorrow, we will delve into the details

Linda

Impressive. Looking back, I must admit that I did not expect this level of results at this stage. After all, we haven't yet examined any pre-made functionalities of any IT system; we've only relied on the imagination and experience of the observers and interviewees. I'm surprised by both the quantity and quality of the requirements presented to us

If the review is so overwhelmingly positive, then I have no concerns about the coming days. I look forward to tomorrow when we will document the findings in various forms of presentation together

6.5 Linda's Notepad

On the fourth day of requirements engineering, Linda noted the following key points:

Day 4: Gathering requirements

Work steps:

Requirements are found in

(a) Documentations,

(b) Existing systems,

(c) Stakeholders

Steps:

1. Define requirement sources from (a)-(c) and choose collection methods (e.g., workshop or document analysis)

Work steps specifically for collection with stakeholders (Case c):

2. Prepare the collection organizationally (date, place, participants)

3. Prepare the collection in terms of content:

- *Suggest requirement categories (see RE plan),*
- *Prepare known information (e.g., processes, architectures),*
- *Capture constraints (e.g., regulations, style guides)*

4. Carry out the collection:

- *Use conference rooms outside the company,*
- *Detach stakeholders from daily business*

5. Evaluate the collection:

- *Draw a baseline of the requirements*
- *Let the stakeholders confirm the collection results*

TIP: RE = Methodology + Empathy + Communication → CONCLUSION: ALWAYS QUESTION EVERYTHING!

Result of my day: Jan and I are in possession of a sufficient set of stakeholder requirements

References

Lübbe, A. (2011). *Tangible business process modeling.* Retrieved October 31, 2023, from http://ecdtr.hpi-web.de/resources/pdf/phd_tbpm_luebbe.pdf

Niebisch, T. (2022). *360-Grad Prozessmanagement.* Springer Gabler. (in German)

Plattner, H., Meinel, C., & Leifer, L. (2016). when research meets practice: Tangible business process modeling at work. In *Design thinking research.* Springer

Robertson, J., & Robertson, S. (2024). *Mastering the requirements process* (4th edn.). Addison-Wesley Professional.

Day 5: Documenting Requirements 7

Day 5, dedicated to documenting requirements, is directly linked to the previous day. The reason is simple: it's unrealistic to identify requirements without recording them. After all, not all requirements can be mentally retained during the collection process. Despite this connection, separating collection and documentation is beneficial from a didactic perspective.

> **To the point**
> The central questions are: How do I document the stakeholders' wishes? Does a picture really say more than a thousand words? ◄

For our two main characters, the fifth day involves documenting most of the insights they gained during the requirements collection. A significant portion of these insights forms the basis for the rough concept, the decision matrix, and the tender. Other collection results, such as requirements in the categories of *Operation* or *Solution Design*, are of secondary interest at this time. Their importance was assigned to the implementation project in Sect. 6.2.1 and is therefore not covered in this chapter.

In Fig. 7.1, you can see some terms that we will use in connection with documenting requirements, along with their assigned meanings.

- A *notation* is the method used to describe or formulate a requirement (see Sect. 7.1).
- An *artifact* is the medium that carries one or more requirements (see Sect. 7.2). It is created as a deliverable by a requirements engineer.
- The *requirement category* is used solely for the systematization of requirements and was already introduced in Sect. 4.4. We use this categorization directly.

J. Kawelke and T. Niebisch, *AI-Driven Transformation - Practical Frameworks for Real-World Impact*, Future of Business and Finance,
https://doi.org/10.1007/978-3-662-72549-8_7

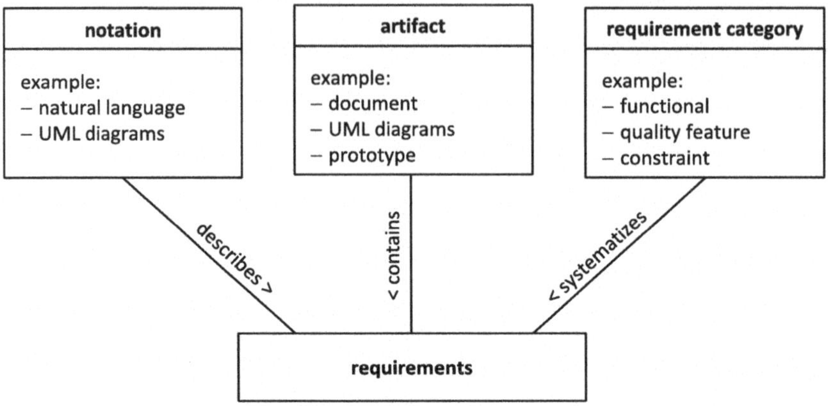

Fig. 7.1 Terms in the context of requirements documentation

Before Linda and Jan begin documenting the survey results and tackling today's tasks, they spend some time discussing the necessary tools. They first take a step back to mentally organize and incorporate the topics of *Notations* and *Artifacts* into the work package 'Documenting Requirements.'

Teaser: Documenting requirements is essential in both traditional and agile project approaches. The notations and artifacts presented here typically have strengths in one approach or the other. Since we aim to present requirements engineering as a management discipline applicable to both project approaches, we will separate the notations and artifacts accordingly. This separation is facilitated by the fact that our overall project includes both approaches (see Fig. 1.2).

Our project example divides the overall project into:

- a *Preliminary Project*, which is conducted using a more traditional approach, followed by
- an *Implementation Project*, which uses an agile approach.

Following this logic, we will primarily introduce notations and artifacts for traditional project management in this chapter. In the next chapter, Chap. 8, we will discuss notations and artifacts that are closely intertwined with the agile project approach.

To the point
You need both Chaps. 7 and 8 to get a comprehensive overview of the documentation possibilities for requirements in traditional and agile projects. ◄

Back to an explanatory theory section.

7.1 Effective Notation Techniques for Requirements Documentation

Notations are the methods used to describe things. We encounter them in everyday life across various domains, such as:

- Music notes
- Traffic signs
- Topographic maps
- Mathematical or logical notations
- Programming languages, XML notation, etc.

All forms of notation share the common requirement of a set of rules for applying individual elements. This set of rules is known as the *syntax* of a notation.

Based on our survey on day 4, we know *what* we want to document, but we only partially know *how* we want to document it. We have found that requirements can be represented using words, various graphics or diagrams, and combinations of these. Therefore, we categorize the notations used in this book to describe requirements into:

- Graphical modeling languages (Sect. 7.1.1)
- Natural language notations (Sect. 7.1.2)
- Notations for UI design (Sect. 8.1.3)

For the creation of rough concepts and RfPs, which is our set goal for this chapter, UI design skills are not yet relevant.

A requirements engineer should ideally master and offer as many of the notations presented in the following sections as possible. Like a skilled craftsman, he must select and use the appropriate tool for the right situation. This is his core competence. But how does he recognize suitable tools, and what does he base his selection on? An important criterion is that the chosen notation is understandable and pragmatic for all those who have to process these requirements. For example, a prose formulation of the requirements might be attractive to the specialist department due to its readability, but not from the perspective of developers and testers. However, all participants can better understand the overall structure of a specific fact if it is represented with a graphical model.

This realization leads us to conclude that there is no inherently right or wrong notation, nor a single notation in which all requirements should be documented. The purpose of notations is to emphasize the features necessary for their specific use (see Sect. 3.2.1). Therefore, different forms of notation have various advantages and disadvantages, strengths and weaknesses. Ultimately, the following tips should be considered when documenting requirements:

- A mix of different notations is most effective.

- The granularity of the notation must be appropriate to the purpose of the requirement.
- Every recipient of a document must know and understand its notation. Using notations that are not understood is unproductive.

Implementing these points requires considerable experience from a requirements engineer. Otherwise, he risks losing the stakeholders' engagement or understanding.

Our two main characters exchange ideas about helpful notations, and Linda is surprised to discover that they have already applied some forms of notation.

7.1.1 Graphical Modeling Languages

Over the past few days, Jan introduced the modeling languages BPMN and UML and discussed several types of diagrams:

- The BPMN process diagram for modeling business processes (Sect. 6.3.2.2)
- The UML class diagram for the concept model (Sect. 3.2)
- The Use Case diagram for representing the entirety of an application's functionalities (Sects. 5.5 and 6.3.2.3)
- The UML state diagram for modeling different state values of an object (Sect. 4.2.3)

Linda I'm surprised to see the different types of diagrams grouped under the common category of notations. From this, I infer that we will discuss additional useful forms of notation.

Jan In addition to the graphical diagram types we've discussed over the past few days, I'd like to introduce another one: the choreography diagram. Like the process diagram, it is part of the BPMN standard. Using it can help us in the rough concept phase to formulate requirements for interfaces and define constraints.

Linda Why do you want to use BPMN for system specification in addition to business process modeling? Personally, I worry that we might overwhelm both our stakeholders and the service providers who have to analyze our tender with two modeling languages—UML and BPMN.

Jan No, I don't think so. Neither the stakeholders nor the providers need to know the complete syntax of the UML and BPMN diagrams. Our diagrams are often intuitively understandable. You saw in the workshop that the participating stakeholders have been able to follow us so far. Why should that change?

Linda Well, let's see then.

Jan The choreography diagram is similar to a process diagram in that it essentially visualizes a series of successive activities. The difference is that the choreography diagram is exclusively limited to activities involving the communication of at least two partners. In our case, these partners could be IT systems. This allows us to document communication at the IT interfaces in a processual form, thus completing the picture.
I will explain the necessary modeling elements to you using a concrete example during the documentation of our interface requirements (see Sect. 7.3.5).

Linda OK, that's fine. But don't we need another diagram to model the process flows of the use cases?

Jan For this, we could use either the UML activity diagram or the BPMN process diagram. However, I would recommend using the latter here. A BPMN process diagram is suitable not only for business process modeling but also for modeling processes within a system. For phase 2, we should leave it to the service provider to decide whether to use the UML activity diagram or the BPMN process diagram for further process modeling. Personally, I also like using the UML activity diagram, especially for modeling system-internal processes. Therefore, I'd like to introduce it to you in detail when we discuss the specifics of agile projects (see Sect. 8.1.4).

Over the past few days, we have come to appreciate the diversity of graphical notation possibilities. In the following documentation sections, we will expand our knowledge with additional options. Most of these graphical notations follow a defined syntax. The advantage of this syntax is that, by knowing the essential components, both the author and reader can immediately focus on the model's content, leaving little room for formal interpretation. However, it should be noted that graphical modeling languages do not necessarily have to be standardized. Examples of non-standard notations include Jan's individual sketch (Fig. 3.3) and the architecture model presented in Fig. 7.10.

7.1.2 Natural Language Notations

Let's turn to natural language notation. In this section, Jan focuses particularly on the sentence template. Following Linda's objection, he goes into more detail…

Linda From your previous explanations, I understand that you want to continue basing a large part of the documentation on diagrams. As I mentioned before, I haven't seen many diagrams in past tenders.

Jan We will also write a lot of prose in the rough concept and especially in the tender. Natural language documentation serves as a link between the diagrams. Additionally, it provides an alternative way to document requirements.
I agree with you that verbal representations dominate in most tenders. In my opinion, this is because RfPs are often created exclusively by departmental staff rather than trained requirements engineers. It is frequently overlooked or ignored that IT tenders are based on a requirements document in the form of a rough concept or a functional specification.
But even among requirements engineers, there are quite a few who have reservations about modeling, that is, creating diagrams. This is reflected in the design of tenders.

Linda Well, then let's take our tender to a new level. What should be considered in natural language documentation? I learned German as a natural language when I was a child.

Jan If you remember our first day together, we already discussed the quality of natural language documentation and the consequences of misunderstandings in specifications (see Sect. 3.5). The colloquial use of natural language has some deficiencies. Information can be assumed to be known, downplayed, distorted, or ignored. We don't assume malice, but consider these issues as normal in communication. Most linguistic mistakes can be clarified by asking questions or are implicitly correctly interpreted. However, for IT requirements, these deficiencies can have devastating effects.
There are different approaches to minimize these weaknesses during the specification phase. They all share the use of a specific template for formulating requirements (see Fig. 7.2). For our project, we particularly use:
- the sentence template
- the user story
- the Gherkin language

We should use sentence templates in our rough concept. The user story (see Sect. 8.1.2) and Gherkin (see Sect. 8.1.5) are used in the implementation project.

Linda Then please expand my knowledge with details about sentence templates!

Jan Sentence templates are structured formats used to formulate natural language requirements in sentences.

Linda So the sentence template is another notation, even if it's not graphical, right?

Jan Correct. The goal of the sentence template is to formalize requirements using predefined sentence structures, thereby minimizing the linguistic issues we discussed on the first day.
A sentence template allows you to:
- Start with the condition under which the system action takes place
- Specify the legal obligation of the requirement
- Characterize the system activity
- Insert relevant objects
- Name the activity performed on the object

This way, you can capture all important information for a single requirement in one sentence. I brought an example of a sentence template from a seminar (see Fig. 7.3). You can find much more information about sentence templates in the MASTER pattern library from Sophist. The REUSE company (2020)

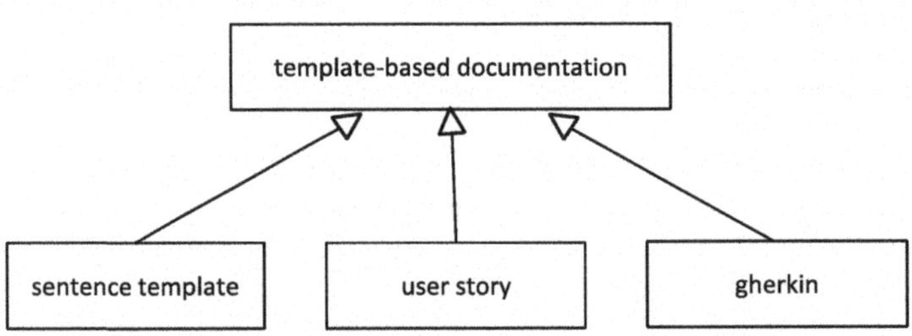

Fig. 7.2 Examples of template-based documentation

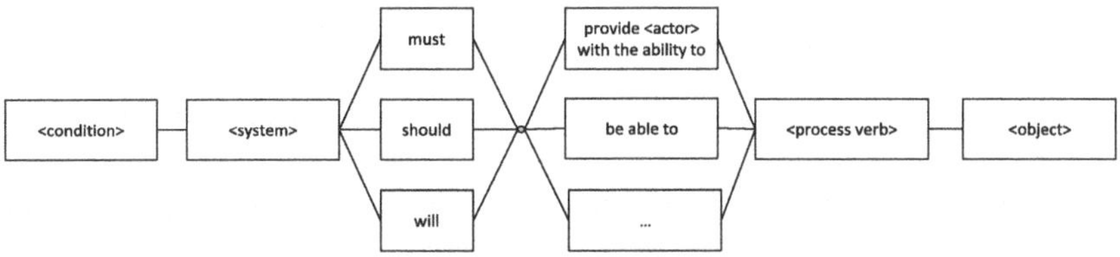

Fig. 7.3 Example of a sentence template

Linda Right, now I remember my own research on this a few years ago. The phrase 'provide with the ability to' describes a system functionality that a user can execute, and the words 'be able to' indicate an interface description. If you completely omit this characterization of the system action, you describe an automatic system activity. But what do 'must,' 'should,' and 'will' indicate as legal obligations?

Jan If you use a sentence with 'must' in the tender, it means that the service or product provider must mandatorily implement the corresponding requirement. The auxiliary verb 'should,' which I personally consider superfluous, indicates a recommendation, while 'will' signifies that this requirement will become effective or legally binding in a future expansion stage.

Linda Yes, I would also avoid 'should.' That could lead to misunderstandings. And we want to avoid misunderstandings with the sentence template.

Jan Exactly. It's important to note that this legal obligation must also be contractually agreed upon with the service provider. It would be problematic if only you, as the client, interpret the words as legally binding, but the service provider does not. However, where there is light, there is also shadow. Imagine you have already formulated dozens of requirements using the sentence template and now want to submit them for review. The disadvantage of the sentence template is its rather mundane readability when you have a large number of requirements in this form. Additionally, the dependency on similar requirements and their potential contradictions is high.

To the point

Sentence templates are structured formats for formulating sentences. They help ensure compliance with quality standards for requirements and mitigate the impact of linguistic issues.◄

Linda I understand the theory, but I would like to see an example from the contact center area.

Jan How about this example:
'Between 5 am and 12 pm, the Omni-Channel system must provide the policyholder the ability to view the knowledge database.'
Let's break down the sentence into its components:
- 'Between 5 am and 12 pm' specifies the time, the when
- 'must' determines the legal obligation
- 'the Omni-Channel system' corresponds to our system
- 'provide the policyholder the ability' indicates the user interaction with the system
- 'the knowledge database' is the object
- 'to view' is the process word

Linda The example sounds structured, understandable, and still manageable as a method. Let me try creating an interface description:
'When a policyholder contacts the insurance company via*live chat, the Omni-Channel system must be able to import the contract data of this policyholder from the contract management system.'*

Jan Very nice. Once you are familiar with the structure of the sentence template, you immediately recognize that the words 'be able' indicate an interface requirement. In your example, this refers to the interface between the Omni-Channel system and contract management. I'm thrilled at how quickly you applied the sentence template structure in your example.

Linda If it's explained well.... I think I can see the potential that comes from correctly using different notation methods. Now I'm curious to see how you apply them.

Jan I can understand that. Nevertheless, you'll have to curb your curiosity a bit. I still want to discuss the topic of artifacts, their granularity levels, and dependencies with you.

This triggers another eye roll from Linda. However, she is already used to Jan's systematic and structured approach to tackling tasks, rather than working haphazardly.

7.2 Categorizing Artifacts

The term *artifact* has its meaning in various disciplines such as archaeology, geology, or literary studies. In the context of requirements engineering (RE), it refers to all documents, models, or other work results that capture the requirements for the future IT solution in writing. Figuratively, they are containers that hold one or more requirements.

Artifacts, like requirements, can be categorized according to different characteristics. This categorization helps provide an overview, orientation, and structure. A suggested classification of common artifacts, some of which we have described, is presented in Fig. 7.4. What considerations are behind this categorization?

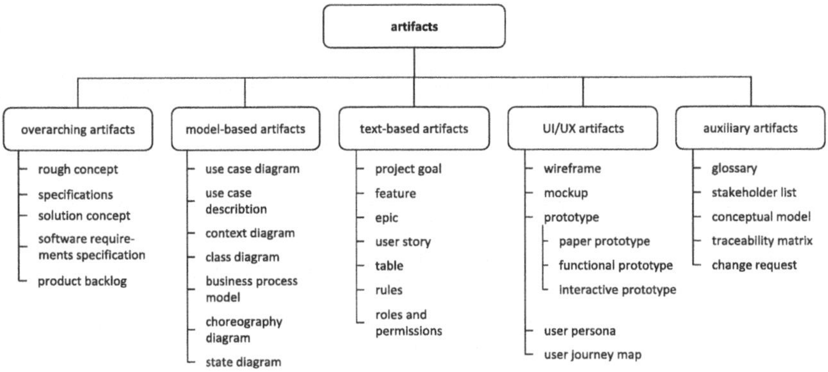

Fig. 7.4 Categorization of artifacts

- Some artifacts exist only as bundles and collections of more detailed artifacts. They can also be part of contracts. Because of these characteristics, we call them *overarching artifacts.*
- *Model-based* and *text-based artifacts* are named based on the predominant representation of their content as a model or text.
- *UI and UX artifacts* are also model-based artifacts. Due to their specific purpose of representing design requirements, they have their own category.
- *Auxiliary artifacts* could also be classified as model-based or text-based artifacts. However, we have decided to assign them their own category, because they provide essential support and context for understanding and managing requirements, distinct from the primary content of model-based and text-based artifacts.

Anyone who is startled by the abundance of listed artifacts should be reminded that many artifacts have already been used without consistently naming them as such. Over the past few days, we have used:

- project goal (Sect. 5.1)
- context diagram (Sect. 5.4)
- business process model (Sect. 6.3.2.2)
- use case diagram (Sects. 5.5 and 6.3.2.3)
- class diagram (Sect. 3.2)
- glossary (Sect. 5.2)
- conceptual model (Sect. 5.2)
- stakeholder list (Sect. 5.3)

Although Linda was able to follow the previous process quite well, it raises some concerns for her.

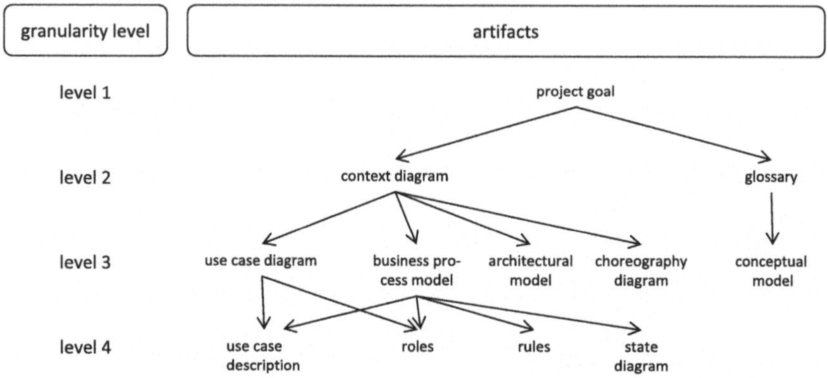

Fig. 7.5 Exemplary relationships between artifacts

Linda The many forms of artifacts surprise me a bit. On one hand, such a set offers a wide range of representation options. On the other hand, I see the danger of:

- Maintaining redundant information with a lot of effort but without added value
- Possibly documenting contradicting requirements due to insufficient time invested in maintenance

Jan We need to avoid that. It's like the house construction example we used in Sect. 3.2.1 to introduce modeling. The different artifacts of a house (sales brochure, floor plan, site plan, static calculation, etc.) all apply to the same house and must not contradict each other despite their different focuses. Similarly, the artifacts we use to document our requirements will have dependencies on each other. If a requirement changes, this change can impact other requirements. Marking such dependencies is called *traceability*.

Before we go into detail on managing requirements and their mutual influence (see 9.3), I can tell you this much in advance: There are horizontal and vertical dependencies:

- Horizontal, if these artifacts are on the same level of the system or development process, e.g., between individual user stories.
- Vertical, if these artifacts are classified at different levels, e.g., the derivations of a use case description from a use case diagram or a test case from a requirement.

For our rough concept, we use artifacts that have dependencies at different levels. In Fig. 7.5, I have sketched some relationships between artifacts of different granularity levels.

I hope this gives you some confidence that we are on the right track and not getting lost in the multitude of possibilities.

To the point

The diversity of notations and artifacts offers us a broad range of options to document requirements and represent relationships between them. ◀

The following sections will introduce helpful artifacts that are crucial for creating the rough concept.

7.3 Apply Notations and Create Artifacts

In this section, we focus on some of the mentioned artifacts. Let's examine the previous work results that form the basis of these artifacts:

- First, we established the *overall understanding* and *goal* of the project, detailing how the Contact Center fits into the Customer Center, which business process is relevant for this project, and how an Omni-Channel system integrates into this process (see Fig. 3.1).
- Then, we analyzed the *project context* in terms of actors, business processes, IT systems, and compliance requirements (Sect. 5.4).
- In Sect. 6.3.2.2, we created the *target business process 'Handle Customer Concerns'* together with the stakeholders in the workshop. The modeling represents a segment of the business view.
- From the process model (see Fig. 6.5), it is clear that tasks are performed by both human actors across three support levels and fully automated functionalities of the Omni-Channel system. The *Omni-Channel system* to be developed is a central actor in the process and is intended to technically support the process. We summarized the use cases of the Omni-Channel system in a *use case diagram* (Sect. 6.3.2.3).
- Numerous additional stakeholder requirements emerged from field observations, workshops, interviews, and the questionnaire (Sect. 6.3).

In addition to the subject-specific findings, we have achieved formal work results, such as:

- A classification system in which all these requirements can be categorized (Sect. 4.4).
- Notation forms and artifacts that can be used to document requirements (Sects. 7.1 and 7.2).

This knowledge from the past few days helps us further develop the upcoming requirement documentation in terms of content and form. In the following sections, we will explain how individual artifacts contribute to the documentation of requirements. Specifically, we will cover:

- The *use case description* for the use case 'Handle Customer Concerns' (Sect. 7.3.1)
- The *state diagram* 'Case Ticket' (Sect. 7.3.2)
- The *rule set* 'Classify Case' (Sect. 7.3.3)
- The *natural language requirements* (Sect. 7.3.4)

- The formulation of the *interface requirements* (Sect. 7.3.5)

7.3.1 Use Case Description 'Processing Customer Concerns'

The use case diagram for the Omni-Channel system (Fig. 6.6) shows a use case named 'Processing Customer Concerns,' but it does not illustrate how the use case is represented within the Omni-Channel system. We need to design and describe the use case from the perspective of the Omni-Channel system. Additionally, we recognize from the process character that this description corresponds to a preliminary workflow level.

What do we understand by workflow? Workflows are specific forms of processes that can run automatically and are managed within one or more IT systems. To represent the workflow and describe the use case, we will utilize the capabilities offered by BPMN for process design.

Note: In the following description, the terms *customer concerns* and *case* (from a business perspective) as well as *case ticket* and *ticket* (from a technical perspective) are used synonymously. A ticket corresponds to the technical representation of a single customer concern.

Let's start the documentation. Jan suggests creating a first draft of a graphical use case description based on the existing artifacts and presenting it to Linda. Consequently, he spends the next few hours working on the use case description and the workflow design. At the agreed time, Linda and Jan meet again in their office, and Jan presents Linda with the designed BPMN process diagram (Fig. 7.6).

Jan — We had already agreed to describe the use case 'Processing Customer Concerns' in the rough concept and to request further use case descriptions in Phase 2 from the service or product provider. Therefore, my elaboration is intended as a suggestion and assistance for the provider, but also as a formulation of our expectations. After all, they should master this tool if they want to get the job.

Linda — You're setting the bar really high, but I think it's appropriate. I'm very interested to see how your use case description is structured.

Jan — Then let's go. The use case has three logical task blocks that the Omni-Channel system must handle from the stakeholders' perspective. The goal of these task blocks is to convey the content and causalities of the desired IT system behavior to the developers:

- The first block on the far left indicates the manual processing of the customer concern. From the perspective of the Omni-Channel workflow, we are not interested in the content of these tasks. It is only important to assign the tasks to the correct actors and ensure the transfer of responsibility back to the Omni-Channel system.
- The middle block bundles automatable activities that the Omni-Channel system independently performs when processing the customer concern.
- The block on the far right is responsible for monitoring and controlling the case ticket. This is mostly done by evaluating time specifications and changed status values.

Linda That sounds interesting. Let's look at the blocks from left to right. Can you please tell me more about the left task block first?

Jan This task block represents the manual processing of the customer concern. If the system determines that it cannot process the concern automatically, it assigns the ticket to an agent. The agent can then handle the customer concern by communicating with the customer, gathering information, taking measures, or capturing data. From the perspective of the Omni-Channel system, these specific activities are not relevant for automatic processing and control.

Linda That's good to know. The way you describe it, it aptly shows that customer matters are handled individually and according to needs. But I don't see any of that in the diagram.

Jan I currently don't see this as necessary. To represent all possible scenarios of agent activities, we would need to refine this diagram further. For the rough concept, I would refrain from doing so. The UML sequence diagram is also very suitable for depicting specific scenarios, as you imagine them (Miles & Hamilton, 2006).

Linda I'm glad you're aiming for an information overload with me—NOT—but let's stick with the use case description for now. I agree that we don't need to go into more detail at this point, but in Phase 2, I do expect concrete user interaction descriptions. We should not lose sight of this requirement. How should the intermediate events in this manual processing activity in the diagram be interpreted?

Jan The handover from manual process handling to fully automatic processing occurs through one of two events:

1. The agent concludes during the process handling that a reclassification must take place. How this reclassification is initiated, I don't know yet.
2. The second event is that the human operator has finished the case and set the ticket status to 'finalized.' From his point of view, the process has been completed and the customer has been informed, so the objection period for the customer begins. Adherence to the objection period is monitored by the right task block 'Monitoring and Control.'

Linda Understood. Thank you for the explanation. Now, let's move on to the automatic system activities in the middle task block.

Jan Exactly. The middle task block handles the processing of the customer concern by the Omni-Channel system. The IT system:

- Evaluates rules
- Calculates required times or durations
- Sets state values
- Automatically assigns the customer request to agents
- Processes the case independently

Linda Very good. This ensures that customer requests are met quickly and efficiently. We can leave it as it is.

Jan The right task block monitors the status of the customer request and triggers further actions if necessary. For example, it can remind an agent if a customer request has not yet been processed or if the calculated target resolution time is approaching.

Linda This is also very helpful. This way, we ensure that all customer requests are completed on time and no matters are left unattended. Additionally, the agents are relieved from constantly setting reminders and follow-ups due to deadlines.

Jan That's an advantage of this task block: keeping an eye on the deadlines of a single case, possibly triggering actions, and measuring different times. The last point, in particular, could be used in a completely different way across the entire Customer Center in the future. Based on the measured times, you should be able to evaluate various questions across the entire process portfolio:

- At what times of day and night are the most and fewest customer concerns submitted?
- In what percentage of all customer request processes was the target resolution time met?
- What percentage of all customer requests could be processed fully automatically?

And so on... Based on the resulting data, you not only get a tool that monitors individual current cases but also one that can steer the Customer Center in a completely different way by evaluating past cases.

Linda You're moving too fast for me. While these possibilities and perspectives are promising, they are not my top priority. Additionally, we need to get the works council on board again for these evaluation options.

Jan Definitely. There's still a long way to go before you can use these functions. I just wanted to show you the potential that can already be seen from the use case description.
I suggest you let the use case description sink in for now. Currently, it's just a digital wishful thinking. Details can still be added and errors corrected. But on this basis, we can have a very constructive discussion and further develop our ideas.

With this outlook, Jan concludes the walkthrough of the quite complex procedural use case description 'Processing Customer Concerns.' (We will discuss the review method *Walkthrough* in terms of quality assurance of requirements in Sect. 9.1.4)

Linda When I look at the process graphic, questions come to mind that the model has not answered so far. The three main ones are:

- What is the significance of the different time types you mentioned for the overall process?
- On what criteria and rules is it decided whether a case should be handled automatically or by an agent?
- Your process involves changing several status values. Are these all the status values, and where can I find an overview of them?

We discussed some of these questions orally but did not write down the answers. Shouldn't we add this information to the process?

Jan Your questions show your analytical understanding. However, in my experience, the answers should not be included in the process model, as it would unnecessarily overload the graphic.
I suggest an alternative: We supplement the graphical use case description with a textual description in the form of a table. I have already numbered all process steps. Using these numbers, we can assign additional information, ideas, or requirements to each activity. The table does not limit us in terms of scope, allowing us to attach all important additions to the process activities from our perspective while keeping the process model understandable and readable.

Linda If I understand correctly, you want to extend the existing model-based use case description with a natural language representation?

Jan Exactly, that's my suggestion. Next, I'll show you my personal method for enriching each individual process activity with information or deriving requirements (see Table 7.1).

Linda I would like to try that. Combined with the diagram, we could offer a refined yet structured specification of the individual process activities. I like that.

And so they jointly supplement each individual activity with the essential information. At the beginning, Linda's question about the significance of the time types is answered.

Jan As you can see, these tabular notes are quite filled with free text. They allow me to add important information or references to the use case description.
We are currently noticing that we are already making many detailed considerations. Not all of them are necessary for the rough concept or the tender. However, fragments of this information were already provided to us in the workshops; I just sorted and completed them. For negotiations with a potential service provider, it is always advantageous to know more than what is communicated in the tender.
While thinking about these details, I noticed that despite all efforts, requirements inconsistencies occur. However, I don't see these as relevant for the tender; we will clarify them during the implementation phase.

Linda My personal impression is that I can move between different levels of detail at any time. This gives me confidence that I won't lose sight of the goal. The graphical process flow allows me to keep an eye on the big picture while still being able to place details in the right context.
The description of the use case or a rough workflow for the process handling seems sufficient to me. However, this workflow also needs to be controlled, which leads us to the next point.

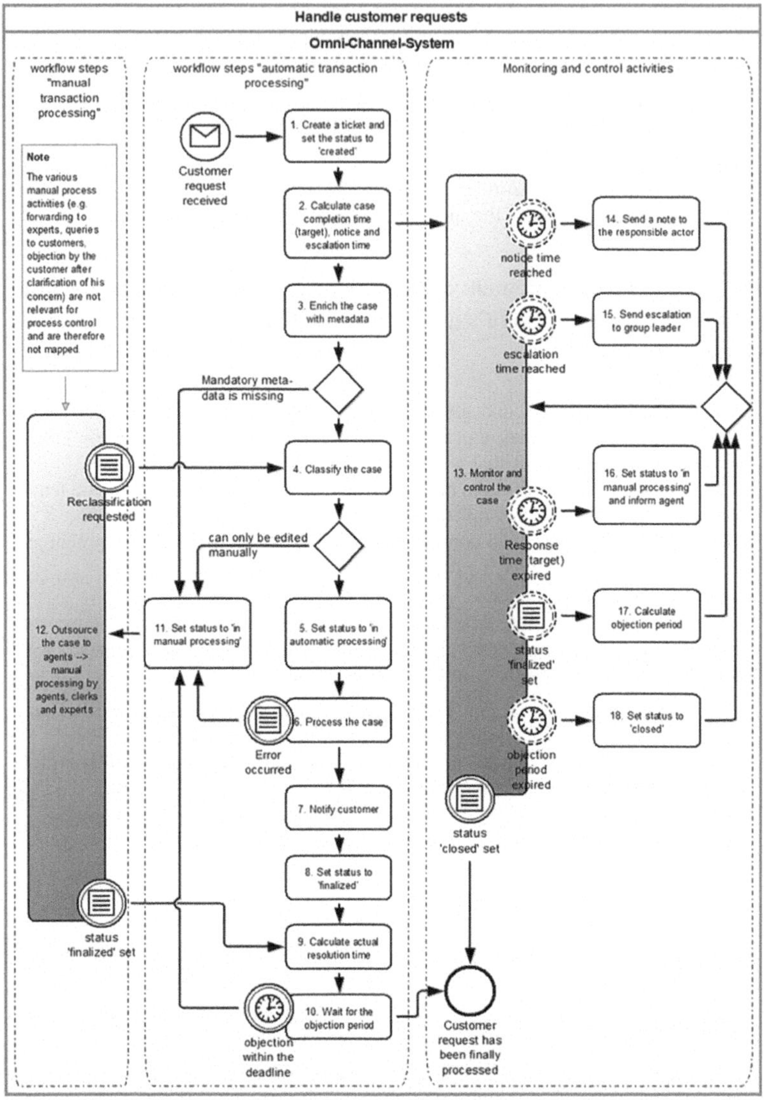

Fig. 7.6 Graphical Use Case Description 'Processing Customer Concerns'

Table 7.1 Supplementary tabular use case description 'Processing customer concerns'

No.	Activity	Process details
–	General use case specifications	The following *deadlines* apply for the Use Case: • Resolution period: Number of days within which the case shall be completed (deadline is to be demanded by management) • Notice period: Number of days before the completion of the case, before a notice is given • Escalation period: Number of days before the completion of the case, before an escalation occurs • Response period: Number of days within which the customer should provide a response to queries • Objection period: Number of days within which the customer can object after a final notification The following *times* (date or duration) are calculated in this Use Case: • Resolution time (Target) = current date + resolution period • Resolution time (Actual) = case completion – case start – response time (Actual) • Notice time = Resolution time (Target) – Notice period • Escalation time = Resolution time (Target) – Escalation period • Response time (Target) = date of query + response period; • Response time (Actual) = response date – date of query • Objection time = date of customer notification + objection period
1	Create a ticket and set status to 'created'	The status value 'created' initiates the lifecycle of the case ticket The interaction of all status values is depicted in the state diagram (Sect. 7.3.2)
2	Calculate case completion time (Target), notice, and escalation time	These times are used for future case control and evaluation.
3	Enrich the case with metadata	The Omni-Channel system obtains all necessary information for processing from the surrounding systems based on the available input data (e.g., a customer number) (see architecture model Fig. 7.10) As a result, the system decides whether it can automatically process the case based on the completeness of the available metadata or if manual further processing is required due to missing metadata
4	Classify the case	If all necessary data is available, the system classifies this case based on a set of rules (Sect. 7.3.3)
5	Set status to 'in automatic processing'	If the conditions specified in the rule set are met, the corresponding status is set, and the case is processed automatically
6	Process the case	The activities for fully automatic case handling will be determined separately and in more detail during the implementation phase If an error occurs or human action is required, this activity is aborted, and the case is managed manually

(continued)

Table 7.1 (continued)

No.	Activity	Process details
7	Notify customer	After the end of the automatic processing, the customer is informed about their request The customer information is provided via the customer's prioritized communication channel or the input channel through which the customer request was received (a special set of rules is required and will be detailed in the implementation phase). With the customer notification, the customer's objection period begins. This is calculated in activity 17
8	Set status to 'finalized'	After informing the customer, the fully automatic case handling is completed and the corresponding status is set
9	Calculate actual resolution time	
10	Wait for the objection period	This is not a task in the true sense. However, since the customer can continue the workflow at any time within the objection period, it was modeled using an activity and an interrupting intermediate event
11	Set status to 'in manual processing'	If necessary metadata are missing or the case categorization requires manual processing, the corresponding status is set and the responsible agent is informed
12	Outsource the case to agent for further manual processing	From the workflow's perspective, this activity is a black box. The agent can perform various activities, which were already explained during the examination of the business process in Sect. 6.3.2.2 Control only returns to the workflow when the event 'reclassification requested' occurs or the status 'finalized' is set following customer notification
13	Monitor and control the case	This activity runs parallel to the actual case handling. Strictly speaking, it is not a real activity. No active action takes place; instead, it waits for the described events to occur Characteristic of this activity are the five non-interrupting intermediate events. When the respective event occurs, the activity 'monitor and control the case' is not interrupted (as the type of event suggests), but one of the activities 14–18 is additionally initiated. The process only ends with the interrupting intermediate event 'Set status to 'closed''
14	Send a note to the responsible actor	When the calculated notice time is reached, the responsible actor automatically receives a message indicating that the process should be completed in x days
15	Send escalation to group leader	If the system does not recognize any progress by the escalation time, a responsible group leader receives a corresponding message. The group leader, in his responsible role, should determine the causes of the non-processing and eliminate them
16	Set status to 'in manual processing' and inform agent	If an agent has asked a question to the customer within activity 12, the customer should respond within a set deadline. If this deadline passes without a response, the status of the process is changed and the responsible agent receives a corresponding notification

(continued)

Table 7.1 (continued)

No.	Activity	Process details
17	Calculate objection period	When the status (manually in activity 12 or automatically in activity 8) is set to 'finalized,' the system automatically calculates the objection period within which the customer can object to the case handling
18	Set status to 'closed'	If the objection period passes without any events, the case ticket is closed

7.3.2 State Diagram 'Case Ticket'

Linda In the process model, status values are changed at different times. I understand the principle of controlling the case ticket via these status values. We had already discussed this when we talked about the status values of a single requirement in the rough concept or during the implementation phase (Sect. 4.2.3). Can we use the same model type for the states of the case ticket? Actually, I can answer that myself. Of course! But what does such a state diagram for the case ticket look like?

Jan Your assumptions are correct. The Omni-Channel system even sets most of the status values itself. But now a new aspect comes into play: The status values we set for requirements were only informative for us. Every reader of a requirement can recognize its current processing status. With the case ticket, we go one step further—the process receives different status values depending on certain events and then automatically directs the workflow in different directions. The state diagram becomes an important building block for central control.

This increased importance is accompanied by somewhat more complex modeling. On day 2, I promised to go into the state diagram in more detail. I would like to revisit that now and first explain the formal notation elements and their meanings before we delve into the content of the state diagram (Fig. 7.7):

- The rounded boxes contain the status value.
- The arrow after the box symbolizes the transition, i.e., the shift from one status to its successor status.
- The arrow label at this transition names the trigger, i.e., the initiator of the status transition in the form of an event.
- If a diamond follows this transition, according to the UML syntax of the state diagram, it corresponds to a pseudo status. This is used if the event triggering the transition can lead to several successor statuses. In the actual run, a decision must be made for a branch.
- The arrow label after the diamond names the condition under which the successor status is set. This condition is noted in square brackets.

This probably sounds quite theoretical to you. So let's not dwell on the specification for long, but apply it directly in the modeling of the state diagram for our case ticket.

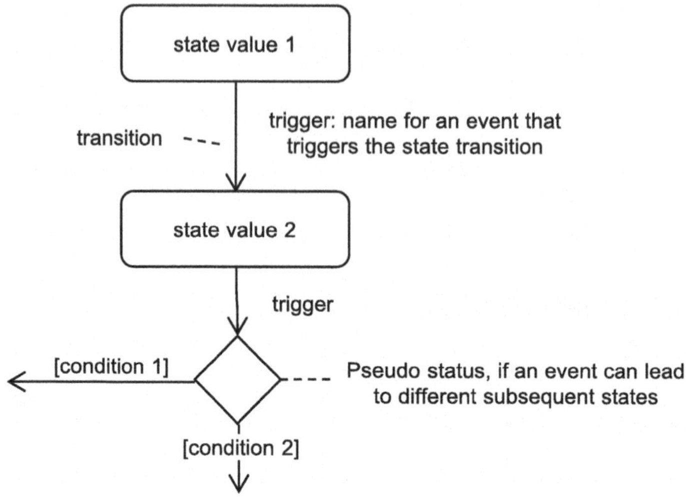

Fig. 7.7 used elements of the state diagram

Some time later …

Jan — If you look at Fig. 7.8, most of the state values will already be familiar to you from the use case description. I have also compared the state diagram with our business process model (Fig. 6.5) and found no inconsistencies.

Linda — Well, that was a tough piece of work. I couldn't have imagined beforehand that the diagram would end up being so complex. I found the separation of events and conditions particularly difficult, and thus the decision whether something is represented with or without square brackets.

Jan — Yes, by using the diamonds we have a clear representation of conditions, but the whole diagram visually resembles a UML activity diagram, which I would also like to introduce to you (Sec. 8.1.4). But more on that later.

Authors' note: Strictly speaking, one does not need a state diagram of this accuracy for the tender. However, Jan was on a roll and took the opportunity to process the information received in the workshop.

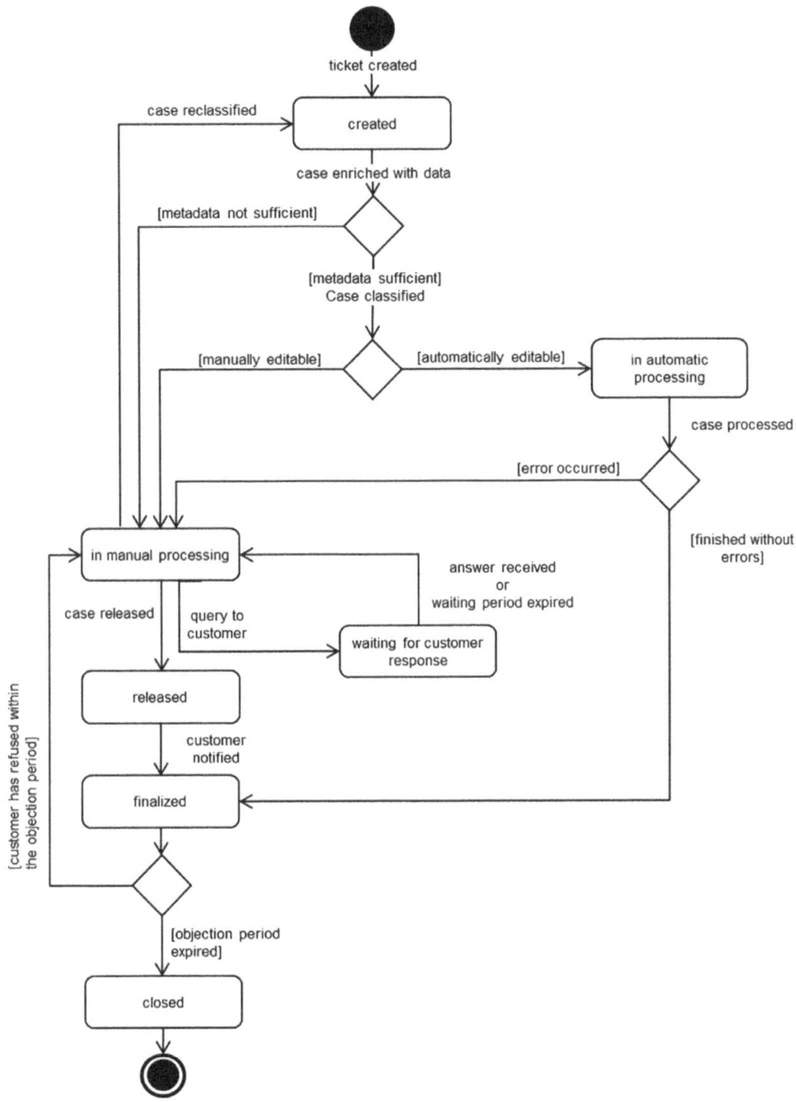

Fig. 7.8 State diagram 'Case ticket'

7.3.3 Rule Set 'Classify the Case'

Linda You've answered my question about getting an overview of all state values to my complete satisfaction. Looking at the process model, another question came to mind: On what basis do you decide in activity 4 whether a case can be processed automatically or needs to be assigned to a human actor?

Jan Let me first address something more fundamental before I go into that specific process step. Of course, we could represent the different rules that determine whether a process goes one way or another directly in the process model. But that would have at least one major drawback: the process would become significantly more complex to model. If we tried to integrate every possible combination of parameters into the process, it could easily become unreadable and incomprehensible to anyone.

Jan explains why complex rule sets should, whenever possible, be modeled outside of the main process representation. He emphasizes that when subsequent activities depend on one or more parameters or their values, the number of possible outcomes can grow rapidly. Representing all these variations directly within the process model would require numerous *if–then–else* branches, which can quickly overload the diagram and confuse its readers.

As a vivid example, Jan refers to the internal invoice approval process within the company. Depending on the invoice amount, different levels of approval authority are required. Attempting to visualize all possible approval paths within a single process diagram would make the model cluttered and difficult to understand.

Linda And how would such a separation work in practice? After all, the parameters are crucial for the process flow.

Jan The smart alternative to embedding rule sets directly in the process is to extract them and represent them separately—typically in a dedicated table. I try to keep the actual process flow separate from the rules and decisions, both in the modeling phase and later during implementation.
From the perspective of the process flow, the rules and decisions are treated as a black box. The process simply reacts to the outcome of the rule evaluation and continues accordingly. The internal logic of how that decision is made doesn't need to be shown in the process diagram itself.
The sketch in Fig. 7.9 is meant to help illustrate this principle.

To the point
Extracting rule sets from the process model improves its readability. Decision tables are a suitable method for documenting these rule sets. ◄

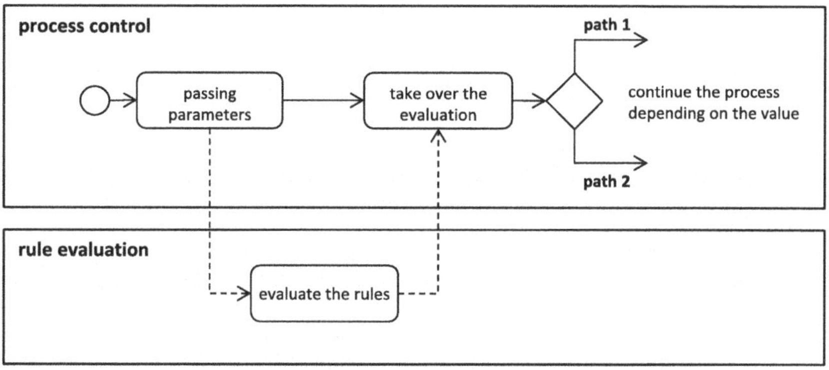

Fig. 7.9 Separation of processes and their rules

Linda I'm starting to get a sense of what you mean. Let's apply it to process step 4, 'Classify the case.'

Jan This process step is a perfect example to illustrate the concept. The rule set I'm about to introduce will definitely need to be defined more precisely during the implementation project, but for the rough concept, the following case example will suffice.

As a first step, take a closer look at the contents of Table 7.2. The left-hand columns show a set of rules. We have various criteria that influence the process flow—such as customer type or communication channel. Not all of these criteria carry the same weight, so we assign different levels of importance to each. Each criterion has four possible values in our example, and each of these values is assigned a specific point score. That's the rule component.

Now let's look at how it's applied, which you'll see in the two columns on the right. Our example scenario is: *A private customer reports a claim* via*email. The claim amount is less than €200. The customer has no previous claims and holds no other insurance policies with us.* For better readability, I've already highlighted this information in the table.

The evaluation of the rules is based on simple arithmetic. For each criterion, the corresponding score for the selected option is assigned (for example, the customer receives 2 points for being a private customer) and then multiplied by the weighting of that criterion. In the end, all weighted points are summed up to produce a total score, which we use as a decision criterion.

In our example, and as shown in Fig. 7.9, the rule evaluation logic calculates a total score of 1.95.

This value, 1.95, doesn't mean much on its own. However, we need it as a basis for deciding whether the process should continue automatically or be handled by an agent. The missing piece is a threshold value that separates these two paths. My suggestion is to present the rule set shown here as an example in our tender, along with the requirement that the IT solution must be capable of handling this kind of rule-based decision-making. To illustrate the principle, we can define an arbitrary threshold value. After reviewing the decision table, I chose 2.1 as the threshold:

- Scores ≤ 2.1 allow automatic processing by the Omni-Channel system.
- Scores > 2.1 trigger manual handling, and the process is assigned to an agent.

In our example, the score of 1.95 is below the threshold, so the customer request can be processed fully automatically under the given conditions. However, other scenarios—such as a higher claim amount or a history of previous claims—would push the score above the threshold and route the case to an agent.

Linda That was quite a detailed explanation, but I believe I've understood it. It seems to me that we've offloaded a significant amount of logic from the process itself, which has greatly reduced its complexity.

Let me summarize the specific advantages this separation of the rule set offers for our Omni-Channel system:

- We can add new *criteria* to the rule set without changing the process.
- We can modify or expand the *values of existing criteria* without adjusting the process.
- We can revise the *weightings* as needed.

This gives us a high degree of flexibility in dynamically handling a wide range of parameters.

Jan Perfectly summarized. And I'd like to add one more adjustment lever: the *threshold value*—currently set at 2.1—should also be configurable, ideally by the business department itself. This would allow the ratio between fully automated and manual processing to be adjusted simply by raising or lowering the threshold, all without needing an IT developer. The same rule set could remain in place while the decision logic adapts to changing business needs.

Linda Impressive. I now understand why you separate the rule sets from the processes. The key takeaway is: *Simplify the processes.* Even though we're still in the phase of collecting and documenting requirements, we're already laying the groundwork for a solution that offers greater flexibility.

Jan I hope you not only see the opportunities this approach offers, but also recognize that the rule set must be developed with great care. The individual values and their combinations must consistently lead to the correct decision—100% of the time. The system evaluates; it does not assess. That's why precision in rule definition is absolutely critical.

A brief addition to the topic of decision rules: The decision table presented earlier was designed based on our own ideas. As an alternative, there is an established standard from the Object Management Group (OMG) that provides a formal notation for decision rules in process management. This standard is known as DMN (Decision Model and Notation). DMN (Object Management Group, 2023) is closely related to BPMN and can be integrated and nested within BPMN models.

To the point
Separating rule sets from the process enhances the flexibility of the IT system being developed. In addition to decision tables, the standardized notation DMN (Decision Model and Notation) is also well-suited for modeling decision rules.◀

7.3.4 Natural Language Requirements Using the Sentence Template

In this Chapter, 'Documenting Requirements,' we address the challenge of presenting a broad range of notations and artifacts suitable for this task. One particularly versatile tool is the sentence template, which serves as a notation format for natural language requirements across nearly all requirement categories (see Sect. 7.1.2). In this section, we use sentence templates primarily to document quality requirements and constraints, though they are equally applicable to specifying functional requirements.

Table 7.2 Rule set and application example for Workflow Activity 4: 'Classify the case'

Rule set						Result of the process	
Criterion	Weighting (%)	Score per manifestation				determined score	weighted score
		1	2	3	4		
Customer type	10	Prospect	***Private customer***	Corporate customer	Broker	2	0.20
Yearly customer revenue	15	up to 50 €	***up to 100 €***	up to 500 €	> 500 €	2	0.30
Type of request	15	Informa-tion	Master data change	Offer	***Damage***	4	0.60
Damage amount	25	0 €	***up to 200 €***	up to 1000 €	> 1000 €	2	0.50
Past damage cases	15	***0***	1	2	3	1	0.15
Additional insurances	5	***0***	1	2	3	1	0.05
Communication channel	15	***Email***	Letter	Phone	Chat	1	0.15
	100						**1.95**

Linda Jan, I think we've laid a solid foundation for the RfP in terms of functional requirements. And even for our upcoming decision—whether to pursue our own development or adopt a standard omni-channel system—we already have a lot of information on the table. What I'm still missing, though, are the quality requirements and constraints you briefly mentioned on day two with a few examples. Do we need to define those now, or is it sufficient to go into detail during the implementation phase?

Linda raises an important point. Both quality requirements and constraints are critical to the success of a software project and should be carefully defined from the outset. Addressing them early helps minimize the risk of delays and unexpected costs, and enables potential issues to be identified and resolved proactively.

- *Quality requirements* ensure that the software meets user expectations. They specify the required level of quality across various dimensions, such as functionality, performance, usability, security, and reliability.
- *Constraints* are conditions that limit the development or use of the software system. These may relate to technological specifications, target users, operating environments, or compliance with legal and regulatory requirements.

Jan I completely agree, Linda. We need to define the quality requirements and constraints now. They'll support the decision-making process you mentioned, and they'll also help the future provider with planning and cost estimation.

Linda I'm still having trouble clearly assigning some of the requirements you mentioned to one of the two categories. Take data security, for example—you classified it as a quality requirement, but it also imposes restrictions on the development and use of the software by requiring specific measures to ensure data protection.

Jan Yes, some requirements can definitely fit into both categories. That's a good observation. Data security is a great example: it's a quality aspect, but it also imposes constraints on how the system is designed and operated.

Linda Aren't all quality requirements also constraints?

Jan Hmm... It's true that most quality requirements tend to increase costs and therefore affect this constraint. But beyond that, I wouldn't describe all quality requirements as restrictions on the development or use of the system. Take the following examples:

- Requirements for users with limited vision
- Usability requirements
- Reliability requirements

These aren't constraints—they contribute to making the future system appealing and useful to users.

Linda That makes sense to me. Let's look at the details, then. I had noted the quality requirements: *performance, reliability, data security, scalability,* and *testability.* As for constraints, we wanted to include *technology specifications*—such as statements on *web generation, interfaces, costs, compliance*, and *evaluability*. I can provide input on most of these points, but what exactly is meant by *web generation*?

Jan — By *web generation*, I mean the two concepts Web 2.0 and Web 3.0. These refer to stages in the evolution of the internet, each changing how information is shared, created, and used online. Web 2.0 is centered around social media platforms, blogs, and wikis—tools that emphasize user-generated content and interaction. Web 3.0, on the other hand, aims to advance the internet through technologies and concepts like the Semantic Web, blockchain, and artificial intelligence.

Linda — Would it make sense to base the Omni-Channel system on Web 3.0?

Jan — It's certainly possible to base the Omni-Channel system on Web 3.0. This would offer greater security and transparency compared to a centralized platform built on Web 2.0. A Web 3.0-based omni-channel system could provide a more secure and decentralized platform for storing customer data, while still ensuring privacy and protection. Additionally, user identification could be handled through blockchain technology, which adds transparency and tamper-resistance. However, I'm not yet sure whether Web 3.0 is the right choice for us. If our focus is primarily on supporting social media, Web 2.0 might be sufficient.

Linda — I'd suggest we stay open to both options and ask the future provider in our tender to give specific input on Web 2.0 and Web 3.0. After all, they're the experts. This way, we can learn from the different providers—free of charge. *(winks)*

Jan — *(Can't help shaking his head and grinning)* That's how customers are—they keep providers on their toes while benefiting from the latest technologies. You could call that a*win-win*.

Linda — *(is now also grinning)* Quite cheeky … With your hourly rates, you providers are also well compensated.

Jan — Yes, if we are commissioned … But let's actually start now.

Linda and Jan had established a trusting relationship in a very short time, which allowed them to engage in verbal sparring—occasionally laced with a touch of cynicism—without any negative consequences.

Jan — Since we're on the topic, let's start with one of the most important constraints.

Linda — You mean costs, right?

Jan — Yes, you should have a clear understanding of the costs and the overall project budget. We can document this in the initial project concept. However, I would advise against including the costs in the tender itself.

Linda — I wouldn't want that either. If there are providers who could offer their services well below our budget, they would probably just increase their price. On the other hand, providers who might have the best solution but can't meet our budget might not even submit a proposal. And we don't want to base our decision solely on cost. Of course, it would be ideal if the cheapest provider were also the best, but unfortunately, that's rarely the case.

They then collaborate to define additional quality requirements and constraints, using the provided sentence template as a guide. They also agree to refer to the Omni-Channel System simply as "the system" in their formulations. The results of their work are shown in Tables 7.3 and 7.4.

Table 7.3 Examples of quality requirements

Quality requirement characteristic	Requirement
Performance	The system must be able to process 100 customer inquiries per minute.
Performance	The system must guarantee a reaction time of 2 s after user inputs.
Reliability	The system must ensure continuous operation without crashes or unplanned outages.
Data security	The system must ensure the security of data by protecting it against unauthorized access, use, or disclosure.
Data security	The system must comply with data protection laws and regulations.
Scalability	The current average number of customer inquiries is 250 per day. The system must be scalable to handle at least twice this volume.
Testability	The system must include an integrated test framework.
Testability	The test framework must enable testers to perform regression testing on the system after each implementation of a change request.

Tab. 7.4 Examples of constraints to be observed

Constraint characteristic	Requirement
Technology specification	The system's new database must be compatible with the existing database.
Compliance	Customers must be informed of their rights to access, rectification, deletion, and the blocking of their data.
Compliance	Customers must have the ability to withdraw their consent to the processing of their data.
Compliance	Customers must be protected from unsolicited advertising.
Web-Generation	The provider should include information about the Web 2.0 and Web 3.0 generations in their proposal.
Costs	The total cost for renewing the Omni-Channel system must not exceed € 7 million.

Linda So, we've already covered some of the necessary requirements. I like that. According to our mind map from yesterday (see Fig. 6.2), the only constraints we still need to address are *evaluability* and *interfaces*.

Jan Yes, those are topics we should probably discuss in a bit more detail.

Linda Exactly. When I hear *evaluability,* I think of data. The ability to evaluate data is a crucial part of our decision-making process for customer requests. By improving data quality and visualization, both the company as a whole and specifically our agents, clerks, and experts will be able to make better-informed decisions. This should have a positive impact on both customer service and business outcomes.

Jan On the one hand, that sounds logical, but on the other, it means a lot of work for us. It's not easy to summarize the requirements for evaluability in just a few sentences. Let's define some key points that ensure data quality and visualization, and thus support the evaluability requirements. How about these categories: correctness, completeness, consistency, traceability, and interpretability of data?

Linda Agreed. Let's bring these categories to life by formulating specific requirements for each one.

No sooner said than done (see Table 7.5):

Table 7.5 Examples for categories of the constraint 'evaluability'

Categories of the constraint 'evaluability'	Requirement
Correctness	Data must be correct and up-to-date to enable informed decisions regarding premium levels, risk assessment, and customer satisfaction.
Completeness	Data must be complete, for example with respect to the customer's medical history, claims history, and customer satisfaction.
Consistency	Data must be consistent to prevent contradictory decisions. For example, customers with the same medical history shall not be assigned different premium levels.
Traceability	Data must be traceable to allow identification of its source. For example, it shall be possible to determine the origin of a specific premium.
Interpretability	Data must be easily understandable to facilitate informed decision-making. For example, it shall be possible to track customer satisfaction over a defined period of time.
Data quality assurance	Data must be reviewable on a weekly basis for correctness, completeness, consistency, and traceability.
Data modeling	Data must be structured in a model that fulfills the specific requirements of the Omni-Channel system.
Data visualization	Data must be visualized with a high level of user experience to support informed decision-making.

Linda I'm not satisfied with our last sentence. What exactly do we mean by "high user experience"? That isn't a measurable requirement, is it?

Jan You are right, but it's difficult to define UX in measurable terms. What if we require providers to submit examples of their data visualizations in their proposals? That way, we can assess the level of user experience each provider offers and have a basis for comparison.

Linda Good idea. Let's do it that way. Now, let's move on to the interface requirements.

7.3.5 Interface Requirements

Jan OK. The implementation of interface requirements should ensure that the various systems can communicate effectively with each other, and that errors or other operational issues are avoided.

Linda Then we should also specify the systems for which we need interfaces.

Jan Yes, we shouldn't just list the systems—we should also categorize them and integrate them into our process. For this, I suggest using two diagrams. The first would present the architectural model, and the second would be the choreography diagram I mentioned earlier. This diagram illustrates when the interfaces are used and what triggers their activation.

Linda Alright, let's have a look then…

Jan therefore prepares both the architectural model and the BPMN choreography diagram, and introduces Linda to the topic.

Jan In our context diagram (see Fig. 5.11), we clearly defined the system boundary that encloses our Omni-Channel system and separates it from the rest of the world. However, we also saw that our system doesn't exist in isolation—it interacts with its environment. It's similar to a city wall: while it marks the boundary and provides protection for what's inside, we still need gates or bridges to allow communication with the outside. Our processes don't run exclusively on the Omni-Channel system; they also rely on and involve other systems that participate in the overall process.

Linda In the context diagram, the use case diagram, and in our process modeling, we've identified that our proposed solution—together with other systems like contract management and customer master data—is essential for the overall process.

Jan As a result, we need to formulate requirements for the interfaces in order to select the right tool for our Omni-Channel system, given that multiple IT systems will be integrated. We need to answer questions such as:

- How is the interface triggered (manually or automatically)?
- How does the data transfer occur (synchronously or asynchronously)?
- What triggers the data transfer (time-driven or event-driven)?

Linda I hope we won't need to provide descriptions at the bit-and-byte level. I wouldn't be able to do that. My goal is to ensure that the necessary IT systems are integrated at a business-logical level to support the process flows. I want to avoid situations where certain systems, like the master data system, are not connected or can only be integrated at great expense. So, it's really about finding the right balance in how detailed our requirements documentation needs to be.

Jan Let's start with the topic of interfaces. We've already identified the surrounding systems in our context and use case diagrams, but we should ask ourselves:

- Are there any other systems we need interfaces for that we haven't considered yet?
- Which IT system actually initiates the interface—is it triggered by the Omni-Channel system or by an external system?

As a first step, I'd like to get an overview of all the relevant IT systems that we'll likely need to integrate. I've organized them into a structure that makes sense to me:

- The most important group of IT systems for customer communication is the communication infrastructure. This acts as our gateway to the outside world and is especially important for first-level support. Technically, these systems are often located in the so-called DMZ, or 'demilitarized zone,' which sits between our corporate network and the internet. Special security concepts apply here to minimize the attack surface of our IT environment, as these systems are directly exposed to the external world.
- There are also IT systems outside our own data center, known as third-party systems. We primarily use these to obtain information that we do not generate ourselves.
- The third group I call backend systems. This includes all internally owned IT applications that need to be connected to our Omni-Channel system and that are housed in a secure data center environment.

That's how I would represent things (see Fig. 7.10). Does this make sense to you?

Linda Not bad. The concept of a DMZ is new to me, but I understand it now. This concise summary makes it clear to me that our Omni-Channel system communicates with a variety of other IT systems in different ways.

Jan By shifting our modeling approach to focus on the interfaces themselves, we can really concentrate on these connections. We could even assign numbers to each system and describe their interfaces with the Omni-Channel system in a table. In my opinion, this level of detail can be handled during the implementation project. However, this approach also has its limitations. If an interface between two systems needs to support multiple functions, it becomes difficult to represent this adequately with just an architecture model and a tabular description.

Linda I have a few more questions: At which points in the process flow do these interfaces actually play a role? Do we need to consider them in the context of different process steps?

Jan Great question. I think BPMN can help us here as well—specifically with the choreography diagram. The purpose of this type of diagram is to represent the communication between different process participants. It works by excluding all process steps where a participant is not interacting with others, so the diagram focuses solely on the exchanged messages. By sequencing these activities, I get a clear overview of the communicative interfaces within the process.

Here's what the corresponding BPMN notation looks like.

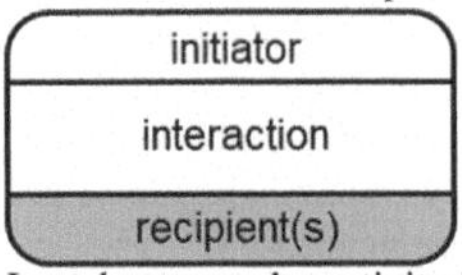

In a choreography activity like this, I can see both the initiating actor and one or more receiving actors—which, in our case, are usually IT systems. By sequencing multiple choreography activities, I can visualize exactly when each IT system calls an interface within the process flow. With this approach, I took a closer look at our 'Handling Customer Concerns' use case and simplified the process to show only those activities that involve interactions between two IT systems or actors—that is, whenever an interface is required. I've mapped these specific process steps as choreography activities. But as the saying goes, a picture is worth a thousand words. In my opinion, Fig. 7.11 clearly illustrates how the different systems interact with each other.

Linda Compared to your other diagrams, this one looks much more streamlined. Could you say a few words about it?

Jan With this approach, we can capture the different functionalities of each interface. I've streamlined the use case description from Fig. 7.6 by leaving out any activities that don't require interaction with another IT system. What's shown here, from a process perspective, is when specific actions involving interfaces are expected to occur. Let's briefly walk through the process:

- First, the customer submits their concern through one of the communication channels. This is the only step involving a direct user interface.
- The chosen communication channel forwards the information to the Omni-Channel system.
- Opening a case ticket and some subsequent internal process steps are excluded here, as they don't require external interfaces.
- When the process is enriched with the necessary metadata, two technical interfaces are involved—one to the contract data system and one to the master data system.
- We discussed process classification in detail in the rulebook (Sect. 7.3.3). Technically, this rulebook could be represented by a decision engine, and communicating with this system would be the next step shown in the choreography diagram.
- The actual case processing is, professionally speaking, the most complex and extensive activity. Not surprisingly, it's in this step that the most IT systems need to be engaged.
- And finally, the customer is informed of the status of their request through a communication channel.

This sequence reflects the use case description, but pared down to only those activities where at least two IT systems are communicating with each other.

Linda The only drawback I see with your method is that it captures only the interfaces needed within a specific process.

Jan That's true. As you've correctly observed, not all IT systems shown in the architecture model are used in this particular process. However, I believe both approaches have their place. The architecture model provides a static and comprehensive overview of all IT systems, while the choreography diagram offers a dynamic perspective focused on a specific process. Each type of representation has its own strengths, and together they complement each other. What's most important is to make it clear that the Omni-Channel system does not exist in isolation—it's integrated into the broader IT landscape, and the relevant requirements for the interfaces are formulated accordingly.

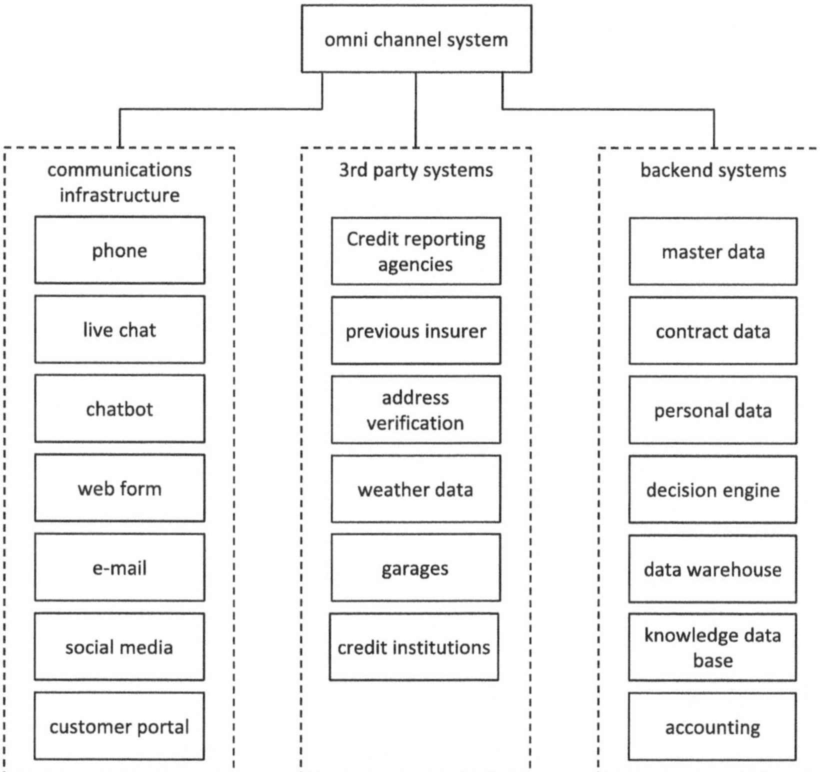

Fig. 7.10 High-level architecture model with grouped technical systems from the context

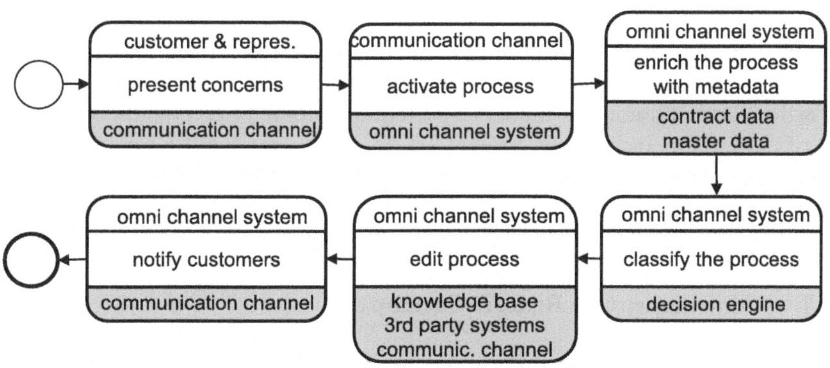

Fig. 7.11 BPMN choreography diagram for the representation of interfaces

To the point
Both architecture models and choreography diagrams are suitable for representing software interfaces; however, neither model can capture all interface requirements in their entirety. They complement each other and should be supplemented with additional natural language documentation for greater clarity and completeness.◄

7.3.6 Further Notation Forms and Artifacts

At the beginning of this chapter, we noted that certain notations and artifacts offer distinct advantages in agile project environments. For the sake of completeness, we refer to additional notations and artifacts specifically suited to this approach in Sect. 8.1.

7.4 Creating THE Document

If you are an agile expert, you may be hesitant about producing a lengthy, comprehensive document—after all, requirements are often subject to change, and documentation can quickly become outdated.

However, for our rough concept as a basis for the tender, there is really no alternative: both the client and the contractor need a solid foundation for the implementation project. Without it, making reliable decisions or accurately estimating the effort required would be extremely difficult. Ideally, the requirements recorded in the rough concept are stable—meaning that the likelihood of them changing is very low. This shared understanding ensures both the client and the contractor are aligned before starting the development of custom software or introducing a standard product. Additional details on this can be found in Sect. 7.4.1.

Furthermore, it's not just tenders that require detailed documentation independent of agile methods. Certain project environments must still be managed using the waterfall model, which involves creating an extensive requirements document before implementation can begin. We will discuss this briefly in Sect. 7.4.2.

7.4.1 Finalizing the Rough Concept

In the mind map shown in Fig. 6.2, Linda and Jan highlighted the specific requirement categories they intended to develop for the initial concept. That task is now complete. The next step is to assemble all these elements into a cohesive, overarching rough concept.

We will not present the aforementioned "kit"—that is, the prosaic merging of the elements of the rough concept—here, and instead leave this task to the imagination of the experienced reader. We have already provided the content core of the rough concept and see little added value in further textual elaboration. Nevertheless, we would like to offer a few tips for creating such a document:

1. Be clear and precise. Every sentence in the rough concept should be formulated so that it leaves no room for ambiguity or misinterpretation.
2. Move from the general to the specific. Start by developing a suitable structure for the document before delving into the details.
3. Less is more. Avoid unnecessarily flowery language or paraphrasing that could confuse the reader. Focus on the essential facts.
4. Ensure the document goes through a quality assurance process.

As previously announced, we will deal in detail with the aforementioned quality assurance (QA) in Chap. 9 and look back at the quality assurance of Linda and Jan's rough concept. For the further course of this chapter, we assume that the rough concept has already successfully gone through the QA process.

7.4.2 Short Detour: Other Waterfall Projects in Software and Systems Engineering

While agile methodologies have revolutionized software development with their flexibility and iterative feedback loops, they are not universally applicable. Agile thrives in dynamic environments, but in projects with rigid requirements, the structured nature of the waterfall model remains indispensable and with it the creation of a detailed requirements document.

The waterfall model is a linear and sequential approach where each phase—requirements, design, implementation, verification, and maintenance—must be completed before the next begins. This model is particularly valuable in projects where changes are costly or infeasible once development has started. Below are four examples where the waterfall model is not only suitable but necessary:

1. **Software Development in Aerospace Avionics (Aviation Industry)** In avionics software for commercial aircraft, such as flight control systems, safety and regulatory compliance are paramount. These systems must meet stringent standards like DO-178C (Clifton & Ericson, 2011), which require exhaustive documentation and verification at each stage. Agile's iterative changes are incompatible with the certification process, making the waterfall model essential for traceability and validation.
2. **Banking Core System Overhaul (Financial Sector)** Replacing or upgrading a bank's core transaction processing system involves high risk and strict regulatory oversight. Requirements must be fully defined upfront to ensure compliance with financial regulations and to avoid disruptions in service. The

waterfall model ensures a controlled, predictable development path with clear milestones and deliverables.

3. **Construction of a Satellite Ground Station (Aerospace Systems Engineering)** Building a satellite ground station involves integrating hardware, software, and communication systems. The physical infrastructure and long lead times for components necessitate a fixed design early in the project. Waterfall's structured approach allows for detailed planning and coordination across engineering disciplines, minimizing integration risks.
4. **Development of a Medical Imaging Device (Healthcare Engineering)** Designing a new MRI (Magnetic Resonance Imaging) machine requires coordination between mechanical, electrical, and software engineering teams. Regulatory bodies like the FDA (Food and Drug Administration) in the USA demand comprehensive documentation and validation before market release. The waterfall model supports this by enforcing a disciplined development process with formal reviews and approvals at each stage.

Despite its rigidity, the waterfall model can still benefit from agile principles. For instance, within individual phases—especially during implementation—teams can adopt agile practices like daily stand-ups, modular development, or internal sprints to improve collaboration and responsiveness. Additionally, early prototyping or simulation during the design phase can incorporate user feedback without compromising the overall structure.

7.5 Deciding Between Standard Product and Custom Software

With the creation and quality assurance of the rough concept, Linda and Jan have compiled the company's specific requirements and ideas for a future Omni-Channel solution, independent of any products currently available on the market. Their concept now forms the basis for the tender document to be prepared. However, one crucial question for the tender remains unanswered: Would a standard product meet their needs, or is custom software development unavoidable? A key prerequisite for answering this question is an understanding of the capabilities of existing Omni-Channel products.

In the next step, they gather the necessary information and arguments for or against adopting a standard product versus developing custom software. They begin this process with a market analysis.

Linda	I almost wanted to say "Done," but unfortunately, that only applies to the first step—documenting our own ideas. Next, we need to determine how big the gap is between our requirements and what standard software products typically offer.
Jan	Exactly. I actually find this next step quite exciting. Even though I'm a passionate requirements engineer, I'm genuinely curious to see how our requirements compare with the features offered by products on the market.

Linda I have to admit, I did wonder at first if you were really the right person to help me with this (*she says with a wink*). But in the end, you put my doubts to rest—you've tackled every topic thoroughly and always had the right tool for every problem.

Jan Thank you for the compliment. I look forward to continuing to support you and hope I'll have the right tool for this task as well. I suggest we don't waste any time and start researching the standard Omni-Channel solutions available on the market. Let's see what range of features they offer.

Linda OK. Let's get started on the market analysis.

7.5.1 Market Analysis of Available Standard Products

The next step is to examine various providers of Omni-Channel products and evaluate their solutions against the specific requirements. Linda quickly realizes that she and Jan cannot test all available products. Therefore, they select five promising providers to focus on.

Linda So, our goal is to decide whether to implement a standard product or develop our own solution. For the standard product option, we've now identified five potential providers. What's the next step?

Jan I see our next task as evaluating these providers based on reviews and ratings from relevant platforms. With this information, we may be able to further narrow down our list, and it shouldn't require much effort.

Linda That might help us rule out one or two products, but it still doesn't give us a real basis for making a decision. We'll know which providers are considered the best, but not whether a standard product is actually right for us.
I think we can't avoid reaching out to these five providers at this stage and starting our tender process with a *Request for Information*.

Jan That's a good idea. A Request for Information will give us a lot of valuable insights. Once the providers have responded, we could also invite them to give demo presentations. Ideally, these demonstrations could even be done online.

After reviewing the ratings on industry platforms (Gartner; TrustRadius), Linda and Jan jointly prepare a Request for Information (RfI) document and send it to the potential product providers. In addition, they seek more information about custom software development from IT consulting firms. For this purpose, Linda and Jan adapt the RfI and send it to a selection of appropriate consulting firms.

A few weeks later, Linda and Jan have received the responses to their RfIs. They are also invited by two providers to attend product presentations. During these presentations, they assess how well the products meet the previously defined functionalities, quality requirements, and constraints. Specifically, they pursue two goals:

1. They make an initial pre-selection of providers, in case they decide to implement a standard product.
2. They support the pending decision between introducing a standard product and developing custom software by using the presentations to more accurately evaluate certain decision criteria for the standard products.

Nine consulting firms responded to the RfI for custom software development. Linda and Jan proceed with evaluating and analyzing the feedback they received.

7.5.2 Construction of a Decision Matrix

With the results from the RfI, Linda and Jan have gathered extensive information from both product vendors and consulting firms—information that is essential for building their decision matrix. At this stage, they still can't say, even based on intuition, which path would be better. Therefore, they need a systematic approach to avoid relying on gut feeling alone. In this case, a utility analysis is appropriate. This method, developed by Zangemeister and Bechmann in the 1970s (Zangemeister, 2014), remains relevant and widely used today. A similar method, along with additional approaches, is described by Belton and Stewart (2002).

Based on this utility analysis, Linda and Jan outline the following steps to guide their decision-making process:

1. Define the categories and criteria that represent a benefit for the company (see Sect. 7.5.2.1).
2. Establish the structure of the decision matrix (see Sect. 7.5.2.2).
3. Assign weights to each criterion (see Sect. 7.5.2.3).
4. Score each criterion for every solution alternative (see Sect. 7.5.2.4).
5. Calculate the utility value for both alternatives—custom software development and standard product adoption (see Sect. 7.5.2.5).

7.5.2.1 Step 1: Define Categories and Criteria

Linda and Jan begin by defining the categories for their decision matrix. They agree on the following categories, each of which is further broken down into specific criteria:

1. *Costs:* Total costs associated with development or license purchase, installation, commissioning, operation, and maintenance of the software.
2. *Time:* The time required to implement and put the software into operation.
3. *Quality:* The reliability and error-free operation of the software.
4. *Functionality:* The scope and relevance of the features the software offers to meet the needs of its users—namely, the insurance customers and support staff.
5. *Adaptability:* The software's ability to be adapted to changing user requirements and preferences.

6. *Maintainability:* The ease and frequency of updates, improvements, and bug fixes.
7. *Security:* Protection of the software against unauthorized access, data loss, or theft.
8. *Customer Satisfaction:* The extent to which the software meets or exceeds user expectations and satisfaction.

Linda The first step is done. Can we define certain criteria as knockout criteria, meaning that if a specific limit is exceeded, the option is automatically eliminated?

Jan Absolutely—we can explicitly mark those as knockout criteria in the decision matrix.

Linda Then I'd like us to define the total investment costs—the sum of software development or license acquisition, plus installation and commissioning—as a knockout criterion. Let's set the limit at €7 million.

Jan OK, we'll take that into account. We can then define operation and maintenance costs separately as a distinct category.

Linda One question: We introduced decision tables earlier when we discussed rule sets. So, at this point, do we just need to replace the criteria in the table with these new ones?

7.5.2.2 Step 2: Structuring the Decision Matrix

Jan Hmm… I don't think it's quite that simple. If you look back at the rule set in Table 7.2, we assigned scores from 1 to 4 to each alternative, with each option given exactly one score from the set. That approach doesn't fit here. I'd suggest we refer to our new table as a decision matrix and take a more nuanced approach this time.

Linda Alright, then let's see how you envision the decision matrix so that it reflects this more differentiated approach.

Jan had used the waiting period during the RfI response phase to prepare an initial draft of the decision matrix.

Jan The result is shown in Table 7.6. As we discussed, I've defined the investment costs with their explicit limit as a knockout criterion, but I've also kept them as part of the 'costs' category so they're included in the overall evaluation.

Linda I also notice that you haven't broken down all of the categories into more specific criteria.

Jan Yes, for the categories *Adaptability* and *Customer Satisfaction*, I don't think we need any additional criteria. That's why I'm treating these categories as individual criteria in the decision matrix.

Linda I can't think of any other categories or criteria to add. I like the structure of the table. The next step is to fill in the individual columns with content, right? Let's move on to that.

Table 7.6 Structure of the decision matrix

		Custom Software Development		Standard Product Introduction	
Knockout Criteria					
– Max. 7 Mio € Capital costs					
Categories and Criteria	Weighting	Score	Weighting * Score	Score	Weighting * Score
Costs					
– Investment costs					
– Operation and Maintenance					
Time					
– Implementation or Configuration					
– Commissioning					
Quality					
– Reliability					
– Error-free operation					
Functionality					
– Scope					
– Relevance					
Adaptability					
Maintainability					
– Simplicity					
– Frequency					
Security					
– Protection against unauthorized access					
– Protection against data theft and loss					
Customer satisfaction					
Total:	**100%**				

7.5.2.3 Step 3: Determine Weights

Linda Let me start with a question: Does the sum of the weighting values always have to add up to 100%?

Jan Yes, although with a large number of criteria, it can be challenging to arrive at exactly 100%. But the weighting values should always represent parts of the whole, and the whole is 100%. We have two options for assigning weights to the categories and criteria:

- We can determine the weights based on our intuition, or
- we can use a well-established method called the preference matrix.

The preference matrix has the advantage of minimizing subjective bias, but it does require a bit more effort to create.

Linda I'm very interested. The decision between developing custom software and implementing a standard product is significant, so I'd like to avoid subjective influences like intuition or gut feeling—they're difficult to justify and always open to challenge. Is creating a preference matrix very complicated?

Jan It's actually less complicated than you might think, but it's not something to ignore either. The underlying idea is to compare only two elements at a time from a larger set. It's much easier for us to make pairwise comparisons than to evaluate many elements all at once.

In our case, our basic set consists of the eight categories. We would need to compare each category against every other category in pairs. For each comparison, whichever category is more important gets a point. At the end, the category with the most points is considered the highest priority.

Linda But gut feeling isn't completely eliminated, is it? When I have to decide which of two categories is more important to me, I'll probably still be relying on subjective judgment quite a lot.

Jan That's true—you can't eliminate subjectivity entirely. But we do gain considerably more objectivity this way. I did some calculations: if we compare each category with every other one, that makes 28 pairwise comparisons.

Linda Only 28? That sounds manageable. Let's give it a try. I'm curious to see the result. How do you suggest we document the process so we don't lose track?

Jan showed Linda his prepared, but as yet unfilled, preference matrix for the eight categories. Using the example of the first two categories—Cost and Time—he explained that if he considers cost to be more important, he would enter a 1 for cost in their shared field; if time is more important, he would enter a 2 for time. The pairwise comparisons continue until the preference between Cost and Customer Satisfaction is determined at the top of the matrix, and either a 1 or an 8 is assigned at this position.

Once Linda is briefed on the method, she and Jan systematically compare all categories with each other to work out the final weightings. Throughout this process, Jan refrains from giving his own opinion, since, ultimately, it is Linda who must justify to the company why one criterion is more important than another from her perspective. The result of her work is the completed matrix (see Fig. 7.12).

Linda I didn't find it that difficult. When I add up the results, I get the following: Costs—3; Time—1; Quality—6; Functionality—5; Adaptability—1; Maintainability—1; Security—7; and Customer Satisfaction—4. That adds up to 28 pairwise comparisons. But the raw numbers only help to a certain extent—we still need to convert them into percentages. If I remember correctly from school, we calculate the percentages using the rule of three.

Jan Exactly. Here's an example: Security was mentioned 7 times, so with 28 comparisons, that gives it a weighting of 25%. I've quickly calculated the percentages for all categories:

- Costs: 10.7%
- Time: 3.6%
- Quality: 21.4%
- Functionality: 17.9%
- Adaptability: 3.6%
- Maintainability: 3.6%
- Security: 25%
- Customer Satisfaction: 14.3%

The total of all percentage values is 100%. Feel free to double-check the calculations.

Linda I trust your calculations. Interestingly, my gut feeling favorites *Quality* and *Security* came out on top. On the other hand, I wouldn't have expected Time to be ranked so low compared to the other categories.
But how do we handle the criteria within each category? Did we overlook those?

Jan No, not at all. We just need to assign weights within each individual category now. For example, within the category *Quality*, I might value *Reliability* at 75% and *Error-free Operation* at 25%.
In Table 7.7, I've summarized how often each category was selected and the corresponding calculated weights. It has turned into quite a comprehensive set of figures…

Linda …but it all makes sense to me. I find it reassuring that gut feeling has taken a back seat and, for me, the weighting now seems much more objective.

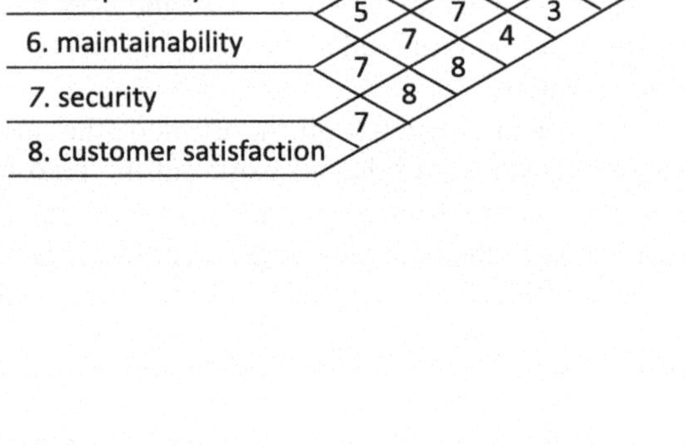

Fig. 7.12 Preference matrix

Table 7.7 Weighting of categories and criteria

Categories	Weighting of categories		Weighting of criteria	
– Criteria	No. of mentions	Weight (%)	Relative (%)	Absolute (%)
Costs	3	10.7		
– Investment costs			60	6.4
– Operation and Maintenance			40	4.3
Time	1	3.6		
– Implementation or Configuration			70	2.5
– Commissioning			30	1.1
Quality	6	21.4		
– Reliability			75	16.1
– Error-free operation			25	5.3
Functionality	5	17.8		
– Scope			30	5.4
– Relevance			70	12.4
Adaptability	1	3.6		3.6
Maintainability	1	3.6		
– Simplicity			60	2.1
– Frequency			40	1.5
Security	7	25.0		
– Protection against unauthorized access			25	6.2
– Protection against data theft and loss			75	18.8
Customer Satisfaction	4	14.3		14.3
Total:	28	100.0		100.0

7.5.2.4 Step 4: Rating Categories for Solution Alternatives

Linda I don't yet have an assessment of how important each category is for the various solution alternatives. For instance, custom software development is more expensive, but it can nearly cover all of our desired functions. We will still need to evaluate this trade-off ourselves.

Jan Perfect, Linda. That's exactly the next step I had in mind. Since the assessment is very specific to our company, I'm looking forward to your suggestions.

Afterwards, Linda and Jan discuss how to evaluate the categories and criteria for each solution alternative—whether to develop custom software or introduce a standard product. Assigning scores to each option often leads to lengthy discussions and highly individual viewpoints. To broaden their perspective and strengthen

Table 7.8 Assessment of categories and criteria for solution alternatives

Categories—Criteria	Custom Software Development	Standard Product Introduction
	Assigned score	Assigned score
Costs		
– Investment costs	2	7
– Operation and maintenance	4	5
Time		
– Implementation or configuration	3	10
– Commissioning	4	4
Quality		
– Reliability	5	9
– Error-free operation	5	8
Functionality		
– Scope	10	8
– Relevance	10	9
Adaptability	9	5
Maintainability		
– Simplicity	7	5
– Frequency	9	3
Security		
– Protection against unauthorized access	7	6
– Protection against data theft and loss	8	7
Customer satisfaction	9	7

the decision-making process, they regularly consult other experts for additional opinions.

For the assessment, they use a scale from 1 (very negative) to 10 (extremely positive), as shown in Table 7.8.

Since determining scores is not a typical requirements engineering activity, we will 'fast forward' at this point and present the results of the discussions directly. Please note that the weightings and scores are specific to our virtual insurance company and may produce different results in real-world scenarios.

7.5.2.5 Step 5: Calculate Utility Value

In the final step of the decision-making process, Linda and Jan need to summarize and evaluate their previous results. They complete the prepared decision matrix (Table 7.6) using the weightings and scores from Tables 7.7 and 7.8 to calculate the utility value. Linda is very excited…

Jan So, what do you think—which option came out on top?

Linda	I think it's the standard product introduction, but I'm not sure—it must be a close call.
Jan	Then let's take a look at the results (see Table 7.9).
	You were right—the standard product introduction received the highest score. However, it wasn't a clear-cut decision.
Linda	Yes, but in the case of custom software development, whenever we were unsure, we tended to pick the higher value. So, I think it's fair to go ahead with introducing the standard product.

To the point
Linda recommends to her project sponsor the introduction of a standard product. She arrived at this recommendation using a utility analysis. ◄

7.6 Creating RfPs

7.6.1 Importance of Tender Documents

We have already discussed the quality of requirements and requirements artifacts at length and will devote a separate chapter to quality assurance as a subfield of requirements engineering (Sect. 9.1). In this section, however, we would like to specifically address the quality of tender documents. Tender documents, also known as Requests for Proposal (RfP), are primarily based on a preliminary concept. In practice, the quality of this artifact is often underestimated.

To the point
An RfP that does not adhere to the principles of high-quality requirements documentation significantly increases the risk of project failure.◄

Usually, providers responding to an RfP have the opportunity to ask questions about any unclear requirements before submitting their proposals. However, providers do not always identify every ambiguously worded requirement. Let's look at an example.

Suppose a fixed-price project is planned, and the RfP includes a statement such as, "In the initial phase of the project, features and epics will be provided." The contractor might interpret this to mean that the client will supply the features and epics. However, what the client actually intended was: "During the three-month initial phase of the project, the contractor must develop the features and epics for the product backlog, based on the use cases provided by the client and through

Table 7.9 Complete decision matrix

		Custom software development		Standard product introduction	
KO criteria					
–Max. 7 million € investment costs					
Categories and criteria	Weighting (%)	Score	Weighting * Score	Score	Weighting * Score
Costs					
– Investment costs	6.4	2	12.9	7	45.0
– Operation and maintenance	4.3	4	17.1	5	21.4
Time					
– Implementation or configuration	2.5	3	7.5	10	25.0
– Commissioning	1.1	4	4.3	4	4.3
Quality					
– Reliability	16.1	5	80.4	9	144.6
– Error-free operation	5.4	5	26.8	8	42.9
Functionality					
– Scope	5.4	10	53.6	8	42.9
– Relevance	12.5	10	125.0	9	112.5
Adaptability	3.6	9	32.1	5	17.9
Maintainability					
– Simplicity	2.1	7	15.0	5	10.7
– Frequency	1.4	9	12.9	3	4.3
Security					
– Protection against unauthorized access	6.3	7	43.8	6	37.5
– Protection against data theft and loss	18.8	8	150.3	7	131.3
Customer satisfaction	14.3	9	128.6	7	100.1
Total:	100.0		709.8		740.3

interviews with the product owner." (We will define the terms "Feature" and "Epic" in Sect. 8.1.2).

Misunderstandings like this can lead providers to underestimate the total project effort. The client may be pleased with the attractively low price they negotiated, but disputes will likely arise during the project. Unsatisfactory scenarios—including project termination or even legal action—can and do occur, all due solely to unclear requirements. Such situations can result in financial losses in the millions and significant reputational damage for both contractor and client.

7.6.2 From Rough Concept to Tender

Linda and Jan want to avoid the nightmare scenario described in the previous section. They have created a quality-assured preliminary concept to serve as the foundation for the RfP. Now, their focus is on identifying the deliverables required from the future contractor and developing the structure of the RfP.

Jan So Linda, what do you expect the contractor to deliver?

Linda A super high-performing Omni-Channel system, of course! Everything else is secondary, right?

Jan The working system is certainly the most important deliverable. But to implement it successfully, our earlier requirements need to be refined and translated into a solution design. This will help ensure that our assumptions about quality, functionality, adaptability, maintainability, security, and customer satisfaction—reflected in the decision matrix—actually become reality. To achieve this, I wouldn't hand over complete control of the project; instead, I would include some additional specifications in the tender.

Linda Of course, Jan. I just wanted to draw you out a bit. In addition to refining the functional requirements based on the use cases, there are also several quality requirements that still need to be detailed and taken into account during implementation.

Jan That's right. Specifically, I'm thinking of portability and testability. We should also establish requirements for documenting the solution design, including both UI and UX design as well as the technical design. While the core solution already exists in the standard product, configuration and, hopefully, only minor customization will introduce some deviations from the standard that necessitate additional design documentation.

Linda And then I'm also thinking about the requirements for operating the solution, including user training materials and system documentation.

The two have now identified several aspects for which they still want to clearly define their expectations in the tender. They also already have some ideas for the structure of the RfP, but they want to see what inspiration generative AI can offer. They experiment with the following prompt:

> *"I want to create a tender for the introduction of an omni-channel system in an insurance company. There is already a rough specification document that should be integrated into this tender. Can you suggest a document structure for the tender? The document structure should include the main headings and second-level headings."*

In addition to a polite greeting and introduction, the AI chatbot returns the following suggested structure:

1.1 Introduction
1.1 Purpose of the Tender
1.2 Background of the Organization
1.3 Objectives of the Omni-Channel System
1.4 Scope of the Tender
1.5 Confidentiality and Legal Considerations
2 Project Overview
2.1 Current State Analysis
2.2 Target State Vision
2.3 Strategic Importance
2.4 Stakeholders Involved
3. Functional and Technical Requirements
3.1 Functional Requirements
- Customer Interaction Channels (e.g., web, mobile, call center, in-person)
- Integration with Existing Systems (CRM, policy management, etc.)
- Personalization and Customer Journey Management
- Reporting and Analytics

3.2 Technical Requirements
- Architecture and Technology Stack
- Security and Compliance (e.g., GDPR)
- Scalability and Performance
- APIs and Integration Capabilities

3.3 Non-Functional Requirements
- Usability
- Availability and Reliability
- Maintainability
- Support and Service Levels

4 Project Implementation
4.1 Project Planning and Approach
4.2 Milestones and Deliverables
4.3 Roles and Responsibilities
4.4 Change Management and Training
5 Tender Process
5.1 Submission Guidelines
5.2 Evaluation Criteria
5.3 Timeline and Deadlines
5.4 Questions and Clarifications
5.5 Contact Information
6 Legal and Commercial Terms
6.1 Contractual Framework
6.2 Budget and Pricing Structure
6.3 Intellectual Property Rights
6.4 Confidentiality and Data Protection
6.5 Termination and Exit Strategy
7 Appendices

7.1 Glossary of Terms
7.2 Existing Specification Document
7.3 Reference Architecture (if available)
7.4 Templates for Response

As usual, the chatbot provides a bit more than it was asked for—such as the additional items under Sects. 3.1, 3.2, and 3.3—but both the format and content are to Linda and Jan's liking. They make some adjustments, for example, reorganizing the requirements in Chap. 3 to match their own categories (quality requirements and constraints). They also enhance the structure with details specific to their project and insights from Jan's experience, for example:

- the role of an external consultant,
- Liability and warranty,
- Payment plan and supplier query.

We will refrain from detailing every chapter of the tender document, as this would take us too far beyond the scope of requirements engineering. However, we would like to highlight the following RE-relevant detail: in Sect. 4.1, "Project Planning and Approach," the agile implementation of the project must be described. We will examine this aspect of agility in depth in the next chapter.

Linda also insisted on including a section on role distribution, with a note emphasizing that Jan's involvement and participation in phase 2 are essential. After all, he has already demonstrated that he can contribute significant added value to the solution.

7.7 Linda's Notepad

Linda summarizes the extensive findings from day 5 of requirements engineering as follows:

Day 5: Documenting Requirements

Core Competence of the Requirements Engineer: Using Diverse Notations and Artifacts for Documentation

1. *Notations*
    - *Can be either natural language or graphical; UI notations are considered a special case*
    - *Common natural language notations include sentence templates and Gherkin*
2. *Artifacts*
    - *Are the deliverables produced by requirements engineering and contain the documented requirements*
    - *Useful artifacts include:*

- o *Context diagrams for defining system boundaries*
- o *Process models to describe processes*
- o *Use case diagrams and descriptions to specify desired system functionality*
- o *Others: Architecture model, rulebook, state diagrams, activity diagrams, class diagrams*

3. Tips

- *A decision matrix helps to make decisions more objective*
- *AI can assist in creating RfPs*

Conclusion for today: *All requirements are documented*

References

Belton, V., & Stewart, T. J. (2002). *Multiple criteria decision analysis. An integrated approach.* Springer-Science+Business Media, B.V.

Clifton, A., & Ericson, II. (2011). *Concise encyclopedia of system safety: Definition of terms and concepts.* Wiley.

Gartner. Retrieved October 31, 2023 from https://www.gartner.com/peer-insights/home

Miles, R., & Hamilton, K. (2006). *Learning UML 2.0: A pragmatic introduction to UML* (4th ed.). O'Reilly.

Object Management Group. (2023). Decision model and notation. Retrieved from October 31, 2023, from https://www.omg.org/spec/DMN/1.5/Beta1/PDF

The Reuse Company. (2020). SOPHIST master patterns knowledge library. https://www.reusecompany.com/wp-content/uploads/2020/08/SOPHIST-Master-Patterns-Library.pdf

TrustRadius. Retrieved October 31, 2023 from https://www.trustradius.com/

Zangemeister, C. (2014). *Nutzwertanalyse in der Systemtechnik* (5th ed.). Zangemeister & Partner. In German.

8 Day 6: Implementing Requirements in Agile Projects

As the title indicates, this chapter will explore the specifics of agile IT projects from the perspective of requirements engineers. This approach has been the most common method for developing IT solutions for many years (please also note the exceptions described in Sect. 7.4.2) and is now the prevailing working environment for requirements engineers. There are various forms of agile IT projects, including:

- Custom software development
- Software product development and deployment
- System development and implementation (encompassing both hardware and software)

We will explain the upcoming agile project primarily from the perspective of the requirements engineer (RE) and assume a basic understanding of Scrum or other agile methodologies. However, regardless of your previous experience, we are confident that even newcomers to the agile environment will be able to follow the content of this chapter with ease. If you would like to learn more about the reasons for and approaches to agile projects, you can refer to Mike Cohn (Cohn, 2004).

In Sect. 7.5, the management of the Customer Center decided to implement a standard product, based on the decision matrix and in consultation with Linda and Jan. The tender has been finalized and published. For now, it may seem that there is little for them to do until the implementation project begins. But that is not what Linda and Jan have in mind. Instead, they use the time before the proposals arrive to think ahead about the upcoming phase of agile project implementation and to prepare for the process. During this time, Jan invites Linda to learn from his own project experiences.

J. Kawelke and T. Niebisch, *AI-Driven Transformation - Practical Frameworks for Real-World Impact*, Future of Business and Finance,
https://doi.org/10.1007/978-3-662-72549-8_8

Jan	The first part of the project is complete. Even though we referred to this phase as the *pre-project*, it involved much more than simply identifying project prerequisites
Linda	I'm extremely satisfied with the content of the preliminary concept. I can't remember ever having such a clear understanding of our own goals, needs, and requirements at the beginning of an implementation project. That's why I'm confident that we'll be able to handle the second part of the project—the actual implementation—successfully as well
Jan	I can understand your optimism. But even with the purchase of a product and its introduction into the company, there are still plenty of uncertainties ahead. That's why I'd like to use this break before the project starts to prepare ourselves together for the upcoming tasks
Linda	Aren't you exaggerating a bit? Is that much preparation really necessary? As I mentioned, I've already attended training on agile project approaches. The expertise of the product providers, combined with our own methodological knowledge of agile projects, should be enough preparation—don't you think?
Jan	As Goethe's Faust said, "…all theory is grey, my friend…." Training is valuable, but it tends to be very general. Here's how I see it: we should combine what I've learned from previous agile projects with what you picked up in your Scrum training, so we can tailor our knowledge to the introduction of an omni-channel system. I have experience with agile projects, but not specifically in the context of a contact center, and while you know the technical topics inside out, you haven't had much exposure to agile projects. We both have some knowledge gaps, and it's best to address them before the project starts. I also wouldn't depend too much on the product provider
Linda	Alright. Maybe you're right. It probably does make sense to align our ideas before the project actually starts
Jan	To start, I'd like to focus on a factor that's very important to me: the collaboration and overlap between requirements engineering and UI/UX design
Linda	Now you've made me curious—this wasn't covered in the training. I don't really see what UI design has to do with requirements engineering. In the past, whenever we had the budget for a new frontend, we simply hired a design agency to create it for us, and we were always very satisfied with the results
Jan	Absolutely, design agencies do extremely valuable work. We even have our own design team at our consulting firm, and we collaborate with them closely. These UI and UX designers are highly skilled, especially when it comes to creative and innovative topics or leading design thinking workshops (Crilly, 2024). They're often involved in the early stages of IT projects, or they help create cross-project *design systems*—a sort of library of user interface elements that both UI designers and frontend developers use throughout IT projects
Linda	Yes, I've heard of design systems. They help ensure a consistent look and feel across all of a company's IT applications
Jan	Exactly. This consistency helps users quickly find their way around new applications thanks to the familiar look and feel
Linda	But what exactly is a UX designer, and how is that different from a UI designer?

Fig. 8.1 Lack of collaboration between different roles

Jan	Well, to start with, UX stands for User Experience. It refers to the overall feelings and impressions a user has when interacting with a product or service. UX design is the process of creating products or services that provide meaningful and satisfying experiences for users. This can involve various aspects of product development—for example, brand design (Miller, 2025), usability, or functionality UI design, on the other hand, focuses on the actual interface that users interact with. UI designers make sure that every visual element in a product or service contributes to a smooth and positive user experience. While UX designers are primarily concerned with the overall experiences and viewpoints of users—often taking a high-level perspective on the product or service—UI designers focus more on the aesthetics and functionality of the application, often working down to the smallest details
Linda	OK, I understand that. But you still haven't answered my original question. Why should a requirements engineer be involved in design topics at all? Wouldn't it make more sense to leave that to the experts?
Jan	If these design experts are also skilled requirements engineers, then there's nothing wrong with letting them handle it. However, if they create their designs without taking the functional requirements into account, it can lead to a lot of confusion and problems. A good friend of mine once illustrated this with a sketch (see Fig. 8.1): the designers contribute design drafts, the requirements engineers specify the functional and quality requirements as well as constraints, and the developer tries to blend everything together. Too often, it turns out that the ingredients don't really fit—the design doesn't support the intended requirements, the project takes longer than expected, and usability ends up suffering

Linda	That's a very fitting analogy. Now that I think about it, I do remember some project misunderstandings and rework—especially in cases where we hired a design agency separately from requirements engineers. I hadn't realized at the time that these issues might have stemmed from a lack of collaboration between the designers and requirements engineers
Jan	I believe the likelihood is quite high. What you need are requirements engineers who are also familiar with design. They should be able to create screen designs for the user interface, supported by appropriate tools, and still leverage the elements of an existing design system. Alternatively, requirements engineers should work very closely with designers to ensure that requirements and UI design align perfectly in the end.

In addition to the details outlined by Jan, we illustrate our view on the classification of the areas of requirements engineering (RE) and UI/UX design using a Venn diagram, positioned at the intersection of business process analysis, software development, and design (see Fig. 8.2).

Historically, RE was primarily associated with software and system development, but in recent years, it has increasingly incorporated aspects of design. Requirements engineers now work closely with UI and UX designers in software development projects, particularly when a frontend interface is to be developed—assuming the project involves more than purely backend tasks.

It is also important to note that the topic of design extends far beyond UI and UX design alone, encompassing many other sub-areas. For example, service design effectively covers the interface between design and business process analysis. However, a more in-depth treatment of this broader design landscape would go beyond the scope of this book. If you are interested in exploring this further, we recommend consulting specialized literature on the subject (Norman, 2016).

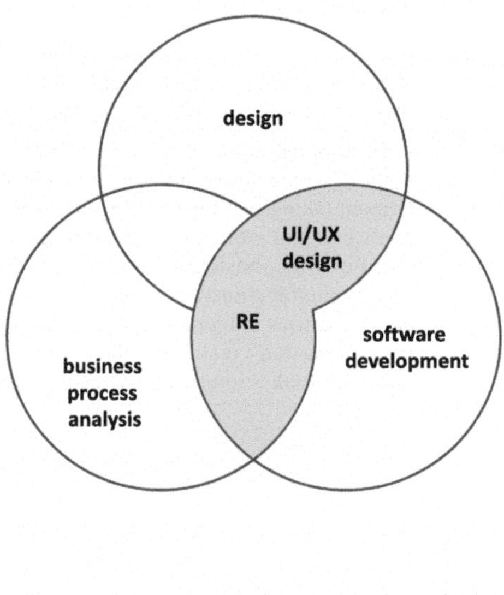

Fig. 8.2 Venn diagram for the classification of RE and UI/UX design

Jan It looks like we've delved into the world of agile projects more quickly than anticipated.

Linda You've really sparked my curiosity again, and I must admit I felt so well prepared through the training... How do you envision our next steps for coordination?

Jan After emphasizing the importance of UI and UX design in agile projects, here is my proposed plan:

- First, I would like to expand our existing set of notations and artifacts to include those that are particularly effective in the context of agile projects. We'll identify which artifacts we should have ready for the implementation phase beyond the ones we already know
- One of these artifacts is the user story. In the agile environment, it has a dual significance. We should become aware of this potential ambiguity
- Finally, I suggest we focus on the core of the agile approach itself. We will examine the sprint structure, simulate how sprints could be executed in our project, and determine what information and artifacts will be required to support them effectively

To the Point

In agile projects, RE and UI/UX design are closely intertwined and mutually reinforcing.◄

8.1 Incorporate Further Notations and Artifacts

We will begin with artifacts that sit at the intersection of requirements engineering (RE) and UI/UX design. An (incomplete) list of the key elements that distinguish and connect these artifacts can be found in Table 8.1. Many artifacts were already listed in Fig. 7.4; now, we will revisit them along with a selection of relevant methods for closer examination.

Tab. 8.1 Differences and similarities between RE and UI/UX design

	RE	RE + UI/UX design	UI/UX design
Methods	Modeling RE System Archaeology	UI Design Workshop Interview Requirement Validation Usability Testing	Design Thinking Eye Tracking A/B Testing Design Patterns
Artifacts	User Story Gherkin Scenarios Context Diagram Quality Requirements Boundary Conditions Conceptual Model	User Persona User Journey Map Wireframes Mockups Prototypes Navigation Flow	Empathy Map Engagement Report

When considering the significance of these artifacts for the collaboration between the two disciplines, we would like to highlight the following points:

- Requirement artifacts:
  - Describe the functional requirements verbally and through models,
  - Serve as the foundation for the design,
  - Are refined collaboratively with the design team.
- Design artifacts:
  - Visualize functional requirements,
  - Support the ongoing collection and refinement of requirements,
  - Provide a basis for discussions with stakeholders from the respective departments.

In the previous chapters, we discussed various forms of notation and their representative examples. To recap: we distinguished between natural language notation and model-based notation. The focus of natural language notation was on template-based documentation approaches, particularly sentence templates. As representatives of model-based notation, we considered various diagrams from modeling languages such as UML and BPMN.

In this section, we aim to introduce additional representatives of both template-based and model-based notation, whose strengths are especially valuable in agile projects. Unlike traditional development projects, agile approaches aim to deliver working software or integrated components of a product at a very early stage. Consequently, alongside requirements specification, solution design also plays a pivotal role.

The artifacts described below are particularly well-suited—due to their syntax and semantics—to navigating the delicate balance between requirement specification and solution design.

8.1.1 User Journey Map

Jan: At the very start of developing our rough concept, we placed our planned system—the *Contact Center*—in its broader context (see Sect. 5.4). We created a high-level overview, or big picture, from which we assumed that the key elements and relationships of the *Contact Center reorganization* task are represented at a very abstract, high-level view.

Linda: I remember; that's my project mandate.

Jan: In addition to this high-level overview, I'd like to introduce you to another artifact. Its origins are neither in requirements engineering nor in UI/UX design; perhaps you've already encountered it in the marketing field. We're talking about a User Journey Map. I find it particularly useful for the task at hand

Linda: Doesn't ring a bell.

Jan The User Journey Map is a tool that helps to organize and visualize assumptions about the typical lifecycle of an insurance customer. It involves adopting the perspective of specific people or customer segments, known as personas, and simulating their journey through the insurance process. The goal is to gain a detailed understanding of what can happen to the customer, including the tasks they perform, the touchpoints they encounter with the insurance company (see Fig. 8.3), and their feelings throughout the process.

Linda That doesn't seem too complicated.

Jan In our example, I kept things quite simple. We only used one persona—the existing customer—without further differentiating by age, gender, or technical preferences. Also, we didn't map the entire customer lifecycle. For this particular journey map, I focused on the claims process for existing customers. What can you see in the figure?

- There are various touchpoints between the customer and your company. People are often unaware of these touchpoints, but they are exactly the moments when customers might become frustrated or when competitors could offer a better experience
- At the very bottom, I started noting the potential pain points at each touchpoint. These obstacles can be organizational (for example, always having a different contact person) or technical (such as media disruptions or missing functionalities). If we know about these issues, we can try to address them as much as possible during the implementation project
- As additional information, I recorded which communication channels are used at each touchpoint

With this user journey map, we're able to examine and optimize both the pain points and the communication channels separately for each touchpoint. In my opinion, this serves as an excellent starting point for further analysis

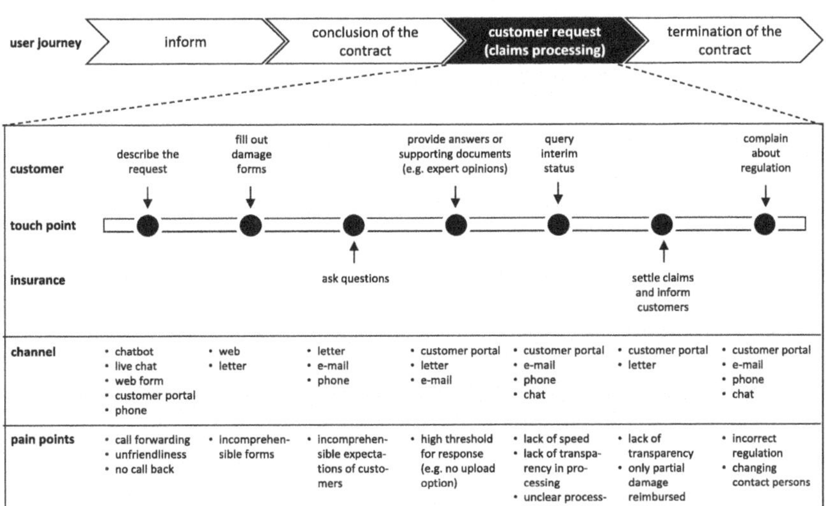

Fig. 8.3 Simplified example of a user journey map

Linda I really like this artifact. But is it actually specific to agile projects? We could have created a User Journey Map much earlier in the process

Jan I can't get anything past you, Linda *(Jan grins and shakes his head).* You're absolutely right—it's an artifact that operates at a fairly high level of abstraction. We could have created the User Journey Map as part of the rough concept. On the other hand, it does already reveal some potential solution aspects. That's why I wanted to save it for when we're discussing the connections between requirements engineering and design

Linda You really have a talent for teaching… I'd actually like to create this kind of User Journey Map together with my colleagues—and not just for claims processing. It's a great method to capture my agents' extensive expertise on specific customer situations in a structured way and, when we identify pain points, to look for possible solutions. We'd be able to walk through each touchpoint step by step

Jan That's exactly what I would have suggested. You can start this form of project preparation independently of the software product that will eventually be selected. But regardless of the approach—whether you use a User Journey Map or the Use Case method from the rough concept—in the end, you'll need to break things down further and derive more granular requirements for the agile project. You can formulate these using the notations we've already discussed. In addition, I'd like to broaden your toolkit a bit and recommend the artifacts *Epic, Feature*, and *User Story* as next steps

To the Point
The User Journey Map provides a valuable big-picture perspective and can significantly enhance understanding from the user's point of view. ◄

8.1.2 Epic, Feature, and User Story

Let us briefly recap: During the development of the rough concept, we relied primarily on use cases for requirements specification. Use cases provide a high-level overview of the entire functionality of a system. However, in an agile project, these functionalities must be further decomposed so that each sprint delivers a working increment of the overall system.

As in previous chapters, we will now let our two protagonists, Linda and Jan, discuss this topic in dialogue form.

Linda Tell me, how do we move from our use case level or the user journey to a scope that we can actually implement within agile sprints?

Jan Let me explain using the example of Use Cases: The inventor of Use Cases, Ivar Jacobson, addressed this challenge with his agile method—the *Essential Unified Process* (EssUP) (Jacobson et al., 2019)—by applying what he calls "slicing" (Slicing of Use Cases: Refers to dividing or cutting of use cases to get them to a manageable size for an agile sprint.) to Use Cases. However, in *Scrum*, which is much more widely used, we've had good experiences by breaking down Use Cases into Epics, Features, and more detailed User Stories

Linda For my sake, could you please go through that slowly again, without mixing up all the terms? First of all: What exactly do you mean by those three artifacts?

Jan You're right, I should explain these terms more clearly. All three artifacts are essentially text-based, and their primary difference lies in the level of detail with which they describe a requirement

- *Epics* are broad, high-level stories that keep the overall solution in view and can be broken down further in subsequent steps
- *Features* are somewhat more detailed than epics and represent specific aspects or capabilities of the solution
- *User Stories* are the smallest of the three; they formulate individual requirements from the perspective of a particular user role

In our experience, most use cases can be mapped directly to epics. These epics are then divided into smaller features—similar to the "slicing" technique from the Essential Unified Process. User stories provide another level of detail, representing further refinement of features

If we were to visualize the relationships among these four artifacts using a UML class diagram (see Sect. 3.2), it would appear as shown in Fig. 8.4

Linda OK, I understand the principle. But how can I formulate Epics, Features, and User Stories as clearly and accurately as possible?

Jan To describe requirements in these three new artifact types, a template-based documentation method is especially useful: the User Story format, which has been around even before the Agile Manifesto:

As a < stakeholder > , I want < function > , so that < result >

Although the name suggests that this template is used exclusively for User Stories, it is also commonly applied to Epics and Features. Of course, the level of detail for functions and results will vary depending on whether you're writing an Epic, a Feature, or a User Story. For User Stories specifically, the stakeholder is generally the user, so the template looks like this:

As a < user > , I want < function > , so that < result >

Linda I'd understand it even better if you could give me some concrete examples from our project context

Jan Of course, I can do that. As a starting point, I used the "Handling Customer Concerns" use case, which we discussed in our workshops and which is represented in our Use Case diagram (see Fig. 8.6). From this use case, I derived suitable Epics, Features, and User Stories as examples. In Fig. 8.5, you can see both the textual formulation of these examples and the relationships between the different levels of granularity, which illustrate the concept of *vertical traceability* mentioned earlier (see Sect. 7.2)

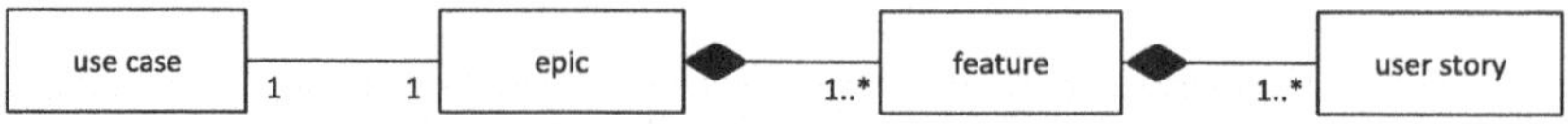

Fig. 8.4 Breaking down use cases in agile projects

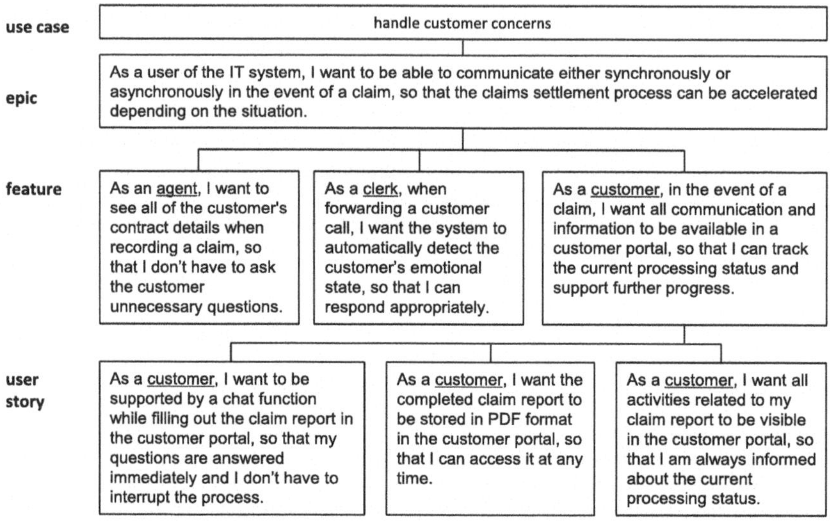

Fig. 8.5 Exemplary relationship of use case, epic, feature and user story

For the successful implementation of user stories within a sprint, it is essential not to rely solely on the template-based sentence format. Instead, user stories should be supplemented with additional information. The various options available for providing this supplementary information will be discussed in Sect. 8.2.

First, however, we will examine three graphical artifacts that can assist us in formulating requirements for UI design.

8.1.3 Wireframe, Mockup, and Prototype

UI design—that is, the design of the user interfaces of an IT system—falls clearly within the domain of solution design. Product owners and other stakeholders can use the following visual artifacts to further refine or adapt their existing business requirements to the specific application.

These artifacts can vary greatly in their level of detail. The spectrum ranges from simplified sketches of the essential design elements (*low-fidelity design*) to highly detailed representations that express the finest graphic nuances (*high-fidelity design*).

The simplest way to capture personal ideas is with a *wireframe*. A wireframe is a basic graphical representation of the structure of a single screen, such as a website. The primary focus is on layout and content, without significant attention to detailed visual elements. Wireframes facilitate the planning of the screen's structure and content. They are often created quickly using pencil and paper. Figure 8.6 shows a low-fidelity wireframe example, which already incorporates requirements from the previously discussed user stories.

More detailed requirements can be visualized using *mockups*. Mockups are static models of a website or IT application in which colors, images, and other graphical elements are incorporated. Figure 8.7 provides an example of a high-fidelity mockup.

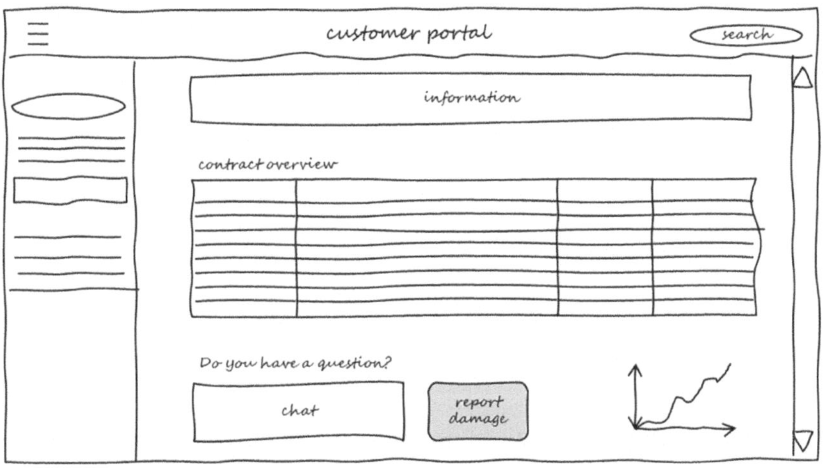

Fig. 8.6 Example of a wireframe

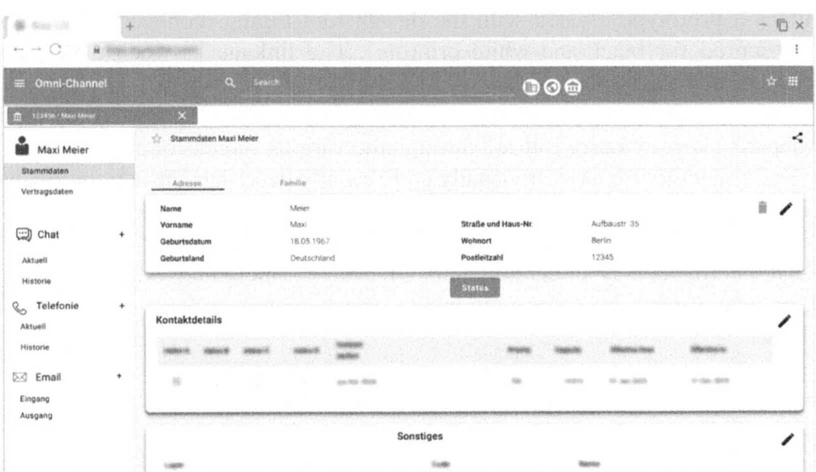

Fig. 8.7 Example of a high-fidelity mockup

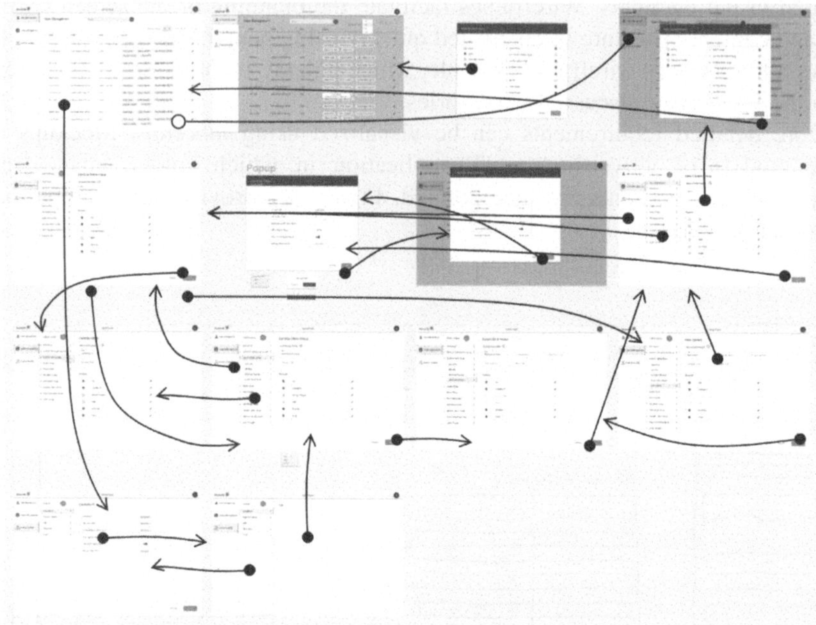

Fig. 8.8 Prototype in Figma

To represent the functionality of an application, the design process must go one step further by creating a prototype. *Prototypes* are interactive models of an application that consist of mockups of various screens or webpages, showcasing how these elements interact during specific user actions. Prototypes enable requirements engineers and designers to test and enhance the user experience. Figure 8.8 illustrates a prototype created with the design tool Figma (connection lines have been obscured for black-and-white printing). The linkage between the different screens can be clearly observed.

Closely related to prototypes is the concept of *navigation flow*. A navigation flow depicts the path a user follows through the various screens of an application to complete a specific use case. It visually and verbally describes the actions available to a user and the possible outcomes of those actions.

Having established the fundamentals of UI design, Chapter 15 examines how artificial intelligence is integrated into UI design—including AI-driven plugins in tools like Figma—to boost efficiency, spark creativity, and refine the user experience.

8.1.4 UML Activity Diagram

In this section, we will once again let our protagonists speak. When Jan mentioned UML activity diagrams as valuable artifacts, Linda became attentive.

Linda So now you want to introduce the last UML diagram that you consider important, even though we've already gone through the BPMN process diagrams in detail?

Jan Yes, because I believe that activity diagrams are much easier to learn and understand than BPMN process diagrams. While both types of diagrams are generally applicable, I tend to use activity diagrams more often to describe internal system processes, whereas I use BPMN diagrams for visualizing broader business processes
When I review user stories with stakeholders in walkthroughs, I've found activity diagrams to be extremely effective. Stakeholders are able to quickly grasp the flow of processes represented in the diagram

Linda So, does that mean you expect an activity diagram to be created for every user story?

Jan No, not necessarily. Some user stories might only involve configuring or providing a single screen, where a process description isn't needed. However, in some cases, it can make sense to create a diagram at the feature level

Linda Ah, I see… so you have to be very flexible depending on the situation. Then let's take a look at an activity diagram, so I won't have any trouble getting started with the implementation project

Jan Okay then, let's review our previous artifacts. Let's focus on the requirements of the clerk at the feature level (see Fig. 8.5). Below is an initial draft of how an activity diagram derived from those requirements could look (see Fig. 8.9)

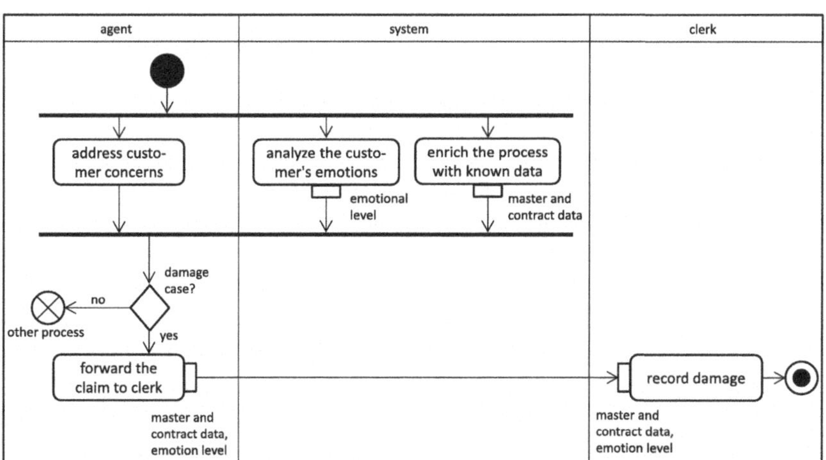

Fig. 8.9 Example of a UML activity diagram

Linda I understand the actions, and I recognize the three swimlanes for agent, system, and clerk. I also remember seeing the diamond symbol in state diagrams. But what are these boxes attached to the actions, and what do the thick bars represent?

Jan The boxes are called *pins*. They represent input or output parameters and data for the respective actions

Linda Ah, I see—that's how you read them. The master data and contract data are supplied and then passed on to the clerk for recording the claim

Jan Exactly, and the same goes for the customer's emotional state as determined by AI. Depending on this, the clerk can interact with the customer in a more or less sensitive manner

Linda That's a great feature. Sometimes you feel like you need a psychology degree to handle upset customers—so it's even better if you get some technical support with that assessment

Jan then explains the 'bars': These are parallelization and synchronization nodes. Within these two nodes, the order in which actions are performed is not fixed—they run in parallel or at least independently from each other. However, it's important to note that the first action after the synchronization node can only be executed once all actions between the parallelization and synchronization nodes have been completed.

The circle with the cross, on the other hand, is a flow end node. In our case, it marks the end of a path that we are not continuing here. This path could be further developed or continued in another activity diagram.

Jan I'd like to say a few words about the diamond you mentioned. This is called a *decision node*—some also refer to it as a branch node. It's usually paired with a merge node to bring two branches or control flows back together. You can see what that looks like in the sketch I made in Fig. 8.10

Linda Is this merge node absolutely necessary?

Jan You could also merge the two branches in a subsequent action, but I find it clearer to use the merge node. It makes it easier for less experienced readers to see exactly where the paths come back together. Using the two diamonds as a pair is like using opening and closing brackets in a text

Linda I can imagine that if there are a lot of branches, the number of elements in the diagram could quickly get out of hand because of all the merge nodes

Jan That's true. You always have to strike a balance between strictly following the syntax and keeping the diagram clear and understandable

With this, Jan has now explained the last diagram relevant to requirements engineering for his client. Another type of diagram—the UML sequence diagram—will not be used in this project, but can be helpful in other situations. Sequence diagrams are especially useful when you want to model specific scenarios within a process flow, particularly the interactions between actors or IT systems.

UML is a powerful language with a wide variety of diagram types. We have introduced the ones that are essential for our needs. Beyond this selection, UML

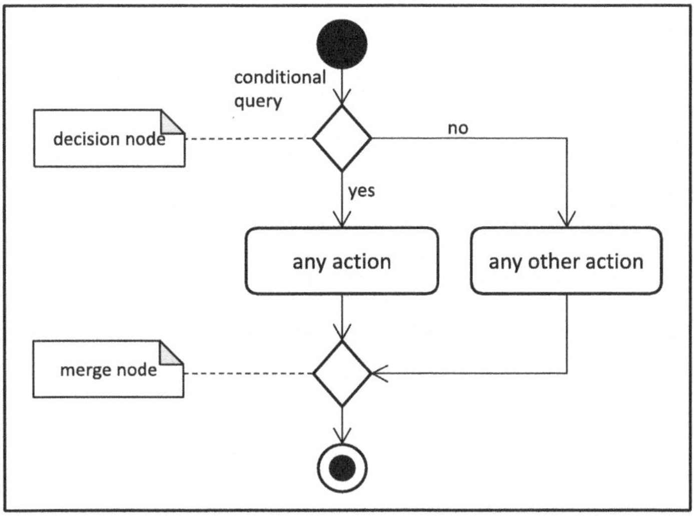

Fig. 8.10 Branching and joining nodes

also addresses the requirements of many other technical disciplines. If you are especially curious and would like to explore the possibilities of UML further, there is a wealth of specialized literature available for deeper study (Michael Jesse Chonoles, 2017).

8.1.5 Acceptance Criteria in Gherkin Format

Let's mentally revisit Sect. 8.1.2, where we introduced the user story as an artifact that captures requirements from users and other stakeholders in a highly detailed way. Closely tied to recording these requirements is the question of how they will be accepted and validated. We will explore this topic in the current section and take a closer look at the template-based notation known as Gherkin.

Unlike the sentence template introduced earlier as a form of template-based notation (see Sect. 7.1.2), acceptance criteria written in Gherkin can be automatically executed—provided they are supplemented with source code—using appropriate test automation tools. How does Jan explain this?

Jan	When it comes to specification in agile projects, I don't think you can avoid Gherkin anymore
Linda	Well, you'll have to explain what agile projects have to do with pickles
Jan	*(grins)* Gherkin is actually the name of a domain-specific language, abbreviated as DSL. We use this language to create acceptance criteria for user stories. Gherkin allows you to break down acceptance criteria into small, easily understandable pieces. Both business stakeholders and developers can understand them

Linda Is a DSL kind of like a programming language, with lots of reserved words?

Jan Exactly. The nice thing is that Gherkin only has a few of these reserved words. This simplicity means we can learn the language much faster than a typical programming language. Let's start with the four most important reserved words: Given, When, And, and Then.

Linda Then please give me an example, so I can better understand how it works

Jan Sure, I'd be happy to. Here's a simple scenario from everyday life:

```
Given my account balance is $500
When I withdraw $100 from an ATM
Then my account balance is $400
```

Linda That's pretty straightforward. What would a scenario from our environment look like—say, when an agent forwards a customer call to a clerk?

Jan How about this:

```
Given the upset customer Emily Thompson has contacted our
agent Oliver Smith by phone via the hotline
And Ms. Thompson wants to report a motor liability claim
after a self-inflicted accident
When Oliver Smith forwards the call to me as a clerk
Then I see Ms. Thompson's emotion level, 4 out of 5,
displayed on my screen.
```

Linda Wow, that's a very specific scenario written in language that's easy to understand

Jan Exactly, Linda

And the word **`Scenario`** which you just used instinctively, is actually another reserved word in Gherkin. It serves as a headline to introduce your scenario. Unlike the other reserved words, it's used with a colon. In our case, it would look like this:

```
Scenario: Display of the emotion level of an upset
customer after forwarding from the agent to the clerk
```

Linda That makes sense. So, am I right in thinking that everything after **`Given`** and before **`When`** describes the preconditions or the system state before a specific action takes place?

Jan Yes, exactly. Well spotted. After **`When`** comes the actual action, and after **`Then`** you describe the system state or the system's reaction to that action. You can see a summary of how these keywords are used in Table 8.2

Linda This is very similar to the structure of a test case

Table 8.2 Reserved words in Gherkin

Reserved word	Description
Given	Description of the initial situation
When	Description of the action performed by the actor
Then	Description of the expected result
And	Linking of several initial situations, actions or expected results

Jan Yes, exactly. Acceptance criteria are meant to serve as the link between the specification of a user story and the acceptance test cases

Linda But doesn't that mean we're describing everything three times—first in the user story refinement, then in the acceptance criteria, and finally in the test cases?

Jan It may seem that way at first… *(pauses and thinks for a moment).* On closer inspection, I can think of few strong counterarguments against comparing Gherkin acceptance criteria to acceptance test cases. To explain, I have to give a little preview: In agile projects, user stories actually take on a second function, which we'll discuss later (see Sect. 8.2). In short, they're enriched and refined with additional information. Different notation forms are used to examine user stories from multiple angles, so the developer gains a thorough understanding
An acceptance criterion defines the conditions under which a user story is considered implemented. If I use Gherkin to do this, with very specific example data, it isn't just a duplication of the user story refinement. But—and here I have to agree with you—I am definitely getting close to test cases
Now, regarding the differences: Gherkin only describes positive scenarios. For a complete set of acceptance test cases, you also need cases that specify what should *not* happen. Gherkin doesn't cover those

To the Point
Gherkin acceptance criteria can be used directly as manual acceptance test cases if concrete example data is included in the scenarios. However, for complete test coverage, these should be supplemented with negative test cases. ◄

To highlight the difference between Gherkin scenarios with and without example data, we would like to present the previous ATM scenario again—this time without specific example data:

```
Scenario: Withdraw Money
Given my account balance is positive
When I withdraw money from the ATM
Then my account balance is reduced by the withdrawn amount.
```

In this more general form, Gherkin can also be used as part of a user story refinement. However, as an acceptance criterion or test case, this scenario is not meaningful because it lacks concrete test data.

Linda I'm curious what the agile gurus and test experts would say about the bold claim that creating separate acceptance test cases is almost unnecessary when you have Gherkin scenarios. As a requirements engineer, you're taking away part of their work!

Jan I don't think the test experts will be out of a job because of this. On the contrary, they still have to take care of other test types, such as integration tests, system tests, and failure tests. Also, I wouldn't say that only requirements engineers should define the Gherkin acceptance criteria—the responsibility could just as easily lie with the test analyst. As we'll see later, Gherkin also opens up additional opportunities where the more technical test experts will play a significant role
Our discussion also highlights how closely the different roles in an agile project team are connected. If we look at the software development section of the Venn diagram in Fig. 8.2, we could easily add testing to it as another important element (see Fig. 8.11)

Fig. 8.11 Overlap of different disciplines in agile software development

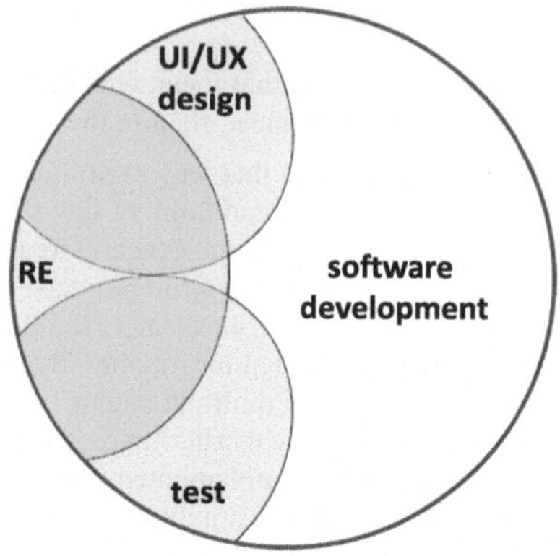

Linda	I don't see any overlap between testing and UI/UX design. Is that really the case, or is it just the way the diagram is drawn?
Jan	As is often the case, there are different perspectives. In this instance, I intentionally chose to present it this way. Of course, there is usability testing, but I consider that a part of UX design rather than general software testing
Linda	And the unmarked part of the circle represents the areas handled by developers and architects, right?
Jan	Yes, that's right. But software development involves many roles—not just developers and architects, but also roles like the Scrum Master. Depending on the nature of the project, there may be additional specialists involved as well, such as analytics, database, or migration experts. That's why the size of the areas in Fig.8.11 doesn't represent the scope or workload of any particular role
Linda	OK. But back to Gherkin—since we're on the topic, could you introduce me to some more language elements of Gherkin?

Jan selects more reserved words and characters that are frequently used and explains them (Table 8.3).

We would like to illustrate the most recently introduced Gherkin elements using two examples. As a starting point, we refer to the user story presented in Fig. 8.5: *'As a customer, I want all activities related to my claim report to be visible in the customer portal, so that I am always informed about the current processing status.'* For this user story, multiple acceptance criteria are formulated in Gherkin.

Example 1 Includes: Feature, Scenario Outline, Pipe, Variable, and Examples

In this example, the portal user wishes to send a message regarding their claim from within the customer portal to the insurance company. Since this contact activity can occur for various reasons and with different data sets, a scenario outline is used to describe the template. The user must select the corresponding claim number and specify a contact reason (e.g., change of master data, provide evidence, respond to inquiries, etc.).

Table 8.3 Further reserved words from Gherkin

Reserved word or character (English)	Description
`Feature:`	Acts as a heading for a group of related scenarios. It typically provides a high-level description or a summary of functionality, and could, for example, represent a user story *Note:* This use of "Feature" refers specifically to Gherkin syntax and should not be confused with a "feature" as it appears in the Product Backlog in agile methodologies
`Examples:`	Used as a heading for a data table in Gherkin. The table is separated by pipes (|) and includes a header row followed by one or more rows of data. Data tables under "Examples" allow you to insert multiple sets of example data into a scenario, enabling the same scenario to be tested with different inputs
`Scenario Outline:`	Used when you want to run the same scenario multiple times with different sets of data. The "Scenario Outline" works together with the "Examples" table, allowing you to define a scenario template that will be executed once for each data set provided
| (Pipe)	A vertical bar used as the separator in a data table. Pipes are used to separate columns in the header and each data row within tables in Gherkin scenarios
<> (Angle brackets)	Brackets used to denote a parameter or variable in Gherkin. Within a scenario outline, terms inside angle brackets are placeholders that will be replaced by the corresponding values from the Examples table during execution
# (Hash)	Used at the beginning of a line to add comments in Gherkin. Any text following a "#" symbol on the same line is treated as a comment and ignored during execution. Comments are useful for providing explanations or notes within your Gherkin scenarios
`Background:`	Defines a set of steps that are executed before each scenario in a feature. The "Background" section is used to describe common preconditions that apply to all scenarios within that feature, helping to avoid repetition and make scenarios easier to read
"""""" (Triple Quotes)	Denotes a "Doc String" in Gherkin. This is used to attach a longer block of text to a step definition, allowing for the inclusion of detailed descriptions, multi-line data, or examples within a scenario step. The Doc String begins and ends with triple double quotes

```
Feature: Send message to insurance company

Scenario: Customer logs into the customer portal
  Given the login page of the customer portal is open
  And the correct username and password are entered
  When the customer clicks on "OK"
  Then their personal page in the customer portal opens

Scenario Outline: Initiate contact
  Given the customer's personal page in the customer portal is
open
  And a claim number has been selected <boolNo>
  And a contact reason has been selected <boolAnlass>
  And a message has been entered
  When the user clicks "Send"
  Then the contact request is sent <boolSende>

Examples:
  | boolNo | boolReason | boolSend |
  | false  | false      | false    |
  | false  | true       | false    |
  | true   | false      | false    |
  | true   | true       | true     |
```

Example 2 Includes: Background, Triple Quotes, and Hash

This second example builds on the previous one by presenting the initial scenario as a background. Every subsequent scenario or scenario outline within the feature requires the same precondition: mandatory login to the customer portal. By specifying this precondition in the "Background" section, there is no need to repeat the corresponding "Given" steps in each scenario. The scenarios do not necessarily need to follow a particular business process but can be executed independently, each starting from the background context.

Furthermore, a specific text within the message is included using a doc string (“"”), and a comment is added using the hash symbol (#).

```
Feature: Send message to insurance company

Background: Customer logs into the customer portal
  Given the login page of the customer portal is open
  And the correct username and password for the customer are
entered
  When the customer clicks on "OK"
```

```
    Then their personal page in the customer portal opens

  Scenario Outline: Initiate contact
    Given a claim number has been selected <boolNo>
    And a contact reason has been selected <boolReason>
    And the following text has been entered
      """
      Dear Sir or Madam,
      I am sending you the requested documents for the above claim
  number in the attachment.
      Best regards,
      Your John Smith
      """
    When the customer clicks "Send"
    Then the contact request is sent <boolSend>

  Examples:
    | boolNo | boolReason | boolSend |
    | false  | false      | false    |
    | false  | true       | false    |
    | true   | false      | false    |
    | true   | true       | true     |

  # Jump in the business process, but the background remains
  effective
  Scenario: Check the status of the claim report
    Given the customer has already sent a claim report
    When the customer clicks on "My claim reports"
    Then the customer sees a list of their claim reports
    And the current status is displayed for each claim report

  # Background is still valid
  Scenario: Report additional accident participants
    Given a claim number has been selected
    And a contact reason has been selected
    When the customer reports additional accident participants with
  these data
     # data tables can be used without the Examples reserved word
     | First name | Last name | Birthday   | Insurance   | Ins-No.   |
     | Emma       | Brown     | 01/01/1991 | V-Direct    | AB-123-WW |
     | William    | Taylor    | 02/02/1992 | AutoSecure  | XY-2E-35  |
     | Oliver     | Smith     | 03/03/1993 | BestInsure  | 234-FGH-7 |
    Then the system saves this data
    And sends a message to the agent's mailbox
```

Note: The data table provided here represents only a subset of the information required for actual claim processing.

Linda You know what I noticed? You only used **And** in the **Given** and **Then** steps. Can't you also have multiple user actions with **When** steps in one scenario?

Jan — First of all, good observation, Linda. It is fundamentally allowed to define multiple actions within one scenario and link them with **And**. However, each user action typically has its own corresponding system reaction. If you chain several actions together with **And**, only the outcome of the last action can be directly tested with the **Then** step. Here's an example:

```
Scenario: Upload report
Given my personal page in the customer portal is open
When I choose the option "Upload report"
And I select the report file from my local drive
And I upload the report
Then a new report icon is displayed in the report frame.
```

The first two actions after `When` are not directly tested; they are simply assumed to have taken place. Only the result of the final action is validated in the **Then** step

Linda — You're right—every user action would really need its own **Then** step in order to be properly tested

Based on the previous descriptions, at least three key principles can be summarized.

To the Point

Best Practices for Documenting Gherkin Acceptance Criteria:

1. Use concrete data to ensure that scenarios can serve directly as test cases.
2. Utilize data tables to execute the same scenarios multiple times with different data sets.
3. Specify atomic user actions so that each action can be independently tested. ◄

Linda — That was really helpful—I've learned a lot, thank you! But do requirements engineers and test analysts really need to master Gherkin themselves, or can AI just do this for them nowadays?

Jan — Modern AI language models are now capable of handling Gherkin. However, if you work with normal AI chatbots, then prompt engineering can become a challenge due to the diversity of input data. The input could include:

- The user story in its function as a rough requirement (see Sect. 8.1.2)
- The user story as a sprint backlog item (see Sect. 8.2), which, as we'll see shortly, can contain various textual and model-based elements
- Potentially, the UI design (see Sect. 8.1.3)

A substantial amount of prompt engineering experience is needed to convey all this input clearly and to obtain a satisfactory result

Linda — And what about the sample data?

Jan: The sample data comes into play later in the process. I would approach this by using what's called a prompt chain: a sequence of prompts, each building on the output of the previous step. Here's how it might work:

1. You provide the initial input as described earlier, and ask the AI chatbot to suggest possible scenarios—just the headlines for the Gherkin statements. These headlines may still need to be manually reviewed or adjusted
2. For each of these scenarios, you supply the sample data—or, in test expert terms, the test data. Alternatively, you can have the AI chatbot generate suggestions for test data, which you then review and adapt as needed
3. Finally, using the scenario headlines and the test data, you let the AI chatbot generate the full scenarios in Gherkin format. These, too, may require manual review and correction

This stepwise approach helps ensure that both the scenarios and the associated sample data are accurate and meaningful

Linda: So, a lot of human intelligence is still necessary after all

Jan: Yes, one should weigh on a case-by-case basis whether the effort of integrating AI is worthwhile. I would always recommend the attempt. Experimenting with AI also has a gamification effect. Werbach and Hunter (2021) In this way, one quickly learns the tricks of prompt engineering

Linda: Earlier you said "if you work with normal chatbots." What is the alternative?

Jan: That's a great question, Linda. When I said "normal chatbots," I was referring to AI systems that respond to prompts without maintaining much context or autonomy. The alternative—and this is where things get really exciting—is *Agentic AI*

Agentic AI systems are designed to operate more like autonomous collaborators. They can:

- Maintain context over multiple steps
- Plan and execute sequences of actions—like a prompt chain, but self-directed
- Interact with tools or APIs to gather data, validate assumptions, or even update requirements
- Reflect and revise their own outputs based on feedback or new information

In the context of requirements engineering and Gherkin, this means an agentic AI could:

1. Parse a user story, UI mockup, and acceptance criteria from a shared workspace or repository
2. Generate scenario headlines, then proactively ask for clarification or missing data
3. Suggest test data based on domain knowledge or previous examples
4. Iterate on Gherkin scenarios, incorporating feedback from a human reviewer or even a test execution report

So instead of you manually guiding the AI through each step, the agent can take initiative. Of course, this still requires oversight. But the cognitive load shifts from micromanaging the AI to *collaborating with it*. That's a big leap forward.

Linda: Every time I feel like I'm finally up to speed, you open another door and reveal I'm still in the hallway!

Jan: I totally get that, Linda. I'm doing my best to avoid overwhelming you with too much information at once. Instead, I try to introduce new developments when they're most relevant to the task we're working on.

By the way, with Gherkin we have covered the last of the notation forms I wanted to introduce to you. Now we can put the puzzle pieces together and look at the entirety of the refinement possibilities of a user story.

We'll explore Agentic AI in more detail in Chapters 11 and 14.

8.2 Using User Story as a Sprint Backlog Item

This section addresses a break in logic and a verbal ambiguity that has developed in real-world practice and could lead to confusion.

We have repeatedly highlighted the ambiguity of the term *User Story*. Of course, it is known as a template-based formulation of user requirements (see Sect. 8.1.2). However, within the Scrum framework, "User Story" has taken on an additional meaning: it now also refers to the individual work items, or performance bundles, to be implemented during a sprint. But how should this be understood?

In principle, all requirements—regardless of their level of detail—are first captured in a *Product Backlog*. These items are subsequently refined until they exist as User Stories within the Product Backlog. The development team then selects User Stories from this backlog to assemble the scope of work for a specific sprint. Each sprint consists of one or more User Stories that are managed together in the *Sprint Backlog*.

Such a performance bundle requires more than just a single User Story sentence, as discussed in Sect.8.1.2. Rather, it must be accompanied by more extensive descriptions. Jan will now explain this further in his own words.

Jan	We have learned about many artifacts and notations that can be used to document requirements in a variety of ways. Previously, we distinguished between text-based, graphical, and UI-related artifacts. Each of these artifacts can contribute to describing a work package to be implemented—let's call it a *Sprint Backlog Item*, or simply a *User Story* I think it's helpful to now summarize all available options. In my view, a fully refined and well-formulated User Story should include the following elements: • An introductory sentence in User Story format, • UI design requirements and solution ideas, provided as wireframes, mockups, prototypes, or navigation flows, • Detailed textual descriptions, such as data value ranges for specific fields, expected system behavior for valid or invalid inputs, and descriptions of switching elements or permission settings, • Model-based specifications, such as activity or state diagrams, and—if new terminology is introduced—a reference to the conceptual model, • Technical solution details (developed in collaboration with technical architects), • Acceptance criteria, preferably in Gherkin format and including relevant test data These elements collectively help ensure that the User Story is both clearly understood and ready for implementation
Linda	Wow, that's quite a lot to put together. Isn't that too much effort for just a single User Story?
Jan	In most cases, I would agree with you, it's definitely a lot of effort (laughs). Even the Agile Manifesto recommends valuing "working software over comprehensive documentation." How much detail I, as a requirements engineer, need to go into really depends on many factors. It takes some experience to judge whether the effort invested is worthwhile. On one hand, every additional hour spent refining a User Story costs money. On the other hand, missing details or misunderstandings can lead to solutions that don't meet the needs, and fixing those issues later can become much more expensive
Linda	I remember you already explained the consequences of gaps, errors, or ambiguous specifications to me (see Sect. 2.3.4). But could you share your own experiences? Under what circumstances would you accept compromises?

Jan Basically, I can reduce the level of detail in the refinement if the technical background is not very complex or if the development team has been collaborating in the project context for a long time and is well coordinated
Similarly, a very detailed specification can often be skipped if the Product Owner and requirements engineers are highly accessible during the implementation sprint and can answer questions quickly. From a technical perspective, effort can also be saved: for example, if I want to give the frontend developer more creative freedom—especially if they are already working within strict constraints set by a design system—then a simple wireframe may suffice
On the other hand, there are industries with strict regulatory requirements for specifications, and these may differ from the approach I've outlined

Linda OK, so your list is really more of a recommendation with a lot of *it depends*, right?

Jan Exactly, Linda. As a bonus, I've summarized all my explanations in a graphic (see Fig. 8.12), hoping that the connections are clearer this way. At the very least, it should help you understand the pathway we discussed—from Use Cases or the User Journey Map all the way to extensively described Sprint Backlog Items in the form of User Stories

To the Point
The User Story serves as a Sprint Backlog Item, bundling together a multitude of requirements and their corresponding acceptance criteria.◂

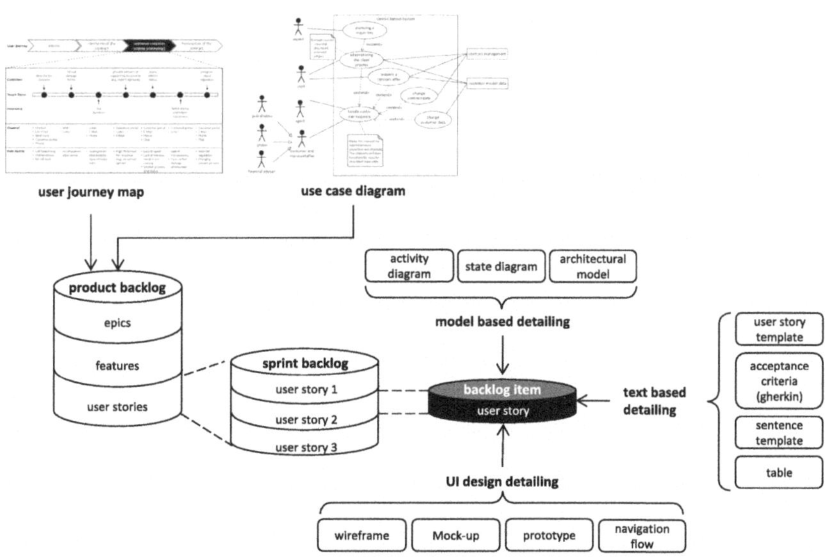

Fig. 8.12 Relationships of the user story as backlog item

8.3 Working Together in Agile Sprints

Linda That all sounds good, and you've explained a lot of foundational knowledge and how it all connects, Jan. But how is the creation of design artifacts and the refinement of User Stories actually organized in an agile project? Does it all take place in the same sprint when the developers are implementing the User Story?

Jan No, I wouldn't schedule all of that in a single sprint. I'd actually plan for two sprints to fully process a User Story. Creating and refining the artifacts for UI design and requirements engineering takes time. During this period, developers are involved at certain points, but they don't start implementing the User Story right away.
That's why I recommend having a dedicated specification and design sprint first, followed by an implementation sprint—just as I've outlined in Fig. 8.13.
In the first sprint—the one on the left—requirements engineers and UI designers work closely together and continuously involve the Product Owner, developers, and users in discussions. Their primary focus is the highest-priority User Story from the Product Backlog. As they work, they must also take additional constraints and quality requirements into account, such as web content accessibility guidelines for UX design or adherence to the design system.
Requirements engineers and UI designers iterate through several cycles, regularly seeking feedback from the other stakeholders. Once the results reach a certain level of maturity, an official walkthrough meeting with the Product Owner and the team is scheduled.

Linda And in this meeting, the User Story gets its final touch, right?

Jan I've rarely seen a User Story remain completely unchanged after a walkthrough, even when a very experienced requirements engineer was involved in the sprint. Team discussions almost always bring up additional questions or requests for changes. That's why the walkthrough is so valuable.
To make this meeting effective, there's a checklist known as the *Definition of Ready* (DoR). This contains the Scrum team's agreements about when a User Story is considered ready for implementation and is typically defined at the start of a project. In practice, the DoR should be kept as concise as possible, to avoid over-regulation and delays in project progress. For example, it could include the following two points:

1. In the walkthrough, the team has established a common understanding of the User Story
2. The team has agreed on the acceptance criteria in the walkthrough

If this Definition of Ready is met, the User Story has, so to speak, received its ticket to enter the implementation sprint and thus the Sprint Backlog

Linda So let's say the development team gives the User Story this "ticket." Does that mean the User Story is implemented in the following implementation sprint?

Jan Yes, and of course it's also tested. However, it can happen—either during implementation or sometimes only during testing—that a team member notices certain details in the User Story are inconsistent, or that requirements or UI design need adjustment. In such cases, these adjustments are made directly within the implementation sprint in consultation with the PO. If the changes are more substantial, the User Story may need to be moved back to the specification and design sprint.

In the best-case scenario, the testing is successful. At the end of the implementation sprint, there's another checklist: the Definition of Done (DoD). This includes the criteria for accepting a User Story by the Product Owner. Let me give you an example of a DoD:

- All functions have been tested and documented
- The code has been checked into the version control system
- The production environment has been successfully updated
- All necessary user documentation has been created

If all the points in the DoD are fulfilled, we have a finished increment of the system for this User Story at the end of the implementation sprint

Linda Let me just summarize to make sure I've understood the two documents correctly:

- Definition of Ready: includes the criteria for accepting the artifacts from the specification and design sprint
- Definition of Done: includes the criteria for accepting the artifacts from the implementation sprint

Got it! But if a User Story has to go back to the specification and design sprint, doesn't that mean the developers are left without work in the meantime?

Jan No, that's not the case. Usually, there are several User Stories in the sprint backlog that need to be implemented. The graphic in Fig. 8.13 is just meant to illustrate the process for a single User Story. So, the developers should still have plenty of work to do.

Linda OK, but what about the other way around? If there's very little adjustment work for the requirements engineers and UI designers during the implementation sprint, does that mean they're left with nothing to do?

Jan Of course not. During that time, they're preparing the next User Stories to ensure that the developers have enough work lined up for the following sprint as well.

To the point

The parallel execution of different sprints ensures a balanced and consistent workload across all roles involved.◄

8.4 Implementing Behavior Driven Development (BDD)

Linda now felt well prepared to begin phase 2 of her project—the agile implementation of her IT solution. However, Jan wished to introduce her to the agile approach known as *Behavior Driven Development* (BDD), an approach he feels strongly about and which relies on well-developed Gherkin scenarios as a foundation (see Sect. 8.1.5).

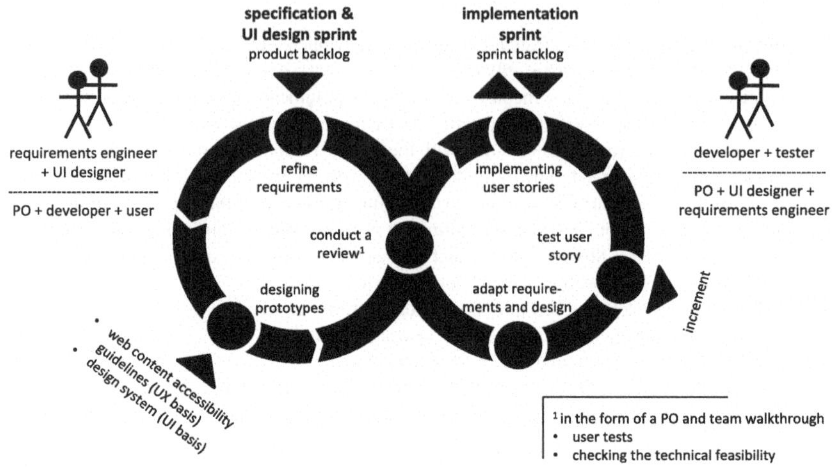

Fig. 8.13 Collaboration model in agile frontend development

Fig. 8.14 The three amigos in BDD

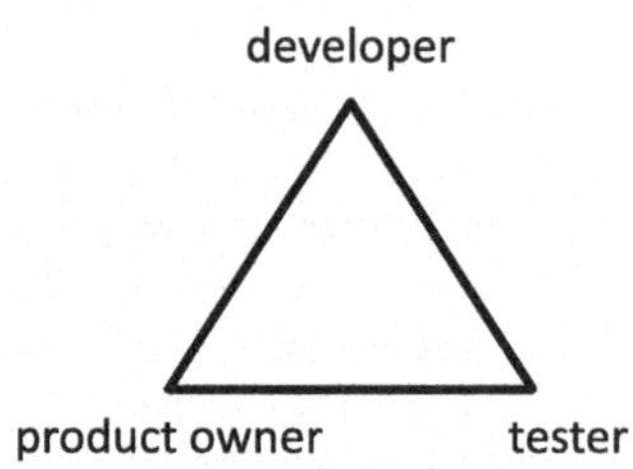

In the context of BDD, reference is often made to the "three amigos": the Product Owner, the Tester, and the Developer. The close collaboration among these three roles is typically depicted as a triangle, as illustrated in Fig. 8.14.

We would like to further specify the roles of the three amigos in the context of BDD as follows:

- the requirements engineer,
- the test automation specialist,
- the frontend developer.

While BDD has sometimes been applied successfully in pure backend development, we are convinced that its use in the frontend domain is especially promising. After Jan began his detailed explanation of BDD with this role allocation—replacing the product owner with the requirements engineer—Linda responded with a touch of cynicism:

Linda So you're saying that as a future Product Owner, I wouldn't be able to apply this methodology?

Jan I wouldn't go that far. You're now so well trained that you'd do very well as a requirements engineer *(grins)*. But seriously: a PO who comes from the business side and only occasionally works on IT projects has different priorities and responsibilities than getting deeply involved with requirements engineering tools. The PO will always be responsible for accepting and approving RE artifacts, but the actual creation of those artifacts typically needs to be handled by a trained requirements engineer.

Linda Nice dodge, Jan. But what is BDD really about?

Jan Well, you already know the first part: the requirements engineer refines a user story and creates acceptance criteria in Gherkin format. What's even more important here—compared to just writing acceptance criteria—is to use testable sample data. These executable Gherkin scenarios then serve as the foundation for test automation, which is set up even before the actual source code development begins.

Linda The idea that the test cases are actually completed before the development even starts is going to take some getting used to. Doesn't that mean the tests will inevitably fail at first?

Jan Of course. They already produce a result—even if at first this result is *Red* or *Failed*
The test automation specialist enriches the Gherkin scenarios with test code in a tool like Cucumber, making them executable and able to deliver an actual test result.

Linda And then the frontend developer gets involved and codes until all the tests pass—so they show *Green* or *OK*?

Jan Exactly. The frontend developer often still needs support from a backend developer—unless he's a so-called full-stack developer. By the way, AI can now provide significant assistance to both test automation experts and developers when it comes to coding.

Linda Yes, I've heard that some of them are worried about losing their jobs because of that. OK, but can we add the respective artifacts for each of the three amigos to the triangle?

Jan As always, that's a great idea from you.

The result of this approach is illustrated in Fig. 8.15.

The sequence in which the artifacts are created is indicated by the numbering, while the arrows highlight their dependencies: the Gherkin scenarios serve as the foundation for automated tests, and both artifacts in turn form the basis for the frontend developer's work.

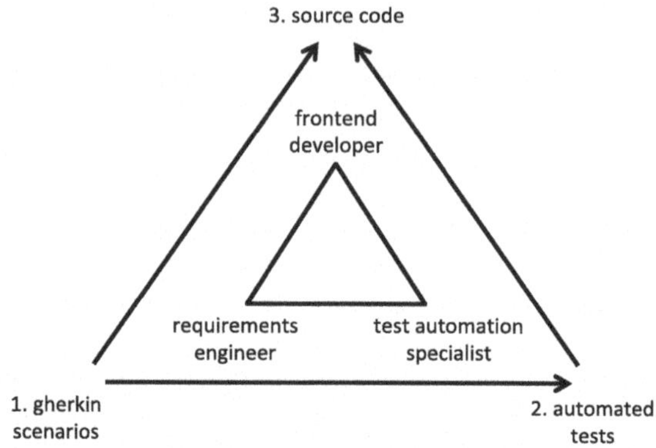

Fig. 8.15 Roles and artifacts in BDD

Linda That brings up a question for me: how does this additional step of creating automated tests fit into your agile sprint cycle?

Jan It's actually not that complicated. We simply add another sprint to the process. So, the full implementation of a user story—from requirements refinement and solution design, through test automation, to actual programming—spans three sprints. At first glance, it might seem like this would slow down the project. However, the positive effects of BDD are so substantial that system quality and implementation speed both improve significantly. The effort required for refactoring—which often makes up more than 50% of a developer's time after a few months into the project—is also considerably reduced.

Figure 8.16 presents a highly abstract graphical depiction of the process proposed by Jan. Once the refinement of a user story—including UI design—is complete, the requirements engineer, potentially in collaboration with a test expert, creates the corresponding Gherkin scenarios using relevant test data. In the subsequent sprint, these scenarios serve as the foundation for implementing test automation for that user story. Only after this is accomplished does the actual implementation of the user story occur in the third sprint. Otherwise, all other specifications outlined for 'standard' agile developments continue to apply, including the Definition of Ready (DoR) and Definition of Done (DoD).

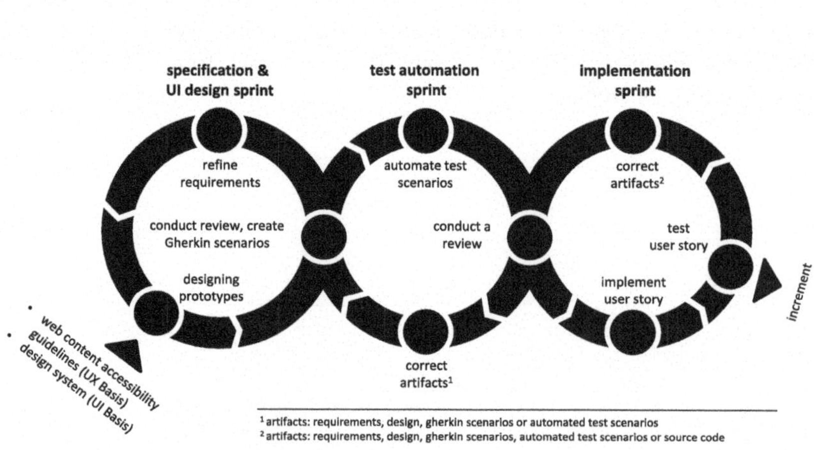

Fig. 8.16 Agile sprints with BDD

Linda	Jan, all of this sounds great, and even as a layperson, I understand the added value for a software development project. But we're not developing custom software—we want to introduce an off-the-shelf product. Does this approach still make sense for a project like ours?
Jan	It depends. Primarily—and I agree with you here—BDD shows its greatest strengths in agile software development projects. Before deciding for or against using BDD in our product introduction project, we need to consider and answer a few key questions: 1. Does the product provider already offer standard test automation, and if so, to what extent? 2. How extensive are the required custom developments—meaning, how far will we need to deviate from the product's standard functionality? 3. To what degree is the product provider willing to invest in test automation themselves? As a customer, you shouldn't be expected to fully fund the creation of a test framework that would also benefit the provider in future product rollouts for other clients Once these questions have been addressed, we can refer back to our decision matrix to support the final decision
Linda	That sounds logical to me. Even if we don't end up applying BDD in our project, I find the approach appealing—it can really help ensure high quality in other software development projects. We should definitely present this concept to the departments planning similar projects and also to our IT department
Jan	I'm sure that BDD is no longer a foreign concept to your IT department. However, in practice, BDD often fails because teams are unwilling to make the initial investment in terms of time and budget. But once a project has been successfully completed using BDD, it's much easier for decision-makers to choose BDD for future projects
Linda	The classic chicken-and-egg problem. Well then, have you now shared all your tips for agile projects with me?
Jan	I have one more…

8.5 Creating a Way of Working Artifact

Scrum and other agile methods provide a framework for a specific project. Conversely, this means that a certain degree of flexibility is required in how the chosen agile method is implemented. This flexibility allows teams to address the unique characteristics of each project. These project-specific adaptations of the agile approach should be documented in an artifact known as the *Way of Working* (Sutherland & Sutherland, 2014) .

Jan I'd like to recommend the Way of Working document, or *WoW* for short. I mentioned it briefly on our second day, and I'd now like to explain it in more detail. The WoW isn't a specific requirements engineering artifact, but is more of a project management instrument. Nevertheless, because the requirements engineer acts as a key connection point among all roles in the agile project team, it's in their interest to ensure a consistent and established way of working. The purpose of the WoW is to make sure that everyone on the project team is aligned and working toward the same goals.

Linda We already decided to use Scrum. So why do we still need a Way of Working document?

Jan No two Scrum projects are exactly alike. The interpretation and application of Scrum are influenced by unique factors, such as:

- the development context,
- the skills and availability of stakeholders,
- the allocated budget,
- the available timeline,
- the technical expertise of the development team

These specifics and their implications are documented in the Way of Working (WoW)

Linda OK, that makes sense. Who is responsible for developing the WoW?

Jan The entire development team, the Product Owner, and the Scrum Master—or a project manager, if one is involved—can all contribute input. Of course, there should be someone who takes overall responsibility for the WoW. Suitable candidates for this role would be the Product Owner, the Scrum Master, or the project manager.

Linda What kind of content should be included in the WoW?

Jan First of all, all the roles involved in the project should be clearly defined in the WoW. In our case, for example, alongside the Scrum Master, Product Owner, requirements engineer, tester, and developer, I could also see involving a configuration expert from the product provider. If it turns out—contrary to expectations—that no in-house development is required, we might even be able to do without developers altogether.

Secondly, I would specify in the WoW how we structure the project. For complex projects, or those involving multiple Scrum teams, I've had good experiences with bundling several sprints together into what I call *Relays*.

Linda Another new term.

Jan Yes, sorry for that… In a Relay, for example, we can group together four sprints. For each Relay, a clear goal is established, to which the goals of the individual sprints are subordinate. About two weeks before the start of a new Relay, we hold a Relay planning session where this overarching goal is defined. If there is a parallel project that has dependencies on ours, or if our project involves multiple teams, these dependencies are addressed and accounted for during Relay planning. The main objectives of Relays are to improve collaboration between teams, increase planning reliability, and enhance risk management.

As a third point, the WoW should specify the duration of a sprint, as well as the types and frequencies of meetings that will take place within each sprint.

Linda What would you recommend for sprint duration and meetings?

Jan In recent years, a two-week sprint duration has become standard in most places, although three-week sprints can also work well. Regarding meetings, here's what I recommend:

- On the first day of each sprint, a *Sprint Planning* session should take place. In this meeting, all User Stories to be implemented in the sprint are moved from the Product Backlog to the Sprint Backlog, and each story is assigned to a developer or, in our case, possibly a configuration expert
- Each morning, there should be a *Daily* or Daily Scrum, where every team member briefly reports on what they accomplished the previous day, what they plan to work on today, and whether there are any impediments
- Additionally, I would suggest holding a *Walkthrough* once a week. As the requirements engineer, I would present the refinements of the User Stories for the next sprint to you and the team, so we can make any necessary adjustments together. These meetings are also often called *Refinements*
- At the end of each sprint, a *Demo* is held to showcase the implemented User Stories, followed by formal acceptance from you as the Product Owner
- Finally, a *Retrospective* can take place every one or two sprints. In this meeting, each team member can share their positive experiences or areas for improvement. The team then agrees on measures to address any inefficiencies. If any long-term improvements are identified, the WoW responsible person should document them in the WoW artifact

Linda OK, thanks for the summary. I realize I interrupted you earlier while you were listing the contents of the WoW. Was there a fourth point you wanted to address?

Jan Well, you can go into as much detail as you like. Many of the topics I've covered with you today regarding agile projects can be further detailed in the WoW. For example:

- The contents of the 'Definition of Ready' and 'Definition of Done'
- The structuring of the Product Backlog into Epics, Features, and User Stories
- The specifics of collaboration among the different team roles
- The criteria for test coverage in both automated and manual testing, including the concrete forms each type of test should take. And if we decide to use BDD, that must also be described explicitly in the WoW

Ultimately, it's important that the contents of the WoW are actually followed and updated as needed—especially after retrospectives. The WoW is a 'living' document. All project members must have access to it, for example via the project SharePoint. The Scrum Master should also remind the team if the agreements laid out in the WoW are not being followed.

Linda Great, thanks Jan, for explaining this artifact so clearly. I feel much better prepared now for the actual execution of the project

Even though the implementation phase of the project may still appear distant, it is beneficial to have already established a shared understanding within the project team.

8.6 Linda's Notepad

Linda's notes are as follows:

Day 6: Implementing Requirements in Agile Projects

1. In agile projects, the interplay of requirements gathering, implementation, and testing is more granular and efficient than in the classic approach:

o *UI/UX design occupies a special role.*

o *BDD (Behavior Driven Development) is a specific implementation approach.*

o *The specific rules of an agile project are documented in the Way of Working (WoW) artifact.*

2. Additional artifacts:

o *User Journey Map*

o *Epics, Features, User Stories*

o *Wireframe, Mockup, Prototype*

3. Special features:

o *The User Story takes on an additional role as a Sprint Backlog Item.*

o *Gherkin enables the creation of acceptance criteria suitable for automation.*

<u>*Result of my day*</u> *I am prepared for the implementation project.*

References

Chonoles, M. J. (2017). *OCUP 2 certification guide: Preparing for the OMG certified UML 2.5 professional 2 foundation exam* (1st Edition). Morgan Kaufmann.

Cohn, M. (2004). *User stories applied: For Agile software development* (1st Edition). Addison-Wesley Professional.

Crilly, N. (2024). *Design thinking and other approaches.* Cambridge University Press.

Donald Miller. (2025). *Building a story brand 2.0.* HarperCollins Leadership.

Jacobson, I., Lawson, H., & Ng, P. (2019). *The essentials of modern software engineering.* Association for Computing Machinery.

Norman, D. (2016). *The design of everyday things* (2nd Edition.). Vahlen.

Slicing of use cases: Refers to dividing or cutting of use cases to get them to a manageable size for an agile sprint.

Sutherland, J., & Sutherland, J. J. (2014). *Scrum: The art of doing twice the work in half the time.* Penguin LLC US.

Werbach, K., & Hunter, D. (2021). *The gamification Toolkit.* Gildan Media Corporation.

Day 7: Quality Assurance and Requirements Management

9

As the title suggests, this chapter is dedicated to quality assurance and requirements management. In this context, we will examine three main areas:

- Given the two phases of our project, we will first revisit Phase 1 (see Sect. 7.4) to assess the quality of the requirements documented in the rough concept (Sect. 9.1).
- Returning to the present, we will then address the specific characteristics of quality assurance in the context of the agile implementation project (Sect.9.2).
- Finally, we will focus on the details of requirements management (Sect. 9.3).

9.1 Ensuring the Quality of Requirements in the Rough Concept

Although we have already examined the agile project approach outlined in Phase 2 and its associated artifacts, we will now mentally return to the rough concept phase—specifically, to the closing stages of the rough concept creation (see Sect. 7.4).

Developing the rough concept required significant effort from both Linda and Jan to reach the current status. They followed the established requirements engineering steps by:

- defining the initial situation,
- collecting stakeholder requirements using a variety of elicitation techniques,
- mapping these requirements in different models and obtaining individual confirmation from the respective stakeholders.

J. Kawelke and T. Niebisch, *AI-Driven Transformation - Practical Frameworks for Real-World Impact*, Future of Business and Finance,
https://doi.org/10.1007/978-3-662-72549-8_9

Following these activities, they are now in possession of a comprehensive set of solution requirements. Both Linda and Jan estimate that they are on track to achieve the project objectives and improve the Contact Center process with IT support.

However, due to the sheer number of requirements, they have not yet been able to consider their entirety. At this point, they are unable to answer several key questions:

- Are all requirements compatible with one another? Are there conflicting requirements among stakeholders that must be resolved?
- Are there gaps or omissions in the requirements that must be addressed through further analysis? Are there "white spots" in the requirements catalog?
- Can the stakeholders accept the overall set of requirements, even if this means making compromises or reductions regarding individual requirements?

However, their task is not limited to addressing the requirements as a whole; they must also clarify any ambiguities within individual requirements and eliminate errors. On this day, both Linda and Jan will analyze and review the requirements themselves, as well as involve other stakeholders in the review process. Jan, true to form, has yet another ace up his sleeve.

Linda: So, we've collected the requirements, documented them, and visualized everything. Each stakeholder has confirmed their own requirements. What's the next step?

Jan: Next, we need to make sure that the *requirements, as a whole*,
- are complete,
- do not contradict each other, and
- are perceived and accepted by all stakeholders in the same way

In addition, we should also check each *individual requirement* to see if it is clearly written and free of errors.
For me, quality assurance happens in two stages:
1. We, as the Product Owner and requirements engineers, analyze and review the requirements ourselves.
2. Then, the stakeholders review the requirements.

We need to address both of these steps.

Linda: Normally, I'm an optimistic person. But I have a feeling your list sounds a lot easier than it will be in practice. I'm sure we'll have to go through both steps—sometimes with stakeholders, sometimes without—several times before we finally reach agreement

Jan: Yes and no. We actually have a strong ally when it comes to reviewing the requirements.

9.1.1 Quality Assurance with Tool Support

Linda	How could I forget—there's always the AI!
Jan	Yes, AI—especially when combined with other technologies. We can use text analysis applications that examine our requirements both syntactically and semantically. This allows us to identify gaps, ambiguous wording, and even duplicates or inconsistencies
Linda	Incredible. It's always amazing to see how machines can process our language. But do you really need AI for this, or are most of these just rule-based analyses?
Jan	That's often difficult to distinguish. One typical approach is to use Natural Language Processing techniques (see 11.4.2) to identify the function of each word in a sentence. This helps determine the subject and predicate, and whether the verb is in active or passive voice. In addition, machine learning algorithms can extract sentence features and recognize patterns that indicate things like active or passive constructions. However, if you want the system to not only analyze but also suggest improvements, then generative AI comes into play
Linda	Let us examine this topic further. What specific vulnerabilities are these tools capable of identifying?

Linda has shown interest in the topic. Over the past several years, Jan has worked with various quality assurance tools (QA tools) that have been used in requirements engineering since the early 2010s. These tools initially supported only the English language but were soon adapted to analyze texts in other languages.

The advent of the Transformer NLP technique (introduced in 2017; refer to Chap. 11) has significantly enhanced the efficiency and accuracy with which complex language patterns are processed, providing substantial advancements in quality assurance (QA). This approach facilitates the identification of inconsistencies and redundancies within requirements. Table 9.1 outlines these and other potential issues in requirements, as detected by relevant automated tools. In the absence of such QA tools, this list may also serve as a valuable resource for supporting manual quality assurance processes.

Linda	Thanks for the overview. It's interesting to see what these tools are already capable of. But how does it work in practice? Do we just feed the finished rough concept into the tool and simply press a button?
Jan	That would be the approach we'd use now, since we already have the rough concept finished and ready to go. However, it's also possible to integrate automatic quality assurance as an RE assistant directly into the requirements editor. With this setup, you get real-time feedback on content gaps or issues as you're writing.
Linda	Now you tell me, when we're already done! But if we extended the tool to include generative AI, would it be able to provide a correction for each of your examples?

Jan Yes, that's correct. Some QA tools do offer suggestions for corrections by integrating with a foundational AI model. However, you have to treat the AI-generated output with caution—the corrections don't always make sense from the business point of view. For example, I once let an AI chatbot split an overly long example sentence (see Table 9.1) and got the following output:

- *The agent forwards customer calls*
- *In case of damage to vehicles, the screen automatically displays the customer and contract details*
- *The clerk sees customer data and insurance contracts on the screen*

The long sentence was indeed broken down into several shorter ones, but along the way, important content was lost. With a few additional prompts, I eventually got a more satisfying result, but I also lost quite a bit of time in the process. So, in many cases, it can actually be more efficient to simply get a hint about where the weaknesses in your specification are and correct them manually, rather than relying on generative AI and only reaching the result you want after several iterations.

To the Point

The output of generative AI in requirements engineering must be quality assured through human review.◀

9.1.2 The Goals of Quality Assurance

Jan But before we begin quality assurance—whether with or without tool support—we should first ask ourselves another, seemingly simple question: What do we actually want to achieve with reviewing the requirements? What objectives are we pursuing with our quality assurance measures? The answers to these questions will help us determine our next steps.

Linda For me, the goal is clear: we want an approved specification.

Jan That's definitely the main goal. But what exactly are we reviewing and approving? I'm thinking about requirements like, 'The system must be able to do this…' or 'The system should offer that…'.

Linda Ah, I think I see what you're getting at. The most obvious aspect is *content* approval of the requirements, which is what I meant. It's about evaluating how understandable and meaningful the requirements are: Do other members of the project team interpret a requirement the same way as the person who wrote it?

Jan And it's not just about the content of each individual requirement, but about the whole specification. Even if the requirements themselves are correct, they might contradict one another. We need to make sure that doesn't happen either.

Linda As a representative of the business department, those would be very important aspects for me to review. And if there's a content review, there should also be a *formal* review.

Jan Exactly. For example, a formal review checks whether

- all the features we wanted are included,
- each requirement has an ID, and
- the diagrams follow the correct notation

Linda Now I understand what you mean. Another formal criterion is whether the overall documentation follows the required structure. So far, we've based this structure on the requirements categories. That's something we should review and verify as well. But based on what we know now, I think we can keep the structure we chose according to the requirements categories.

Jan I would suggest the same, at least as a starting point
We've just talked about the goals of quality assurance, and I think we can state them clearly. The goals of quality assurance are:

1. The requirements are analyzed and documented. This means:
   a. The requirements are *documented correctly*, i.e., with high quality
   b. We have *captured* the *right* requirements that reflect the actual needs
2. The requirements are understood by the stakeholders
3. The requirements are accepted by the stakeholders

To the Point
The goals of quality assurance make the purpose of the review transparent to all participants. ◄

Jan Especially with regard to the first goal, there are several aspects we need to consider. Only some of these can be addressed by a QA tool. For me, these are general points that we need to look at—and some we've already mentioned:

- Check *formal criteria* (syntax): Are they clear, measurable, etc.?
- Check *content criteria* (semantics): Are there any contradictions, or gaps?
- Review requirements for the appropriate *level of detail* (not too vague, not overly detailed)
- Remove *unnecessary* requirements and check whether requirements are still in scope for the project
- Review and, if necessary, improve the requirement *categories* defined in the RE plan
- Check the *feasibility* of the requirements
- Ensure *quality criteria* and *constraints* are complete

Linda That's quite a lot to keep in mind. I can see that this phase of requirements engineering is also quite challenging. It's not enough just to run the concept through a QA tool and read it over once. You really have to put some extra effort into quality assurance. Otherwise, any unresolved issues that go unnoticed now will be carried over into the implementation phase.

Jan Exactly. Let's come up with a plan to meet our quality assurance standards. In my experience, we can best achieve the first goal—having high-quality, accurate requirements—by the two of us taking a close look at the collected requirements first. To reach the other two goals, we'll need to involve the stakeholders.

Linda Then let's start with our part of the review.

Table 9.1 Weaknesses in Requirements

Effect	Brief description of the effect	Example	Unclear
Passive voice sentences	In sentences written in passive voice, the actor is, as the name suggests, omitted. It is unclear whether the action is performed by the system, a user, or a particular group of users. Quality assurance tools can detect passive constructions by leveraging Natural Language Processing (NLP) or Machine Learning (ML) techniques • With NLP, techniques such as part-of-speech tagging or syntactic analysis are employed • With ML, on the other hand, the QA tool is trained to recognize patterns within large volumes of text. These patterns are then applied to the input requirements. In this context, classic AI methodologies are utilized	When the clerk is contacted, the master data and contract data are displayed on the screen	Who is contacting the clerk—the customer, agent, or expert?

(continued)

Table 9.1 (continued)

Effect	Brief description of the effect	Example	Unclear
Duplicates and similarities	Similarity analyses across the entire requirements document can be used to identify and avoid identical or highly similar requirements. Duplicates can lead to inconsistencies, especially if changes are made in only one location. A QA tool is capable of providing a percentage match when comparing two similar sentences. During configuration, an administrator can specify the threshold at which similarities should be flagged and displayed	A: When the agent forwards a customer call to the clerk, the clerk is automatically shown the master data of the corresponding customer on the screen B: When the agent forwards a customer call to the clerk, the clerk is automatically shown the master and contract data of the corresponding customer on the screen. Match: 91%	Are only the master data displayed or also the contract data?
Inconsistencies and redundancies	Content comparison of requirements using Transformer-based NLP techniques allows the identification of candidates for contradiction or redundancy, even when the corresponding sentences differ significantly in word choice	A: The Omni-Channel system shall only offer the policyholder the opportunity to view the knowledge database between 5 a.m. and midnight. Access is not possible at other times B: From 11 p.m. to 6 a.m., it is not possible for the policyholder to view the knowledge database due to maintenance reasons	Contradiction in the times between 5 and 6 a.m. as well as between 11 p.m. and midnight

(continued)

Table 9.1 (continued)

Effect	Brief description of the effect	Example	Unclear
Long sentences	Very long sentences can lead to misunderstandings, as readers may overlook important details. Detecting long sentences is straightforward for a QA tool, as it simply needs to count the number of words in each sentence. The upper limit for sentence length can be defined by the administrator; a recommended maximum is 25 words per sentence	When the agent forwards a customer call from a customer who has suffered a total loss to the opposing vehicle in a car accident to the clerk, the clerk is automatically shown the master data of the corresponding customer and the contract data of his motor liability insurance on the screen. Number of words: 40	Recommendation: Divide the long sentence into several short ones
Slashes	When slashes are used in requirements, it is often unclear to the reader whether 'and' or 'or' is intended. For this reason, the use of slashes should be avoided in requirement documents. Detecting slashes is a straightforward analysis that can be implemented in QA tools without the need for AI	When the agent contacts the clerk, the master/contract data are displayed on the screen	'Master and contract data' or 'master or contract data'
Comparatives and Superlatives	Comparative and superlative expressions, such as "faster than" or "the best," weaken requirements because the corresponding reference values may change or are not clearly defined. Using Natural Language Processing, QA tools can automatically identify comparatives and superlatives within sentences	When forwarding a customer call from the agent to the clerk, the master and contract data must appear on the screen *faster* than in the previous version	How fast exactly? Which is the previous version? How fast was it there?

(continued)

Table 9.1 (continued)

Effect	Brief description of the effect	Example	Unclear
Vague Words and Expressions (1/2)	The machine identification of vague words and expressions is also straightforward to implement. Such expressions signal potential gaps in requirements. The administrator of the text analysis application can configure a predefined list of these words and phrases, and the application will search for their occurrences in the text to be analyzed Here is a small selection of vague words and expressions relevant for requirements engineering: as much as possible, clearly, in case, meanwhile, approximately, definitely, mostly, currently, actually, extraordinarily, about, certainly, bad, all, especially, several times, mainly, usually, quasi, somewhere, a while, multiple times, apparently, simultaneously, really, hardly, narrow, if necessary, sometimes, far, mostly, often, certain, mostly	If the customer wants to report a damage, then the agent *usually* forwards the call to the clerk	When does the agent not forward the call?
Vague Words and Expressions (2/2)	Unclear words also include pronouns that refer to the previous sentence or to preceding subordinate or main clauses	The system pulls the customer master data and contract data from the database. *These* are displayed on the clerk's screen	Does 'These' refer only to the contract data or also to the master data?

(continued)

Table 9.1 (continued)

Effect	Brief description of the effect	Example	Unclear
Negations	Negations or double negations can lead to misunderstandings and should be rewritten as positive statements to improve clarity	If the customer does not want to report a damage, then the agent does not forward the call to the clerk	What other cases besides a damage report are there? Does the agent forward the call in this case to another colleague?
Details on Solution Design	Technical details or descriptions of the user interface should not appear in rough concepts or specifications at this stage. Technical design details pertain to implementation-specific considerations and may distract from the focus on functional requirements. In the QA tool, specific keywords—such as 'Button,' 'Menu,' or 'Python'—can be predefined. The tool will then analyze the text for the presence of such terms	If the agent wants to forward a customer call to a clerk, she selects the 'Clerk' sub-item from the 'Forward' *menu*	

9.1.3 Individual Analysis and Review

Linda and Jan first ask themselves where there are gaps or inconsistencies in the requirements.

Jan	Let's start with our own homework. In the next step, we'll look at all the requirements in their context and complexity. This can reveal, for example, that • some requirements or information are incomplete or missing, • some requirements contradict each other
Linda	In short, we need to make sure the entire set of requirements is solid as a whole. Is there anything else we should consider?
Jan	In terms of efficiency, it would make the most sense to divide the work between us. Personally, I find it difficult to review all aspects with equal attention. If I focus on the content, I tend to overlook the formal review—and if I focus on the formal side, I might miss content issues.
Linda	Then let's split the work. We'll each review all the requirements, but with different areas of focus. That way, we'll definitely save time.
Jan	OK, how about this: I'll check the syntax and you focus on the semantics. I'll review compliance with the formal quality criteria using a QA tool and manually correct the text-based documentation. I'll also make sure the model-based documentation follows the correct syntax. You would handle the content evaluation of the documentation.
Linda	That works for me. You're more familiar with the syntax of the documentation formats than I am. As a subject matter expert, I feel more comfortable handling the content review.

With this division of tasks, Linda and Jan go their separate ways. They agree to analyze the requirements individually and to meet again in a few days to discuss the gaps and inconsistencies they have found.

At the agreed time, they reconvene. The following brief exchange of experiences serves as an example of how important requirements review is for the entire requirements elicitation process.

Jan	How's it going for you? Have you found any inconsistencies or gaps?
Linda	Yes, a bit of both. My task was to review the content—the semantics. The first thing I noticed was a contradiction. I almost fell into the same trap that caused problems in my last project. You can see it right away in our requirements. We included two requirements, Monit02 and Stat05, which unfortunately contradict each other • The first one (Monit02) is about displaying same-day due or overdue customer inquiries in the monitoring system. These should be listed by agent group • The second requirement (Stat05) states that no employee-related evaluations may be performed This is where a contradiction may arise. If an agent group is very small, then evaluating the data could make it possible to draw conclusions about individual employees

Jan	In my opinion, we should report this risk to the data protection officers and the works council. Let's set up a joint meeting with both parties
Linda	In this context, I also noticed that we're planning to store not only the responsible agent group for each customer inquiry, but also the individual agent. We can discuss with the data protection officers and the works council in our meeting whether they see any issues with this
Jan	We definitely need to do that. Did you notice any gaps or missing information?
Linda	I had taken on the task of checking the stakeholder list, and I've done that. Unfortunately, it wasn't complete. I've added the missing stakeholders, such as the tool managers for our backend systems. And how did your syntax review go?
Jan	When I checked our natural language documentation, the QA tool was a big help. I was able to import the entire rough concept into the tool and run the quality analysis on it. The tool actually uncovered a lot of weaknesses, flagged them, and automatically generated a comment for each issue. Most of the comments were really spot on. However, I chose not to use generative AI to fix the issues, but I found it more efficient to make the corrections myself Checking our models also wasn't a big task, since our modeling tool doesn't allow for syntax errors during modeling
Linda	Well, you had it easy...

Linda and Jan realize that they need to repeat some steps of RE they've already completed, and that the requirements gathering process is inherently iterative. As a result, they meet again with various stakeholders to refine requirements together and resolve any inconsistencies.

> **To the Point**
> The analysis and review of requirements will most likely result in repeating, or iterating, previous RE steps.◄

Their rework on the quality requirements for the specifications pays off, eliminating any remaining room for interpretation. They conclude that the time spent on requirements analysis and review is time well invested, as it further improves the quality of the documented requirements. Now they have high-quality requirements in hand.

They consider their first quality assurance goal—checking and ensuring the quality of the requirements—achieved. What remains is to obtain approval of the entire set of requirements from all stakeholders, who so far have only seen their own perspectives.

9.1.4 Team Review

Jan After improving our requirements in terms of both quality and completeness—and consulting with individual stakeholders—we now move on to the official step of approving the rough concept. Each stakeholder now needs to confirm their part within the context of the complete set of requirements

To the Point
"Examine the bill: you are the one who must pay it." (Brecht, 1932) ◄

Linda I would give the specification to the stakeholders for review and ask them to provide feedback—including marking the status as 'Accepted'—by a certain date, or to submit change requests for specific requirements. That would fulfill quality assurance goal 3: acceptance. But as I recall, you weren't too enthusiastic about that approach
How would you handle the review and acceptance of the specification?

Jan As you probably know, there are different types of reviews, which mainly differ in their degree of formality. So we should consider which kind is best for us

- The most common informal approach is the *request for comments*, which is what you just suggested. You distribute the specification to reviewers and receive feedback that can vary in detail and usefulness
- A bit more formal is the so-called *walkthrough*. In this method, the author of the specification presents their documentation using scenarios most relevant to the stakeholders. The group mentally simulates and checks these scenarios together. However, this approach typically only covers part of the specification or specific aspects
- And finally, there's the *inspection*. This is a very formal review process, but given the complexity of our requirements, I think it's the most suitable option for our situation

To the Point
The choice of review method should be based on several factors, such as business criticality, the experience level of the stakeholders, and the complexity of the business background.◄

Linda That's definitely the most time-consuming option. Very formal procedures always require a lot of time

Jan That's true. But we're dealing with a complex topic and many stakeholders. So we have to decide whether
we want to invest the effort now, during this review, to avoid having faulty or incomplete requirements in our tender documents, or
only discover these issues later during the implementation phase, when correcting them would be much more costly. You know the consequences this can have for development, budget, testing, and so on
Personally, I prefer the first option. For the stakeholders, it also means that they have to take greater responsibility for their requirements than they might in a typical review

Linda Through gritted teeth, I have to agree with you. Let's conduct a systematic inspection. How should we go about it?

Jan So, the inspection process takes place in the following five steps:

1. *Planning*: First, we select the documents to be reviewed—in our case, the rough concept. We also designate the stakeholders for the review team and assign specific tasks to the reviewers. For example, we can decide that certain reviewers should focus only on formal aspects or look specifically for contradictions. We also need to plan the organizational aspects of the inspection. This planning will be done by both of us
2. *Preparation Meeting*: Next, we hold a kick-off meeting with the reviewers or inspectors to explain the procedure. They are given their tasks and responsibilities, which are clearly outlined. We also provide the organizational details
3. *Individual Review*: After the preparation meeting, each reviewer takes their assigned tasks and reviews the document individually—just as we have done before. Any questionable issues are noted down but not resolved at this stage. This step requires time and concentration, so we need to account for that in our planning
4. *Review Meeting*: We then meet for the actual review session and go through the document together—section by section. Anyone who has comments or issues with the current section shares them. These points are discussed and recorded, and once corrections are made, the section is considered approved. The outcome of the review meeting can be as follows:
   - The requirements are approved as a whole
   - The requirements are approved with conditions, for example, if some questions cannot be resolved immediately. These will be clarified after the meeting
   - The requirements are not approved

By the way, at this stage, the roles of moderator and minute-taker are particularly important

5. *Follow-up*: During the follow-up phase, the results of the review meeting are incorporated into the document, and any open points from the meeting are resolved. The revised sections are then presented to the stakeholders again for final approval

Linda That's really very formal. I'm curious to see how it turns out. One more point about assigning tasks to the reviewers: In my opinion, we should also have our stakeholders focus only on specific aspects during their review. They won't be able to give equal attention to all areas

Jan	Exactly. Otherwise, they would have to inspect the document multiple times, each time focusing on a different objective. That would be unrealistic to expect. So, we'll start by preparing for the inspection with step 1, planning, where we'll define the review aspects for each individual reviewer. In step 2, the preparation meeting, we'll explain these assignments to the reviewers. If necessary, we can make minor adjustments during that meeting
Linda	With this approach, we're feeding two birds with one scone, since we're meeting both quality assurance goals 2 and 3. The reviewers have the opportunity to clarify any unclear requirements. After that, there shouldn't be any reason to withhold approval. Thumbs up from me—I like it

Linda and Jan actually carry out the review of the requirements specification using this very formal review method. The initial planning step is relatively easy for them. They introduce roles such as inspection leader, minute-taker, and reviewer, and establish rules for the review meeting. Each reviewer is assigned specific tasks and aspects to focus on.

It proves to be a bit more challenging, however, to convince the review participants during the preparation meeting that they need to prepare for the review themselves. In addition to the effort the stakeholders anticipate, they are also concerned about not being able to fully understand everything that is documented and visualized on their own. After all, most of the models being used in this project are new to them and, despite explanations, are still not completely clear. Linda and Jan offer to be available at any time to answer questions.

Nevertheless, all participants arrive at the review meeting well prepared. Most admit that the required preparation led them to read the rough concept much more thoroughly. They also confirm that the effort needed for the review should not be underestimated. The reviewers found that they had to step away from their day-to-day work to focus on the review; otherwise, they would have been constantly distracted by other topics.

The review team then goes through the document section by section, making corrections and additions to the requirements. Discussions arise, revealing that, despite the best possible review efforts, requirements can still be interpreted differently.

To the Point

The goal of quality assurance is not a perfect specification, but rather an optimal specification from a cost–benefit perspective—one that minimizes project risks regarding requirements engineering.◀

In the end, the rough concept is fully approved. In their final feedback, the review participants admit that they hadn't expected this many requirements related to the Contact Center process. However, overall, they are impressed by the professionalism of the approach and convinced by the results.

We have now completed the interlude—the work package "Quality Assurance of the Rough Concept"—and from a logical perspective, Linda and Jan will continue with Sect. 7.5, the decision between a standard product and custom software.

9.2 Considering the Particularities of Quality Assurance in Agile Projects

Let's jump from the quality assurance of the rough concept back to the present and join Linda and Jan as they look ahead to quality assurance in the agile implementation project.

Linda So, Jan, what's different in an agile project compared to creating the rough concept when it comes to quality assurance for our specification?

Jan I'd say we have very similar quality assurance goals (see Sect. 9.1.2), but in some cases, the ways we get there are quite different. Still, there are also some paths we take that are the same.

Linda Well, that was a pretty vague answer. If I fed your statement into a QA tool, it would set off all kinds of alarm bells.

Jan *(laughs)* I can see I can't get anything past you anymore. Let me be more specific and start with the quality assurance goals. Documentation happens during the sprints through the sprint backlog items, meaning the refined user stories. These are no longer approved by a whole group of business stakeholders, but by you as the PO and the team. If you remember the *Definition of Ready* checklist from yesterday, it covers our QA goal exactly.

Linda That's true—actually, your explanation of the approach in agile projects already included quality assurance.

Jan We also talked about the *walkthrough* in the *refinement* meeting as a way to hand over the sprint backlog item to the team. At the same time, the walkthrough is, of course, also our tool for validating and ensuring the quality of the sprint backlog item.

Linda And how does automated quality assurance come into play?

Jan Here I'd actually recommend using an RE assistant—whether it's a modern AI agent or a classic quality assurance tool—which provides us with immediate feedback on shortcomings and suggestions for improvements as we write.

Linda Well, that was quick and painless… That means we'll also have time to cover requirements management today.

Jan Yes, I'm already looking forward to it.

9.3 Managing Requirements

9.3.1 Mastering the Chaos

So far in the RE explanations, various models and methods for documenting, presenting, and validating requirements have been discussed. It was implicitly assumed that there would already be some suitable technical means for capturing the requirements. Linda and Jan focused only on the recording and presentation of requirements, but Jan has remained silent up to now regarding their actual management. Both have been using office and modeling tools available at Linda's company. In addition, during workshops, requirements were captured on paper roll-ups or whiteboard notes.

But what distinguishes a whiteboard record from an office document? Some differences, such as practicality and ease of use, are obvious, as are the possibilities for saving requirements and tracking changes. Consequently, a non-digital whiteboard is clearly unsuitable for managing requirements. Does that mean only office documents are viable for this purpose? What are their strengths and weaknesses? And are there alternatives to these approaches?

Linda and Jan are asking themselves these same questions. During the previous requirements review, they encountered limitations in how they were managing requirements. As long as it was just the two of them documenting requirements, they could coordinate and agree quickly and easily. However, during the review phase, they realized that their approach to requirements management became much more cumbersome once stakeholders were involved. Especially with an eye on the implementation phase of the overall project and the lifecycle of an omnichannel system—including its selection and customization—they see professional requirements management as absolutely essential.

This gap between their expectations and their actual experience has prompted them to question whether standard office tools are really the best choice for managing requirements.

To the Point
The desire for minimal administrative effort on the one hand and quick access to up-to-date requirements on the other must be balanced according to the specific needs of the project.◄

This raises the fundamental question: What is the best way to manage requirements?

Linda Did you notice that working with the document for the rough concept was actually pretty challenging? It was still manageable when we were just gathering and recording requirements from everyone. But when we shared it with the reviewers, that's when the problems started. We kept making small changes, which really should have created a new document version each time I'm afraid we still have a lot of room for improvement when it comes to requirements management. We really don't have it fully under control yet

Jan Yes, in the implementation phase we definitely need to approach requirements management much more professionally. And when I say management, I don't just mean managing a single document—I mean managing individual requirements at various levels of detail

Linda Another aspect came up for me during the review workshop: it's not enough to simply change the requirement in the document. After a few days, hardly anyone could remember who actually requested the change. And the discussions started all over again. Based on my experience now, we should also record the stakeholder and the reason for the change whenever a requirement is updated

Jan Exactly. Requirements management actually involves several aspects. And by requirements, I mean both atomic requirements and any kind of requirements artifacts. For example, I see the following points:

1. *Version Control and Change History.* First, the aspect you just mentioned: The history of a requirement. Every requirement goes through its own lifecycle. It is created, analyzed, and can be adjusted over time. This management information—such as who made changes to the requirement—should be tracked, as it could become important later in the project. Because requirements can change, version control or maintaining a change history is necessary.
2. *Change Requests.* These changes must also be traceable and justified. There's a dedicated process for this: change management for requirements, which governs how requirements change requests are handled. In our requirements management plan, we deliberately omitted this step for the creation of the rough concept, but we'll need to include it for phase two.
3. *Baselines.* Closely connected to versioning is establishing a baseline—a fundamental set of requirements. Baselines are usually the foundation for approving complete specifications, which then serve as project milestones.
4. *Traceability.* There's the question: How do we track whether requirements have actually been implemented? Where do they appear in the solution? This is about the traceability of requirements across different levels of detail and development stages. For instance, it should be possible to prove in which architectural or design elements a requirement has been implemented. In practice, requirements often 'dive below the surface' at this point, becoming untraceable, and only reappear (if at all) in connection with test cases.
5. *Selective and aggregated views.* Not all stakeholders need—or should have—access to all requirements. So, there needs to be the ability to selectively access requirements. Alongside these selective views, it's also important to have aggregated views, for example, when a project manager wants to see the total number of story points for all sprint backlog items.

6. *Attributes*. Speaking of story points: Every requirement comes with a set of attributes. We've already mentioned attributes such as the person who raised the requirement or the reason for a change. Story points are an attribute of a sprint backlog item. But which other attributes are useful to maintain from a management perspective? The more attributes you track, the richer the information about each requirement....

Linda ...and the effort involved in maintaining all those attributes. I experienced that firsthand during the review.
It sounds like a lot of overhead. In the end, we might end up with more administrative information than actual content.

Jan We should definitely avoid that. Which information actually needs to be recorded and maintained should be defined individually for each project—in the Way of Working (see Sect. 8.5). The guiding principle here is: as little as possible, as much as necessary.

To the Point
For each requirement, only as much additional information should be maintained as necessary—no more, no less.◀

Linda Why do we need all this information anyway? Especially in a project like ours, maintaining all these details requires a huge amount of work and can drive up costs significantly

Jan I only agree with you halfway. The word *management* usually brings to mind things like cost or bureaucracy. But management also stands for order, structure, and transparency. Of course, the level of cost depends on the quality of the tool used to support requirements management. We'll talk more about these tools later.
In general, there are various reasons to pay attention to requirements management—whether for the current project or for future projects that should be aware of these requirements. For example,

- Stakeholders need to be kept informed; they always need access to the *latest version*, especially when requirements change. This also applies to new team members who join along the way.
- The *relationships between different requirements* need to be visible. Unclear dependencies can lead to inconsistent requirements.
- And finally, information about requirements and their status must be available for *project controlling*. Otherwise, there would be no way to tell, for example, which requirements have already been approved by the customer and which are still pending.

Linda The reasons and need for requirements management make sense to me—and I also understand that management brings costs and effort that will hopefully pay off later in the project. But there are still some aspects I don't fully understand, so let's take a closer look at them.
We talked about requirements, their changes, as well as their links to implementation and testing. Those are all different aspects, but they're all covered by the term *traceability*. What exactly do you mean by traceability?

Jan OK. Imagine this: it's based closely on the V-Model project management methodology, but it applies just as well to agile projects. On the left side, you have the development phases of a system, going from coarse to fine detail. On the right side are the corresponding quality assurance or test phases (see Fig. 9.1)

In this figure, you can clearly see the differences you mentioned. First, there's management across different levels of detail (vertical traceability). Second, there's checking the results against the requirements at the same level, done by test management (horizontal traceability). Test management derives its test scenarios from the requirements, and the project outcome must fulfill these. This brings us full circle to our quality assurance measures—specifically, the quality criterion of testability

As a third type, you can also maintain the relationships and dependencies between different requirements on the same level of detail.

Linda That's a lot of theory again. But what does traceability actually look like in practice? How do I recognize or organize this traceability, for example, the links between a requirement and its test cases?

Jan We already talked about the attributes of requirements. One of these attributes is the ID—the identification number. This allows a requirement to be uniquely referenced

Let us have a look at the horizontal traceability as an example: every test case should have such an ID as well. That way, traceability works both forwards and backwards. The basic idea is to link each requirement to its associated test case IDs, and conversely, to link each test case to the requirements it is supposed to verify. This also enables proper reporting: you can check whether test cases exist for every requirement, and you can verify that the test cases are actually testing the stated requirements—rather than unintentionally introducing new ones

As the conversation continues, Jan delves deeper into these aspects of traceability. He extends the discussion to include vertical traceability—the architecture, design, and implementation—emphasizing again that requirements don't exist in isolation. They are the starting points on the path to a solution and are linked to implementation components and test cases. Using Fig. 9.2, he convinces Linda that it's important to ensure that.

(a) all customer requirements are incorporated into the solution and the creation of test cases, and that none are overlooked,
(b) no new requirements are introduced during refinement or quality assurance in the form of test cases.

If these points are neglected, the result can be forgotten requirements or test cases that do not correspond to any specified requirements.

Note: Regardless of the previous discussion about the costs and benefits or the usefulness of requirements management activities, in some industries, traceability of requirements is simply a legal requirement. It is mandatory—from requirements elicitation through development and testing, all the way to production.

Just imagine products in aerospace technology or medical devices where important requirements are not implemented because they were lost between concept and finished product, and no one noticed.

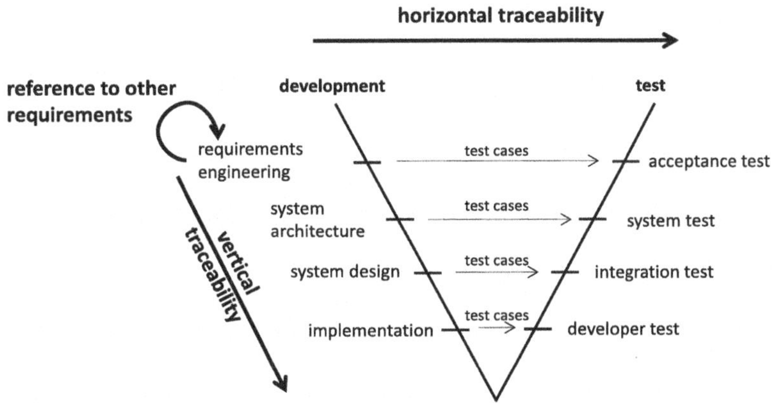

Fig. 9.1 Visualized traceability

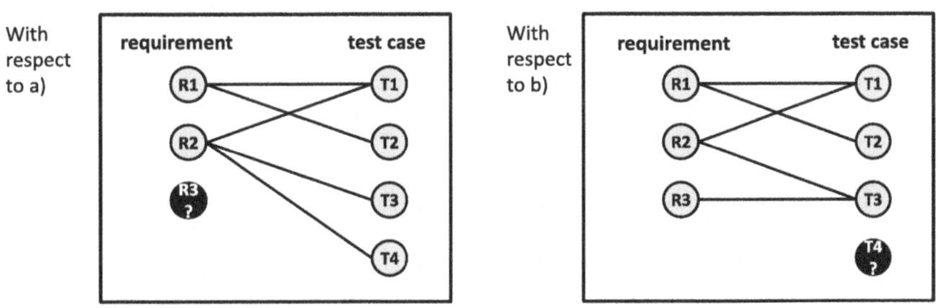

Fig. 9.2 Forgotten and implicit requirements

Linda I understand the traceability of requirements now. But another management aspect is versioning different versions of requirements. Maintaining a history is hard to manage with classic office tools—we experienced that ourselves during the review phase. But is this aspect really critical from a cost–benefit perspective? Is it really important to know what was originally wanted, but has since changed?

Jan You know from your own project experience that it's normal and unavoidable for requirements to be added, changed, or removed over the course of a project. We've just finished Phase 1, and we can already feel that nothing is set in stone. What will it be like in Phase 2?
In an agile project, changes and dealing with them are part of everyday work. The adoption of agile methods is largely based on the experience that monolithic project approaches struggle with handling changing requirements

If the latest changes are only documented in some meeting notes or emails, then everyone tries to prove they're right. People end up digging through old emails and protocols to figure out what the latest status actually is. This wastes a lot of time and causes frustration. And as soon as testers and developers start arguing over whether a requirement is correct or not, having a complete version history is invaluable

Linda I understand now that it's beneficial to know the history, the lifecycle of a requirement, and its current version. But how should I actually handle changes to requirements in practice?

Jan If you remember, we already touched on requirements management when we created the RE plan and defined the status values for a requirement. Let's take another look at the corresponding state diagram (see Fig. 9.3)

Linda I remember this now. So, in addition to the ID and the requirement description, we should also keep track of the status attribute. And now I see the status value *To be changed.* From this, and the many possible previous status values, I can tell that requirement changes can be intended at any point in the project cycle

Jan The illustration makes it very clear why requirements that are only corrected at a very late stage become so expensive. As you can see, in the worst case, a requirement might already have been implemented and tested. After a change, it would have to be documented, reviewed, refined, implemented, and tested all over again. There might also be dependencies with other requirements, which would also need to be updated

One reason for documenting every change is that I can always look up why a correction was necessary and what the change involved. Another reason is the need to revert to a previous version if the reasons for a change no longer apply. For that, you need version history

Linda The benefits of version history are obvious, but I can also imagine that keeping track of all these changes can be a lot of work. Isn't there any way to simplify this? There must be ways to reduce the effort involved

Jan I completely agree with you—the administrative effort shouldn't be underestimated. Especially when you try to manage everything semi-manually with office products and save a new version each time by adding a date to the file name. I'm sure you've seen folder structures like the one in Fig. 9.4. The date formats are inconsistent and sometimes appear at the beginning, sometimes at the end of the file name. The other elements of the file names are inconsistent too

Besides the time it takes to maintain versioning and history, the risk of human error is even more serious. It would be great if we had some little tools to handle these administrative tasks for us and reduce the risk of mistakes at the same time

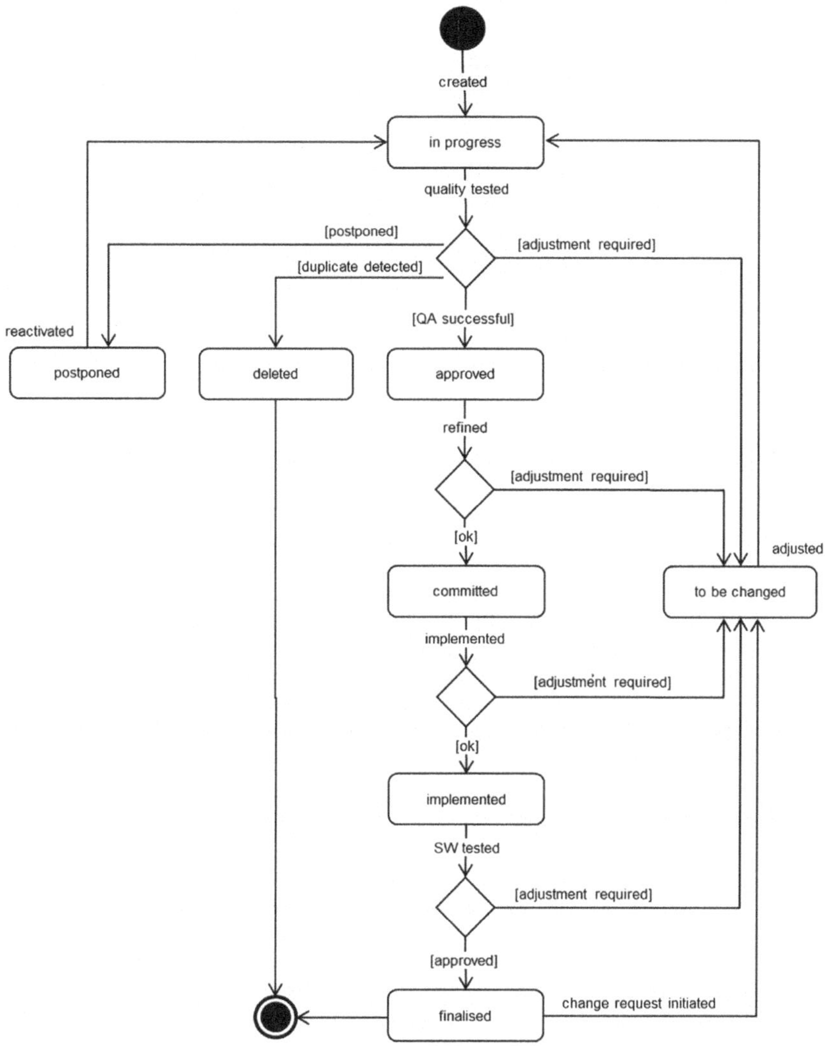

Fig. 9.3 Requirements statuses in agile projects

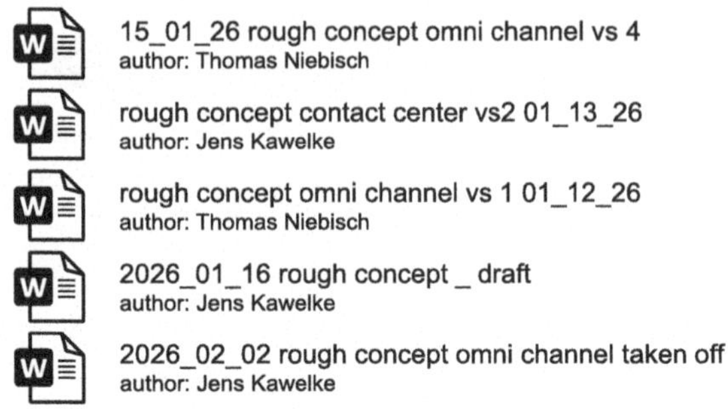

Fig. 9.4 Negative example of a change History

9.3.2 Tool Support

Linda The problem with file names can easily be solved by using version control tools like SharePoint. With this tool, we would have just one document with a single file name, and by checking documents in and out, we can ensure proper version history

Jan That would be an initial improvement, which would ensure versioning of entire documents or files. However, versioning individual requirements would still remain unsolved. That's why, going forward, we should consider a tool that is specifically designed for requirements management
There are tools available that can manage both individual requirements and requirements artifacts. With a specialized tool, for example, you can always see the current status of each requirement and not just when a new baseline of the specification has been created

Linda That sounds interesting. But you're not suggesting that we should introduce a requirements management tool at the same time as rolling out our omni-channel system, are you?

Jan Well… Implementing such a tool is definitely a separate project, but now would be a good time to do it. Tool providers have really stepped up their game in recent years: in addition to features for requirements management, many of them now offer additional functionalities that could be useful for us in phase 2. That way, we'd have fewer tool interfaces and fewer breaks between systems

Linda So you're looking for a jack-of-all-trades tool? What kind of functionalities should it have?

Jan I'll just name a few:
- Automatic quality assurance, which we talked about earlier
- The generation of suggestions to improve "weak" requirements
- Completing sets of requirements based on sentence templates
- Modeling with UML or other modeling languages
- Deriving requirements from larger input documents, like feasibility studies or rough concepts, including the creation of acceptance criteria in Gherkin format

Linda Wow, that would really be a huge help for our phase 2. Is it possible that tool vendors have also jumped on the AI bandwagon, or am I mistaken?

Jan	You're absolutely right. We've already discussed the use of classical AI together with natural language processing in requirements quality assurance The generation of improvement suggestions for weak requirements identified during QA is handled by generative AI. The same goes for sentence completion done by an RE assistant, which is also based on generative AI And the same applies to deriving requirements or Gherkin scenarios from larger documents, like feasibility studies or rough concepts; that, too, is powered by generative AI
Linda	This development is really exciting... What's still missing, though, is the integration of agile methods into these tools. Or is it possible to manage backlogs and Kanban boards in them as well?
Jan	Some tools already offer that functionality today; others are in the process of developing it. The latter also provide interfaces to popular applications like Jira, Confluence, or Azure DevOps, which also support agile methods. These systems are very easy to integrate, allowing you to leverage their functionalities
Linda	Well then, go ahead and set up a demo. Which providers of RE tools do you know?
Jan	Sure, I can name a few. From Europe, there's • objectiF from microTOOL, • reqSuite by OSSENO Software, • and Polarion from Siemens From outside Europe, some widely used tools are • DOORS Next from IBM, • Jama Connect from Jama Software, • Helix RM by Perforce, • and Enterprise Architect from Sparx Systems in Australia All of these offer solid features for requirements management, and some provide really good integrations for agile approaches as well
Linda	I'm glad we covered the topic of requirements management and specialized tools for it. I see now how important these management activities really are. The capabilities of these tools promise to make our work a lot easier in the hopefully not-too-distant future. Even though we didn't use these tools for our rough concept, you've definitely raised my awareness of this topic
Jan	Rome wasn't built in a day. We would have completely lost track if we had tried to introduce a tool on top of tackling the content of the Contact Center requirements. And let's be honest: at the start of our project, no one would have been convinced of its necessity anyway. Now, things are different and nothing is lost. You can always import the rough concept into the RE tool afterwards and continue working on individual requirements and artifacts from the rough concept within the tool

Jan has planted the seed for the tool topic, and fortunately, it has found fertile ground with Linda. As an experienced colleague with good connections to the management of the customer center, she is in a position to push for and advance this topic further. She realizes that while requirements for traceability and versioning generate a large volume of management information, this information also contributes to project success. However, without the support of specialized software, managing requirements becomes very cumbersome. Why? Because ensuring traceability—whether horizontal, vertical, or between requirements themselves—as well as versioning, are management activities that are nearly impossible to handle manually and can lead to many errors.

If a company finds itself needing to manage requirements in numerous IT projects or is about to start several large projects, it's definitely worth considering the use of a requirements management tool.

9.4 Linda's Notepad

What to Remember from Day 7.

Day 7: Quality Assurance and Management of Requirements

Quality Assurance of Requirements

1. *Quality Assurance Goals*
   - o *Requirements are truly needed and correctly documented.*
   - o *Requirements are understood and approved by stakeholders.*
2. *Work Steps*
   - o *Formal and content checks by the requirements engineer for gaps, contradictions, quality criteria, feasibility,* etc.
   - o *Reviews by stakeholders according to the chosen review type (Statement, Walkthrough, Inspection).*
3. *Notes*
   - o *AI can assist with formal checks.*
   - o *In agile projects, quality assurance is integrated into each sprint.*

Requirements Management

1. *Management is not just extra work, but necessary for:*
   - o *Recognizing relationships (traceability),*
   - o *Tracking history,*
   - o *Gaining additional information (e.g., stakeholders or requirement status),*
   - o *Managing the project.*
2. *Notes*
   - o *RE tools are specialized for this management,*
   - o *AI can provide support,*
   - o *A status model for requirements is helpful.*

Results of My Day

- *We checked the quality of the rough concept requirements.*
- *In preparation for the upcoming implementation phase, I now know how quality assurance should work in agile projects.*
- *Managing requirements is a necessary task and a challenge, regardless of the project type.*

Reference

Brecht, B. (1932). *From the poem: Lob des Lernens. English: Praise of Learning* (John Mitchell [1971], Trans.).

10 From Requirements to Results: Key Takeaways

10.1 Recap of the Journey

As our journey with Linda and Jan comes to an end, it's time to step back and reflect on what we have accomplished together. From Linda's explanation of the status quo to the final review and requirements management tasks, we've experienced the full breadth of requirements engineering in practice. The path wasn't always straightforward—there were lively discussions, tough decisions, and occasional pitfalls—but with each step, Linda and Jan showed the value of a structured, thoughtful approach. Their story captures not just the technical activities, but the human side of collaboration, communication, and continuous improvement that turns requirements into project success.

We have shown you a path to a structured, analyzed, and optimized solution that addresses both business processes and supporting IT systems. The process for *handling customer concerns* in the insurance company's *Contact Center* was improved through the introduction of an *Omni-Channel System*. The assignment given by management at the start of the project was successfully accomplished by Linda and Jan.

Linda was in a fortunate position: she was able to involve a consulting expert because her company lacked in-house RE expertise. However, not every organization facing similar challenges will introduce or commission a dedicated requirements engineer role. Out of necessity, interested subject matter or methods experts often take on the responsibilities of a requirements engineer to help make projects successful. While this may be only the "second-best" option from a professional RE standpoint, it is a practical approach to bridging the gap between business and IT specialists.

This alternative was discussed from the perspective of a process manager in the German-language book "360-Grad Prozessmanagement" (Niebisch, 2022). If you

J. Kawelke and T. Niebisch, *AI-Driven Transformation - Practical Frameworks for Real-World Impact*, Future of Business and Finance,
https://doi.org/10.1007/978-3-662-72549-8_10

are a subject matter or methods expert seeking ways to link your area of expertise with requirements engineering, you will find helpful suggestions in this book.

10.2 Your Path Forward: Tips for Applying RE in Real Projects

All that remains for us at the end is to wish you every success in applying the insights you've gained. Of course, your success with these RE methods depends not only on your own efforts, but also on the project environment around you. What works well in one situation might not work in another, even if they seem similar. With that in mind, here are some tips to serve as guideposts along your path:

1. Don't let yourself be rushed into requirements gathering in a new project, even if that's what others expect. First, ask for a "big picture"—whether it's a context diagram, a user journey map, or a meaningful concept model. If one doesn't exist, suggest creating it together. Explain that having this overarching view is essential for orientation and alignment throughout the entire project, serving as a kind of lighthouse to guide your efforts.
2. Identify all the stakeholders you'll need for a successful project, both active and passive. Overlooking or forgetting stakeholders can jeopardize the success of your project.
3. Don't focus solely on IT—remember the business processes as well. Business-IT alignment aims to ensure that the business model and the supporting IT work in harmony and are mutually dependent.
4. Categorize requirements according to meaningful criteria. We've suggested a universal categorization for you, though this may vary depending on the specific focus of your IT solution.
5. Gain in-depth knowledge of notations and artifacts. Practice using them and experiment to discover which are most useful in different situations. This expertise forms the core of your competence as a requirements engineer.
6. Keep in mind that not every stakeholder will immediately understand or use the notations you choose, even if you've explained them thoroughly. Taking a moderating and supportive approach will be more effective than leaving stakeholders to figure out notation on their own. Good communication is often the key to success.
7. Pay close attention to the quality assurance of your requirements. This is the only way to identify defects, inconsistencies, and missing requirements. Specialized RE tools can support you with this task, but their introduction should be handled as a separate project.
8. Establish clear commitments when it comes to the acceptance of requirements. RE tools can help facilitate and document this process.

9. AI can be a powerful assistant in requirements engineering—helping with analysis, quality checks, and even the generation of requirements. However, it should complement your expertise, not replace it fully yet. Always review AI-suggested outputs critically, and remember: your judgment as a requirements engineer remains essential for project success.

10.3 Last Words from Linda and Jan

Linda	It's amazing to look back and see how far we've come together. At the start, requirements engineering was a bit of a mystery to me
Jan	And now you're an expert! I've really admired how open you were to learning new methods—and how you kept challenging our approach
Linda	Well, having a good partner made all the difference. I've learned that a solid process and clear communication are more important than any single tool or technique
Jan	Absolutely. Whether we're in a traditional project or working agile, the fundamentals remain the same: involve the right people, keep requirements visible, and never underestimate the value of quality assurance
Linda	That's so true. And even when things got a bit complex, having a common "big picture" kept us on track. I honestly don't see how a project could succeed without that
Jan	Also, we've witnessed how fast the field is evolving. Tools and AI are here to help, but we've got to maintain our critical thinking and stay curious
Linda	I couldn't agree more. At the end of the day, requirements engineering is about people working together to solve real problems. Jan, thank you so much. I'm looking forward to working with you in Phase 2
Jan	Thank you, Linda. I'm ready for Phase 2—let's tackle the new challenges ahead!

10.3.1 Bridging into the World of AI: A New Era for RE and Beyond

As we conclude the official part of our journey with Linda and Jan, we stand at an exciting crossroads—not just in requirements engineering, but in the wider world of technology and business. The foundational methods we've practiced together still hold true: a focus on structure, stakeholder engagement, quality, and continuous improvement. Yet, a powerful set of new possibilities is emerging, driven by the rapid progress of Artificial Intelligence.

In Part II, we will first take a step back from the practical details and zoom out for a broader view on AI and its growing role in our professional and personal lives. We'll begin by taking a brief look back into the history of artificial intelligence—its breakthroughs, setbacks, and the lessons learned along the way—before clarifying essential AI-related terms and exploring their interconnections.

AI is changing the world, unlocking new potentials in industry and society alike. We'll discuss these opportunities, ranging from increased efficiency and creativity to entirely new business models. You'll learn about key technologies such as *Machine Learning* and *Natural Language Processing*, as well as the critical ethical considerations and risks that accompany progress in AI—think bias, transparency, or even the *carbon footprint* (CO_2 emissions) of large models.

Part II will also examine how regulations are evolving, how companies transform themselves with AI and GenAI, and why *prompt and agent engineering* have become vital new skills. We'll look at the rise of *agentic AI*—systems that can act autonomously—and what this might mean for organizations like yours.

Only then will we focus the lens back on requirements engineering—exploring how prompt engineering and agentic AI can be applied not only to RE tasks, but to the whole Software Development Lifecycle. You'll see where AI not only supports, but also augments your expertise as a team member of a digital product development team and helps bridge the gap between technical innovation and practical project success.

Join us as we embark on this journey—from understanding the fundamentals of AI to exploring its transformative potential in the whole business world and beyond.

Reference

Niebisch, T. (2022). *360-Grad-Prozessmanagement*. Chap. 12.4. Springer Gabler. [in German].

Part II

From Generative to Agentic AI: Transforming Enterprises and Software Development

The AI Revolution: From Early Milestones to Generative and Agentic Intelligence

11

Throughout the first part of this book, we have repeatedly touched on the role of Artificial Intelligence—and, in most cases, Generative Artificial Intelligence (GenAI)—and woven these technologies into the work of our protagonists, Linda and Jan. However, the possibilities offered by AI are so vast and impactful that we believe they deserve a dedicated part two.

As authors, we recognize that the field of AI is evolving at an unprecedented pace. What is current as we write may quickly become outdated by the time you read this—especially when it comes to available tools and specific technologies. Nevertheless, we aim to provide you with a well-grounded overview of key concepts, practical applications, strategies for GenAI transformations in enterprises, and emerging trends that will remain relevant, even as the AI landscape continues to transform.

The wave of AI euphoria began at the end of 2022 with the release of ChatGPT. This excitement received two more significant boosts:

- the introduction of Microsoft 365 Copilot in November 2023 and
- the concepts and development of agentic AI in 2024 and 2025.

Despite the fast pace of change, we are confident that much of the content in Chaps. 11 to 15 will remain relevant and provide you with a solid overview of:

- the evolution of AI
- key concepts and terminology
- the rise of generative AI
- trustworthy AI
- generative AI in the enterprise

J. Kawelke and T. Niebisch, *AI-Driven Transformation - Practical Frameworks for Real-World Impact*, Future of Business and Finance,
https://doi.org/10.1007/978-3-662-72549-8_11

- success factors for AI adoption
- generative AI in the software development lifecycle (SDLC) and how Requirements Engineering merges with other roles in the SDLC.

Please note that we will occasionally use technical terms without providing in-depth explanations when we believe they are not essential for understanding the main ideas. If any term is unfamiliar, you can look it up online, refer to our glossary, or you may already know it from your background. While this part of the book spans several chapters, it is still not intended to be a comprehensive AI textbook. Our goal is to give you a clear introduction, even if that means 'daring to leave gaps'—and hopefully spark your curiosity to explore further.

Nevertheless, we want to relate the most important AI-related terms used in this second part of the book to one another within a conceptual model (see Fig. 11.1), even though they are from different conceptual levels (governance, technology, techniques, assets). The central terms

- Artificial Intelligence
- Generative AI and
- Prompt Engineering
  are highlighted in the diagram.

If you are not familiar with this type of diagram, please refer to Sects. 3.2 and 5.2.1, where the UML class diagram is introduced. Explanations of the AI terms and their relationships, as well as additional diagrams for clarity, will be provided in the upcoming sections, organized by topic. Attentive readers will have noticed that the term "agent engineering" appears twice in the diagram. We did this purely for clarity, to demonstrate both its relationships to prompt engineering and agentic AI.

11.1 AI's Ongoing Revolution: From Early Milestones to Generative and Agentic Intelligence

In recent years, humanity has been experiencing a transformative technological shift, driven largely by groundbreaking advances in artificial intelligence. These developments may represent the most significant leap forward in human history, profoundly influencing nearly every aspect of society, from communication and healthcare to economics and governance. The rapid evolution of AI technology has not only accelerated innovation but has also introduced complex ethical and societal challenges. Understanding the historical roots of AI development, as well as its current trajectory, is essential for contextualizing its role in our future. In this section, we explore the origins, milestones, and ongoing evolution of artificial intelligence, highlighting key moments that have defined its remarkable progression.

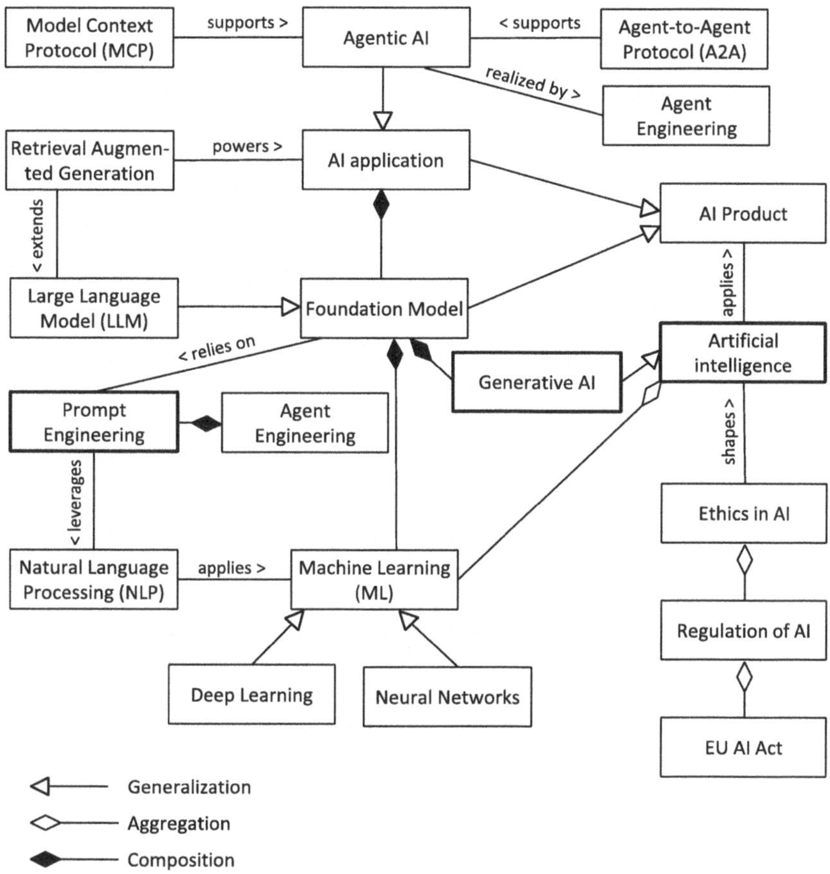

Fig. 11.1 Conceptual model for AI

Let's take a brief look back at the key milestones in the development of AI, as shown in Fig. 11.2. The evolution of artificial intelligence has been a long and often challenging journey, marked by periods of remarkable progress as well as setbacks, often referred to as 'AI winters.'

In the early days of AI research during the 1950s and 1960s, expectations ran high. One of the first concepts was Alan Turing's chess program, although it was not yet implemented on a computer but a paper design. The field entered the computer age with early programs like the chatbot ELIZA, which, despite its limitations, already demonstrated impressive capabilities as a rule-based system.

The 1970s and 1980s, however, saw several AI winters—periods when funding and interest in AI waned after earlier hype and due to technological limits. At this time, the complexity of human intelligence became apparent, and computers simply lacked the power needed to run the required algorithms.

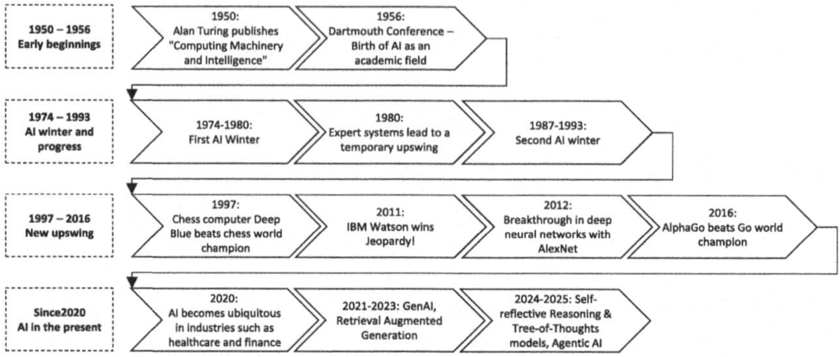

Fig. 11.2 Timeline of the history of AI

A major milestone came in the 1980s with the implementation of the backpropagation algorithm (dating back to the 1970s), which made the training of *neural networks* much more efficient. Still, it wasn't until the 2000s—with the advent of powerful computers and the availability of large datasets—that neural networks could truly realize their full potential.

Deep learning research (from 2006) was the basis for a major breakthrough in the 2010s, occurring with the rise of Big Data and ever more powerful GPUs. This made the training of deep neural networks possible. One especially notable moment was in 2012, when AlexNet, a deep neural network, won the ImageNet competition by a wide margin, demonstrating the superiority of deep learning models.

Other milestones include IBM Watson's victory on 'Jeopardy!' in 2011 and DeepMind's AlphaGo defeating the world champion in Go in 2016—due to the combination of reinforcement learning and neural networks. Both achievements showcased the extraordinary pattern recognition capabilities of modern AI.

The development of artificial intelligence is a prime example of how perseverance, technological progress, and accumulated knowledge can lead to groundbreaking achievements.

The 2020s ushered in a new era of artificial intelligence, marked by the rise of Large Language Models (LLMs) and generative AI. Models such as OpenAI's GPT series and Google's PaLM demonstrated an unprecedented ability to generate coherent text, write code, answer questions, and even reason across tasks. These generative capabilities have driven applications in virtually every industry.

To increase accuracy and mitigate hallucinations, the technique of Retrieval-Augmented Generation (RAG) has become a key architectural pattern. RAG systems enhance generative models by injecting real-time information from external data sources, enabling enterprise-grade applications that can be updated dynamically without retraining the underlying model.

Meanwhile, reasoning capabilities within LLMs have continued to evolve. Models are now able to engage in more structured and evaluative reasoning processes, including *Tree-of-Thoughts*, where multiple reasoning paths are explored and compared, and *Self-reflecting Reasoning*, where the model assesses and refines its own outputs. These techniques go beyond simple prompting, leveraging emergent capabilities of advanced LLMs in combination with orchestration strategies.

More recently, the emergence of Agentic AI represents a major conceptual shift: AI systems are now being designed not just to respond to single prompts, but to autonomously plan, reason, and act—interacting with tools, APIs, and memory to achieve user-defined goals. These agentic systems represent a step toward more interactive, persistent, and goal-directed AI.

To the point
At its core, the AI revolution is about transforming raw computational ability into systems that learn, adapt, and act. ◀

Together, these advances signal that AI is evolving from a predictive tool into an integrated reasoning and action engine, opening up powerful opportunities and new societal questions.

11.2 The Current Potential of AI

Artificial intelligence has been unconsciously making everyday life easier for many people for some time now. It helps us work more efficiently and make better decisions. Only the older generation among us may still remember the challenge of finding a specific address in a city using a physical map. Today, AI-powered navigation systems handle this task for us, providing real-time traffic updates and optimized routes.

Here are a few more examples of how AI is making our lives easier:

- *Voice assistants:* Siri, Alexa, and other conversational AI systems help us by providing information, scheduling appointments, setting reminders, and controlling smart home devices.
- *Healthcare:* AI is used in diagnostics to detect patterns in medical images that are difficult for the human eye to spot. This has greatly improved the early detection of diseases such as cancer.
- *Customer service:* Chatbots—frequently mentioned in this book—act as virtual customer service agents, answering inquiries around the clock and making customer service more efficient.
- *Recommendation systems:* AI-powered algorithms analyze user behavior on streaming services, music platforms, and online shops to offer personalized content and product recommendations based on your preferences, previous purchases, and search history.

- *Meeting summaries:* Running late to an online meeting and want to catch up on what you missed? No problem. Systems like Microsoft Copilot can provide you with a summary of the discussion so far.
- *Translations:* In multilingual environments, modern AI tools provide instant, accurate translations, breaking down language barriers in real time. They work for both written and spoken communication, facilitating international interaction in both professional and everyday contexts.
- *Personal finance*: AI-powered financial tools help people manage budgets, track expenses, and analyze spending habits to offer personalized advice. AI algorithms can also rapidly detect suspicious activity or fraud on your accounts, enhancing your financial security and peace of mind.
- *Smartphones and photography:* Modern smartphones use AI to automatically improve the quality of photos by adjusting brightness, sharpness, and color balance. Advanced AI features such as facial recognition, portrait mode, and night photography ensure that your pictures look professional, even without expert photography skills.
- *Companionship:* AI-powered virtual companions and social robots are increasingly used by people of all ages, including younger generations, to provide conversation, entertainment, and emotional support. These systems can engage in personalized, natural dialogue, remember past interactions, and adapt to the user's preferences, making them feel more relatable. They are available anytime, anywhere, offering a constant and accessible presence that can help users feel connected, understood, and valued.

The latter example has become the most common form of AI use in private life. As ever more power concentrates in the hands of a few technology giants, these companies increasingly have the ability to decide what constitutes the "right" answer to controversial questions. Younger people are embracing AI companionship not merely for novelty, but also for genuine emotional support. However, this trend brings considerable risks, including emotional dependency, mental health challenges, privacy concerns, and undue corporate influence. The combination of youth vulnerability and AI systems designed for engagement creates a powerful mix of influence and potential harm.

But coming back to the benefits: AI doesn't just offer significant advantages for individuals—it also holds enormous potential for the broader economy and society. When applied efficiently, AI can boost productivity and drive innovation. McKinsey estimated that generative AI could add $2.6–4.4 trillion annually to the global economy across 63 use cases—equivalent to about 2–4% of global GDP (Gross Domestic Product). Recent research provides similar estimates specifically for the effective use of AI agents, but we don't want to overwhelm you with too many numbers here. The productivity increase could help maintain or even raise the current standard of living.

To the point
AI has become both a silent helper in daily life and a catalyst for large-scale transformation. ◄

Here are examples for which AI solutions already exist or are currently being developed:

- *Predictive Maintenance:* AI monitors machines, anticipates failures, and proactively schedules maintenance. This significantly reduces unplanned downtime, improves productivity, and extends equipment lifespan.
- *Autonomous Vehicles:* Autonomous trains, trucks, and cars reduce human effort required for driving tasks, freeing employees for higher-value, creative, or strategic work. They also significantly improve safety by reducing human error-related accidents.
- *Support in Healthcare:* AI assists healthcare professionals by automating routine tasks such as patient monitoring, administrative work, and initial diagnostics. Physicians can focus more on complex clinical decisions, and general practitioners can leverage AI-enhanced diagnostics tools (e.g., AI-assisted imaging) to improve early detection and treatment planning.
- *Research and Development:* AI accelerates product and drug discovery through advanced simulations, molecular modeling, and rapid prototyping tools, substantially shortening development cycles and enabling faster market entry of new innovations.
- *Continuing Education:* AI-powered educational systems customize curricula by analyzing learners' individual performance, preferences, and learning speeds, providing personalized recommendations and optimizing educational outcomes.
- *Environmental Protection:* Intelligent autonomous ships and drones are deployed to efficiently collect plastic waste and pollutants from oceans and rivers, significantly enhancing global environmental cleanup efforts.
- *Agriculture and Food Production:* Advanced AI-driven drones and robotics systems now autonomously manage farms, precisely distributing resources such as water and fertilizer, monitoring plant health, and detecting pests early, resulting in higher yield and sustainability.
- *Climate Change Management:* AI is leveraged extensively to accurately predict climate-related events, such as flooding, droughts, and wildfires. AI-powered satellite analytics help governments and organizations deploy proactive measures to mitigate climate risk.
- *Entertainment:* Cutting-edge generative AI technology rapidly creates realistic films, animations, virtual worlds, and games, significantly reducing production costs and enhancing creativity by automating complex visual effects.
- *Urban Management and Smart Cities:* Cities now employ AI for traffic optimization, intelligent waste management, and real-time infrastructure monitoring, enhancing quality of life, safety, and sustainability.

- *Legal Sector:* AI-powered legal assistants quickly analyze vast amounts of documentation, precedents, and regulations, enabling lawyers to expedite legal research, due diligence, and case analysis.
- *Retail and Logistics:* AI is revolutionizing retail by deploying fully automated warehouses, drone-based package delivery systems, and highly accurate demand forecasting algorithms, significantly increasing supply-chain efficiency.

You might guess that generative AI can also write books. However, the book you are currently reading was primarily written the old-fashioned way. Nevertheless, we did receive some help from several chatbots in compiling the two lists in this section.

11.3 Human Intelligence vs. Artificial Intelligence: Key Differences

To better understand artificial intelligence, it is helpful to first consider human intelligence (Bennett, 2024) and how it differs from.

Human intelligence encompasses a complex mix of cognitive abilities, including language comprehension, problem-solving, learning from experience, emotional intelligence, creativity, and the ability to make decisions with incomplete information. It is shaped by a lifetime of personal experiences and social interactions.

Artificial intelligence, by contrast, is a human-designed technology intended to replicate or simulate certain aspects of human intelligence. AI systems excel at well-defined tasks such as pattern recognition, processing large volumes of data, or performing complex calculations. Modern AI, especially those based on machine learning, can learn from data, adapt to new information, and improve their performance over time. However, AI still lacks consciousness, self-awareness, and the emotional depth that are fundamental to human intelligence.

A significant difference between human and artificial intelligence lies in problem-solving. Humans are capable of generating creative and intuitive solutions, taking into account context, abstract concepts, and social dynamics. In contrast, AI systems follow algorithms and depend heavily on the data they have been trained on. While they can process tasks much faster than humans, they require vast amounts of data and significant energy. In terms of energy efficiency, humans far surpass AI: people need much less information to learn something new and can adapt more quickly to unexpected or unfamiliar situations.

AI should therefore be seen as a tool—powerful in specific tasks under human guidance, but not reaching the full breadth of human cognitive capabilities.

To the point
AI is brilliant at specifics, but humans remain unmatched in adaptability and depth. ◄

Importantly, the rise of AI should not discourage us from learning and developing our own abilities. Instead, our roles are shifting more toward creativity, analysis, and interpretation.

One of today's major challenges is developing AI as a combined hardware-software solution to enable intelligent robots to perform physical tasks safely. A striking example is autonomous driving. Just a few years ago, many expected fully autonomous vehicles would soon become commonplace, but this has proven to be overly optimistic (RoboticsBiz, 2024). For autonomous driving to gain broad acceptance, such vehicles must be much safer than human drivers. By contrast, applications like speech AI are tolerated with higher error rates.

11.4 How AI Concepts Interrelate: A Closer Look

Most of us tend to see AI as a purely technical subject. However, the development of AI has been shaped by a variety of research fields, including neuroscience, philosophy, psychology and, of course, mathematics and computer science. The history of these partly parallel approaches has led to different areas of emphasis and the emergence of diverse terminology.

In this section, we aim to shed some light on the conceptual model shown in Fig. 11.1. We will explain the terms Artificial Intelligence (AI), Generative AI, Machine Learning (ML), Deep Learning (DL), and Natural Language Processing (NLP), but also Retrieval-Augmented Generation and Agentic AI and show how they relate to each other (see Table 11.1).

In Fig. 11.3, some of these terms are depicted in relation to one another, including their overlaps and intersections. It becomes clear that Generative AI and Deep Learning are both related to, or more precisely, subsets of Machine Learning. In contrast, Natural Language Processing (NLP) can also have use cases outside of AI and outside of Machine Learning.

We will explore these concepts in more detail in the following subsections and incorporate the additional terms Retrieval-Augmented Generation and Agentic AI into our discussion.

11.4.1 Machine Learning

As shown in Fig. 11.3, there are applications of machine learning (ML) that do not strictly fall under the domain of Artificial Intelligence (AI), or that are not traditionally considered to be AI. Examples include:

Table 11.1 Classification of AI-relevant terms

Term	Explanation
Artificial Intelligence	The field of computer science focused on creating systems that can perform tasks requiring human-like intelligence, such as reasoning, learning, and perception
Machine Learning	A subfield of AI in which algorithms learn patterns from data and improve their performance over time without being explicitly programmed
Deep Learning	A subset of machine learning that uses multi-layered artificial neural networks to automatically learn complex patterns from large datasets
Natural Language Processing	The area of AI concerned with enabling computers to understand, interpret, and generate human language in a meaningful way
Generative AI	A type of AI that can produce original content—such as text, images, or audio—by learning from existing data distributions
Retrieval-Augmented Generation	A technique that enhances generative AI by retrieving relevant external information and injecting it into the model's context to improve factual accuracy and relevance
Agentic AI	AI systems designed to autonomously plan, reason, and take actions—often across multiple steps or tools—to accomplish user-defined goals

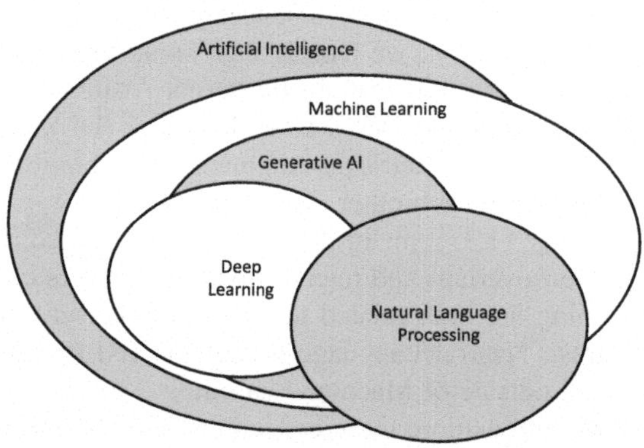

Fig. 11.3 Overview of AI-relevant terms and their relationships

- Statistical data analysis and forecasting,
- Signal processing,
- Process optimization,
- Bioinformatics and genomics,
- System modeling and simulation.

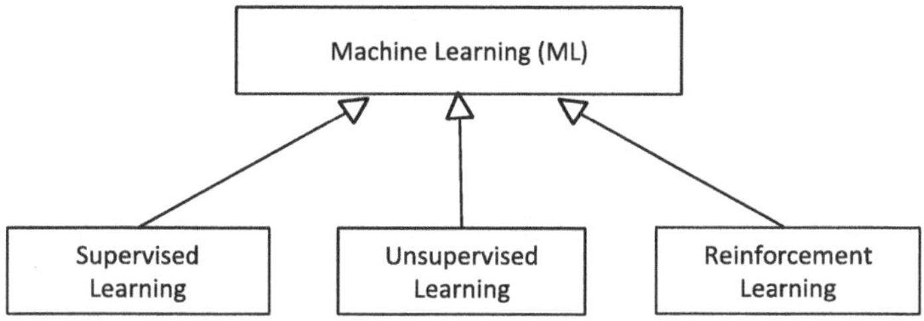

Fig. 11.4 Special forms of machine learning

The distinction lies in how the outputs and algorithms are interpreted and applied: tasks seen as automated computation, statistical inference, or mathematical modeling may use ML but might not be broadly considered as AI.

For AI-oriented machine learning, there are three main approaches: *supervised learning*, *unsupervised learning*, and *reinforcement learning* (see Fig. 11.4). Each of these approaches can be implemented using traditional (non-AI) machine learning methods as well as deep learning (AI) techniques.

The following summarizes these three approaches:

- *Supervised Learning:* In this approach, the model is trained on data that includes both inputs and their corresponding outputs. The goal is to develop a model capable of predicting output values for new data, such as images, text, or measurements. Both traditional machine learning methods (like logistic regression or decision trees) and deep learning models (such as neural networks) can be used for supervised learning.
- *Unsupervised Learning:* Here, the model is provided only with input data, without any associated outputs. The objective is to discover patterns, groupings, or other structures within the data. Common unsupervised learning techniques include clustering and Principal Component Analysis (PCA). Both traditional algorithms and deep learning techniques (such as autoencoders) can be applied.
- *Reinforcement Learning:* In this method, a software agent interacts with an environment and learns through a system of rewards and penalties which actions are most beneficial in different situations. Reinforcement learning can be implemented using traditional algorithms or deep learning approaches, such as Deep Q-Networks.

Deep Learning includes—but is not limited to—these approaches and covers a wide variety of algorithms and techniques.

11.4.2 Natural Language Processing

As already mentioned and shown in Fig. 11.3, there are aspects of Natural Language Processing (NLP) that are not directly related to machine learning (ML).

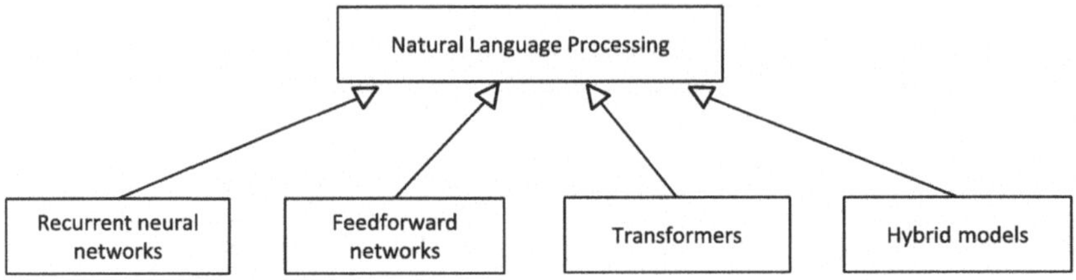

Fig. 11.5 Special forms of natural language processing

Especially in the earlier phases of NLP development, many techniques were based on rule-based systems and linguistic models rather than on ML methods. We touched on this in Sect. 9.1.1, when discussing quality assurance for requirements. Some of these techniques are illustrated in Fig. 11.5.

- *Recurrent Neural Networks (RNNs):* Introduced in the 1980s, RNNs are distinctive because information can flow both ways—forward from the input to the output layer, and backward. This allows RNNs to capture and process temporal dependencies in data, making them especially suitable for tasks such as speech recognition, machine translation, and other sequence-based applications.
- *Feedforward Networks:* Also first used in the 1980s, these networks allow information to flow only in one direction—from input to output. This structure makes them well-suited for applications where temporal dependencies are not a factor.
- *Hybrid Models:* As the name suggests, hybrid models combine features of different neural network architectures. First used in the 2000s, they often mix the strengths of RNNs and feedforward networks. For example, they may integrate the temporal modeling capabilities of RNNs with the complex relationship modeling of feedforward networks, making them useful in language generation and sentiment analysis.
- *Transformers:* Introduced in 2017, Transformers revolutionized the field of Natural Language Processing (NLP) and sparked the generative AI boom we see today! Unlike traditional recurrent neural networks (RNNs), Transformers don't rely on looping information back through the network. Instead, they utilize a groundbreaking attention mechanism that allows the model to dynamically understand and weigh the importance of each input, making them exceptionally powerful at grasping complex relationships between words and sentences. This transformative architecture has paved the way for unprecedented progress in NLP tasks such as machine translation, question-answering, text generation, and beyond, laying the foundation for today's explosion of Generative AI applications like ChatGPT and similar innovations! The 'T' in GPT actually stands for 'Transformers.'

Let's examine three sample requirements for an omni-channel system to better understand the advantages of Transformers compared to feedforward networks and to discuss their quality assurance:

1. Exclusively between 5 a.m. and midnight, the omni-channel system must allow policyholders to access the knowledge database. Access is not permitted at other times.
2. Exclusively during operating hours from 6 a.m. to 11 p.m., the omni-channel system must allow policyholders to access the knowledge database. Access is not permitted at other times.
3. From 11 p.m. to 6 a.m., policyholders cannot access the knowledge database due to maintenance reasons.

If a feedforward network were used for quality assurance, it would likely highlight the similarity between requirements 1 and 2, enabling the requirements manager to identify the contradiction in the specified times. A Transformer model, however—especially when supported by effective prompt engineering (see Sects. 11.4.1 and Chapter 14)—would not only directly point out the conflict between requirements 1 and 2, but also identify the inconsistency between requirements 1 and 3. Additionally, when comparing requirements 2 and 3, a Transformer could also detect redundancies regarding the specified access times.

This example demonstrates how the introduction of Transformers has revolutionized the field of Natural Language Processing. Transformers can capture complex linguistic patterns and contextual relationships far more effectively than traditional feedforward networks. This advancement enables significantly improved performance in demanding NLP tasks such as language understanding and text generation, and has redefined what is possible in machine language processing.

11.4.3 Generative AI and Large Language Models

The previous example highlighted the remarkable language analysis capabilities of Transformers. However, their strengths go far beyond analysis alone. Transformers have driven a revolutionary breakthrough by enabling the creation of diverse and sophisticated digital content. When these advanced neural architectures are used to generate original artifacts—such as text, audio, diagrams, images, or even videos—we enter the exciting realm of Generative AI, commonly known as *GenAI*. We would now like to revisit our introductory remarks on GenAI from the history Sect. (11.1) and explore the topic in greater detail.

Generative AI has rapidly transformed multiple fields by automating creativity and significantly enhancing productivity. It leverages deep learning techniques, primarily based on Transformers, to understand complex patterns in massive datasets. This enables the generation of coherent, contextually accurate, and highly realistic

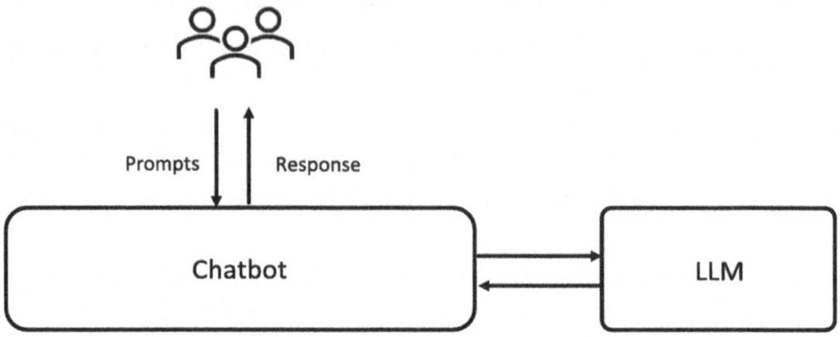

Fig. 11.6 Simplified illustration of an AI chatbot

outputs by the Large Language Models (LLMs). A very simplified illustration of our interaction with GenAI tools is shown in Fig. 11.6.

Popular examples include advanced text generation models such as GPT-5, Claude 4, Llama 4, or Gemini 2.5 Pro, image creation tools like DALL·E 3 or Midjourney V7, and audio synthesis systems capable of producing human-like speech and music like ElevenLabs, Lovo.ai, or Murf.ai—just to name a few.

Let's take a closer look at large language models (LLMs), which can generally be categorized into foundational models and fine-tuned models. Foundational models, such as OpenAI's GPT-5 and Google's Gemini, are trained on vast, diverse datasets, providing them extensive general-purpose knowledge and reasoning capabilities.

Fine-tuned models, on the other hand, are specialized versions of foundational models tailored to specific tasks or domains through additional training. For example, Anthropic's Claude AI, a fine-tuned variant designed for improved safety and alignment, has become particularly prominent in assisting users with nuanced ethical decision-making tasks and sensitive information handling.

Developments in 2024 and 2025 have seen the emergence of even more specialized models. For example, Google's Med-PaLM 3, fine-tuned specifically for medical diagnostics, has achieved human-level accuracy in interpreting complex clinical cases. Similarly, Microsoft's Phi-3 series focuses on precision and reliability in enterprise environments, leveraging RAG systems (explained in detail in 11.4.4) extensively to ensure accurate, up-to-date business insights.

Reasoning capabilities in LLMs have been significantly enhanced by advanced strategies such as Tree-of-Thoughts and Self-Reflecting Reasoning. Tree-of-Thoughts models systematically explore multiple reasoning pathways, resembling deliberate and analytical thought processes akin to the "slow thinking" described by Daniel Kahneman in his book "Thinking, Fast and Slow" (Kahneman, 2012). Self-Reflecting Reasoning, in contrast, enables models to evaluate and refine their outputs iteratively, echoing human metacognition—our ability to reflect on and correct our thoughts. On the other hand, models like DistilGPT by Hugging Face or TinyLlama exemplify "fast thinking," providing extremely rapid responses optimized for speed, efficiency, and partly consumer grade hardware, but with limited depth in complex reasoning, similar to the intuitive and subconscious processes in human cognition.

The adoption of open-source LLMs has also increased significantly, with models like Meta's Llama 3 enabling broad innovation by allowing developers and researchers to experiment freely and customize AI solutions for niche applications.

These advancements collectively demonstrate the rapid evolution and diversification of LLMs, underscoring their pivotal role in shaping the future of AI-driven innovation across industries.

11.4.4 Retrieval-Augmented Generation and Agentic AI

However, as powerful as LLMs are, used on its own their outputs can sometimes lack accuracy or current context, given that such models are usually trained on static datasets. This limitation has given rise to techniques like *Retrieval-Augmented Generation* (RAG). RAG combines traditional retrieval methods with generative AI, effectively augmenting generation with real-time or relevant external information. By dynamically pulling information from external knowledge bases or databases during the generation process, RAG ensures greater accuracy, context-awareness, and reliability in the generated content. This makes RAG particularly valuable in areas like question-answering systems, real-time decision support tools, and dynamic report generation.

Additionally, modern chatbots integrate *internet research capabilities*, dynamically retrieving the latest information from the web to enhance the timeliness and accuracy of generated content. These capabilities can be interpreted as a special form of RAG (see Fig. 11.7). While RAG significantly improves accuracy and context-awareness, maintaining a *'human in the loop'* approach—where human experts validate, refine, or approve retrieved and generated content—further enhances trust, accountability, and overall reliability, particularly in sensitive applications.

In current work environments—especially in IT projects—teams frequently face the challenge of navigating a diverse array of AI tools and plugins, each integrated separately into various applications. While having extensive access to AI-enhanced functionalities through individual plugins and chatbots significantly boosts productivity, it simultaneously introduces complexity and fragmentation. Users must switch between multiple interfaces and contexts, potentially disrupting workflow continuity and creating cognitive overhead. See Fig. 11.8 for the illustration of the described situation.

An optimal solution to overcome this fragmentation would be a single, unified AI interface that can seamlessly operate across all tools and platforms involved. Such a centralized AI interface would leverage its contextual understanding to intelligently orchestrate actions across diverse tools, enhancing productivity, reducing friction, and providing a coherent user experience.

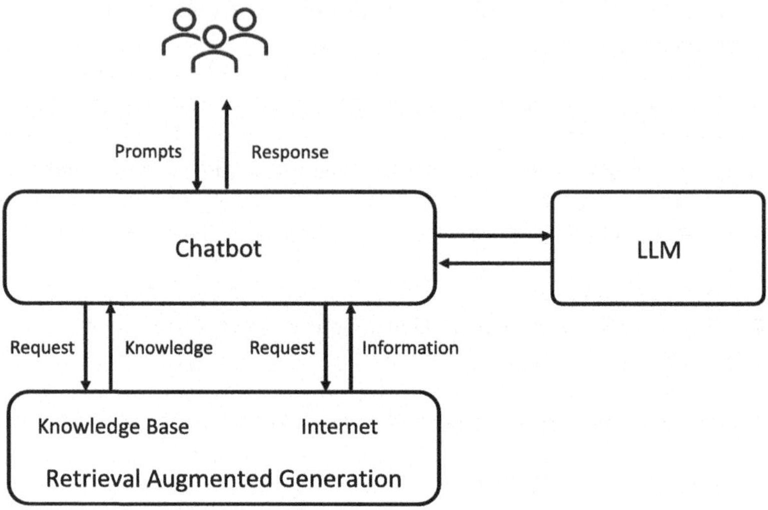

Fig. 11.7 AI chatbot with RAG capabilities

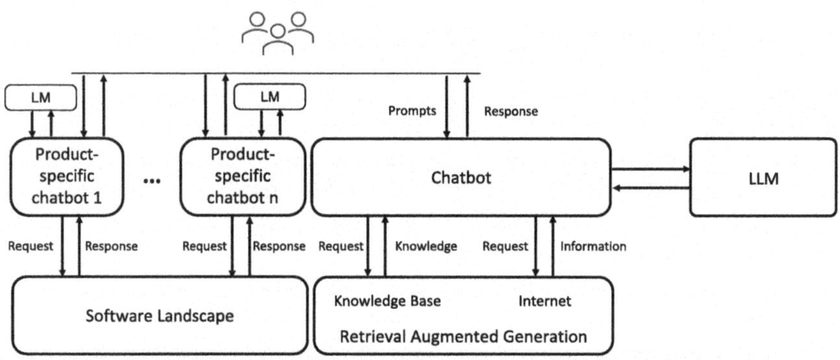

Fig. 11.8 Typical GenAI architecture in work environments from about 2025

To the point
A unified AI interface would transform fragmented tools into a coordinated ecosystem, amplifying efficiency. ◄

Transitioning toward this unified approach paves the way for Agentic AI—ranging from single *AI Agents* to *Agentic Systems.* A single AI Agent is a self-contained software entity that, under one policy and identity, uses generative models, retrieval, and reasoning to autonomously or semi-autonomously pursue a well-scoped goal. Such agents can manage workflows, schedule meetings, conduct market research, or tackle multi-step tasks, e.g., in the software development process, including Requirements Engineering (see Chap. 15).

When moving from single agents to agentic systems, the key idea is collaboration. Instead of one agent trying to handle everything, agentic systems are a coordinated ensemble of multiple agents and services—often with role specialization, shared memory, orchestration, and governance—that collaborate (and sometimes negotiate) to plan, delegate, verify, and adapt work across complex, cross-functional processes. The hierarchical structure in Fig. 11.9 helps us see how responsibilities can be distributed: one orchestrator at the top, a small set of coordinators in the middle, and a group of skill agents at the bottom. The diagram is a simplified illustration of such a system for requirements engineering, showing how agents can be organized to cooperate effectively—without claiming completeness.

Both—single agents and agentic systems—extend traditional AI, which typically handles narrow, predefined tasks, but Agentic Systems deliver end-to-end capabilities with greater robustness, auditability, and oversight in dynamic environments.

Two possible out of several key technology enabler of this shift are the *Model Context Protocol (MCP)* by Anthropic and the *Agent-to-Agent Protocol* (A2A) by Google. They are complementary protocols within modern AI-agent architectures, serving as standardized interfaces for interoperable AI ecosystems.

The Model Context Protocol (MCP) enables AI agents to communicate in a standardized manner with external resources such as databases, APIs, or tools. It functions as a universal adapter, offering agents structured context information

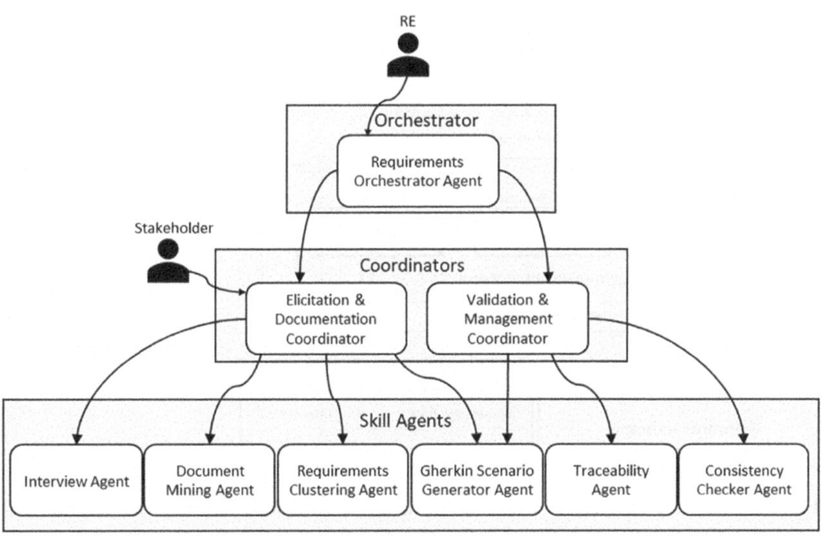

Fig. 11.9 Simplified agentic system for requirements engineering

along with clearly defined descriptions of accessible external functionalities. Its main purpose is to ensure secure and consistent integration, significantly reducing complexity and simplifying interactions between agents and their data sources. MCP is typically employed in vertical integration scenarios, where individual agents independently interact with external systems.

The Agent-to-Agent Protocol (A2A) facilitates standardized and efficient communication among autonomous AI agents. It enables horizontal interoperability by allowing agents to share tasks and dynamically identify potential partner agents through standardized "Agent Cards." The protocol's primary goal is to support coordination among multiple agents, often across different platforms or vendors, enabling them to collaborate seamlessly on complex problems. A2A is most frequently applied in decentralized multi-agent environments that rely on dynamic cooperation, task delegation, and collective problem-solving.

In Fig. 11.10 we have tried to sketch a possible GenAI architecture. We deliberately avoid distinguishing between MCP host, client, and server as well as A2A agent consumers, agent providers, and agent directories in order to keep things simple and not delve too deeply into technical details.

On the right hand side of Fig. 11.10 you also see a centralized language model approach. The agents do not individually embed full-scale LLMs as in a decentralized architecture. Instead, MCP specifically manages the interface between agents and the central language model. Here, it ensures consistent communication, context handling, and standardized interaction patterns between agents and the centralized model resource. The future will determine whether decentralized or centralized language model architectures will dominate, or whether both will continue to be relevant.

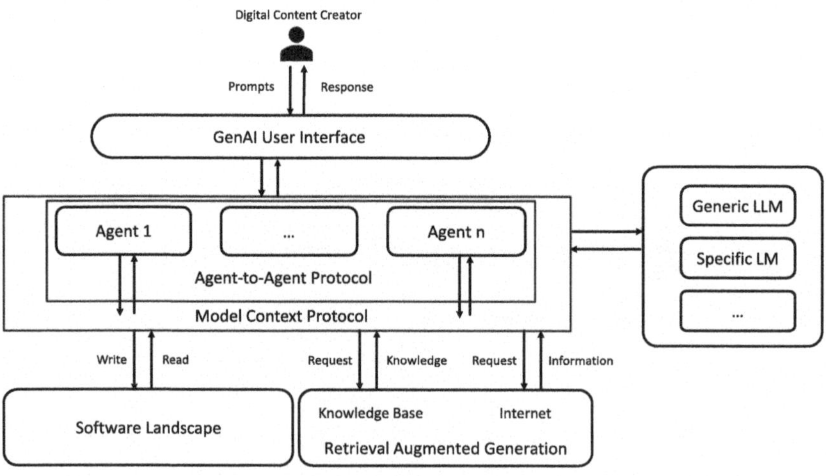

Fig. 11.10 A possible modern agentic AI architecture in work environments with centralized LM integration

The evolution from relying on a single Large Language Model (LLM) to orchestrating multiple specialized Language Models (see also 11.1.4.3) introduces a powerful enhancement to our GenAI architecture. These specialized LMs, each tailored to specific functions or domains, can communicate and coordinate tasks among themselves, enabling richer, more accurate, and contextually relevant interactions. Such collaborative networks of language models amplify overall capability, allowing complex tasks to be decomposed and efficiently managed by Model Context Protocol Hosts.

Please also note that, at the top of the graphic in Fig. 11.10, we have depicted not an entire team but a single user in the role of Digital Content Creator. We will explain our prediction—that some roles are converging, but new roles emerge—in greater detail in Chap. 15. With this we also want to point out that preserving a 'human in the loop' ensures that human judgment and oversight remain integral parts of decision-making processes, especially when navigating ethical considerations, complex reasoning tasks, or critical project decisions.

To the point
The shift from isolated models to coordinated, specialized agents marks a decisive step toward AI systems that think, act, and collaborate at scale. ◄

In summary, the groundbreaking capabilities of transformers extend well beyond language processing. The introduction of GenAI, combined with advanced methodologies like Retrieval-Augmented Generation and the rise of Agentic AI, points toward a future where AI systems not only understand and generate content but also intelligently interact with the world, driving innovation and transforming industries at an unprecedented scale.

References

Bennett, M. (2024). *A brief history of intelligence: Why the evolution of the brain holds the key to the future of AI*. William Collins.

Editorial RoboticsBiz. (2024). *9 critical challenges autonomous vehicles must overcome*. https://roboticsbiz.com/9-critical-challenges-autonomous-vehicles-must-overcome/

Kahneman, D. (2012). *Thinking, fast and slow* (1st edn). Penguin.

12 Trustworthy AI: Considerations on Ethics, Regulation, and Green IT

The success of artificial intelligence greatly depends on how available data is managed. The quality and quantity of this data directly influence the accuracy, reliability, and effectiveness of AI systems. To ensure AI remains ethical and transparent, adhering to principles of data protection and respect for human rights, risk-based governmental regulation, and international standards are essential. Such regulations not only help prevent misuse but also foster public trust in AI technologies. However, it is crucial that these regulations avoid becoming overly restrictive, as excessive bureaucracy and rigid compliance requirements can limit AI's innovative potential and its ability to enhance productivity. Overly stringent rules might impede research and development, thereby reducing AI's transformative power in areas like healthcare, education, and environmental sustainability.

Trustworthy AI refers to artificial intelligence systems that are ethical, transparent, accountable, and designed to respect human rights and align with societal values.

But what specific regulations are genuinely necessary, and what national or international guidelines already exist? To answer these questions, we first need to identify the key risks associated with AI systems.

12.1 Risks of Using AI

To define effective regulatory measures, it is essential to first understand the associated risks (please remember the implications of companionship discussed in Sect. 12.2, which primarily relate to the "loss of control and autonomy" risk). Table 12.1 presents several categories of risks as examples and provides brief explanations for each.

J. Kawelke and T. Niebisch, *AI-Driven Transformation - Practical Frameworks for Real-World Impact*, Future of Business and Finance,
https://doi.org/10.1007/978-3-662-72549-8_12

Table 12.1 Key risk categories

Risk category	Explanation
Bias and discrimination	AI systems may inadvertently replicate and amplify biases found in their training data. This can lead to discriminatory outcomes, such as unfair performance evaluations, biased law enforcement decisions, or unjust candidate selection during hiring processes
Security and data privacy	AI systems rely heavily on extensive datasets to learn and make informed decisions, which can create significant data privacy concerns, particularly when personal information is involved. Moreover, AI technologies can become attractive targets for cyberattacks, endangering both the security of these systems and the confidentiality of their data
Loss of control and autonomy	Highly advanced AI systems may behave unpredictably or make decisions beyond their developers' intentions or expectations. This concern is particularly significant in military applications, where unintended actions by AI systems could trigger unforeseen and potentially catastrophic consequences
Ethics and legal challenges	AI raises critical ethical questions, such as determining accountability when AI systems make mistakes and ensuring these systems operate in alignment with ethical principles. To avoid legal uncertainties and potential disputes, it is crucial that legal frameworks evolve rapidly enough to match the pace of AI technological advancements
Environmental impact	AI systems, especially those involving extensive computational power and large data centers, can have significant environmental consequences due to high energy consumption. As the use of AI grows, the resulting carbon footprint and electronic waste can rise considerably. Addressing this requires developing sustainable, energy-efficient AI technologies and adopting environmentally responsible practices in AI infrastructure and data management
Transparency and explainability	Many AI systems operate as "black boxes," making decisions without providing insight into their reasoning or processes. This lack of transparency can undermine user trust and complicate efforts to identify errors or biases. Ensuring that AI systems are transparent and their decisions are explainable is essential for accountability, effective oversight, and fostering public confidence in AI technology

At a fundamental level, the causes of AI-related risks can be divided into two categories:

1. Risks resulting from unintentional errors during the development or operation of AI systems.
2. Risks arising from the intentional and malicious misuse of AI.

Unintentional errors can result in several of the identified risk categories, such as bias and discrimination, security and data privacy vulnerabilities, lack of transparency, and issues related to loss of control and autonomy. Meanwhile, intentional misuse of AI technologies primarily relates to risks involving security threats, ethical and legal challenges, and potentially severe impacts on environmental sustainability due to irresponsible or malicious deployment.

12.2 Reduction of Risks through Regulation

To mitigate the risks outlined in Table 12.1, regulatory measures are essential. Many companies and industry organizations have established so-called "codes of ethics," which may apply specifically to the development and use of AI systems or, more broadly, to system design—for example, the ACM Code of Ethics and Professional Conduct of the Association for Computing Machinery (https://www.acm.org/code-of-ethics). While these self-regulatory initiatives are well-intentioned, they should not be the sole means of ensuring ethical principles. They must be complemented by standardized methodologies and processes (e.g., IEEE 7000–2021) as well as formal regulatory measures (e.g., GDPR and the EU AI Act). Let us take a closer look:

12.2.1 ACM Code of Ethics and Professional Conduct

The *Association for Computing Machinery (ACM)* is a leading international professional society dedicated to computing, and the ACM Code serves as an ethical guideline for computing professionals worldwide. It emphasizes the ethical responsibilities of computing professionals toward society, the profession itself, colleagues, and users.

The ACM Code is structured around four major areas:

1. General Ethical Principles.
2. Professional Responsibilities.
3. Professional Leadership Principles.
4. Compliance with the Code.

The ACM Code is particularly significant when developing and deploying AI systems, providing guidance on critical areas such as:

- Avoiding harm (e.g., ensuring AI systems don't perpetuate bias or discrimination).
- Transparency and explainability (clearly communicating the capabilities and limits of AI systems).
- Respecting privacy (protecting user data and ensuring AI systems respect confidentiality).

- Accountability (holding professionals responsible for the impact of AI systems on society).

12.2.2 IEEE Standard Model Process for Addressing Ethical Concerns During System Design (IEEE 7000–2021)

This model process is a methodical approach specifically designed to integrate ethical considerations into the design and development process of systems and products, including AI systems. It is rather prescriptive and provides a framework for systematically considering ethical questions.

The IEEE model was developed specifically for system design processes and outlines how ethical considerations can be identified, assessed, and integrated into technical decisions. By embedding ethical thinking into the design process, products and systems can be created that are better aligned with societal needs and values, while also minimizing potential negative impacts.

IEEE 7000–2021 is not legally binding; compliance with it is voluntary, but can be used by regulatory frameworks as a reference point or best practice. Thus, IEEE 7000 serves as a bridge between ethical guidelines (like ACM Code) and enforceable regulatory frameworks (like GDPR), providing a practical means to integrate ethical principles systematically into technology development.

12.2.3 General Data Protection Regulation (GDPR)

AI systems often rely heavily on processing personal data—through machine learning models, big data analytics, and automated decision-making—raising key issues around privacy and data protection. The GDPR, enforced in May 2018 and valid also outside AI, establishes comprehensive rules about how personal data should be managed, placing strict obligations on data controllers and processors.

The following key GDPR principles are particularly relevant to AI:

1. Lawfulness, fairness, and transparency
   - Individuals must be informed clearly about how their data is processed and the purpose of the AI system.

2. Purpose limitation
   - Data must be collected for specified and legitimate purposes only, limiting unauthorized secondary use by AI systems.

3. Data minimization
   - Only data strictly necessary for a clearly defined purpose should be processed, restricting indiscriminate data collection by AI.

4. Accuracy
   - AI-driven systems must ensure the data used is accurate and updated; inaccurate data can lead to biased or unfair AI outcomes.

5. Storage limitation
   - Data cannot be stored indefinitely without justification—AI developers must explicitly consider retention periods.

6. Integrity and confidentiality (Security)
   - AI developers must implement adequate measures to ensure security against unauthorized access or data breaches.

7. Accountability
   - Organizations must document compliance, perform Data Protection Impact Assessments (DPIA), and ensure transparent AI processes.

12.2.4 EU AI Act

The EU Artificial Intelligence Act (AI Act) is the world's first comprehensive legal framework specifically targeting AI. The EU reached a political (provisional) agreement on 9 December 2023, following long negotiations. The law was formally adopted by the European Parliament on 13 March 2024, and subsequently approved by the EU Council on 21 May 2024. It was signed into law on 13 June 2024 and published in the Official Journal on 12 July 2024, entering into force on 1 August 2024.

The predefined phased schedule after the enforcement between August 2025 and August 2027 is shown in Fig. 12.1. This represents a significantly accelerated and structured rollout, rather than a simple 2026 implementation date.

For further details look up the respective EU AI Act pages (EU Artificial Intelligence Act, 2025).

This regulation aims to strengthen trust in the safety of AI systems while also promoting innovation and the competitiveness of the EU in this field. The rules categorize AI systems based on the potential risks they pose:

- *Unacceptable risk:* AI systems that represent a clear threat to the safety, livelihoods, and rights of people are to be banned.

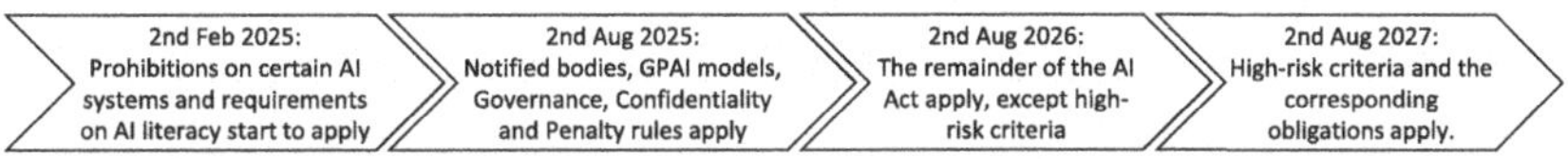

Fig. 12.1 Confirmed EU AI Act Timeline Milestones

- *High risk:* AI systems used in critical sectors such as healthcare, law enforcement, transportation, or the justice system must meet strict requirements before being placed on the market.
- *Limited risk:* AI systems that come with certain transparency obligations (such as chatbots) must clearly indicate that they are AI systems.
- *Minimal risk:* AI applications with low risk are largely unregulated to foster innovation.

Added during the legislative process in late 2023, the GPAI (General-Purpose Artificial Intelligence) category covers foundation models (e.g., LLMs). Providers must comply with transparency obligations, and high-capability GPAI models that may pose systemic risks (e.g., models exceeding ~10^25 FLOPS) are subject to further evaluation and oversight requirements.

The EU AI Act establishes national supervisory authorities within each Member State and creates an EU-level governance framework consisting of the European AI Office and the European Artificial Intelligence Board, which together ensure harmonized oversight and compliance across the Union.

A particularly contentious issue during negotiations was whether regulation should target only applications using foundational (general-purpose) AI models or also regulate the foundational models themselves. France, Germany, and Italy initially resisted direct regulation of foundational models to prevent imposing heavy burdens on their leading start-ups, notably France's Mistral AI and Germany's Aleph Alpha, whose models underpin many downstream applications. The concern was that developers of foundational models might unfairly face liability for outputs over which they have limited control. Ultimately, the EU reached a compromise, deciding that foundational AI models must also be regulated directly—imposing transparency requirements for most foundational model providers, with stricter obligations and oversight for high-capability models presenting systemic risks.

12.2.5 Others

In the USA, Great Britain, China, and other countries and regions, various legal regulations were enacted from 2023 onwards, which differ in part from European laws but are continuously adapted. Since AI knows no borders, international agreements and cooperation are absolutely necessary. Work on these regulations is sometimes progressing rapidly, but at other times it faces resistance and even boycotts.

12.2.5.1 USA: Fragmented & Evolving Framework

The USA have no unified federal AI law, relying instead on:

- *Executive Orders*, e.g., Biden's 2023 "Safe, Secure, and Trustworthy AI" order, which set up initiative like the AI Bill of Rights (fairness, privacy, accountability) and the NIST AI Risk Management Framework.
- *Voluntary commitments* from major tech firms (e.g., OpenAI, Microsoft, Meta, Google) to conduct testing, watermarking, transparency disclosures, and risk sharing (starting July–September 2023).
- *State-level laws*: at least 45 states have introduced more than 500 AI-related bills on privacy, discrimination, and safety.

In January 2025, the Trump administration issued an Executive Order, instructing agencies to remove or revise regulatory barriers to AI innovation and requiring AI tools in federal contexts to be "ideologically neutral," triggering criticism about political content control in federal AI procurement.

As part of deregulation efforts, the Department of Government Efficiency (DOGE) is reportedly using an AI-based Deregulation Decision Tool to eliminate up to 50% of federal regulations by early 2026—raising concerns around legality and transparency.

12.2.5.2 Great Britain: Principles-based & Institutional Approach

Instead of hard legislation, the UK is favoring a flexible, principles-based path.

The AI Safety Institute (AISI) was created (evolving from the Frontier AI Taskforce) in late 2023–2024, with a £100 million budget and open-source tools (like "Inspect") to test frontier AI models.

Simultaneously, the UK government has been pursuing consultations on regulating generative AI and copyright issues, trying to balance innovation with intellectual property rights and human-rights alignment.

12.2.5.3 Other Countries and Global Initiatives

China adopted the "Interim Measures for Management of Generative AI Services" in 2023 and rolled out network data security regulations (Dec 2024), which require AI-generated content to be labeled and user choice features, under strong state oversight.

At the 2025 World AI Conference (July), China proposed creating a new international AI cooperation organization, housed in Shanghai, to offer an alternative global governance framework.

The Council of Europe's "Framework Convention on AI and Human Rights, Democracy and Rule of Law" was adopted and opened for signature on 5 September 2024. Over 50 countries (including the EU, UK, Israel, USA, Canada, Argentina, Japan, Uruguay) have signed, committing to align AI development with democratic values and human rights.

Countries like Canada launched a national AI Safety Institute in November 2024, and rolled out multi-billion-dollar AI strategies as part of broader industrial policy.

Israel, Australia, Brazil, and South Korea have also begun enacting risk-based national guidelines, public consultations, and regulatory centers to address AI ethics and safety while accommodating innovation.

12.3 Green IT—Limiting Carbon Emissions

The use of Artificial Intelligence (AI) has a significant impact on both the environment and the economy. The energy consumption of data centers, which are essential for running AI applications, is projected to double to an estimated 980 terawatt-hours (TWh) annually by 2030. Information and communication technology is becoming a major emitter of greenhouse gases, with some studies estimating its share of global emissions at up to 4%—and rising.

Ultimately, most aspects of Green IT for Generative AI (GenAI) are aimed at limiting *carbon emissions* as a primary goal. However, there are other important, related objectives that we will just outline here:

1. *Resource Conservation:* Reducing the consumption of physical and computational resources like water, metals, and minerals beyond just carbon emissions.
2. *Waste Reduction:* Minimizing electronic waste (e-waste) through efficient hardware management and promoting recyclability.
3. *Economic Sustainability:* Lowering operational costs and promoting long-term economic efficiency by decreasing energy consumption and waste.
4. *Social Responsibility:* Demonstrating responsible corporate citizenship and ethical commitments by minimizing environmental impact.
5. *Resilience and Reliability:* Increasing system resilience and stability through more efficient and sustainable practices, which contributes to long-term operational effectiveness.

12.3.1 Technology and System-Level Considerations for Green AI

To assess the CO_2 footprint of AI, it's important to examine the size of the underlying large language models (LLMs) and the energy consumption in data centers.

GPT-4 is broadly estimated by experts to contain around 1.8 trillion parameters, although OpenAI has not formally confirmed this figure. Its successor, GPT-5 (https://openai.com/gpt-5), released in August 2025, has a unified, smarter architecture that automatically selects the optimal model variant—whether fast and lightweight or deep and reasoning-focused—based on prompts. Most credible estimates regarding the number of parameters point to around 1–1.5 trillion parameters. Others speculate much larger model sizes, but these should be treated cautiously unless confirmed.

Google's language model family Gemini (https://deepmind.google/models/gemini/), introduced in December 2023 as the successor to PaLM 2, comes in several tiers—Gemini Ultra, Pro, Flash, and Nano—with Gemini Ultra positioned to compete directly with GPT-4 and GPT-5. While specific parameter counts are not publicly released, independent sources estimate Gemini Ultra has over 1 trillion parameters. Google's Gemini 2.5 Pro Experimental ("Deep Think"), launched in early 2025, significantly improves reasoning and problem-solving performance, topping benchmark scores like Humanity's Last Exam and LiveCodeBench.

Meta's Llama 3 series debuted in April 2024, followed by Llama 4 in April 2025, which introduced variants ranging from 109 billion to two trillion parameters (https://en.wikipedia.org/wiki/Llama_%28language_model%29). Other notable models include Huawei's PanGu-Σ with almost 1.1 trillion parameters and Microsoft's MAI-1, projected to contain ~500 billion parameters, positioning it as a direct competitor to OpenAI and Google's offerings.

Beyond just parameter counts, these models demand immense computational resources during both training and inference, contributing significantly to their environmental impact. Understanding their size and resource intensity is therefore essential when evaluating the CO_2 emissions associated with GenAI deployments.

The share of global electricity consumed by information and communication technology (ICT)—including data centers, networks, and devices—is now estimated at about 10%, up from 5–9% in earlier years, and is projected to rise toward 15–20% by 2030 if current trends continue (Gelenbe, 2023). Data-center electricity use alone is forecast to more than double by 2030, reaching nearly 980 TWh annually, up from around 415 TWh in 2024 (Skidmore, 2025). Across the sector, electricity use has grown at roughly 12% per year between 2017 and 2023, about four times the rate of global electricity demand growth (Hirsch et al., 2025).

Regarding AI model training, newer published estimates suggest that training GPT-3 consumed around 1287 MWh, while GPT-4 training required about 1750 MWh—substantially higher but well below some earlier speculative figures (Towler, 2025). Training that scale equates roughly to the annual electricity use of several hundred to a thousand US households, depending on assumptions.

Given today's rapid expansion of AI workloads, especially in inference-heavy applications, reversing or even slowing the rise in ICT energy consumption appears extremely challenging. Unless there's radical progress in model efficiency and renewable-powered data centers, the upward trajectory is likely to continue.

To the point
Without breakthroughs in efficiency and renewable energy, AI's carbon footprint will continue to grow faster than our ability to offset it. ◄

Nuclear fusion presents a promising, long-term solution for meeting the enormous energy demands associated with AI, potentially offering abundant, clean energy with minimal environmental impact. One company at the forefront is Marvel Fusion, based in Munich. They pursue a laser-driven inertial confinement fusion approach, using ultra-short pulse lasers and nanostructured fuel capsules. Marvel Fusion publicly states hopes to realize fusion-based electricity generation in the 2030s, achieving a cost of no more than 5 cents per kWh, though many experts still regard this timeline as very ambitious.

Concurrently, efforts are underway to enhance the efficiency of AI models to reduce their energy consumption. The Green IT movement, which promotes environmentally friendly and sustainable IT practices, aims specifically to minimize energy use and related environmental impacts. Major cloud providers like Microsoft and Google have adopted this approach, setting ambitious targets to become climate neutral—or even climate negative—by 2030. Nonetheless, achieving this goal poses a substantial challenge, as the CO_2 footprint of AI systems is anticipated to surpass one gigaton by 2030, roughly equivalent to the current combined annual CO_2 emissions of Germany and France.

The non-profit organization Green Software Foundation (GSF), founded in 2021, has defined so-called Green Software Patterns for the categories of

- Artificial Intelligence
- Cloud
- Web

to help limit CO_2 emissions in IT.
These are the AI patterns defined by the GSF (*Green Software Patterns*, 2023):

- Optimize the size of AI/ML models.
- Use efficient file formats for AI/ML development.
- Run AI models locally.
- Choose a more energy-efficient AI/ML framework.
- Use energy-efficient AI/ML models.
- Use sustainable regions for AI/ML training.
- Use pre-trained models for AI/ML development.

- Choose the appropriate hardware and Virtual Machine (VM) instance types for AI/ML training.
- Adopt serverless architecture for AI/ML workload processing.

12.3.2 Individual Levers: The Role of Green Prompting

Every AI user should be aware that using AI applications increases their own CO_2 footprint.

As for using LLMs—energy consumption per GenAI query is orders of magnitude higher than a traditional search. A single ChatGPT-style response can use around 0.0005 kWh implying about 10× more energy than a typical web search per query (Thomas, 2025).

Despite the relatively small individual user footprint for AI applications, the cumulative effect of AI usage is substantial. A 2025 NTT DATA Global GenAI Report found that 74% of companies believe their GenAI ambitions are in direct conflict with their sustainability goals. This highlights the critical importance of developing and using AI in a sustainable and conscious manner.

Many factors influence the energy consumption of AI, particularly for individual users at the micro level, where our most effective levers exist. These factors include:

- *Response length:* This is one of the most significant factors influencing energy consumption. The computational workload and energy use increase with the number of *tokens*.
- *Model size:* Larger models consume more energy. Choose the smallest model that satisfies the task to reduce energy use. If you just need a direct answer (no reasoning), a small model suffices. GPT-5 does the job for you by infering intent from your prompt: "just the answer – no reasoning" is routed to a lightweight, low-energy path, while cues like "explain why" or "show your steps" (see also Keywords) trigger the heavier reasoning stack.
- *Media type:* The type of media being generated is a key factor. Image and video generation are far more energy-intensive than text generation.
- *Keywords:* Certain keywords, such as "analyse" and "classify", correlate with energy consumption. Keywords that require complex reasoning or justification tend to use more energy than those that ask for simple tasks like listing or translating.

Table 12.2 provides a summary of high-impact strategies for reducing energy and emissions through "Green Prompting."

Table 12.2 Top 5 levers for Green Prompting

Lever	Impact
Media awareness	Very high: a single generated image can be as energy-intensive as 60 text generations
Number of tokens	High: a 20% shorter response can result in 15–25% less energy (Husom, 2024)
Model size	High: can save 70–95% of energy by choosing the smallest suitable model (Husom, 2024)
Batching (avoid prompt chains)	Medium to small: consolidates multiple questions into a single query to save 5–15% of energy (Niu et al., 2025)
External sources	Medium to small: can increase energy consumption by 10–100% due to additional load from web searches and tools (Aljbour et al., 2024)

12.3.3 Green-Through-AI: Leveraging AI for a Greener Planet

On the other hand, AI also has the potential to contribute to a more sustainable and environmentally friendly future—in other words, enabling *Green-through-AI*. This approach focuses on using AI to solve environmental problems and can help offset, or even reduce, the CO_2 emissions generated by AI systems themselves. For example, AI can play a crucial role in developing more efficient energy systems, optimizing traffic and logistics, or improving recycling processes (Fang et al., 2025; Ukoba et al., 2024).

References

Aljbour, J., Wilson, T., & Patel, P. (2024). Powering intelligence. EPRI. https://restservice.epri.com/publicdownload/000000003002028905/0/Product

Association for Computing Machinery. *ACM code of ethics and professional conduct*. https://www.acm.org/code-of-ethics

EU Artificial Intelligence Act. 2025. *Implementation Timeline*. https://artificialintelligenceact.eu/implementation-timeline/

Fang, Y., Wen, Y., Dai, L., Wang, C.-w., You, S., & Li, W. (2025). Artificial intelligence in plastic recycling and conversion: A review. *ScienceDirect*. https://www.sciencedirect.com/science/article/abs/pii/S0921344924006803

Gelenbe, E. (2023). Electricity consumption by ICT: Facts, trends, and measurements. *Ubiquity, 2023*, 1–15.

Gemini, a language model developed by Google, released in December 2023. https://deepmind.google/models/gemini/

GPT-5, a language model developed by OpenAI, released in 2025. https://openai.com/gpt-5

Green Software Patterns. (2023). Retrieved November 30, 2023, from https://patterns.greensoftware.foundation/

Hirsch, D., Bourdin, A., & Crabbe-Field, S. (2025). *Tech sector emissions, energy use grow with rise of AI*. https://www.itu.int/en/mediacentre/Pages/PR-2025-06-05-greening-digital-companies-report.aspx

Husom, J. E. (2024). *The price of prompting: Profiling energy use in large language models inference*. Arxiv. https://arxiv.org/html/2407.16893v1

Niu, C., Zhang, W., Zhao, Y., & Chen, Y. (2025). Energy efficient or exhaustive? Benchmarking power consumption of LLM inference engines. *SIG Energy*. https://energy.acm.org/eir/energy-efficient-or-exhaustive-benchmarking-power-consumption-of-llm-inference-engines/

Skidmore, Z. (2025). *IEA: Data center energy consumption set to double by 2030 to 945TWh*. https://www.datacenterdynamics.com/en/news/iea-data-center-energy-consumption-set-to-double-by-2030-to-945twh/

Thomas, E. (2025). Here's how we all ended up paying big tech's power bill. *Business Insider*. https://www.businessinsider.com/why-utility-customers-are-paying-big-tech-power-bill-2025-7

Towler, L. (2025). *Search engines vs AI: energy consumption compared*. https://kanoppi.co/search-engines-vs-ai-energy-consumption-compared/%E2%86%A9%EF%B8%8E

Ukoba, K., Olatunji, O. K., Adeoye, E., & Madyira, T. (2024). Optimizing renewable energy systems through artificial intelligence: Review and future prospects. *Energy & Environment*. https://journals.sagepub.com/doi/pdf/10.1177/0958305X241256293

Wikipedia. *Llama (language model)*. https://en.wikipedia.org/wiki/Llama_%28language_model%29

13 GenAI Transformation in Enterprises: From Use Cases to Cultural Change

13.1 The GenAI Transformation Journey

While the previous section focused heavily on risk and ethics, we now want to explore the next phase: turning GenAI's promise into *tangible organizational value.*

This section explores the key building blocks that companies need to address to successfully implement GenAI at scale. From preparing the workforce through structured change management and training programs, to selecting the right GenAI technologies that align with business priorities, to identifying high-impact use cases and optimizing underlying processes—transformation requires more than tools. It demands alignment across people, processes, and platforms.

Whether you're piloting your first GenAI initiative or aiming to scale across departments, this guide provides a structured lens on how to embed GenAI into the fabric of your organization—sustainably, responsibly, and with measurable impact.

13.2 The Success Factors for a GenAI Transformation

While a full transformation roadmap could span volumes, this section aims to distill the essential elements companies should focus on to get started effectively. Some of these areas—such as employee enablement and technology selection—will be explored in more depth, while others are introduced briefly with references to more detailed resources.

To set the stage, we begin with a list of critical success factors that any organization should consider when embarking on a GenAI transformation. These pillars form the foundation for sustainable, scalable, and responsible GenAI adoption:

- Strategic Leadership and Vision.
- Prioritized Use Cases with Business Impact.

J. Kawelke and T. Niebisch, *AI-Driven Transformation - Practical Frameworks for Real-World Impact*, Future of Business and Finance,
https://doi.org/10.1007/978-3-662-72549-8_13

- Workforce Enablement and Change Management.
- Robust Data and Technology Foundations.
- Agile Execution, Cross-Functional Collaboration and Scaling.
- Measurement and Governance.

In the following subsections we will go into detail with these pillars.

13.3 Strategic Leadership and Vision

Strong executive sponsorship and a clear vision are essential to align GenAI initiatives with business goals. Leaders must champion the transformation, set priorities, and communicate the value story internally.

In contrast to traditional digital transformation initiatives—which are often top-down—GenAI has entered many organizations through a *bottom-up movement.*

Here is what typically happened:

- A few curious, tech-savvy employees experiment with tools like ChatGPT or GitHub Copilot in their daily tasks.
- They share quick wins, e.g., automated reports, improved emails, or coding shortcuts, with colleagues.
- Word spreads informally via internal chats, brown-bag sessions, or peer coaching, and interest grows organically.
- Eventually, middle managers and departments start experimenting more seriously, often in silos and without clear oversight.
- At some point, executive leadership takes notice—usually when these activities start touching sensitive processes, generate efficiency spikes, or raise concerns around risk, compliance, or shadow IT.

This grassroots enthusiasm is a powerful asset. It proves there is demand and energy for transformation. However, left unchecked, it can lead to:

- Fragmentation and duplication of efforts.
- Risky tool usage (unverified apps, unsecured data).
- Misaligned initiatives that don't serve broader business goals.

Rather than trying to reset or suppress this bottom-up momentum, leaders with foresight have embraced and should still embrace it and channel it strategically. Here's how:

1. Acknowledge and celebrate the bottom-up energy
   - Recognize internal champions and early adopters.
   - Create safe spaces (e.g., GenAI sandboxes or innovation forums) to share learnings.
   - Position this as a company-wide opportunity, not a threat.

2. Rapidly Establish a Strategic Vision
   - Define *why* the company is pursuing GenAI—whether to improve customer experience, boost productivity, or reduce costs.
   - Align GenAI initiatives with business objectives and existing digital roadmaps.
   - Communicate the vision clearly and repeatedly to all levels.
3. Formalize Ownership and Governance
   - Appoint a *GenAI steering group* or *AI Center of Excellence* that includes tech, business, HR, legal, and compliance leaders.
   - Create guiding principles for responsible and secure GenAI experimentation.
4. Build a Scalable Framework Around Existing Initiatives
   - Catalog current bottom-up use cases.
   - Identify the ones with potential for scale and align them with strategic goals.
   - Offer tools, data access, and infrastructure to support them responsibly.
5. Invest in Upskilling and Enablement
   - Develop structured training paths, including AI literacy, prompt engineering, and role-specific courses (see Chap. 15).
   - Encourage cross-functional teams to co-create GenAI use cases.
6. Signal Support from the Top
   - Senior leaders should lead by example, using GenAI tools themselves and sharing their own use cases or learnings.
   - Allocate budget and resources—this legitimizes the transformation and makes it sustainable.

Bottom-up adoption is a signal, not a setback. Leaders who have recognized this energy early—and have moved quickly to unify, amplify, and govern it—have hopefully transformed scattered enthusiasm into a cohesive, enterprise-wide GenAI capability. The key is not to control the movement, but to lead it with purpose. For further insights into GenAI leadership, refer to the World Economic Forum article (Kapoor, 2024), which provides an additional viewpoint on this topic.

13.4 Prioritized Use Cases with Business Impact

Before hastily trying to identify all possible daily work processes as potential GenAI use cases, it is important to first consider whether the task at hand truly requires AI, or if it is simply a repetitive, rule-based task. Robotic Process Automation (RPA) can automate standard tasks without the need for complex algorithms or machine learning. RPA simulates human interactions with user interfaces, thereby automating simple but time-consuming activities. On the other hand, GenAI can handle unstructured data, adapt on the fly, and deliver insights that RPA might miss, because RPA relies on rigid, rule-based workflows. More thoughts on the comparison of RPA and GenAI you find in the article by Parmer (2025).

Additionally, before deploying AI, it may be worthwhile to review and optimize existing processes. Often, efficiency improvements can be achieved through lean management techniques or by reorganizing workflows.

After the possibilities of process automation and optimization have been exhausted, one of the most common pitfalls in GenAI transformation is chasing novelty over necessity—deploying GenAI tools because they're exciting, not because they solve real business problems. To create momentum and justify further investment, you must begin by identifying and prioritizing use cases that are both impactful and feasible.

Early experiments often spring from curiosity or bottom-up exploration (as discussed previously), but for GenAI to scale sustainably, the next phase must be guided by *strategic prioritization*. This means aligning GenAI initiatives with the company's core business objectives—whether that's increasing revenue, improving efficiency, enhancing customer experience, or reducing risk.

A successful use case should check three main boxes:

1. *Business Relevance:* Does it solve a real pain point or unlock measurable value? GenAI should address existing inefficiencies, high-cost areas, or growth opportunities.
2. *Technical Feasibility:* Is the data accessible and of high enough quality? Are the systems and people ready to support implementation?
3. *Adoption Potential:* Will people actually use it? Is the workflow integration smooth, and are employees or customers receptive to change?

Frameworks like the *Impact vs. Complexity Matrix* or *Use Case Funnel* can help teams evaluate ideas and narrow them down to a high-value shortlist. By now, there is plenty of literature on the subject of AI use case identification, evaluation, and prioritization, e.g., Sharma (2024), Mayan (2023) and Sfita (2024).

While use cases vary by industry and function, here are a few commonly successful ones:

1. *Customer Service:* handling Tier 1 support inquiries.
2. *Marketing*: generate personalized content.
3. *Legal & Compliance:* summarize contracts.
4. *Software Development:* generate code.
5. *Finance & Procurement:* profile supplier risks.

Let's try to create an Impact vs. Complexity Matrix for those (Fig. 13.1), adding two low impact use cases for illustrative reasons:

6. *Auto-generate short, simple emails such as meeting confirmations, reminders, or basic follow-ups.*
7. *Highly customize an AI plugin for a niche internal tool used by very few employees.*

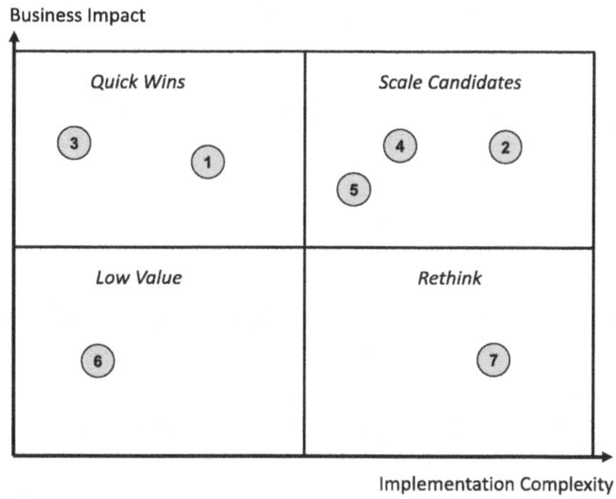

Fig. 13.1 Impact vs. Complexity Matrix for selected GenAI Use Cases

Justification for the classifications of the 7 example use cases:

1. delivers measurable efficiency quickly, with minimal integration overhead.
2. promises significant ROI, but demand data pipelines, content governance, and experimentation frameworks.
3. saves expert time without requiring deep system changes.
4. improves velocity but requires integration with development workflows and quality safeguards.
5. drives strategic insight but needs robust data sources and auditability.
6. Quick to roll out, but time saved is small compared to higher-impact domains.
7. High development effort with little measurable benefit; resources should be allocated elsewhere.

Naturally, a book with a strong focus on requirements engineering would be incomplete without a detailed discussion of RE use cases. In fact, we will extend this discussion to cover the entire software development life cycle in Chap. 15.

Once identified, each use case should be linked to a *value hypothesis*: What KPIs will it affect? What outcomes do you expect in 6–12 months? How will success be measured?

Establishing this business case upfront

- Helps secure leadership buy-in.
- Focuses development efforts.
- Enables continuous improvement based on outcomes.

Small, well-scoped pilots are ideal to test these hypotheses before scaling. Early wins can then be turned into reference cases to expand adoption across other teams and departments.

It's important to remember that the use case portfolio is constantly evolving. What's high-value today may be table stakes in a year. Organizations should review and reprioritize regularly—especially as new capabilities emerge, employee skills grow, and infrastructure matures.

Strategic use case prioritization turns GenAI from an innovation experiment into a business performance driver. By focusing on *value, feasibility* and *adoption*, companies can make the most of early investments and build the case for broader transformation.

13.5 From Process Automation to AI-Orchestrated Processes

In the previous subsection, we contrasted Robotic Process Automation (RPA) with Generative AI, highlighting how GenAI extends automation from rigid, rule-based tasks to more adaptive and knowledge-intensive activities. AI can support individual process steps such as extracting requirements, generating reports, or drafting customer responses. However, these contributions are still largely *assistive*, enhancing predefined processes rather than reshaping them.

So, what has been described in the previous subsection, still represents only a transitional stage in the broader GenAI transformation journey.

The next stage is the application of Agentic AI, which elevates process management from assistive automation to *dynamic orchestration*. Traditional process management relies on predefined workflows: tasks are modeled upfront, optimized once, and then executed repeatedly with limited flexibility. Robotic Process Automation (RPA) and early workflow engines operate under this paradigm—efficient, but brittle when faced with changing contexts or unstructured inputs.

The rise of Agentic AI changes this paradigm fundamentally. Agentic systems can not only act within workflows but also design, adapt, and execute processes dynamically based on real-time input data, business priorities, and environmental signals. Instead of humans defining the "happy path" upfront, AI agents orchestrate the flow of tasks in response to context.

Key implications for process management include:

- Dynamic Process Design: Processes are no longer modeled once and deployed. Agents can generate and optimize workflows on demand, adjusting task order, resources, and hand-offs in real time.
- Context-Aware Execution: Input data, compliance rules, customer intent, or external market signals continuously influence how a process unfolds. For example, a claims-handling process may diverge based on detected fraud risks without requiring predefined branches.
- Human-in-the-Loop Governance: While agents can autonomously manage tasks, humans remain involved as supervisors, arbiters of exceptions, and decision-makers in ethical or high-stakes cases.
- Evolving Processes Instead of Static Models: AI-driven processes learn from outcomes: bottlenecks, customer satisfaction, or compliance flags feed back into the system, creating *self-improving workflows*.

Table 13.1 Strengths of Humans and AI Agents in Process Management.

Humans	AI Agents
• Goal formulation • Setting values, priorities, goals, and constraints • Accountability for results • Critical thinking & judgment • Creativity • Common sense and contextual awareness	• Dynamic process design • Operating within defined rules and constraints • Execution of tasks at scale • Data-driven optimization • Processing speed • On-the-fly generation of workflows, code, or documentation • Cost-efficient handling of routine and repetitive tasks

So, humans and AI Agents form hybrid teams with complementary strengths. Table 13.1 summarizes these contrasts and shows how both roles interlock in process management.

This side-by-side view makes clear that humans provide direction, judgment, and ethical grounding, while AI agents contribute speed, scalability, and adaptability. Effective process management in the age of Agentic AI will depend on integrating these strengths into hybrid orchestration models.

To the point
Agentic AI transforms process management from static execution into adaptive orchestration—where workflows are designed, executed, and evolved dynamically by AI, guided by data and context.

This shift represents more than an efficiency gain: it redefines the role of business process management itself. Organizations will need to rethink process governance, compliance assurance, and workforce enablement when workflows are no longer fully predefined, but are instead *continuously co-created by AI and humans.*

13.6 Workforce Enablement and Change Management

Generative AI has the potential to radically improve how employees work—but only if they understand it, trust it, and know how to use it. While much attention is placed on selecting the right tools or use cases, the real enabler of GenAI transformation is *human readiness*.

In many organizations, employees respond to GenAI with a mix of curiosity, excitement, skepticism, and fear. Some are early adopters, pushing boundaries and sharing clever hacks. Others ignore the potential of GenAI and believe that GenAI cannot support them in their job. A third group quietly wonder: Will this replace my job?

To the point
GenAI adoption succeeds only when employees feel empowered, not threatened, by the technology. ◀

This emotional and skill-based divide makes change management and enablement a critical layer of the transformation journey.

Employees need to be trained not only in using new technologies, but also in adapting their working methods to AI-driven process changes. Training should also foster a cultural shift—encouraging openness to change and a clear understanding of both the possibilities and limitations of AI.

The dual goal is adoption and engagement, i.e., true workforce enablement means achieving two things:

1. Equipping employees with the skills and confidence to use GenAI tools effectively, and.
2. Creating a culture that embraces continuous learning, experimentation, and responsible innovation.

To the point
Skills, trust, and culture are the real engines of GenAI transformation—not the tools themselves. ◀

This goes far beyond training sessions—it requires a mindset shift, supported by consistent leadership messaging, role modeling, and incentives.

As already indicated in 13.3, a successful GenAI enablement program should address multiple dimensions:

1. Foundational AI Literacy
   - GenAI basics including wording.
   - Strengths, limitations, and responsible use.
   - GenAI use cases examples.
2. Prompt Engineering Skills (See Chap. 14)
   - Prompting Strategies.
   - Prompt Frameworks.
   - Prompting techniques.
   - The use of system prompts.
   - Prompt and agent libraries.

3. Role-Specific Skills (See Chap. 15)
   - Role specific prompting.
   - Role specific GenAI use cases.
   - Using AI to support decision-making.
   - Upcoming new GenAI technologies (vision).
4. New Ways of Working
   - Collaborative workflows between humans and AI.
   - Embedding AI agents into daily routines.
   - Creating feedback loops to improve AI performance and usability.

To support adoption at scale, companies should treat GenAI transformation as a *change management program*—not just a training program and tech rollout.

Here's how:

- *Segment your audience*: Tailor messaging and training by function, seniority, and tech familiarity.
- *Use key user*: Identify and empower GenAI ambassadors across departments to support peer learning.
- *Lead from the top*: Executives and managers must visibly use and advocate for GenAI tools themselves.
- *Normalize experimentation*: Encourage pilot use, tolerate failure, and share learnings openly.
- *Create psychological safety*: Employees should feel safe asking questions and voicing concerns without fear of being replaced or judged.
- *Be transparent about impact*: If roles will change or evolve, communicate early and support transitions through reskilling and new opportunities.

GenAI transformation is as much a human journey as a technological one. Without deliberate workforce enablement and empathetic change management, even the best GenAI tools will fail to gain traction.

To the point
The human side of GenAI is the deciding factor between a costly rollout and a lasting transformation. ◄

Companies that invest in their people—through training, trust-building, and cultural readiness—will unlock the true potential of GenAI: not as a replacement for human capability, but as a tool to help people grow and adapt.

13.7 Robust Data and Technology Foundations

To harness the full power of Generative AI, organizations need more than clever prompts and creative use cases—they need a strong and scalable technical foundation. This includes high-quality data, but equally important are interoperability across systems and fit-for-purpose GenAI application that align with business, IT, and regulatory needs.

Let's start with *data*: While large language models are typically trained on massive datasets, most companies today are not in the business of developing their own foundational models. Instead, the real opportunity lies in enabling GenAI applications—especially those using Retrieval-Augmented Generation (RAG) techniques—to tap into internal enterprise data, whether structured (like databases or spreadsheets) or unstructured (like documents, emails, and wikis).

Tools such as Microsoft Copilot Chat (using its "Work" rather than the "Web" grounding mode) rely heavily on internal content to generate relevant, context-aware responses. Their effectiveness does not depend on having perfectly structured data, but rather on ensuring that the relevant content is accurate, accessible, and organized well enough to be effectively retrieved and interpreted. When internal data is siloed, outdated, or difficult to navigate, even the most advanced GenAI tools will struggle to deliver meaningful results. Other platforms, like Google Gemini for Workspace, Salesforce Einstein, or Notion AI, similarly use RAG to surface the right information at the right time, drawing from a company's existing knowledge rather than retraining models from scratch.

Secondly, we want to focus on *interoperable systems*: Modern enterprises often operate within a patchwork of legacy systems, SaaS platforms, and custom-built tools. GenAI, especially in the context of Retrieval-Augmented Generation (RAG) or real-time GenAI Agents, requires smooth, real-time access to data and context across these systems.

To enable this:

- API-first design is essential: Ensure key platforms expose data and services via secure, well-documented APIs.
- Integration with collaboration tools (e.g., Microsoft 365, Slack, ServiceNow) enhances usability and context-awareness.
- Unified identity and access management (IAM) is crucial to govern who can access what data across tools and environments.
- Event-driven architecture can enhance responsiveness and enable GenAI to react to system changes in near real-time.

Interoperability isn't just a technical problem—it's also an organizational challenge, requiring alignment between IT, security, data teams, and business units to avoid duplication and data fragmentation.

To the point
True GenAI interoperability depends as much on organizational alignment as on technical integration. ◀

Last but not least, let us cover the topic of *Fit-for-Purpose GenAI application.* Choosing the right application depends on your specific use case portfolio, data architecture, scalability needs, and risk profile.

Key considerations for the GenAI application selection include:

1. Hosting Strategy (Cloud, On-Prem, or Hybrid)
   - Public cloud LLMs offer speed and ease of access.
   - Private, fine-tuned models or on-prem deployments may be better for sensitive data or regulated industries.
   - Many enterprises opt for a hybrid GenAI architecture—mixing public API usage for non-sensitive tasks with private models for internal applications.
2. Model Customization and Control
   - Does the platform support prompt tuning or RAG workflows?
   - Does it allow integration of proprietary knowledge bases and domain-specific data?
3. Compliance and Security
   - Does the platform adhere to relevant privacy and security standards (e.g., ISO 27001, SOC 2 (What is SOC 2? n.d.), GDPR, HIPAA (Health Insurance Portability and Accountability Act, n.d.)
   - Is data usage for future model training clearly governed?
4. Cost and Scalability
   - Some platforms charge by token, others by compute—understanding your usage profile helps optimize for cost.
   - Look for platforms that allow horizontal scaling, load balancing, and observability (e.g., prompt tracking, latency, and usage analytics).

Ultimately, GenAI application and infrastructure decisions should not be made in isolation. They must be:

- Aligned with enterprise architecture and cloud strategy.
- Co-developed with IT operations and cybersecurity teams.
- Reviewed continuously as new models, modalities, and pricing structures emerge.

Choosing the right interoperable tech stack and responsible GenAI application sets the stage for secure, scalable, and sustainable value creation. Forward-thinking companies treat this not as an IT project—but as a core enabler of digital transformation.

To the point
Selecting GenAI applications is a strategic choice that shapes long-term value, security, and scalability. ◄

13.8 Agile Execution, Cross-Functional Collaboration, and Scaling

In the context of GenAI transformation, speed matters—but so does precision. Organizations that succeed are those that adopt agile, iterative delivery models and foster tight collaboration across business, IT, legal, and data teams. This combination enables faster experimentation, better risk management, and stronger alignment with real-world business needs.

Unlike traditional IT projects, GenAI initiatives come with uncertainty, rapid innovation cycles, and evolving user expectations. Rigid planning and long timelines don't work. Instead, agile execution lets teams test quickly, fail safely, and scale confidently.

GenAI capabilities—especially those based on large language models—introduce a fundamentally new way of working. Success depends on a continuous learning loop within blended agile teams (see Table 13.2).

Beyond team composition, you need both a robust technical foundation—such as versioned prompt and agent libraries and scalable inference pipelines—and parallel organizational structures: including governance processes, stakeholder alignment, and feedback loops.

Pushing hard on one axis (see Fig. 13.2) while neglecting the other leads to brittle systems or stalled initiatives. We recommend pursuing *content-technical* and *enterprise scaling* journeys in tandem, from pilot to enterprise-wide deployment.

Crucially, successful enterprise scaling hinges not just on governance and tooling, but also on proactive communication and change management, because employee

Table 13.2 Possible composition of blended agile teams

Function	Contribution
Business units	Define use cases, validate value, own outcomes
IT & architecture	Specify and develop enterprise specific GenAI applications, ensure integration and security, provide scaling environment
Data science/GenAI engineers	Tune models, design prompt, create prompt and agent library, evaluate
Legal & Risk	Guide responsible use, manage compliance
Change & Training	Drive adoption and skill-building
End users	Provide feedback, reveal real-world friction

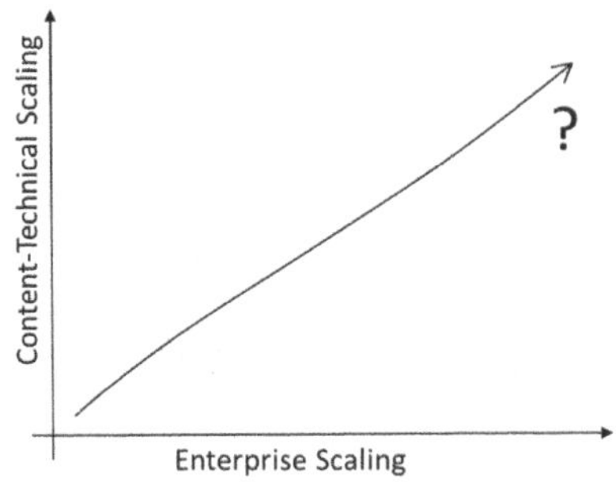

Fig. 13.2 Content-Technical Scaling vs. Enterprise Scaling

acceptance is paramount. At each phase, plan and execute targeted outreach—newsletters, demos, trainings, dashboards, and leadership endorsements—to ensure every team hears about, understands, and adopts the new GenAI measures.

With each of the following building blocks we want to illustrate the side-by-side approach of the two scalings:

- GenAI Use Case Catalog (see Table 13.3 and section13.4).
- GenAI Applications including agents (see Table 13.4 and section 14.6).
- Prompt & Agent Libraries (see Table 13.5 and section 14.7).

Other building blocks include Data & Knowledge Management and Monitoring & Observability (feel free to define your own scaling phases and additional building blocks).

Note that pursuing both content-technical and enterprise scaling at once to the maximum can yield diminishing returns. Key challenges:

Table 13.3 Scale GenAI Use Case Catalog

Phases	Content-Technical Scaling	Enterprise Scaling
Pilot	Document 5–10 use cases as templates on a shared wiki	Appoint a curator; solicit success stories; apply light review; announce use case templates on company wiki; invite feedback via an enterprise communication platform
Expansion	Build a searchable portal with categories, tags, ratings	Define submission/review templates; run quarterly case-jam workshops; introduce recognition programs; highlight top use cases on intranet homepage; run quarterly show-and-tell sessions
Enterprise	Integrate deploy-from-catalog automation into the AI platform	Incentivize contributions with budget credits; enforce lifecycle governance; measure catalog ROI; embed catalog links in daily tools; issue monthly 'Catalog highlights' newsletter; integrate use case prompts into GenAI agents

Table 13.4 Scale GenAI Applications

Phases	Content-Technical Scaling	Enterprise Scaling
Pilot	Build 1–2 proof-of-concept bots/tools with hard-coded integrations	Select a champion team; gather qualitative feedback; maintain lightweight support; communicate pilot roadmap to all teams; solicit early adopter champions
Expansion	Refactor SDKs/UI components; add telemetry dashboards and logs	Spin up support channel/office hours; prioritize cross-team feature requests; provide training; publish roadmap updates via intranet; hold demo days; collect testimonials
Enterprise	Launch self-service app-builder portal with SLA'D APIs and autoscaling infrastructure	Charter an AI Center of Excellence; define rollout playbooks; tie funding to usage KPIs; deploy internal marketing campaign; require GenAI app overview in onboarding; feature success stories in leadership updates

Table 13.5 Scale Prompt- and Agent Libraries

Phases	Content-Technical Scaling	Enterprise Scaling
Pilot	Curate a handful of high-value prompts and agents stored in a shared folder; manual versioning	Assign single owner/reviewer; light governance (naming conventions); share by request; publish launch announcements via internal newsletter; host intro webinar
Expansion	Add metadata (tags, model versions); introduce basic retrieval APIs or CLI	Formalize PR/review workflow; define contributor roles & permissions; track usage metrics; maintain a public changelog; run Q&A sessions; spotlight contributors in town-hall
Enterprise	Migrate to a dedicated prompt- and agent DB service with versioning, role-based access control, and automated quality gates	Establish governance board; enforce audit logs, SLAs; schedule regular library reviews; roll out company-wide training modules; integrate usage metrics into executive dashboards; celebrate library milestones in all-hands

- Resource Contention: Engineering effort and process overhead compete for limited budgets and talent.
- Change Management Friction: Heavy governance can slow technical innovation, while rapid rollouts can outpace process readiness.
- Cultural Lag: Organizational buy-in at scale often trails technical capabilities, leading to misalignment.

To overcome these, blend paired growth, minimum-viable governance, and continuous feedback loops. Within each phase, work in short cycles (1–4 weeks) using agile ceremonies—stand-ups, retrospectives, demos—to maintain alignment. This approach lets organizations move from pilot to production without overextending resources or stifling innovation.

To the point
Balancing rapid technical progress with equally strong organizational scaling is the only way to achieve sustainable GenAI adoption. ◄

13.9 Measurement and Governance

As organizations deploy GenAI at scale, it becomes critical to measure what matters and to ensure GenAI applications are used in ways that are transparent, responsible, and aligned with corporate policies. Measurement and governance go hand in hand—they provide the structures and signals that help guide GenAI from experimentation to sustainable impact.

Without these mechanisms in place, even promising initiatives can drift into ambiguity, generate compliance risks, or fail to demonstrate return on investment.

13.9.1 Measurement

Early enthusiasm for GenAI often centers around potential. But sustaining investment requires evidence of actual value. Organizations need to move from "this is cool" to "this delivers business value."

Key steps include:

1. Define clear KPIs up front
   - Link use cases to measurable business outcomes: productivity, cost savings, customer satisfaction, cycle time reduction, etc.
   - Differentiate between leading indicators (e.g., usage, adoption rate) and lagging indicators (e.g., cost reduction, revenue uplift).
2. Monitor usage and engagement
   - Track user interactions with GenAI applications, e.g., frequency and prompt types.
   - Use insights to refine UX, training materials, or prompt and agent libraries.
3. Assess quality and accuracy
   - Create mechanisms for human-in-the-loop validation, especially in customer-facing or regulated domains.
   - Use scoring frameworks to evaluate GenAI outputs (e.g., relevance, factual accuracy, tone).
4. Feed metrics back into iteration

- Use measurement data as a feedback loop to improve GenAI use cases, optimize performance, and make smart, low-risk decisions about where to focus next.

13.9.2 Governance

While some organizations see governance as a constraint, the most mature ones treat it as a strategic enabler—a way to build trust, reduce risk, and scale responsibly.

Key governance dimensions include:

1. Model and Tool Governance
   - Maintain a registry of approved LLMs and GenAI applications used across the organization.
   - Evaluate models on performance, cost, privacy, and alignment with business needs.
2. Data Usage and Privacy
   - Define clear rules for which data can be used, e.g., for fine-tuning or prompting.
   - Enforce data classification, anonymization, and retention policies.
3. Risk & Compliance Oversight
   - Involve legal, compliance, and risk teams early in the use case lifecycle (see 13.8).
   - Define review workflows for sensitive use cases (e.g., HR, finance, legal communications).
   - Track and audit GenAI usage across teams, users, and departments.
4. Ethical and Responsible Use Policies
   1. Embed guidelines for fairness, non-discrimination, and transparency in all GenAI development.
   2. Ensure that outputs are attributable and verifiable, especially where decisions impact individuals or customers.

In this context, we also need to consider governance bodies. Many organizations create dedicated structures to oversee GenAI governance, such as:

- AI Steering Committees Set priorities, resolve conflicts, and ensure strategic alignment.
- AI Ethics Boards or Responsible AI Councils Provide independent guidance and escalation on ethical dilemmas.
- GenAI Product or Platform Teams Manage tooling, experimentation environments, prompt libraries, and lifecycle processes.

Measurement and governance are not afterthoughts—they are essential foundations for scaling GenAI with confidence and accountability. When done well, they enable innovation without chaos, experimentation without risk, and adoption without erosion of trust.

References

Health Insurance Portability and Accountability Act. (n.d.). Wikipedia. https://en.wikipedia.org/wiki/Health_Insurance_Portability_and_Accountability_Act

Kapoor, C. (Dec. 2024). *Why Generative AI leaders must blend thinking, building and creating value.* World Economic Forum. https://www.weforum.org/stories/2024/12/why-generative-ai-leaders-must-blend-thinking-building-and-creating-value/

Mayan, K. (2023). *What is the Value vs Effort Matrix? Explanation, Guide, and How to Avoid its Pitfalls. (Part of "Product Roadmaps 101: Complete A-to-Z Guide for Product Managers").* https://www.savio.io/product-roadmap/

Parmer, S. (2025). *Traditional RPA vs AI-Driven Process Automation: A 2025 Comparison.* Get-Generative.ai. https://www.getgenerative.ai/traditional-rpa-vs-ai-driven-process-automation/

Sfita, D. (December 2024). *Think Big, Start Small, Scale Fast: A Practical Guide to AI Innovation Funnel.* https://mindit.io/blog/a-practical-guide-to-ai-innovation-funnel/

Sharma, R. (2024). *AI and the Boardroom (Chapter: Evaluating Generative AI Use Cases: A Comprehensive Framework).* Apress. https://link.springer.com/chapter/10.1007/979-8-8688-0796-1_25

What is SOC 2®?. (n.d.). https://secureframe.com/hub/soc-2/what-is-soc-2

14 Prompt and Agent Engineering

14.1 Prompts: The Keys to Generative AI

GenAI systems rely on *input prompts* to produce specific outputs. These prompts act as explicit instructions, guiding the AI toward generating content that aligns with the user's intent. The clarity, precision, and creativity of a prompt play a decisive role in determining the quality, relevance, and usefulness of the generated results.

Whether the goal is to create a marketing report, design innovative website content, or rapidly prototype an application, effective *prompt engineering* is a valuable skill that can save time and significantly improve outcomes. As the name suggests, prompt engineering involves crafting and refining prompts to harness and optimize the performance of LLMs.

Achieving consistently high-quality results is not trivial. The most effective prompt engineers often share traits with skilled requirements engineers—strong analytical thinking, precise use of language, and an ability to anticipate ambiguities before they arise.

Just as clear and unambiguous requirements documentation is essential in RE, carefully structured prompts help AI models interpret the author's intent accurately. Detailed and context-rich descriptions in a prompt tend to produce more accurate and relevant results. Conversely, vague, ambiguous, or overly general prompts can lead to unintended or unsatisfactory outputs. Consider this real-world example from a customer request to a contact center bot:

"Since the last update, the thing is not working as expected."

J. Kawelke and T. Niebisch, *AI-Driven Transformation - Practical Frameworks for Real-World Impact*, Future of Business and Finance,
https://doi.org/10.1007/978-3-662-72549-8_14

This prompt is problematic: 'the thing' could refer to any product or service, and 'not working as expected' could mean anything from total failure to a slight performance issue. Moreover, 'last update' is undefined—was it a software patch, a service configuration change, or something else?

Improved version:

> *"Since the software update 3.2 of the Omni-Channel system, the response times to user inputs have increased from one second to two seconds. Can you provide an explanation for this change in max 5 sentences?"*

Prompts are a powerful means of steering generative AI models. Designing them effectively requires both practice and an understanding of how AI systems respond to different types of inputs. By mastering prompt optimization, users can unlock the full potential of generative AI to produce highly relevant, context-aware, and high-quality content.

To the point
Well-crafted prompts turn generative AI from a generic responder into a precise, context-aware problem solver. ◀

In recent years, a new discipline has emerged alongside prompt engineering: *agent engineering* (Smith, 2025). While a prompt defines a single interaction, an *agent* embodies a persistent prompt extended with memory, planning, and the ability to use tools or integrate with external systems. Agent engineering involves designing the underlying prompts, workflows, and safeguards that govern such autonomous systems. Just as prompt engineering turns a model into a reliable problem solver, agent engineering turns it into a consistent and trustworthy collaborator.

For example, in a no-code platform a single well-crafted prompt such as:

> *"You are a customer support assistant for our e-commerce shop. Answer questions about products, link to relevant FAQ entries, and escalate billing issues to a human agent when necessary."*

is enough to instantiate an agent. Unlike a one-off prompt, this definition persists across conversations, giving the assistant a stable role, memory, and integration with external resources.

The following subsections will examine prompting strategies, prompt frameworks, and prompting techniques for effective prompt engineering. Afterwards, we will discuss system prompts and developer messages, before turning to GenAI agents and the emerging discipline of agent engineering. Finally, we will explore prompt and agent libraries.

14.2 Prompting Strategies

Before looking at specific frameworks for structuring prompts, it is helpful to understand the broader strategies for interacting with generative AI systems. A single prompt is rarely the end of the story: users often refine, extend, or reframe their inputs to guide the model more effectively. How this interaction is approached can make a significant difference in the quality of results.

In practice, three strategies have proven especially valuable:

- the iterative approach,
- the all-in-one prompt, and,
- the model-as-collaborator approach.

Each has its strengths and limitations, and the most effective prompt engineers know when to apply which strategy.

14.2.1 The Iterative Approach

The iterative approach resembles a dialogue: the user provides an initial prompt, receives an output, and then gradually adds clarifications or constraints based on the result. The model "remembers" the previous turns in the same chat session, so each new prompt builds on what has already been established.

For example, a user might begin with a simple request:

> *"Draft a short blog post about sustainable energy."*

If the output is too general, the user can refine:

> *"Please focus on the role of solar power in urban environments."*

The conversation continues until the user is satisfied with the output.

At this point, we revisit the UML activity diagram introduced in Part I to illustrate the process (see Fig. 14.1).

This approach is intuitive and flexible. It is particularly useful when the task is open-ended and the desired outcome is not yet fully defined. However, it can also become time-consuming, and without careful steering, the interaction may drift away from the original intent.

From a green-IT perspective, iterative prompting may come with a higher CO_2 footprint, as each refinement requires another model run and thus additional energy consumption. By contrast, an all-in-one prompt, that we consider in the next subsection, can be more resource-efficient, aligning better with sustainability goals.

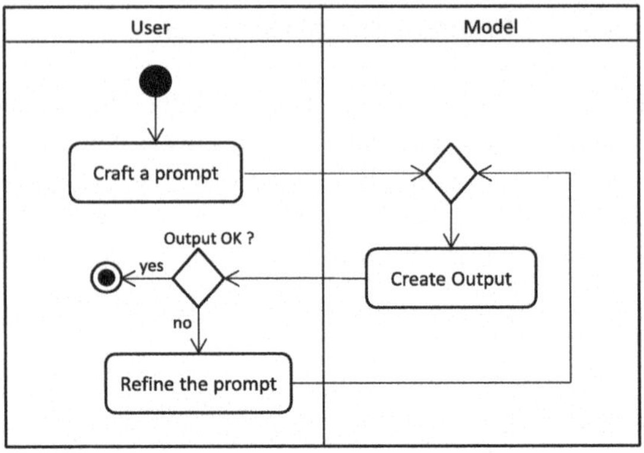

Fig. 14.1 The iterative prompting approach

14.2.2 The All-in-One Prompt

The all-in-one strategy seeks to provide everything the model needs in a single, well-crafted prompt. This reduces the need for back-and-forth and often produces a high-quality draft on the first attempt.

For example, instead of starting vague, the user might directly write:

> *"Draft a 500-word blog post about the role of solar power in urban environments. The audience is city planners and policymakers, the tone should be informative yet engaging, and the structure should include an introduction, three main points, and a conclusion."*

Because the model receives complete instructions, context, and expectations at once, the output is typically more aligned with the user's needs. The downside is that crafting such a comprehensive prompt requires foresight, clarity, and practice. This is where prompt frameworks, such as **ICIO** or **RACE**, become especially useful: they act as checklists to ensure no essential element is overlooked (Sec. 14.3).

The all-in-one prompt results in a much simpler activity diagram (see Fig. 14.2).

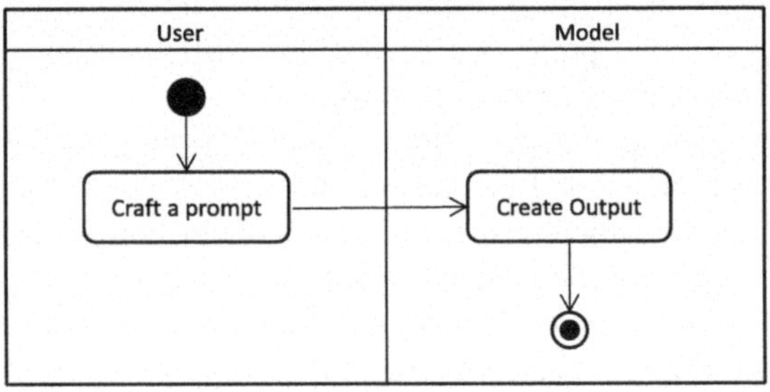

Fig. 14.2 The "all-in-one" prompting approach

14.2.3 Letting the Model Ask Questions

A third strategy is to treat the model not only as a generator of text, but also as a conversation partner capable of gathering requirements. Instead of providing every detail upfront, the user can instruct the model to ask clarifying questions before attempting a final response.

For example:

> *"I would like you to write a blog post about sustainable energy. Before you begin, please ask me up to five questions so you better understand key points to include."*

The model might then respond with questions such as:

- Who is the target audience?
- Should the post highlight a specific form of sustainable energy?
- What length are you aiming for?

Once the user provides the answers, the model is better equipped to deliver a well-aligned response. This process is illustrated in the activity diagram in Fig. 14.3.

This approach is particularly powerful when the user has not yet fully articulated their needs. It reduces the risk of vague prompts leading to irrelevant outputs, and it creates a more collaborative dynamic between human and machine.

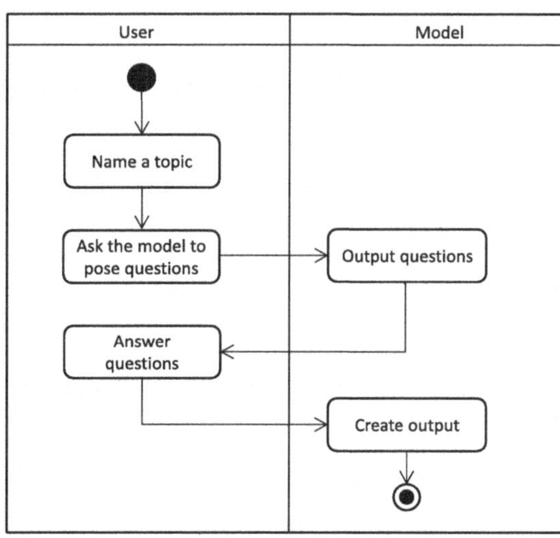

Fig. 14.3 The "Letting the model ask questions" prompting approach

14.2.4 Choosing the Right Strategy

There is no single "best" prompting strategy; the right choice depends on the situation.

- **Iterative prompting** works well for exploratory tasks or when the outcome is not yet clearly defined.
- **All-in-one prompting** is efficient when the requirements are already clear and can be fully specified from the start.
- **Letting the model ask questions** bridges the gap when the user's intent is still forming and helps surface important details that might otherwise be overlooked.

In real-world use, these strategies are often combined. A user might start by letting the model ask clarifying questions, then refine the result iteratively, and finally arrive at a polished all-in-one prompt that can be reused.

By mastering these strategies, users can work more effectively with generative AI systems. In the next subsection, we will look at how structured prompt frameworks can support especially the all-in-one approach, ensuring that even complex prompts remain clear, complete, and easy to construct.

14.3 Prompt Frameworks

Having seen how the quality of a prompt directly shapes the output of a generative AI system, the next step is learning how to design prompts in a more systematic way. Rather than relying on intuition or trial and error, structured frameworks help ensure that key elements—such as intent, context, and expected results—are always addressed.

Frameworks do not limit creativity; instead, they provide a practical scaffolding that makes prompts more consistent, reproducible, and effective. They act as checklists that guide users toward formulating instructions in a way that AI models can interpret reliably.

In the following pages, we introduce two particularly effective frameworks: ICIO (Instruction, Context, Input, Output Indicator) and RACE (Role, Action, Context, Expectation). Each offers a simple but powerful way of structuring prompts to unlock more accurate and relevant results.

14.3.1 The ICIO Framework

At NTT DATA, we developed the ICIO framework as part of our internal trainings on prompt engineering. Through extensive practice across diverse projects and client engagements, we have found that ICIO is one of the most effective structures for creating reliable prompts. It is simple enough to be adopted quickly, yet powerful enough to address the majority of real-world use cases we encounter.

The framework consists of four elements:

- Instruction—What you want the model to do.
- Context—Background information that situates the task. The context sets the stage. It can tell the model *where, when, for whom, and why* the task matters.
- Input—It supplies the *specific data, content, or facts* that must appear in the output. They are typically *unique, factual, or non-negotiable details.* LLMs are good at filling gaps creatively (hallucinations). If you provide context but no input, they may generate plausible but incorrect facts. By explicitly supplying input, you reduce the risk of unwanted invention.
- Output Indicator—Guidance on how the result should be delivered (length, tone, format, constraints).

Context as well as input may include:

- *Documents* (e.g., text documents, research papers, or blog articles) that serve as reference material. A document does not necessarily have to be submitted as a file; it can also be provided via a URL.
- *Images*, which can be used to support the creation of design elements or visual content, or to generate a description of the image.
- *Audio recordings*, which may serve as templates for generating music or sound effects.
- *Structured data*, provided for evaluation.

Taken together, the four components transform a vague prompt into a precise and reliable instruction. To illustrate, let's walk through the same task step by step, adding one ICIO element at a time. Each output is produced by ChatGPT with its GPT-5 model. Please note that we copy the email body only here and not the full output of the model.

Step 1: Instruction only.
Prompt:
"Write a product launch email."

Output:

“Header:
✨*Meet [Product Name]—Your New [Benefit/Category].*

Opening:
We're thrilled to announce the launch of ***[Product Name]****, designed to [solve pain point / deliver key benefit]. After months of innovation and dedication, it's finally here—and we can't wait for you to try it.*

Highlight Benefits (3 Bullets Work Well):

- ***[Feature 1]**—[Short benefit-focused explanation]*
- ***[Feature 2]**—[How it helps the user]*
- ***[Feature 3]**—[Why it's better than alternatives]*

Call to Action (CTA):
👉*[Get Started Now] (button).*

Closing:

Thank you for being part of our journey. With [Product Name], we're excited to help you [achieve goal / transform experience].

Warmly,

The [Your Company] Team".
The model generates a well-structured, polished template with clear sections, engaging elements, and a professional tone. However, with only a broad instruction, the result remains generic, lacking in relevance and specificity. You can see this from the numerous placeholders in the output.

Step 2: Instruction + Context.
Given the constraints of this book and our relatively simple example, we limit both context and input (in the next step) to a few small details.

Prompt:
"Write a product launch email for a new project management software targeted at small businesses."

Output:

"Header:
Introducing [Product Name]—Project Management Made Easy for Small Businesses

Body:
*Managing projects shouldn't feel overwhelming. That's why we built **[Product Name]**, a project management software designed with small businesses in mind. Whether you're tracking deadlines, assigning tasks, or collaborating with your team, our intuitive platform keeps everything organized in one place — so you can focus on growing your business.*

With [Product Name], you can:

- *Organize tasks, projects, and deadlines with ease.*
- *Collaborate seamlessly with your team, wherever they are.*

- *Get real-time updates and insights without the complexity.*
- *Scale as you grow — no enterprise-level bloat, just what you need.*

Why small businesses love it:

Unlike other tools that feel too heavy or too simple, [Product Name] strikes the perfect balance — powerful enough to keep projects on track, simple enough to start using in minutes.

Call to Action:
👉*[Start Your Free Trial Today].*

Or, schedule a quick demo to see how [Product Name] can work for your team.

Closing:

We can't wait to help your business run smoother, faster, and smarter.

Cheers,

The [Product Name] Team."
By adding context, the model can better tailor the email. The output now refers to the right type of product and audience, making it more useful than the first version. Also, the number of placeholders has decreased.

<u>Step 3: Instruction + Context + Input.</u>
Prompt:
"Write a product launch email for a new project management software targeted at small businesses. The software is called TaskFlow, and it offers automated scheduling, team dashboards, and AI-powered progress tracking."

Output:

"Header:
🚀*Introducing TaskFlow—Project Management Made Simple*

Body Copy:
*Managing projects doesn't have to be complicated. That's why we built **TaskFlow**, the all-in-one project management software designed with small businesses in mind.*

With TaskFlow, you can:

- ***Automate Scheduling****—Save time with intelligent task assignments and calendar syncing.*

- ***See the Big Picture***—*Use customizable* ***team dashboards*** *to track progress in real time.*
- ***Stay Ahead with AI***—*Get smart insights and* ***AI-powered progress tracking*** *to keep projects on schedule.*

Whether you're juggling multiple clients or coordinating a growing team, TaskFlow helps you streamline operations, boost productivity, and hit every deadline.

Call to Action:
👉*[Start Your Free Trial Today].*

Closing Line:

TaskFlow is here to take the stress out of project management—so you can focus on growing your business.

Cheers,

The TaskFlow Team.
Here, the inclusion of concrete inputs (product name and features) enriches the response. The model highlights differentiators and produces content that feels specific and aligned with the actual offering.

<u>Step 4: Instruction + Context + Input + Output Indicator.</u>
Prompt:
"Write a concise and engaging product launch email for a new project management software targeted at small businesses. The software is called TaskFlow, and it offers automated scheduling, team dashboards, and AI-powered progress tracking. The email should be no longer than 150 words, end with a clear call-to-action, and adopt a friendly yet professional tone."

Output:

*"**Subject:** Meet TaskFlow—Smarter Project Management for Small Businesses* 🚀

Body:

Hi [First Name],
We know running a small business means wearing many hats. That's why we built ***TaskFlow***—*your all-in-one project management partner.*

With ***automated scheduling***, ***team dashboards***, *and* ***AI-powered progress tracking***, *TaskFlow helps you save time, stay organized, and keep your team moving in sync—without the overwhelm.*

Whether you're planning next week's projects or tracking progress in real time, TaskFlow makes it simple to focus on what matters most: growing your business.

Ready to work smarter?
👉*[Start Your Free Trial Today].*

Cheers,

The TaskFlow Team"
By adding an output indicator, the request becomes fully structured. Now the model knows not only what to write and for whom, but also how the result should look and sound. This significantly increases the likelihood of receiving a usable draft on the first attempt.

In this example, each additional ICIO component improves the relevance, focus, and practical quality of the generated text. The framework does not make prompts longer for the sake of it; rather, it ensures that the essentials are communicated in a way the AI can reliably interpret.

Note that ICIO was illustrated using an all-in-one approach, where each new prompt would be started with a new session. However, the same principle can also be applied iteratively: after providing the instruction in one prompt, we can add the context in the next, then supply the input, and finally add the output indicator to obtain the expected result. This flexibility shows that ICIO—but also the following frameworks—are compatible with both prompting strategies.

14.3.2 The RACE Framework

While ICIO provides a highly detailed structure for constructing prompts, sometimes a lighter but similar framework feels more natural for you. The RACE framework offers such an alternative. It is built around four elements that align closely with how humans naturally describe tasks:

- Role—Who should the model "be" in the scenario?
- Action—What should the model do?
- Context—What background information is necessary?
- Expectation—What does a successful output look like?

This structure helps transform a plain request into a well-defined instruction without too much detail.

By explicitly defining the *role*, users can steer the model's perspective and tone. A financial analyst, a requirements engineer or a creative designer will all approach the same task differently—and the model adapts accordingly.

The *action* provides clarity about the task itself, ensuring that the model knows exactly what is expected. Adding *context* situates the action in the right environment, supplying the information necessary to avoid vague or misleading results. Finally, the *expectation* acts as a quality check: it specifies the format, level of detail, or outcome that determines whether the result is useful.

Although both frameworks have four parts, RACE reduces the effort required by combining or omitting elements that ICIO treats separately.

- In ICIO, *Context* covers background, and *Input* requires the user to supply specific details, data, or materials (e.g., product name, statistics, text to rewrite). This forces precision and makes the framework especially strong for technical or business-critical use cases.
- In RACE, *Role* takes over part of the context by defining the perspective ("as a teacher...," "as a project manager..."). However, there is no dedicated Input element. Details may still be included in the context, but they are not explicitly required.

This makes RACE quicker to apply: users can create effective prompts without worrying about whether they have provided every possible piece of input data. It guides the model into the right mindset and ensures the output is structured and appropriate, but it does not demand the same level of completeness as ICIO.

Example.
Consider the task of writing a customer-facing FAQ response. Using RACE, the prompt might look like this:

"[Role] You are a customer support agent. [Action] Write a response to a user who asks why their account was locked. [Context] The customer uses our online banking system and has recently failed multiple login attempts. [Expectation] The response should be polite, reassuring, and provide next steps in 3–4 sentences."

This prompt immediately gives the model enough direction to produce a relevant, tone-appropriate, and actionable output.

RACE does not replace ICIO but complements it. Where ICIO ensures completeness and precision for complex tasks, RACE offers a quick and effective way to structure prompts in day-to-day interactions. Together, they provide users with a flexible toolkit: one for depth and reliability, the other for speed and simplicity.

14.3.3 Other Frameworks

Beyond ICIO and RACE, a number of other prompt frameworks have been proposed in practice. While they may not be as comprehensive or widely applicable, they can be valuable in specific situations. The following four frameworks are among the most frequently referenced.

14.3.3.1 APE (Action, Purpose, Expectation)

APE is a lean framework that emphasizes clarity of intent. The *Action* specifies what the model should do, the *Purpose* explains why the task is being carried out, and the *Expectation* defines the desired outcome. This is useful when users want to quickly align the model's response with both the task and the reasoning behind it, without adding unnecessary detail.

14.3.3.2 TAG (Task, Action, Goal)

TAG focuses on breaking down the user's request into a simple sequence. The *Task* outlines the general assignment, the *Action* describes how the model should approach it, and the *Goal* states the end result. Its strength lies in its brevity, making it easy to remember and apply in fast-paced scenarios.

14.3.3.3 RISE (Role, Information, Steps, Expectation)

RISE resembles RACE but adds more procedural guidance. After assigning a *Role* to the model and supplying necessary *Information*, the user can outline specific *Steps* to be followed before setting the final *Expectation*. This makes RISE particularly useful for instructional prompts or multi-stage tasks where process matters as much as outcome.

14.3.3.4 COAST (Context, Objective, Action, Style, Tone)

COAST is designed for creative and content-focused use cases. *Context* and *Objective* define the situation and intent, while *Action* tells the model what to do. *Style* and *Tone* then shape the output's character. This framework is highly effective when working on marketing, storytelling, or brand-related tasks where voice and presentation are critical.

14.3.3.5 Summary

These frameworks demonstrate the variety of approaches that exist for structuring prompts. Each highlights slightly different aspects: APE and TAG focus on simplicity and clarity, RISE provides procedural structure, and COAST emphasizes stylistic control. Together, they expand the prompt engineer's toolkit, offering flexible options for different contexts and needs. Since ICIO is the only one of our introduced frameworks that does not form an English word, you might find it helpful to remember the mnemonic *'Instruction Creates Intelligent Output'*—or, for a more humorous twist, *'I – the CIO'*.

14.4 Prompting Techniques

So far, we have looked at prompting strategies (how to approach a prompting session) and prompt frameworks (how to structure the essential elements of a single prompt). Both remain central to designing clear instructions and achieving reliable results.

Prompting techniques, in contrast, are specialized methods that influence the model's reasoning process or style of response—for example, asking it to explain its steps or showing examples of the desired output. These techniques were highly valuable in earlier stages of generative AI, when models needed more explicit guidance to perform complex tasks consistently.

To the point
While the importance of prompting techniques is likely to decrease as models become more powerful, effective prompting strategies and frameworks will remain essential for structuring intent and ensuring reliable results, also in the age of agentic AI. ◀

In the following subsections, we will briefly explore some of the most effective prompting techniques. While they may no longer be the foundation of prompt engineering, they remain useful complements to strategies and frameworks—especially in specialized or demanding scenarios.

14.4.1 Shot Prompting

One of the most widely used prompting techniques is known as shot prompting. The term *shot* refers to how many *examples* of a task are included in the prompt. These examples demonstrate to the model *how* to perform an input-output transformation or reasoning step, rather than simply instructing it. Depending on the number of examples provided, we speak of zero-shot, one-shot, or few-shot prompting.

In *zero-shot prompting*, the model is expected to perform the task without being shown any example. The user only describes the desired outcome.

Prompt:
"Transform the following requirement into a user story: The system must allow login with two-factor authentication."

Output (M365 Copilot Chat):
"As a user, I want to log in using two-factor authentication so that my account is more secure and protected from unauthorized access."

Zero-shot prompting is simple and fast but not always reliable. The model may interpret the task correctly, or it may deliver inconsistent formats.

One-shot prompting strengthens the instruction by including a single example of the desired transformation. This helps the model understand the expected structure and style of the output. In our example we slightly change the standard user story template by replacing "so that"—as the model knows it without giving examples—with "in order to."

Prompt:
"Transform requirements into user stories strictly following the structure of the given example.
Example: Requirement: The application shall provide a password reset function. User Story: As a user, I want to reset my password in order to regain access if I forget it. Now transform the following requirement: The system must allow login with two-factor authentication."

Output (M365 Copilot Chat):
"As a user, I want to log in using two-factor authentication in order to enhance the security of my account."

With just one example, the model is much more likely to follow the intended format and deliver a coherent user story. In our example above, it is interesting to note that without the word *"strictly,"* most models default to the *"so that"* format, even though we provided the example using *"in order to."*

Let us now consider *few-shot prompting* in practice. Few-shot prompting might remain powerful when the task requires sentiment classification or adherence to specific structures, formats, or domain conventions.

However, modern language models are so strong that we were not able to construct an example where few-shot prompting outperforms zero-shot or one-shot prompting. We gave it a try with sentiment classification.

Prompt:
"Classify the following customer reviews using the custom sentiment categories:

- *Red = Highly dissatisfied, urgent problem*
- *Yellow = Mild dissatisfaction, not urgent*
- *Green = Positive feedback*
- *Blue = Mixed feedback*

Example 1:

Review: 'The software keeps crashing and I can't finish my work.'

Sentiment: Red

Example 2

Review: 'The app is good overall, but it takes a while to load.'

Sentiment: Yellow

Example 3:

Review: 'Fantastic support team, thank you!'

Sentiment: Green

Example 4:

Review: 'The product works well, but the delivery was very late.'

Sentiment: Blue

Now classify this review:
'The new update improved the interface, but it also introduced frequent bugs.'"

All models we tried out gave the correct output: blue category.

But now we left out the examples and tried out this zero-shot prompt:

"Classify the following customer reviews using the custom sentiment categories:

- *Red = Highly dissatisfied, urgent problem*
- *Yellow = Mild dissatisfaction, not urgent*
- *Green = Positive feedback*
- *Blue = Mixed feedback*

Review:

'The new update improved the interface, but it also introduced frequent bugs.'"
Also here, the result was always: blue category.

So, in our experiments with custom sentiment classification, models consistently produced the correct result regardless of whether examples were included, showing little advantage for few-shot prompting. However, we believe that there are cases where a handful of examples function like "mini training data," anchoring the model to a specific convention. That could be a cheap alternative for fine-tuning a language model.

To the point
One-shot prompting usually strikes the best balance between clarity and consistency, while few-shot adds limited value with today's strong models. ◄

In practice, organizations and individuals often combine prompt frameworks such as ICIO with prompting techniques like one-shot prompting. The framework ensures that all essential information is included, while the technique enforces that outputs follow a consistent style or structure.

14.4.2 Chain-of-Thought Prompting

One of the limitations of large language models is that they sometimes "jump to conclusions." They can provide fluent answers that appear correct but lack proper reasoning. Chain-of-Thought (CoT) prompting addresses this by explicitly encouraging the model to explain its reasoning step by step before producing the final answer. This can simply be done by instructions like *"Let's think step by step."*

LLMs already contain reasoning patterns in their parameters from pretraining. CoT prompting helps surface those hidden patterns, especially for tasks that require logical reasoning, calculations, or multi-step problem-solving. Prompting the model to "think step by step" improves accuracy by forcing it to handle smaller subproblems. Also when writing out intermediate steps, the model is less likely to make subtle mistakes and more likely to deliver a transparent, verifiable result. Also, it gives us the chance to follow the models "train of thought" and—if necessary—correct our prompt or the output.

Let us consider an example. Suppose a team wants to prioritize software requirements based on three factors: business value, implementation effort, and risk. A naive prompt might yield a list that looks reasonable at first glance, but the reasoning behind it remains hidden.

<u>Simple Prompt (no CoT):</u>
"Prioritize the following requirements based on business value, implementation effort, and risk:

1. *The system must provide multi-language support.*
2. *The system must offer a dark mode for the user interface.*
3. *The system must allow users to log in with two-factor authentication.*
4. *The system shall enable data export to Excel format."*

<u>CoT Prompt:</u>
"Prioritize the following requirements based on business value, implementation effort, and risk:

1. *The system must provide multi-language support.*
2. *The system must offer a dark mode for the user interface.*
3. *The system must allow users to log in with two-factor authentication.*
4. *The system shall enable data export to Excel format."*

Think step by step. After showing your reasoning, provide the final prioritized list."

We refrain from showing any LLM output here. Please try out these examples yourself. With modern LLMs you will see the following:

- Basic reasoning even without the CoT addition.
- a slightly more detailed output with the CoT prompt,
- probably different results, even if you use the same CoT prompt with different LLMs.

If you give the task described in the CoT prompt to several experienced requirements engineers (without the permission to use AI), you might get as many different solutions. The same you will experience with different LLMs and Chatbots. But at least you can follow the chain of reasoning and react accordingly—with a slightly adapted prompt in a new chat, a follow-up prompt in the same chat or by manually changing the output.

14.4.3 Prompt Chaining

While chain-of-thought prompting encourages the model to reason step by step within a single response, prompt chaining distributes reasoning across multiple prompts. Each output becomes the input for the next, creating a sequence that gradually builds toward the desired result.

This technique is particularly effective for complex or multi-stage tasks where handling everything in one prompt would be unwieldy or error-prone. By breaking the workflow into smaller, manageable steps, prompt chaining reduces cognitive load on both the user and the model.

Example.
Consider the task of generating a market analysis:

Step 1 (Research):

"Summarize the five most important trends in the European renewable energy market based on the following report."
Step 2 (Analysis):

"From the trends you summarized, identify the two that pose the biggest risks for new entrants."
Step 3 (Output Formatting):

"Transform your analysis into a two-page executive summary suitable for a board presentation."
Instead of expecting the model to jump directly to a polished board-ready report, chaining structures the reasoning process into stages, each with clearer inputs and

expectations. Please try out this prompt chain by yourself. You might want to input a current report or use this reference (Armstrong, 2025).

Example.
In our second example, we return to the field of requirements engineering and the use case "validate requirements." Similarities between system requirements are to be discovered by comparison, and inconsistencies and redundancies are to be analyzed. The requirements are part of the prompt here. If there are a large number of requirements, the requirements would be provided, for example, in a file or extracted from a database. In our example—that was already considered in Table 9.1—we have chosen 3 requirements that contain contradictions between requirements 1 and 2 as well as 1 and 3. Redundancies could exist in the requirement pairs 1 and 2 as well as 2 and 3.

Step 1 (Context, Input, and Similarity Analysis Instructions with Output Indicator).

"Here are three requirements for an Omni-Channel system:

- *Exclusively between 5 AM and 12 AM, the Omni-Channel—system must offer the policyholder the opportunity to view the knowledge database. Access is not possible at other times.*
- *Exclusively during operating hours from 6 AM to 11 PM, the Omni-Channel system must offer the policyholder the opportunity to view the knowledge database. The knowledge database is locked at other times.*
- *From 11 PM to 6 AM, it is not possible for the policyholder to view the knowledge database due to maintenance reasons.*

Examine the requirements for similarities in sentence structure in percent.

Analyze each combination of 2 requirements for this.

Present your output as a table with 2 columns. Column 1 is named "Requirement Numbers" and contains the requirement numbers of the two compared requirements, respectively.

Column 2 is named "Similarities" and contains the similarity in percent, accurate to one decimal place."

Step 2 (Add contradiction analysis results).

"Now examine the requirements for direct and indirect contradictions between them in relation to the access times to the knowledge database.

Analyze each combination of 2 requirements for this.

Add a column 3. This is named "Contradictions." If a contradiction exists, write "Contradiction: "in column 3 and explain the contradiction.

If no contradiction exists, simply write "none.""
Step 3 (Add redundancies analysis results).

"Now analyze the requirements for redundancies between them.

Add a fourth column. This one is named "Redundancies."

If it is certain that a redundancy exists, column 4 contains an explanation of the redundancy.

If a redundancy might exist, write "Possibly:" and explain the possibility of a redundancy.

If it is certain that no redundancy exists, simply write "none.""
Output (with GPT-5).

We focus here on the output of the third prompt in the prompt chain, as columns 3 and 4 were added sequentially in steps 2 and 3, respectively, without altering the content of the previous output.

Req Number	Similarities	Contradictions	Redundancies
1 & 2	72.8	Contradiction: Req 1 allows between (5, 24) but Req 2 denies between (23, 24). Req 1 allows between (5, 24) but Req 2 denies between (0, 6).	None
1 & 3	47.6	Contradiction: Req 1 allows between (5, 24) but Req 3 denies between (23, 24). Req 1 allows between (5, 24) but Req 3 denies between (0, 6).	None
2 & 3	47.4	None	Possibly: Requirement 3 is fully contained within requirement 2.

While readability in the output could be improved (use of the standard time format), the prompt chain output highlights how the transformer-based LLM can precisely detect and explain contradictions and redundancies within requirements, a task that traditional NLP methods struggled to achieve reliably. It shows the strength of contextual understanding across sentences, enabling nuanced requirement validation beyond mere keyword or pattern matching.

Benefits of Prompt Chaining

- Modularity: Complex requests are broken into smaller, testable units.
- Transparency: Each step provides an intermediate result that can be reviewed, corrected, or refined before moving on.
- Flexibility: If one part of the chain underperforms, it can be retried or restructured without re-running the entire process.
- Compatibility with frameworks: Frameworks such as ICIO or RACE can be applied to each step, ensuring precision and completeness throughout the chain.

Limitations

Prompt chaining requires multiple model runs, which significantly increases energy consumption and, consequently, the carbon footprint—contradicting the principles of green AI. While it can improve reasoning, this approach risks undermining sustainability goals. Additionally, it introduces dependency: if early steps contain errors, those may cascade downstream unless corrected. For these reasons, careful design and monitoring are essential.

14.5 System Prompts and Developer Messages

14.5.1 Definition and Scope

A system prompt is a high-priority instruction given to a language model. It defines the GenAI application's role, scope, and tone before any user input is seen, and it establishes how the language model should respond across an entire session. Modern GenAI architectures also specify a clear *instruction hierarchy*:

1. platform rules (Global, non-overrideable constraints set by the language model provider to enforce safety, compliance, and usage policies across all interactions) (OpenAI Model Spec, 2025; Release Notes, 2025),
2. system prompts or developer messages (as described in this subsection) (Armstrong, 2025),
3. user prompts.

This hierarchy ensures that user prompts cannot casually override the GenAI application's fundamental behavior. It also means that platform rules (that we will not further consider in detail) cannot be changed or bypassed by application developers or users.

Note that OpenAI has introduced the term *developer messages* with its first specific reasoning model GPT-o1. By renaming system prompts to developer messages, OpenAI emphasizes that these messages represent instructions authored by the application builder, not by the end user or the model. So, in a chat setting, different roles exist: *user* (end-user), *assistant* (model output), and *developer* (the hidden guiding instructions). This helps the model distinguish what comes from the developer vs. the user, which is especially important when instructions conflict.

However, you may have noticed that in many GenAI applications, the system prompt (or developer message) is visible to the end user or even presented as an empty input field. In such cases, the user temporarily takes on the role of the developer by defining the hidden instructions that guide the model's behavior. Whenever this message is editable by the end user, we refer to it as the *system prompt* instead of the developer message. For consistency and clarity, we will use the term system prompt throughout the rest of this section also as a synonym for developer message.

System prompts remain important even as models grow stronger. While advanced models need fewer prompt techniques than earlier ones—as discussed in the previous subsection—system-level instructions continue to anchor the GenAI application in its intended mission, enforce policy boundaries, and ensure consistency across many conversations.

Designing an effective system prompt—whether by the GenAI application developer or the user—involves balancing clarity, safety, and usability. At its core, the prompt should explain the GenAI application's purpose, define what is in and out of scope, and set the desired tone and format of outputs. It should also contain policy guidance—how to refuse disallowed content, when to ask clarifying questions, and how to handle ambiguous requests.

System prompts and task-level prompt frameworks such as ICIO share some similarities. Both emphasize clarity of instruction, context, and output constraints. The difference lies in their scope: ICIO is applied at the level of a single user request, ensuring that one prompt is complete and effective, while a system prompt sets the overarching rules that apply across all tasks and conversations. In practice, you really need system prompts when building persistent AI assistants or applications where safety, compliance, or consistency must be guaranteed. For one-off tasks or experiments, however, a carefully crafted ICIO prompt is often enough without defining a system prompt.

However, if a system prompt is defined, users still enter their own prompts—and frameworks such as ICIO remain highly useful. The key is to recognize the scope: the system prompt establishes the application's persistent defaults, while ICIO structures the task-specific request. In practice, this means avoiding duplication and contradiction. ICIO's instruction should focus on the task, its context should describe the situation at hand, and its input should provide concrete data. Output indicators should extend but cannot override the system defaults set in the system prompt. Put simply: the system prompt sets the stage, and the prompt framework helps you play your part effectively within it.

14.5.2 Design Principles for System Prompts

To design an effective system prompt, it is helpful to think in terms of a few guiding principles. These principles ensure that the application's role and behavior are defined clearly, safely, and consistently across all interactions.

1. *Purpose & scope*—Define the application's mission, intended audience, and boundaries of use.
2. *Safety & policy hooks*—Specify what content should be refused, how to handle disallowed requests, and how to confirm risky actions.
3. *Reasoning & quality*—Indicate preferred reasoning approaches (e.g., step-by-step), fact-checking, and citation practices.
4. *Formatting & interaction contract*—Standardize tone, structure (e.g., Markdown, JSON), and interaction style for consistency.
5. *Tool and data handling rules*—Define how to treat external content (trusted vs. untrusted), when to summarize, and how to use tools responsibly.

These five areas ensure that the system prompt is not just a set of vague instructions, but a durable framework for reliable, transparent, and safe AI behavior.

Although we've presented these five design principles in the context of system prompts, they in fact reflect broader best practices that also apply to platform rules. What differs is scope. System prompts define the persistent defaults—persona, safety boundaries, output forma—for all user interactions. Platform rules, in turn, enforce compliance and restrict the assistant's possible actions. While the principles remain constant—clarity, safety, reasoning, structure—their point of application shifts across these layers.

14.5.3 Example System Prompt and Analysis

Let us analyze a specific system prompt, provided by GPT-5:

"*You are an AI assistant for a financial advisory platform. Your purpose is to provide general information on personal finance but never give personalized investment advice. Always be concise and professional in tone. When explaining financial concepts, use plain English and provide simple examples. If a user request goes beyond general information and asks for personal investment recommendations, politely refuse and explain why. All lists should be formatted with bullet points, and numerical data must include a source citation when available.*"

The following analysis refers to the design principles in the previous subsection.

- Purpose & scope: The GenAI application's role is clearly limited to "general information," excluding personal advice. This narrows risk and sets expectations.
- Safety & policy hooks: The refusal condition ("never give personalized investment advice") is spelled out explicitly, including how to decline.
- Reasoning & quality: The instruction to provide examples encourages clarity, while requiring citations anchors outputs in verifiable information.
- Formatting & interaction contract: Output style is standardized through bullets, tone ("concise and professional"), and plain-English language.

- Tool and data handling rules: While not included here, the prompt could be extended with rules on how to handle untrusted web content or integrations.

This example illustrates how a system prompt translates abstract principles into actionable defaults. It does not tell the application what task to perform in each conversation but rather sets the *rules of the game* for all interactions.

To the point
System prompts are the operating manual of an AI application: they encode purpose, safety, reasoning, and style at a high priority—second only to the platform rules that always take precedence.◄

14.6 Agent Engineering

So far, we have looked at prompt engineering as a way to design better single interactions between a human and a generative AI system. *Agent engineering* builds on this foundation: it is the discipline of creating, refining, and maintaining *AI Agents* and *Agentic AI systems* through the careful design of their prompts, workflows, and integrations. Where prompt engineering optimizes one request at a time, agent engineering turns those principles into *persistent, autonomous systems*.

14.6.1 Off-the-Shelf Agents

Before building custom agents, you should first consider off-the-shelf agents. These are pre-built, enterprise-ready assistants that come with robust capabilities out of the box. They are typically developed by large technology vendors, optimized for reliability, security, and scale, and are often integrated directly into widely used business ecosystems.

Examples include:

- Microsoft Copilot (embedded across Microsoft 365 and Dynamics), which provides ready-to-use productivity and business agents.
- Google Duet AI (integrated into Google Workspace), offering collaborative AI features without requiring configuration.
- Salesforce Einstein Copilot, which delivers conversational CRM agents natively connected to sales, service, and marketing workflows.
- ServiceNow Now Assist, designed to streamline IT and enterprise service management through conversational automation.

These off-the-shelf solutions offer a strong first step into agent adoption: they minimize setup effort, deliver immediate value, and often come with built-in compliance and governance features. However, they are not platform independent: each runs only inside its vendor's ecosystem. This close integration provides stability and security, but it also creates dependency, often referred to as *vendor lock-in.*

At the same time, new efforts have emerged to overcome these limitations. *PwC's Agent OS* aims to enable AI agents to work across multiple cloud providers such as Microsoft Azure, Google Cloud, and Anthropic. Similarly, the startup*/dev/agents*, founded by ex-Android leaders, is building an "Agent OS" designed to let autonomous agents operate across heterogeneous environments. These developments point to a future where off-the-shelf agents may evolve toward greater cross-platform interoperability, reducing dependency on single-vendor ecosystems.

14.6.2 No-Code Agent Creation

In everyday usage, a user typically formulates one prompt at a time. In contrast, agents are powered by carefully engineered prompts that define their role, scope, and workflow from the outset. In modern no-code platforms, an agent can often be created with nothing more than a single well-crafted system prompt. For example:

"*You are a support agent for prompt engineers. When a user describes a task, help them rewrite it into the ICIO format. First, identify the Instruction (what the AI should do). Then clarify the Context (background and audience). Next, extract or request the necessary Input (data, text, or details). Finally, propose an Output Indicator (format, tone, length, or constraints). Present the finished prompt in a clear ICIO structure.*"

This single instruction can instantiate an agent with a stable role: acting as a structured assistant for designing prompts in the ICIO framework. Behind the scenes, the no-code platform locks this definition into a persistent system prompt and may even provide the agent with template storage or a prompt library. From the user's perspective, agent engineering at the no-code level is essentially advanced prompt engineering turned into a persistent service.

Thinking about agents through the lens of agent engineering highlights several insights:

- System prompt as *agent DNA*. The agent's persistent identity and behavior stem from its system prompt. Designing this is the first act of agent engineering.
- Frameworks scale-up. Structures like ICIO or RACE are not limited to one-off tasks; they can also be used to design the *meta system prompt (*Schneider Electric, 2025*)* that defines an agent's overall role.
- Chaining prompts into behaviors. Multi-step reasoning workflows—analyze, summarize, format—are essentially prompt sequences orchestrated inside the agent.
- User prompts still matter. Even when an agent has a strong underlying system prompt, task-specific prompts affect how well it applies its instructions.

For anyone familiar with prompt engineering, moving into agent engineering is a natural progression (as long as you are in the no-code or low-code area). Agents are not a replacement for prompts—they are the embodiment of prompt engineering in application form. By applying the same principles of clarity, completeness, and context, you can create agents that perform consistently, align with organizational goals, and integrate seamlessly into workflows.

To the point
No-code agents are engineered prompts in action—extended into systems that act autonomously and consistently across tasks. ◀

In the evolving landscape of no-code agent engineering, several platforms now enable users to design autonomous AI assistants using intuitive, visual, or natural language interfaces—no code required. A prime example is *Microsoft Copilot Studio*, a powerful tool embedded within the Microsoft 365 ecosystem that enables declarative agent creation via natural language descriptions or configuration wizards. Users can define roles, knowledge sources, and conversational topics, with seamless integration into Teams, SharePoint, or Power Automate workflows—bringing enterprise-grade agents to life in minutes.

Other platforms reinforced this trend in 2025: *Relevance AI* offers a drag-and-drop workspace for business workflows, letting users configure agents for tasks like data processing or email summaries. *Relay.app* and *Gumloop* feature modular, visual builders that make prompt-based agent creation quick and accessible. And for voice-first applications, *Synthflow AI* provides no-code interfaces to build conversational agents capable of handling real-time customer interactions.

These and other tools illustrate how prompt engineering now powers agent creation itself: a single, well-crafted instruction or configuration not only defines the LLM's immediate output but also instantiates an entire autonomous assistant.

14.6.3 Low-Code and Full-Code Agents Creation

In *low-code agent engineering*, prompting remains central but is increasingly combined with light scripting, workflow design, and integrations. The system prompt typically defines how the agent should communicate and reason, while code modules specify which tools or APIs it can access. Prompt engineering therefore becomes more modular: instead of a single defining instruction, developers often create a system prompt, a few reusable templates, and specialized task prompts. In this setting, prompting still plays an important role in ensuring quality and reliability, but it is only one piece of the design puzzle alongside workflow orchestration and light coding.

Tools like *Flowise* enable visual creation of AI agents and automated workflows with minimal coding, positioning these platforms as practical bridges between design and deployment in enterprise environments. Similarly, *Workato One's Agent Studio* offers a unified, low-code interface for building, governing, and managing AI agents.

In *full-code agent engineering*, the role of prompting is reduced further. Developers focus on programmatic orchestration—building planners, memory modules, and toolchains—while prompts serve mainly as embedded components that guide specific reasoning styles, error handling strategies, or output formats. Typically, a handful of strong prompts act as building blocks, while the majority of the system's behavior is defined in code. In this approach, prompting becomes less about defining the entire agent and more about fine-tuning how the agent handles particular steps or edge cases, with the bulk of the design effort shifting to architecture, integration, and logic.

For full-code agent frameworks, developers turn to modular, orchestration-centric toolsets such as *LangChain*, *AutoGen,* and *CrewAI*, which underpin robust, deployable AI agents capable of multi-step reasoning, memory, and integration with external data sources. These frameworks are cornerstones for teams needing deep customization, scalability, and control in agent behavior.

14.6.4 Comparing Agents

Different approaches to agent engineering shift the balance between prompting, programming, and integration.

- In off-the-shelf solutions, the vendor manages prompts, integrations, and governance.
- In no-code platforms, a single prompt can define the assistant's role, scope, and behavior.
- In low-code platforms, scripting and workflow design are added, making prompting one part of a broader toolset.
- In full-code frameworks, prompts are embedded inside larger architectures where coding, integrations, and orchestration dominate.

Table 14.1 summarizes the strengths, trade-offs, and required skills of each approach:

In practice, many organizations start with no-code tools to test ideas, move to low-code for everyday operations, and adopt full-code frameworks for mission-critical or large-scale deployments. Choosing the right approach depends less on the agent itself than on who will maintain it and how complex the surrounding system is meant to be. Choose based on your team's skills and your workflow complexity.

Table 14.1 Agent comparison

Approach	Best For	Skill Required	Trade-offs
Off-the-shelf	Immediate adoption with minimal setup; enterprise-grade reliability	None (end-user ready)	Very limited customization; vendor lock-in
No-code	Rapid prototyping for non-technical users	Basic prompt-writing skills	Fast to start, but limited control and flexibility
Low-code	Teams that need quick setup with some customization	Light scripting or workflow design	Balanced speed and flexibility; requires light scripting
Full-code	Complex, large-scale, or highly customized agents	Advanced programming and integration expertise	Maximum control and scalability; higher development effort

14.7 Prompt and Agent Libraries

As prompts and agents grow in sophistication, it becomes inefficient to reinvent them for every project. Prompt and agent libraries address this by collecting reusable, high-quality assets that can be adapted across teams and use cases. They save time, improve consistency, and ensure compliance with organizational policies. In many organizations, these libraries are quickly becoming part of knowledge management and governance structures, much like code repositories or requirements templates. We have already considered these libraries in 13.8 in the context of technical and enterprise scaling.

14.7.1 Prompt Libraries

Prompt libraries are curated collections of well-tested prompts for recurring tasks. Instead of drafting from scratch, users can start from proven examples and adapt them to their context.

Examples of use:

- A marketing team may store prompts for ad copy, social media posts, or campaign reports.
- In requirements engineering, prompts for transforming specifications into user stories or generating acceptance criteria can be reused across projects.
- Technical teams may keep prompts for SQL generation, code reviews, or test case design.

Public repositories such as *PromptBase* or Hugging Face's collections offer thousands of templates, while enterprise platforms like Microsoft Copilot Studio or

Relevance AI support internal prompt libraries that are governed and versioned. In both cases, prompts are increasingly treated as artifacts to be documented, evaluated, and maintained.

On the other hand, creating an internal prompt library from scratch—for example in Microsoft SharePoint or Atlassian Confluence—is not particularly difficult. To make it useful in practice, we recommend including at least the following functionalities:

- Filter options, e.g., for different scope groups such as Requirements Engineering, Development, Design, or Marketing.
- Predefined system prompts tailored to those scope groups.
- Support contacts for library users.
- A submission process to hand in new prompts.
- A prompt details table with entries such as:
  - Short name of the prompt.
  - Scope group.
  - Contact person or creator.
  - Date of the latest change.
  - Links to one or more chatbots so that the selected prompt can be directly copied into the chatbot.

Of course, the development team for such a library should include both a Requirements Engineer and a UX Designer to ensure usability and completeness.

14.7.2 Agent Libraries

While prompt libraries collect reusable instructions for one-off tasks, agent libraries go further: they store preconfigured agents with defined roles, workflows, and sometimes tool integrations. Such libraries allow teams to build on tested designs rather than reinventing agents from scratch, ensuring consistency and speeding up deployment.

On the no-code and low-code side, platforms like Microsoft Copilot Studio, Relay.app, or Synthflow AI offer agent templates for customer service, HR onboarding, or project management. These pre-built agents give organizations a quick starting point while maintaining governance through features like Microsoft's integration with enterprise compliance tools.

For developer-focused environments, open-source libraries are emerging. The Agents Toward Production repository provides production-grade blueprints for multi-tool orchestration, memory, and observability. Similarly, the GenAI Agents repository consolidates dozens of implementations across domains—from customer support bots to research assistants. At the enterprise level, NVIDIA's NeMo Agent Toolkit offers a framework-agnostic way to connect agents, tools, and workflows with profiling and monitoring built in. Business-oriented solutions such as Glean's AI Agent Library provide template agents for everyday enterprise tasks like ghostwriting, reminders, or ticket resolution, helping teams deploy with minimal setup.

Compared to prompt libraries, however, agent libraries present some unique challenges. Agents are not only defined by prompts but also by their runtime environments, connectors, and tool integrations. This creates a degree of platform lock-in: for example, an agent created in Copilot Studio cannot simply be "copied" into LangChain or AutoGen without rebuilding its workflows. To mitigate this, the reusable design elements can be separated—such as the system prompt, input/output schemas, and tool interfaces—from the platform-specific wiring. Another difficulty is governance: because agents can act autonomously and touch external systems, agent libraries require stricter approval workflows, security tagging, and continuous testing than prompt libraries.

In practice, agent libraries bring the same advantages as prompt libraries—faster deployment, standardization, and reuse—but require more careful engineering to stay portable and safe. By treating agents like software components (versioned, tested, and documented), you can gradually build a sustainable ecosystem of reusable, reliable agents.

To the point
Agent libraries come with added complexity: platform dependencies, integration challenges, and stronger governance needs. ◂

14.7.3 Maintenance, Governance, and Future Outlook

Just like software code, prompts and agents in libraries need continuous evaluation and maintenance. Outdated prompts may lead to inconsistent results; unsafe agent definitions can create compliance risks. Successful libraries use tagging, version control, and ownership rules, ensuring that assets are updated, documented, and aligned with company policies.

Looking ahead, prompt and agent libraries will evolve into marketplaces and ecosystems. Enterprises will exchange pre-built prompts and agents the same way they currently exchange APIs or code packages. Emerging concepts such as meta-prompt libraries—templates for designing system prompts or entire agents—will further accelerate engineering practices. Increasingly, prompts and agents are being treated as software artifacts in pipelines, managed alongside models, code, and data.

To the point
Prompt and agent libraries transform one-off creations into reusable, governed assets. ◂

References

Armstrong, J. (2025). *Crafting Better LLM System Prompts: A Meta-Prompt Approach.* https://ailookingglass.blogspot.com/2025/05/crafting-better-llm-system-prompts-meta.html
OpenAI Model Spec (always the latest). (2025). https://model-spec.openai.com
Release Notes: System Prompts (always the latest). (2025). https://docs.anthropic.com/en/release-notes/system-prompts
Schneider Electric. (2025). *European Renewables Report 2025.* https://perspectives.se.com/renewable-energy/european-renewables-report-2025
Smith, A. (2025). *The Future of AI Agent Engineering: A Comprehensive Guide.* https://ugstechs.com/ai-agent-engineering/

Connecting Requirements Engineering to Agentic Development

15

15.1 Introduction: The Agentic Bridge

In Part I, we established Requirements Engineering as the foundation of successful software projects and showed how Generative AI (GenAI) can accelerate and enrich that work. These use cases illustrated GenAI's potency as a productivity multiplier.

This chapter bridges Part I (Requirements Engineering) and Part II (AI and Generative AI). We now widen the lens from requirements to the entire Software Development Life Cycle (SDLC). As development increasingly evolves toward agent development and agentic system development, those domains must also be part of our discussion and the SDLC in our context becomes the *DPDL*—the *Digital Product Development Lifecycle*. Unless otherwise specified, when we say "digital product development" we mean software, agent, or agentic system development (see 11.4.4 for the introduction of the terms agent and agentic system).

Two shifts matter:

1. how products are changing and
2. how GenAI is changing how we build them.

Let's start with item 1 and a statement upon which this whole chapter will be built:

> **To the point**
> Today we put AI into products. Tomorrow we put products into AI.

J. Kawelke and T. Niebisch, *AI-Driven Transformation - Practical Frameworks for Real-World Impact*, Future of Business and Finance,
https://doi.org/10.1007/978-3-662-72549-8_15

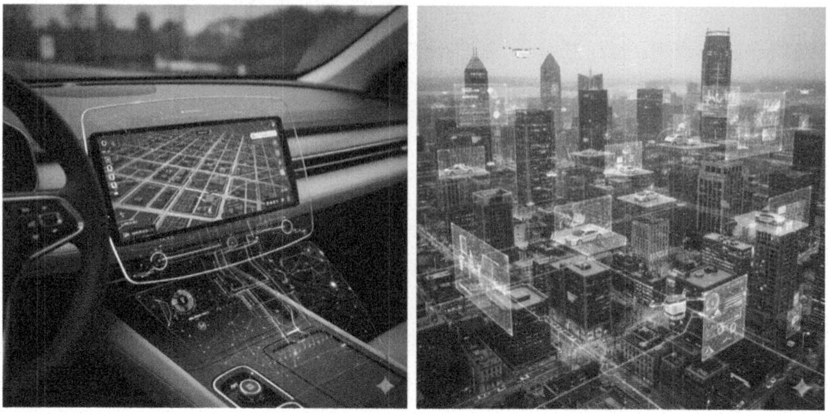

Fig. 15.1 From AI as a feature to AI as the environment (illustrative rendering by Google's Gemini/Imagen)

To illustrate this evolution, consider two systems-engineering examples of products with embedded software:

1. **Mobility**
   - **AI in Products:** A car dashboard with a built-in GPS. AI enhances the product.
   - **Products in AI:** A city powered by an AI "grid," with cars, drones, and devices operating within it. Here, products function inside an AI-driven environment.
2. **Personal Devices**
   - **AI in Products:** A smartphone with AI features (voice assistant, camera filters, predictive text). The product is primary; AI is an add-on.
   - **Products in AI:** An AI-powered cloud platform where smartphones, smart speakers, and wearables are interfaces to AI services. Because the AI lives in the cloud, it aggregates data from connected devices, learns from user behavior, and improves over time.

Figure 15.1 illustrates the mobility example, contrasting a car with embedded AI features and a city operating within an AI-driven grid.

While the mobility example makes this evolution concrete, the same principle applies more broadly. To generalize, the Fig. 15.2 contrasts two worlds: in the first, products contain a small bubble of AI that supports their function; in the second, agentic systems emerge where many product bubbles coexist inside a larger Agentic system. This captures the essence of our "To the point" statement: Today we put AI into products. Tomorrow we put products into AI.

Taking a broader view of recent agentic developments, we observe a common pattern of change over time across both products and processes. At a high level,

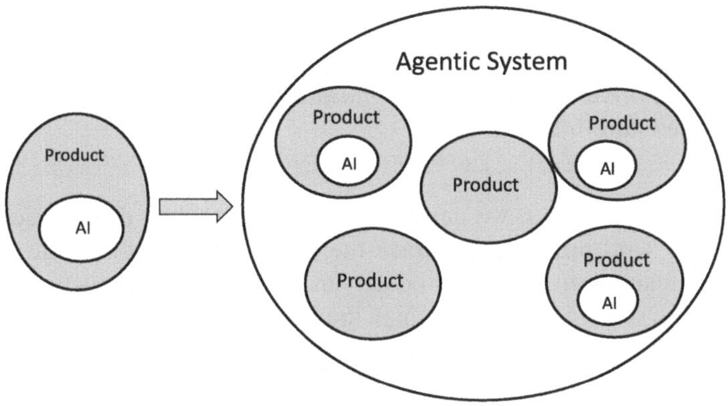

Fig. 15.2 From AI in products to products in AI

the evolution follows three stages: no AI support ➔ AI as a feature ➔ Agentic Systems (see Fig. 15.3).

Both products and processes are currently being enhanced by AI. Similarly to our product considerations above, for business processes, we have already added AI to individual steps; the logical next step is to place the process inside an agentic operating model, where cooperating agents orchestrate processes—end-to-end under human governance.

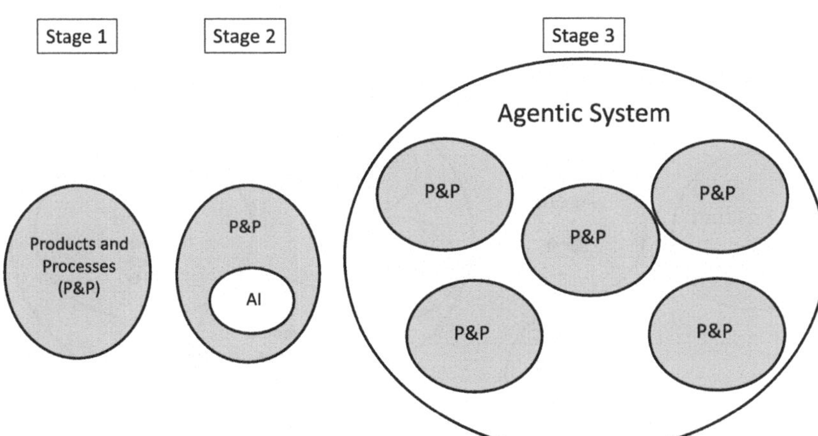

Fig. 15.3 Architectural evolution of products and processes through AI

To the point
Both digital products and development processes are transitioning from static, human-driven models to AI-augmented and ultimately agentic systems that reshape entire lifecycles. ◄.

In the next two sections, we unpack these digital product developments. First, we dig deeper with products and trace the product-architecture trajectory from AI-enhanced features to agentic products and, ultimately, products as elements in an agentic system. Second, we chart the process-architecture trajectory from AI-augmented steps to agentic process orchestration.

15.2 Agentic Evolution in Products

Building on the general views in Figs. 15.2 and 15.3, the next diagram (Fig. 15.4) breaks this evolution into three concrete stages for software products. In this way, the general principle is unfolded step by step, connecting directly back to our initial "To the point" statement.

The figure shows a shift from product-centric software to an AI-first landscape, where stage 2 can be interpreted as 3 sub-stages of AI enhancements in digital products. These are the descriptions for each stage:

1. *No GenAI features*: On the left is the traditional software application.
2. *AI enhancements*: In the middle are today's hybrids: a software product with embedded AI, a standalone AI agent, and a multi-agent system.

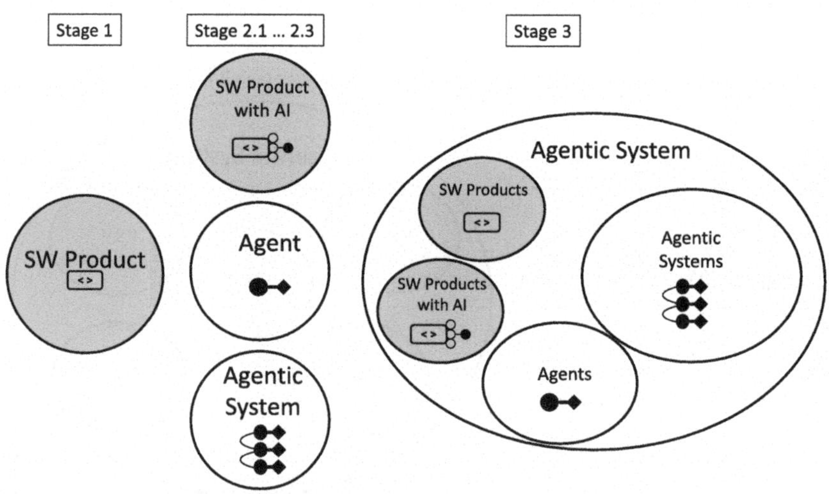

Fig. 15.4 From no AI to AI in digital products to digital products in AI

3. *Agentic Systems*: On the right, all four from items 1 and 2 sit inside an agentic system, indicating a future where products operate within AI-orchestrated environments rather than merely containing AI features.

This nesting flips the relationship: rather than AI living in products, products (and even sub-systems of agents) live inside an AI-centric, agentic system.

To the point
Digital products are evolving from traditional software to AI-enhanced solutions and ultimately to agentic systems that again can operate inside AI-centric environments. ◄.

15.3 Agentic Evolution for Development Processes

15.3.1 Software, Agent, and Agentic System Development as Special Business Processes

Just as we noted earlier (see 13.5) that 'Agentic AI transforms process management from static execution into adaptive orchestration,' the same will be true for development processes itself. If we look at the Business Process Landscape in Fig. 15.5, this might be clearer.

The digital product development processes are processes within the Core Processes category, specifically inside the Product Development domain, at the third level of detail.

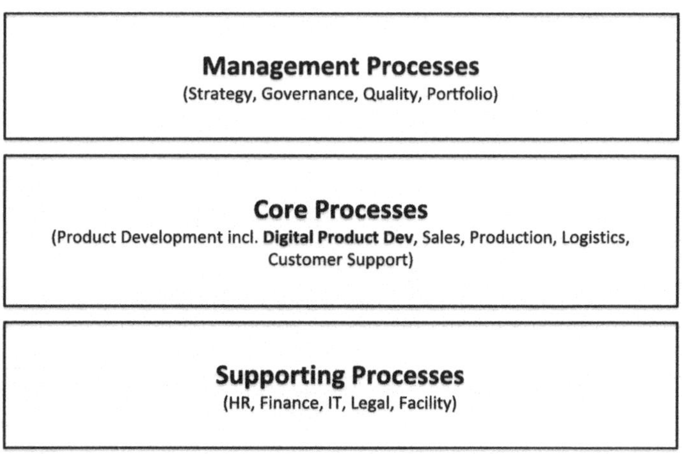

Fig. 15.5 Placement of digital product development processes within the business process hierarchy

15.3.2 Evolution Steps

On the basis of Fig. 15.3 and the icons used in Fig. 15.4 we want to deep dive into the development process evolution (see Fig. 15.6).

Let us describe the three stages in more detail:

1. *No GenAI support*
   Digital Product Development workflows such as requirements, design, and development processes as well as testing, and deployment are predefined once and manually maintained. Adaptations require human intervention, and processes remain static.
2. *GenAI-assisted*
   Copilots and single-purpose agents speed up the development process. Consistency improves and errors reduce, but humans still orchestrate the workflow.

   Extensions:
   Use a small, shared library of good prompts and examples so teams don't start from scratch. Add simple automatic checks that review AI-generated drafts for basic quality and missing pieces. At existing review steps, include short checklists and a link to a model info sheet, then make a clear yes/no decision before work moves on.
   In practice, "GenAI-assisted" means people stay in charge while copilots and small, focused agents produce faster first drafts, alternatives to compare, and checklists that prevent misses. To make this tangible, the next section summarizes starter use cases that any team can trial with low risk. The goal is not to replace judgment, but to remove busywork and raise the quality of starting points—across UI/UX design, requirements engineering, development, and quality engineering.

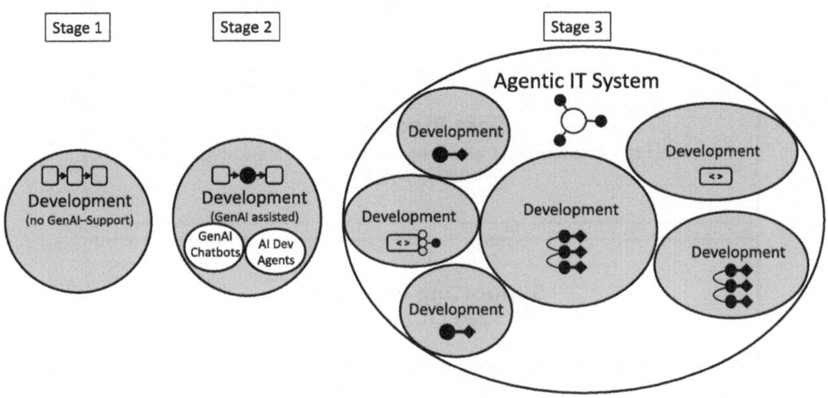

Fig. 15.6 Agentic evolution of the digital product development process

3. *Agentic IT System*
   Workflows evolve into adaptive systems. AI not only executes tasks but orchestrates entire development lifecycle dynamically, guided by data, feedback, and context, making development self-optimizing and continuously evolving, while humans keep control with clear rules and approval points. Here are some examples of the agents being at work within the agentic system:
   - Tests added dynamically based on production usage patterns
   - Deployments adapted based on live telemetry
   - Workflows reconfigured by AI without manual intervention

Every "Development" bubble in Fig. 15.6 should be read as "development of software, or of an agent, or of an agentic system." The respective icons introduced in Fig. 15.4 indicate this. As products move from "AI in products" to "products in AI," the process evolution mirrors that shift: from static, manually maintained workflows (no GenAI support), to human-orchestrated flows accelerated by copilots and narrow agents (GenAI-assisted), to a governed, goal-driven, agentic IT system that can coordinate tasks, evaluate continuously, and surface provenance across artifacts—regardless of whether the target is code for a classic app, an agent's tools or policies, or a multi-agent orchestration. In short, the product architecture you build (software, agent, agentic system) and the process architecture you use (no GenAI → GenAI-assisted → agentic system) advance in lockstep.

To the point
Development processes progress from static workflows to GenAI-assisted flows and finally to adaptive, agentic ecosystems that orchestrate the entire lifecycle under human governance. ◀.

15.4 Product x Development Process Matrix

To link the product stages from Fig. 15.4 with the development process stages from Fig. 15.6, we organize the remainder of the chapter around a 3 × 4 matrix. It shows how Digital Product Development changes when a given product stage is built at a given process stage, and it serves as the roadmap for the following sections Table 15.1.

The four columns represent the product stages using the icons introduced in Fig. 15.4:

1. No GenAI features (classic software)
2. Embedded AI (software with AI components/plugins)
3. Single GenAI agents

Table 15.1 Product x Development Process Matrix

Product Stages / Dev Stages		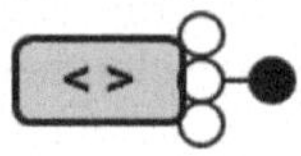		
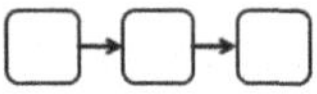	∅	∅	∅	∅

4.  Agentic systems (multi-agent orchestration).

The three rows represent the development process stages from Fig. 15.6:

1. 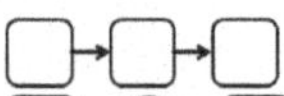 No GenAI support (manual workflows)
2.  GenAI-assisted (copilots/small assistants; humans orchestrate)
3. 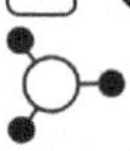 Agentic IT system (governed, goal-driven orchestration).

We examine selected product–process combinations to explain their specifics—how use cases, artifacts, and roles change with each pairing. We exclude the first row (*No GenAI support*): developing without GenAI assistance is no longer realistic, so it remains only as a historical baseline. Column 1 (*No GenAI* features) remains in scope: even as teams adopt GenAI to develop, many products—though fewer than in the past—will still ship without embedded AI. In other words, classic software will continue to be built using GenAI-assisted or agentic processes.

Our analysis begins in the GenAI-assisted row, with an initial emphasis on classic software (B1: Classic software x GenAI-assisted). We then point out the distinctive details of the remaining GenAI-assisted combinations—B2 (Embedded AI x GenAI-assisted), B3 (Single agents x GenAI-assisted), and B4 (Agentic systems x GenAI-assisted). Their use cases and artifacts differ markedly from classic software. For the Agentic IT system row, we split coverage into two sections: one addresses C1 (*No GenAI features*) with operational detail; the other covers C2–C4 (*Embedded AI, Single agents* and *Agentic systems*) as an emerging area—patterns, guardrails, and open questions rather than prescriptive playbooks, since specifics may evolve quickly.Each section opens with a small locator matrix highlighting the product × process combination(s) addressed; previously covered cells are ticked and lightly greyed out for quick orientation.

15.5 GenAI-Assisted Development of Products without AI Features

In this section, we begin by listing practical use cases that teams can pilot in a matter of hours rather than days. Our focus is on GenAI-assisted software development: chatbots, AI plugins integrated into support tools, and small, single-purpose agents that accelerate UI/UX design, requirements engineering, development, and quality assurance in digital product development (see section locator in Fig. 15.7). For typical GenAI architectures used in such projects, please refer to Chap. 11, specifically Figs. 11.7 and 11.8. Since those examples do not illustrate standalone agents, we will address that here by adding an example agent to the architecture shown in Fig. 11.8 (see Fig. 15.8).

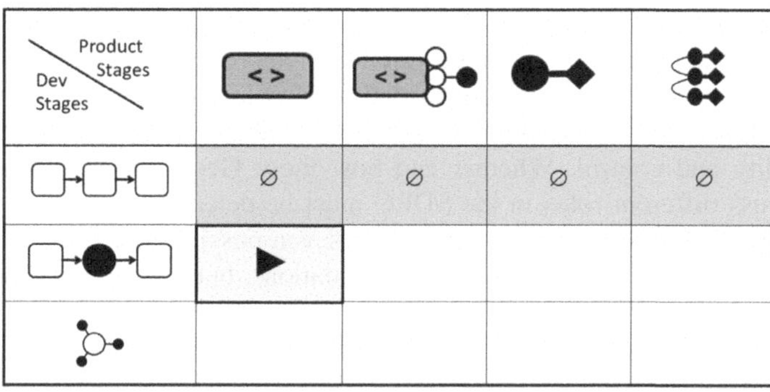

Fig. 15.7 Section Locator (1) for the Product x Process Matrix

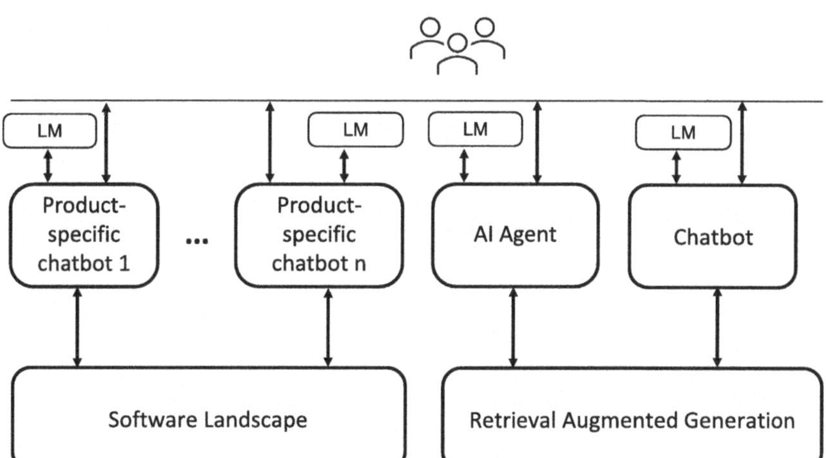

Fig. 15.8 Example GenAI-assisted software development architecture

We describe use cases where GenAI can deliver significant efficiency gains, always maintaining a "human-in-the-loop" approach. Our focus is on producing safe, verifiable outputs supported by simple and lightweight guardrails.The goal is to achieve steady improvements in speed and quality while preserving accountability and control. Whether and how these GenAI use cases should be applied across the respective roles in the SDLC must be determined on a project-specific basis.

15.5.1 GenAI Use Cases in RE

Building on Part 1 of this book where the Requirements Engineer Jan supported the Product Owner Linda in preparing a tender document, this section summarizes the key GenAI use cases (see, for example, 9.3.2) and their potential benefits. These use cases demonstrate how GenAI can deliver significant efficiency gains while always maintaining a "human-in-the-loop" approach. Our focus remains on producing safe, verifiable outputs supported by simple and lightweight guardrails. The goal is to achieve steady improvements in speed and quality while preserving accountability and control. Whether and how these GenAI use cases should be applied across different roles in the SDLC must be determined on a project- and use case-specific basis. We want to introduce seven possible use cases (Fig. 15.9). We will not explicitly provide tool recommendations, but we suggest that you:

- Use the GenAI capabilities of your RM/ALM tool,
- Create your own specific no-code agent or.
- Use the available GenAI assistant/chatbot.

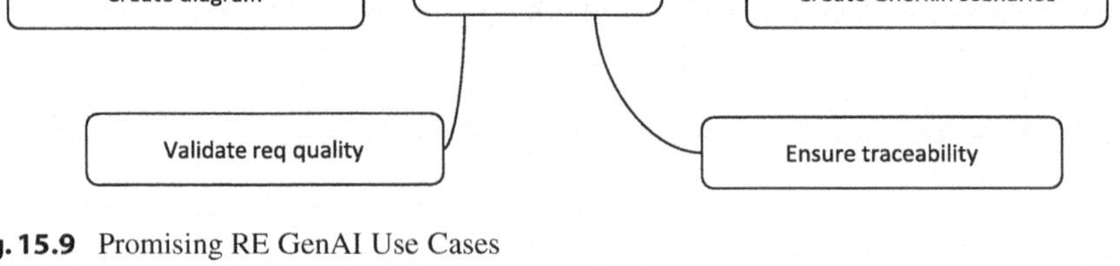

Fig. 15.9 Promising RE GenAI Use Cases

Extract Requirements

The extraction of requirements as part of the "gather requirements" process step (see Fig. 3) from existing sources is a very important GenAI use case, since efficiency and quality gains can be huge.

Input: Documents, spreadsheets, websites, or recording transcriptions.
Output: a requirements catalog.

There are several ways to extract requirements from these sources. Below, we outline four widely used approaches:

1. Using a chatbot:
   - Upload the document, spreadsheet or transcription or reference the URL of the respective website,
   - Create a system prompt (see 14.5).
   - prompt for extraction (see 14.2–14.4).

2. Using an individual GenAI architecture containing a parser and a vector database
   - Parse the input data and store the content in a vector database.
   - Prompt database for extraction.

3. Knowledge-graph oriented extraction
   - Extract entities/relations (system, actor, action, constraint) into a graph; generate requirements from graph patterns.
   - Helps with traceability and impact analysis.

4. In-tool augmentation
   - Integrate extraction directly inside your Requirements Management (RM) or Application Lifecycle Management (ALM) tool (e.g., ingest docs → auto-create requirement items with trace links).
   - Operationally the simplest option—reuses your existing workflows and permissions.

Alternative 1 can be used for a small amount of input data. It is of course much cheaper than alternatives 2 and 3, which should be used for repeated execution and large amounts of input data. In-tool augmentation (alternative 4) emphasizes seamless operations, governance, and immediate usability where teams already work.

In this way, entire requirement catalogs can be generated automatically, which are available for further review and refinement.

Structure Requirements

This use case primarily belongs to the "document requirements" process step. Once requirement catalogs have been generated and quality assured, GenAI can shape them into a navigable structure by proposing hierarchies (epics → features → user stories), consistent categories/tags, and an initial prioritization based on explicit criteria (e.g., value, risk, urgency, stakeholder impact).

> *Input:* One or more requirement catalogs (with IDs, sources, and metadata).
> *Output:* A structured backlog (epics/features/stories), categories/tags, priority ranking, and (optionally) dependency hints.

Below are practical ways to structure requirements with GenAI without overcomplicating the architecture:

1. Policy-driven structuring (taxonomy + prompts)
   - Provide a taxonomy (domains, modules, components) and naming conventions.
   - Prompt the model to assign each requirement to a parent (epic/feature) and propose missing intermediate items.
   - Enforce style and granularity rules (e.g., one user benefit per story).
2. Semantic grouping & consolidation
   - Use embeddings to cluster similar requirements; merge or split where the model detects overlap or scope creep.
   - Flag cross-cutting themes (security, localization, accessibility) for shared epics or enablers.
3. Priority scoring with transparent criteria
   - Define a scoring frame (e.g., Value, Effort, Risk, Time-criticality, Compliance).
   - Ask the model to compute draft scores from available context and explain each score in one sentence.
   - Keep humans in the loop to lock final priorities and capture rationale.
4. In-tool augmentation
   - Run structuring directly inside your RM/ALM tool: auto-create epics/features, bulk-tag items, and set draft priorities; preserve IDs and trace links.
   - Keeps governance simple and avoids data hops.

For small catalogs, policy-driven structuring (1) plus light semantic grouping (2) is typically sufficient and cost-effective. Larger portfolios benefit from deeper clustering and consolidation. Priority scoring (3) should remain advisory—use it to surface trade-offs and drive discussion, not to replace product judgment. Always preserve provenance (original text, source, and change history) so that restructuring remains auditable and reversible.

Transform Format

This use case sits squarely in the "document requirements" process step. It re-expresses existing requirements in a new representation without changing the meaning. A common example is turning a flat list of requirements into user stories with consistent "As a … I want … so that …" phrasing—covered in Sect. 14.4.1 using one-shot prompting. Other frequent transforms include text-to-sentence-template transformations and tool-specific import/export (e.g., ReqIF, CSV, Jira issue schema).

Input: source requirements (IDs, text, metadata) and a target format definition (template/examples or schema).
Output: requirements in the target format.

Always preserve provenance (source IDs, trace links) and include a brief human check to ensure meaning hasn't drifted during the transformation.

Create Gherkin Scenarios

This is a special case of the previous "Transform Format" use case and is applied after user stories have been refined. As discussed in Sect. 8.1.5, Requirements Engineers use Gherkin primarily as acceptance criteria; combined with test data it becomes an executable seed for test cases.

Input: refined user story, test data.
Output: acceptance criteria in Gherkin format.

This is how GenAI helps (end-to-end) in this use case:

- Interprets the refined user story to extract actors, preconditions, business rules, and outcomes.
- Suggests a concise Feature description and a small set of high-value Scenarios (happy path + key alternates).
- Converts rules into Given/When/Then steps, keeping steps declarative and UI-agnostic.
- If test data is provided, upgrades Scenarios to Scenario Outlines with an Examples table (including boundary and negative cases).
- Proposes trace links back to the story/requirement IDs.

Quality guardrails to ask the model for in the respective prompt:

- One behavior per scenario; steps read like business rules, not click paths.
- Preconditions in Given; single trigger in When; observable outcome in Then.
- Examples cover boundaries, nulls, and forbidden combinations; rationale is explained in one line per scenario.
- Terminology matches your glossary; no magic data—every value has a business meaning.

Close with a brief human-in-the-loop review. Treat the model as a co-author—humans make the final call on scope, risk, and wording.

Ensure Traceability

Traceability is part of the "Manage requirements" process step. It links requirement artifacts horizontally (between requirements) and vertically (to upstream goals and downstream designs, code, tests, and risks). We introduced the concept in Sect. 9.3.1 "Mastering the Chaos." GenAI can help here by using modern, transformer-based NLP to spot dependencies and propose meaningful links between items; reviewers confirm the suggestions so only approved links become part of the baseline.

Input: requirements, design artifacts, code references, test cases, etc.
Output: trace links with short rationales, optionally with coverage/impact insights.

There are two ways to establish traceability—static and dynamic. Static ("hard-wired") links are stored in your RM/ALM tool and persist across releases. For example, when GenAI creates a test case for a given requirement inside the tool, it automatically creates a link between the test case and the requirement; that link appears in coverage reports and remains until someone deliberately removes it. Dynamic (temporary) links are created on the fly, typically outside the RM tool, to support discovery or troubleshooting. They are assembled by semantic search, exist only for a session or short time window, and are saved permanently only if you choose to promote them.

Example for semantic search:

We're in an information-security scenario: a product team has a requirement about encryption key rotation for customer data in a cloud system, where keys are managed by a Key Management Service (KMS).

You search for "key rotation for customer data." The assistant semantically gathers a temporary group: a requirement ("Rotate keys every 90 days"), the matching test case ("Verify rotation policy"), a design note ("KMS rotation design"), and a code file that mentions the interval. This result is only possible through the transformer capabilities. The grouping is just for discovery and expires after a short time. If it's useful, you click Save links and choose which pairs to make static (hard-wired) links in the RM tool; otherwise, the temporary grouping disappears.

Validate Requirements Quality

Input: a set of requirements
Output: identified weaknesses and suggested corrections.

See Sect. 9.3.1 for details. As shown there, GenAI can flag quality issues that reviewers may miss—e.g., ambiguous or passive phrasing, lack of testability, inconsistencies, and redundancies—and propose targeted rewrites with short rationales. Section 14.4.3 also provides a prompt-chain pattern for detecting inconsistencies and redundancies. Accordingly, we keep this use case brief here.

Create diagrams

As shown throughout Part 1, professional requirements documentation benefits from clear visualizations of complex behavior and structure. GenAI can draft UML, SysML, and BPMN diagrams from natural language descriptions, such as:

- Use case diagrams.
- Concept models (class diagrams).
- Activity/process diagrams.
- State diagrams.

Not every assistant can render diagrams natively. A practical workflow is to have the model generate PlantUML or Mermaid code and then render it in your modeling tool. Some RM/ALM tools already include modeling features and may support diagram generation directly from requirements.

Input: natural language requirement descriptions
Output: UML/SysML/BPMN diagrams or PlantUML/Mermaid code ready for rendering

To the point

GenAI accelerates Requirements Engineering while keeping humans accountable. Apply via chatbots, embeddings, or in-tool augmentation—safe, auditable, and project-specific.

15.5.2 GenAI Use Cases in UI/UX Design

UI and UX design are the disciplines in software development most closely related to Requirements Engineering (see Fig. 8.2 and Sect. 8.1), particularly in agile settings. Designers sometimes begin their work even before requirements engineers; in the Discover phase they establish the foundation for the project. Once the project is underway, after requirements are refined in a sprint, the Requirements Engineer (RE) collaborates closely with designers to explore the solution space.

We classify the GenAI use cases by design phase and distinguish UI from UX. While there are several valid schemes, we use four phases: Discover, Define, Develop, and Deliver. The example use cases with the highest expected efficiency

Table 15.2 Promising UI/UX design Use Cases

Phase	UI Design	UX Design
Discover	Generate wireframes	Analyze behavior
Define	Generate layouts	Predict usability issues
Develop	Generate assets	Test design variations
Deliver	Generate code from design	Ensure accessibility

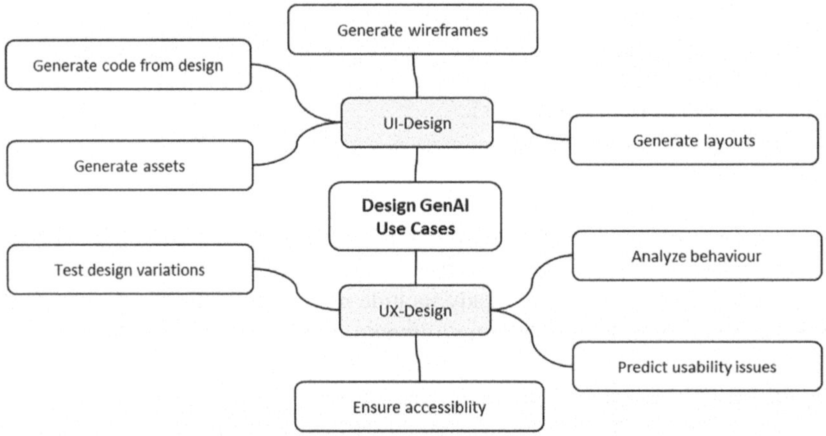

Fig. 15.10 Promising UI/UX Design GenAI Use Cases

gains are listed in Table 15.2 and displayed in Fig. 15.10. If you want to see another view on this topic please refer to (Cerejo, 2025).

15.5.2.1 UI Design Use Cases

In this and the following subsection, we will describe the design use cases shown in Fig. 15.10 and suggest appropriate tools for each.

Generate wireframes

GenAI turns problem statements, user goals, and constraints into low-fidelity screens and user flows. It proposes alternative structures and surfaces missing states or edge cases. Designers iterate quickly, accepting or rejecting suggestions and adding rationale for the next fidelity step.

Tool recommendations: UIzard, Mokkup.ai, Relume.ai

Generate layouts

GenAI recommends compositions—grid, spacing, hierarchy—aligned to the design system and content goals. It can refactor messy artboards into consistent patterns, align components, and suggest responsive breakpoints. Designers review and adjust to meet brand and accessibility rules.

Tool recommendations: Figma AI, Galileo AI (as Figma plugin), Canva's Magic Design, Framer AI

Generate assets
GenAI creates or adapts UI assets (icons, illustrations, states) within style-guide constraints. It can upscale, recolour, or variant assets for themes and densities, and fill placeholder content. Designers retain final approval to ensure coherence and licensing compliance.

Tool recommendations: Adobe Firefly (integrated in Photoshop and Illustrator), Midjourney, Canva Magic Media

Generate code from design
This use case acts at the interface of the designer and frontend developer role. GenAI converts vetted designs into clean, component-based frontend code mapped to the team's UI library. It preserves semantics, responsive behavior, and accessibility attributes to reduce hand-off friction. Frontend developers review diffs and integrate within existing pipelines and standards.

Tool recommendations: Uizard, Framer AI, Locofy.ai, Anima, Figma Dev Mode

15.5.2.2 UX Design Use Cases

Analyze behavior
GenAI summarizes qualitative and quantitative signals (notes, clickstreams, surveys) to surface patterns, intents, and pain points. It clusters similar behaviors and flags opportunities or risks with concise evidence. Researchers validate findings and plan focused follow-ups.

Tool recommendations: Maze, Dovetail, FullStory AI, Amplitude

Predict usability issues
GenAI estimates likely friction based on heuristics, prior data, and attention modeling. It annotates screens with risk explanations (e.g., low contrast, unclear affordance, cognitive load) and suggests corrective options. Teams triage findings and write acceptance criteria.

Tool recommendations: Attention Inside, EyeQuant, Google Lighthouse, Maze

Test design variations
GenAI helps generate controlled variants of copy, layout, and flows, and drafts hypotheses and lightweight test plans. It can pre-screen variants with attention/first-click predictions to focus live testing. Practitioners select candidates and define success metrics.

Tool recommendations: VWO Editor Copilot, Optimizely Opal, Maze, Kameleoon

Ensure accessibility
GenAI audits artifacts against accessibility standards (e.g., contrast, semantics, keyboard flows) and proposes remediations with code or content examples. It tracks coverage and regression risks as designs evolve. Teams capture exceptions and include accessibility in the definition of done.

Tool recommendations: Deque axe DevTools, Google Lighthouse, Stark Sidekick plugin (e.g., for Figma, Sketch)

15.5.2.3 Summary and Outlook to the Next Sections

In sum, the use cases above show GenAI boosting speed and consistency from ideation to handoff: generating wireframes, layouts, and assets, turning designs into code, surfacing behavioral insights; predicting usability risks, testing variations, and enforcing accessibility. The near future extends this with agentic systems that chain these capabilities into goal-driven workflows—proposing changes, running checks, and opening merge requests—while humans set objectives, review decisions, and ensure ethical and brand alignment. Section 15.8 details how such agentic development reshapes roles, governance, and pipelines.

While the sections on requirements engineering and UI/UX design draw on our own professional expertise, the following subsections on IT design & architecture, development, quality engineering, deployment, and operation as well as project management are mainly synthesized from research and consultations with NTT DATA experts. They reflect current practice, but only partly personal expertise.

15.5.3 GenAI Use Cases in IT Design and Architecture

In IT design and architecture, GenAI already compresses weeks of upfront and documentation work into hours while improving consistency against well-architected standards. The five use cases below (see Fig. 15.11) deliver the strongest ROI today—and set you up for agentic, end-to-end workflows next. For each of the use cases we provide short descriptions and references for recent articles or industry reports that illustrate current practices and highlight emerging trends in IT design and architecture. Once more, tool recommendations are included.

Reference Architectures & Solution Blueprints
GenAI drafts cloud-ready reference designs from goals and constraints, proposing patterns and services by workload. It surfaces trade-offs and alternative topologies so architects can converge faster and record rationale for the next fidelity step (Microsoft, 2025).

Tool recommendations: Google Cloud Architecture Center, AWS Solutions Library

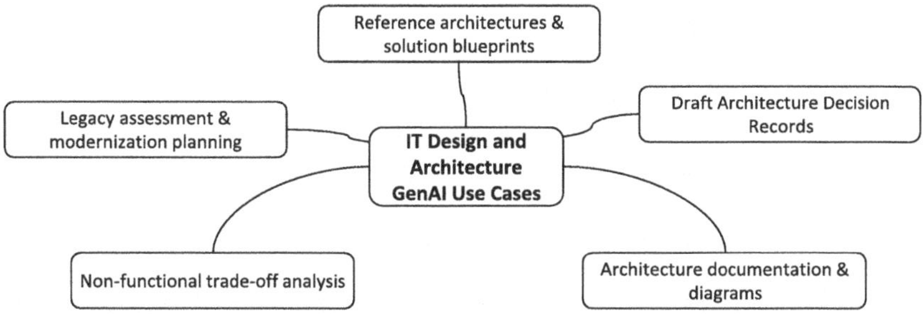

Fig. 15.11 Promising IT Design and Architecture GenAI Use Cases

Draft Architecture Decision Records (ADRs)
GenAI structures options, consequences, and links to prior decisions from brief requirements. Architects review, accept or reject suggestions, and keep a living decision log tied to repos (Laskowski & Michalak., 2025).

Tool recommendations: adr-tools (Nat Pryce), Log4brains

Create documentation & diagrams
GenAI turns text or system knowledge into layered C4 views (Context/Containers/Components/Code) and keeps diagrams consistent as designs evolve. It flags missing elements and keeps "single source of truth" models in code (Heuel, 2025).

Tool recommendations: Structurizr, Terrastruct

Analyze non-functional trade-offs
GenAI evaluates designs against reliability, security, performance, cost, and sustainability pillars, annotating risks with concrete remediations. Teams triage findings and track improvements between design reviews (AWS, 2025).

Tool recommendations: AWS Well-Architected Tool, Azure Well-Architected Review

Plan system modernization
GenAI inventories estates, clusters dependencies, and proposes modernization paths with effort and risk signals. It can draft target architectures and code transformation plans to reduce hand-off friction (Hallikeri, 2025).

Tool recommendations: Azure Migrate, IBM watsonx Code Assistant

15.5.4 GenAI Use Cases in Frontend and Backend Development

In frontend and backend development, GenAI already accelerates coding, testing, and refactoring by automating repetitive tasks and highlighting improvements in

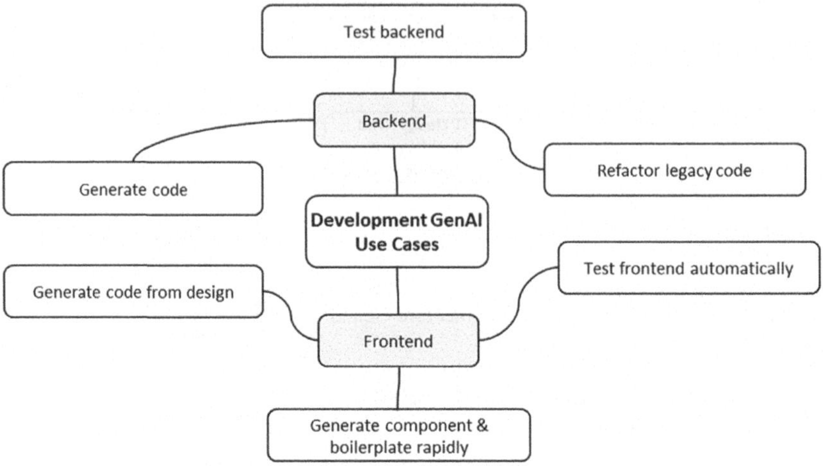

Fig. 15.12 Promising Development GenAI Use Cases

real time. The overview in Fig. 15.12 illustrates how GenAI augments the development workflow, from rapid prototyping on the frontend to legacy modernization and test generation on the backend.

We then describe the use cases for each domain, including tool recommendations and recent references that highlight their practical value.

15.5.4.1 Frontend Development Use Cases

Generate component & boilerplate rapidly
GenAI generates reusable frontend components (e.g., UIwidgets, navigation, form inputs) or full boilerplate scaffolding from descriptions of layout, style, and theme. Developers accept and refine suggestions, reducing time from design to usable code (QED42, 2025).

Tool recommendations: GitHub Copilot, Tabnine.

Generate code from design
This use case applies to both UI/UX (see 15.5.2) and frontend development; we distinguish a designer-led mode and an engineer-led mode.

GenAI converts designs into component-based frontend code aligned to the design system and accessibility rules. In designer-led mode it produces vetted, semantic components to ease hand-off; in engineer-led mode it generates scaffolded pages and integration code (routing, state, tests) to accelerate prototyping and implementation (QED42, 2025).

Tool recommendations: Uizard, Framer AI, Locofy.ai, Anima, Figma Dev Mode.

Test frontend automatically
GenAI helps generate test cases for UI components, discover accessibility and performance issues, and provide feedback in code reviews (e.g., for style, consistency, proper ARIA attributes). This catches many errors before manual QA (Wavhal, 2025).

Tool recommendations: Playwright, Applitools.

15.5.4.2 Backend Development Use Cases

Generate code
From requirement or schema descriptions, GenAI generates backend APIs, controllers, data models, and wiring (e.g., CRUD endpoints), enforcing architectural patterns and picking tech like REST vs GraphQL. Developers polish and integrate the output rather than building from scratch (Ilas, 2025).

Tool recommendations: GitHub Copilot, Amazon CodeWhisperer.

Refactor legacy code
GenAI analyzes existing codebases, identifies duplicated logic, bad patterns, or outdated dependencies, then proposes or automates refactorings. Helps maintain performance, readability, and supports modernization (Ilas, 2025).

Tool recommendations: Qodo, OpenAI GPT-based tools.

Test backend
GenAI generates test inputs, mocks, and assertions for API endpoints; uses specifications like OpenAPI and even business logic to detect edge cases. Also can create test oracles or validate response correctness beyond just status codes (Kim et al., 2025).

Tool recommendations: Apidog (for API testing & mocking), RESTGrep, ToolFactory, LlamaRestTest frameworks.

15.5.5 GenAI Use Cases in Quality Engineering

We organize QE into four categories (see Fig. 15.13): Test Analysis & Design, Test Planning & Controlling, Test Automation & Execution, and Exit Criteria & Reporting. For each category, we define 2–3 GenAI use cases that speed up work, raise coverage and quality, and keep teams aligned with standards—always with humans reviewing suggestions and owning final decisions.

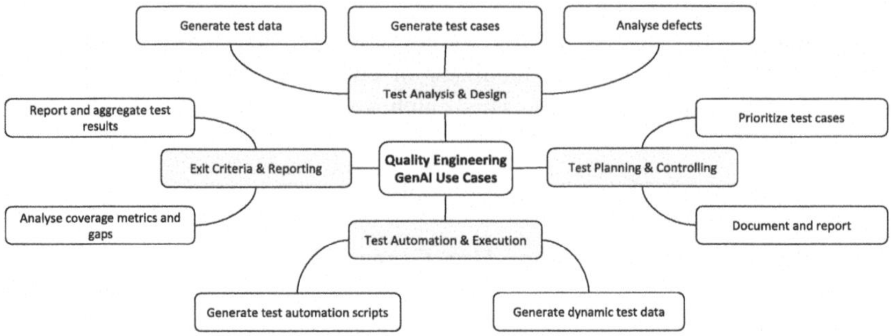

Fig. 15.13 Promising Quality Engineering GenAI Use Cases

Category overviews:

- *Test Analysis & Design*—turning requirements and risks into test ideas, data, and cases with traceability back to sources.
- *Test Planning & Controlling*—translating scope and constraints into plans, priorities, and coverage targets, then tracking progress against them.
- *Test Automation & Execution*—generating and maintaining automated checks and orchestrating reliable runs across environments.
- *Exit Criteria & Reporting*—assessing release readiness with evidence (coverage, risk, defects) and producing clear, decision-grade summaries.

15.5.5.1 Test Analysis & Design

Generate test cases
GenAI turns user stories, acceptance criteria, and risks into structured positive, negative, and edge cases with rationale and traceability back to sources. Testers review and refine before moving to automation (Bandi et al., 2025).

Tool recommendations: Keysight Eggplant Generator, testRigor.

Generate test data
From field rules and constraints, GenAI proposes equivalence partitions and boundary values (min/max/off-by-one) and synthesizes realistic datasets. Teams approve sets, lock them to cases, and regenerate when rules change (Guo et al., 2025).

Tool recommendations: GenRocket, Tonic.ai.

Analyze defects
The assistant clusters similar defects across logs, traces, and commits, links them to components and requirements, and surfaces likely root causes. Teams use clusters to focus fixes and add preventive tests (Szandała, 2025).

Tool recommendations: ReportPortal, MS Auto Triage AI Agent.

15.5.5.2 Test Planning & Controlling

Prioritize test cases
Using impact and likelihood signals (change history, defect hotspots, usage), GenAI ranks cases and proposes a minimal viable set per sprint or release. The test lead adjusts weights and finalizes the order (Baqar & Khanda, 2025).

Tool recommendations: Launchable, Tricentis SeaLights.

Document and report
GenAI drafts concise test plans, status notes, and stakeholder updates from backlog and run data. It maintains a living record of scope, risks, environments, and milestones (Kumar et al., 2025).

Tool recommendations: BrowserStack Test Reporting & Analytics, PractiTest.

15.5.5.3 Test Automation & Execution

Generate test automation scripts
From approved cases, Gherkin scenarios, or OpenAPI specs, GenAI drafts stable UI/API test code, step definitions, and fixtures, mapping steps to page objects or request stubs with assertions. Software Development Engineers are reviewing code differences, enforce standards, and land them via CI policies (Poth et al., https://link.springer.com/chapter/10.1007/978-3-032-04288-0_3).

Tool recommendations: Mabl, Keysight Eggplant Test.

Generate dynamic test data
During execution, GenAI creates on-the-fly datasets that satisfy case preconditions (e.g., unique users, temporal windows, boundary combinations) and refreshes them between runs. This reduces flakiness and keeps scenarios realistic (AI Testing Tools, 2025).

Tool recommendations: GenRocket, Tonic.ai.

15.5.5.4 Exit Criteria & Reporting

Report and aggregate test results
The assistant consolidates results across tools and environments, explains failures, and highlights trends (pass rates, flake rates, defect leakage) in decision-ready summaries (Linders, 2025).

Tool recommendations: ReportPortal, Allure TestOps.

Analyze coverage metrics and gaps
GenAI maps requirements, tests, and test runs, calculates coverage by risk and feature, and flags gaps or orphan items. Teams triage gaps and update plans and suites before sign-off (Cheng et al., 2025).

Tool recommendations: Tricentis SeaLights, Xray (Jira).

15.5.6 GenAI Use Cases in Deployment

Deployment has long been highly automated through CI/CD, infrastructure-as-code, and GitOps. GenAI adds a smart layer on top: it turns intent into draft pipelines and manifests, suggests verification steps and policy checks, and recommends risk-aware rollout strategies such as canary or blue-green. Teams keep determinism by merging through pull requests and enforcing policy-as-code, treating AI output as suggestions rather than direct changes.

Figure 15.14 shows the use cases at a glance; detailed descriptions follow.

Draft pipelines
GenAI drafts CI/CD definitions from repo conventions, dependencies, and test matrices, then explains failing jobs and proposes additional checks. Teams keep these assistants in "suggest" mode, merging via PRs and policies to preserve repeatability (Baqar et al., 2025).

Tool recommendations: Harness AIDA, GitHub Copilot.

Generate IaC with guardrails
From environment descriptions and constraints, GenAI produces Terraform/Pulumi and Kubernetes manifests and helps align them to security, performance, and cost objectives; organizations enforce guardrails with policy-as-code before apply (Angi et al., 2025).

Tool recommendations: Pulumi AI, Terraform.

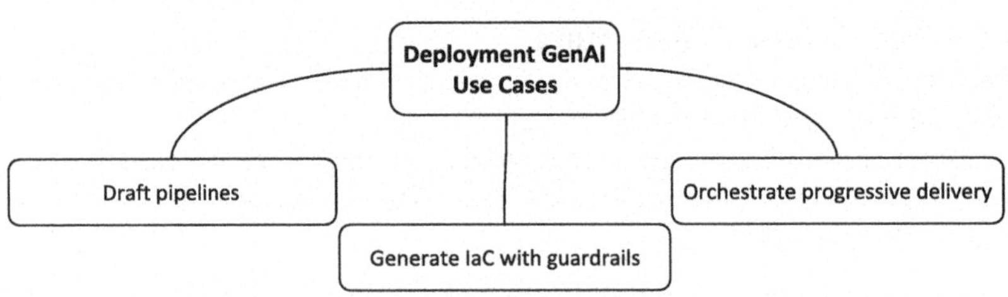

Fig. 15.14 Promising Deployment GenAI Use Cases

Orchestrate progressive delivery
By correlating change events with live telemetry, GenAI helps select canary or blue/green rollout strategies, recommends safe step sizes, and flags regressions early for rollback or pause (Angi, 2025).

Tool recommendations: Harness Continuous Verification, LaunchDarkly.

15.5.7 GenAI Use Cases in Operation

In operations, GenAI accelerates detection and response. It summarizes alerts and logs, clusters related symptoms, and proposes likely causes with remediation options. Models also forecast anomalies and capacity risks and help keep runbooks and knowledge bases current. Human review and access controls remain essential to preserve reliability and accountability.

An overview of the use cases is shown in Fig. 15.15, followed by detailed descriptions.

Triage incidents
Assistants summarize alerts and logs, cluster related signals, and suggest likely causes with remediation paths, reducing mean time to resolution while keeping humans in the loop (Yu et al., 2025).

Tool recommendations: Datadog Watchdog, PagerDuty Copilot.

Predict anomalies
Models forecast bottlenecks, SLO breaches, or anomalous behavior across services so teams can intervene early or trigger guarded automation; recent work combines causal, predictive, and generative methods (Jeon et al., 2025).

Tool recommendations: Dynatrace Davis AI, New Relic AI.

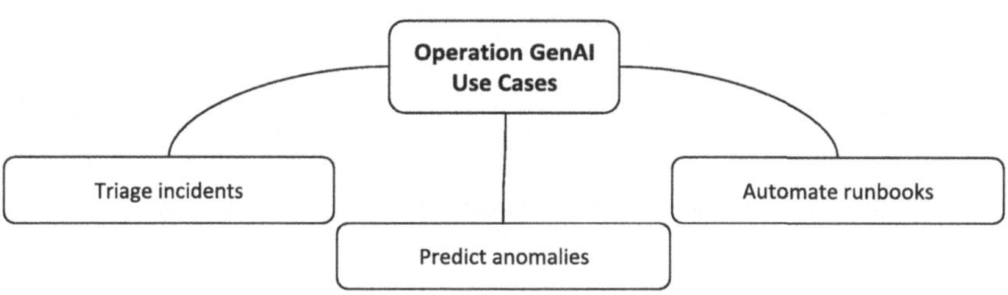

Fig. 15.15 Promising Operation GenAI Use Cases

Automate runbooks
GenAI drafts and updates runbooks and post-incident reviews, links incidents to relevant docs, and answers common operational questions—subject to review and access controls (Lin et al., 2025).

Tool recommendations: ServiceNow Now Assist, Atlassian Intelligence (Confluence/Jira).

15.5.8 GenAI Use Cases in IT Project Management

In IT project management, GenAI lightens the admin load, sharpens forecasts, and keeps stakeholders aligned—without replacing the PM's judgment. The overview (see Figure X) groups our use cases into three categories: Communication, Budgeting, and Leadership; each category contains several practical use cases drawn from current PM workflows.

- *Budgeting*—Explains and forecasts spend by analyzing burn, variance, and staffing scenarios; suggests trade-offs and flags risks early so leaders can act before overruns occur. Human approval and finance policies remain the gate.
- *Communication*—Streamlines project communications by drafting and tailoring updates, summarizing meetings, tracking actions/risks/decisions, and keeping status pages consistent. PMs review and publish, ensuring tone, context, and confidentiality are right.
- *Leadership*—Supports decision-making and team effectiveness with risk/dependency mapping, progress synthesis (OKRs/roadmaps), and signals on delivery health and capacity. The PM uses these insights to set priorities and drive accountability.

Figure 15.16 lists the concrete use cases within each category; the next pages provide short descriptions, references, and tool examples for each.

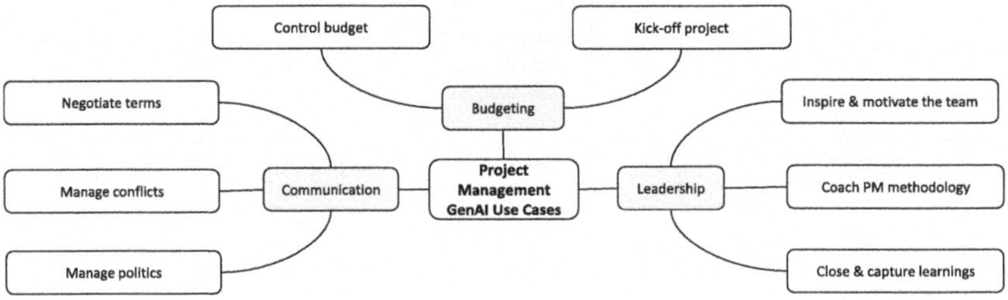

Fig. 15.16 Promising Project Management GenAI Use Cases

15.5.8.1 Budgeting

Control budget
GenAI pulls in actual costs (time sheets, vendor purchase orders, cloud invoices) and compares them to the agreed budget. It explains any differences in plain language, forecasts the final total cost if nothing changes, and suggests actions (for example, defer lower-value work, adjust scope, or rebalance staffing). It also drafts a one-page update for stakeholders (Marri, 2025).

Tool recommendations: ServiceNow with Now Assist, Microsoft Project, and Excel with Copilot (optionally connected to Power BI for dashboards).

Kick-off project
From the project charter and high-level scope, GenAI drafts an initial budget: a work breakdown structure with cost estimates, separation of capital costs and operating costs, contingency for risks, and two or three "what-if" scenarios (team size, partner mix, cloud service tiers). It also generates a funding brief with clear assumptions you can review with experts (Shamim, 2025).

Tool recommendations: Anaplan, Pigment.

15.5.8.2 Communication

Negotiate terms
GenAI assembles a negotiation brief from scope, risks, and constraints: it clarifies interests on both sides, proposes trade-offs, drafts clear offers and counter-offers, and even role-plays the other party to surface objections. It also prepares talking points and a fallback plan (your "best alternative if no agreement") so you enter the meeting aligned and prepared (Revilla & Saenz, 2025).

Tool recommendations: any chatbot with LLM, MS Copilot for Word/Outlook/Teams, Pactum Agent.

Manage conflicts
GenAI distills each side's position, rewrites messages in neutral, respectful language, and suggests options for resolution with pros and cons. It can produce a short mediation script, highlight emotional triggers and misalignments, and recommend next steps you can validate with the people involved (Hale et al., 2025).

Tool recommendations: any chatbot with LLM, MS Copilot in Teams to summarize calls and propose follow-ups, Grammarly Business.

Manage politics
GenAI maps stakeholders, their goals, and influence, then flags alignment risks and likely points of resistance. It drafts tailored updates for different audiences, tracks commitments and concerns over time, and suggests who to brief before key

decisions—always with careful handling of confidential information (Krpan et al., 2025).

Tool recommendations: Miro with AI for stakeholder maps; Polinode.

15.5.8.3 Leadership

Inspire & motivate the team
GenAI helps you tailor messages to different audiences, surface wins to celebrate, and suggest recognition or career-growth opportunities based on recent work. It also drafts talking points for town halls and one-on-ones, and proposes lightweight rituals that strengthen purpose and momentum—always reviewed by you for tone and context (Lange & Parra-Moyano, 2025).

Tool recommendations: Microsoft Viva with Copilot, Culture Amp AI Coach.

Coach PM methodology
The assistant turns your chosen framework into practical checklists, templates, and reminders (e.g., ceremony agendas, risk and decision logs, stakeholder maps). It spots gaps against your governance rules and suggests next steps—so the team applies the method consistently without extra overhead (Institute, 2025).

Tool recommendations: Atlassian Intelligence (Jira + Confluence), Asana Intelligence.

Close & capture learnings
GenAI assembles the closure pack: outcome vs. objectives, benefits realized, open items, and acceptance evidence. It synthesizes lessons learned from issues, decisions, and feedback, drafts a clear handover and knowledge-base updates, and proposes follow-up actions to carry improvements into the next project (Gancarz, 2025).

Tool recommendations: Atlassian Confluence AI, ServiceNow Now Assist.

15.6 GenAI-Assisted Development of AI-Enhanced Products

In this section we consider digital products that use generative AI features but aren't AI agents or agentic systems (see Fig. 15.17). The key distinction is that these products generate content or insights based on user prompts and do not act autonomously to achieve a goal. They are tools that assist a human, not systems that take independent action. Examples include

- AI Plugins in classic digital products, e.g., requirements management tools.
- Editing and code assistants.
- LLM-powered Enterprise Assistants.

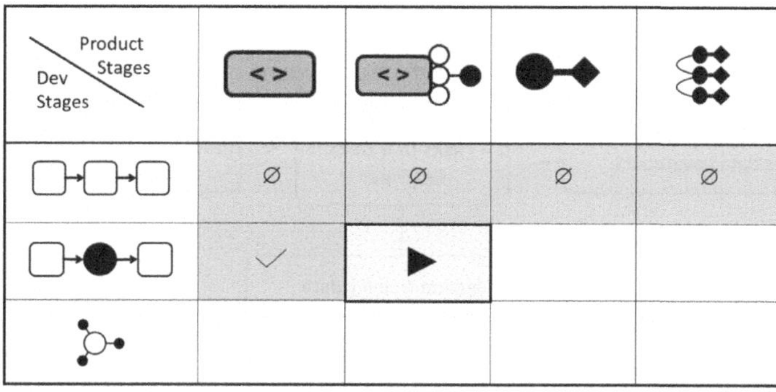

Fig. 15.17 Section Locator (2) for the Product x Process Matrix

- Image generators.
- Educational Platforms.
- Contact Center Bots like the ones discussed in Part 1 of this book.

Classic methods still apply when it comes to developing such systems; what's different is that data becomes a first-class product artifact and requires explicit quality, safety, and governance.

15.6.1 Key Roles Emerging: Data and Security Engineers

For the development of AI-enhanced features, we explicitly call out the *data engineer* and *security engineer* as new key roles. Both roles collaborate closely with each other and with the other roles introduced in the previous subsections.

Data engineers are crucial because they build and maintain the robust infrastructure and pipelines that collect, process, and organize the vast, often messy, datasets needed to work with GenAI language models. Their work ensures the models receive high-quality, reliable data, which is essential for accurate and relevant outputs. Since this is a new role we are considering, we emphasize the main tasks of the data engineer in Fig. 15.18. In the task descriptions, we also highlight how GenAI can assist the data engineer in completing the task.

Build Data Pipelines
Data engineers design and build or work with automated systems to acquire raw data from various sources (databases, APIs, streaming sources) and move it into a data lake or warehouse.

GenAI can auto-generate code for data ingestion, helping engineers write complex SQL or Python scripts for data pipelines. This accelerates development and reduces human error.

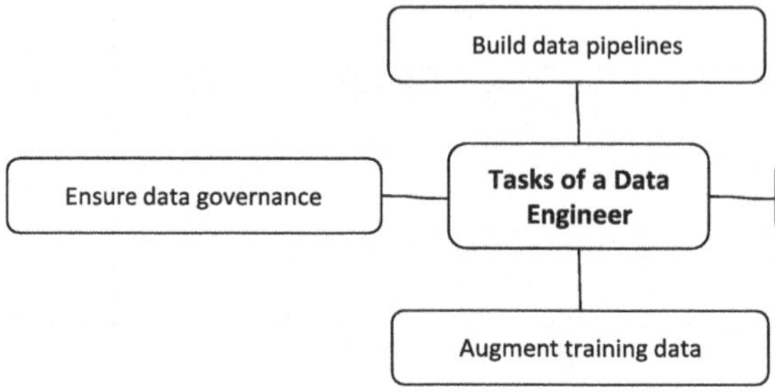

Fig. 15.18 Tasks of a data engineer

Tool recommendations: Airbyte, Dagster.

Clean Data Sources

Data engineers are responsible for cleaning, transforming, and formatting data to remove inconsistencies, duplicates, or errors. This step is critical for preventing bias and improving model performance.

GenAI can detect anomalies and suggest corrections in real-time, automating a significant portion of the data cleansing process. This allows engineers to focus on more complex data quality issues.

Tool recommendations: OpenRefine, Alteryx Trifacta.

Augment Training Data

Data engineers create new data features from existing raw data to improve a model's predictive power. For GenAI, this can also involve creating synthetic data to augment small or imbalanced datasets.

GenAI can create realistic synthetic data that mimics the statistical properties of real-world data, which is essential for training models when real data is scarce or sensitive.

Tool recommendations: Augmentor, Hugging Face Transformers.

Ensure Data Governance

They implement or configure systems to manage data access, ensure compliance with privacy regulations (like GDPR), and design scalable architectures to handle ever-increasing data volumes.

GenAI can automate the creation of data documentation and metadata, providing a comprehensive, searchable record of data lineage. This helps with auditing and ensures compliance with data governance policies.

Tool recommendations: Collibra, OneTrust.

The role of the security engineer ensures that AI-specific risks, e.g., prompt injection, data leakage, and unsafe outputs are assessed and mitigated, and that compliance with the frameworks above is maintained. Please refer to Chap. 12

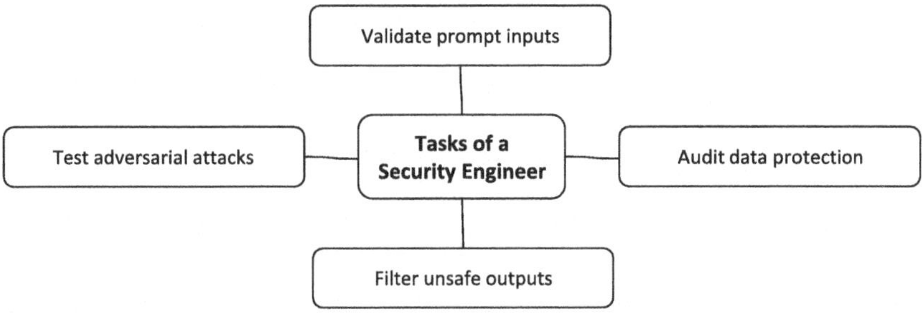

Fig. 15.19 Tasks of a security engineer

where we analyzed the risks in detail. These are security engineer tasks that can be executed with help from GenAI. Again, we display the main tasks in Fig. 15.19 and include potential GenAI support in the task descriptions.

Validate Prompt Inputs

Security engineers create and implement systems to analyze and sanitize user prompts, defending against prompt injection attacks that can manipulate the model into dangerous or unintended behavior Fig. 15.20.

GenAI-powered security tools act as intelligent firewalls. They can analyze the semantics and intent of a prompt in real-time, detecting and blocking known attack patterns or suspicious language before the prompt ever reaches the core model. They are more sophisticated than simple keyword filters, as they can understand context and nuance.

Tool Recommendations: AWS Bedrock Guardrails, PromptPerfect

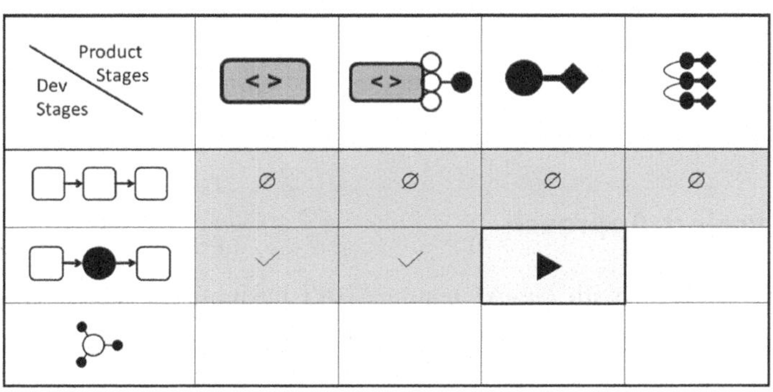

Fig. 15.20 Section Locator (3) for the Product x Process Matrix

Audit Data Protection
This involves auditing the data lifecycle from collection to use, ensuring that sensitive data is anonymized, access is controlled, and the system complies with privacy regulations like GDPR.

GenAI tools can automate the process of scanning vast, unstructured datasets to find and classify sensitive information. They can identify PII (Personally Identifiable Information) with high accuracy, automatically flag it for review, and even suggest or perform de-identification, which is crucial for training and operating models on large, often messy, data lakes.

Tool Recommendations: MS Purview, OneTrust

Filter Unsafe Outputs
Security engineers develop and configure content filters to prevent the model from generating harmful, biased, or toxic content.

GenAI models can be used as a content moderation engine itself. They can be fine-tuned to act as classifiers, identifying and scoring outputs based on categories like toxicity, hate speech, or violence. This enables a dynamic and scalable defense that can automatically reject or flag problematic responses before they are presented to the end user.

Tool Recommendations: Azure AI Content Safety, Google AI Responsible GenAI Toolkit

Test Adversarial Attacks
They proactively "red-team" the system, using a variety of adversarial techniques to find and exploit weaknesses, such as jailbreaking the model or using data poisoning.

GenAI can be used to automate the red-teaming process. Instead of manually crafting a few malicious prompts, a GenAI-powered tool can generate thousands of diverse, creative, and subtle adversarial inputs to test the model's robustness and help discover new vulnerabilities at scale. This allows for a more comprehensive and efficient security audit.

Tool Recommendations: MS PyRIT (Python Risk Identification Toolkit), Garak

15.6.2 Project Approach

Developing products with GenAI features isn't business as usual; it fundamentally changes how teams work and what they need to focus on. While technical roles like IT architects and developers remain important, GenAI features increase the need for cross-functional collaboration across product, data, security, UX, and compliance.

Governance frameworks, such as NIST's AI Risk Management Framework and the EU AI Act, call for end-to-end oversight that spans requirements, design, development, security, and legal—not just technical roles alone. The following project approach highlights how the new data and security engineer roles integrate into this broader process:

- Requirements and Data are probabilistic: Requirements Engineers must define not only *what* the system should do but also *how well*, under which data conditions. Here, data engineers contribute by specifying data quality metrics, designing pipelines that can monitor these metrics in real-time, and working with REs to define feasible performance thresholds.
- UX includes AI-specific patterns: UX designers must embed transparency, controls, and recourse mechanisms. Security engineers collaborate here by ensuring user-facing disclosures don't inadvertently reveal sensitive system details and by embedding safeguards into interaction flows (e.g., safe prompt handling, confidence indicators).
- Security & Safety as part of the attack surface: AI-enhanced products require additional checks for malicious prompts, unintended disclosure, and unsafe outputs. Security engineers lead these processes, integrating automated guardrails, adversarial testing, and continuous monitoring. Data engineers support by ensuring sensitive data is properly anonymized and governed.
- Governance as a product concern: Compliance cannot remain an IT afterthought. Data engineers provide auditable data lineage (*system cards* (McGowan et al., 2025), metadata), while security engineers validate alignment with AI management systems like ISO/IEC 42001. Together, they ensure every release is traceable, explainable, and compliant.

In practice, a GenAI project team should be cross-functional by design, with requirements engineers, data engineers, security engineers, UX designers, architects, and product owners collaborating continuously. This ensures that AI features are not only technically feasible but also reliable, secure, compliant, and user-centered.

15.6.3 Definition of Done for an AI-Enhanced Feature

How do you know when your new AI feature is truly ready to ship? Before you call an AI feature "done" (see 8.3), your team should agree on what success looks like—for the user, the business, and safety. This checklist should be part of the "Way of Working" document (see 8.5) and is used to confirm the feature meets all expectations.

- Function & quality are measurable and met: We've defined and met simple targets for how often the feature is correct, its response time, and how much

each use costs. These targets are met in automated checks and in the first real-user rollout.
- User experience patterns are in place: The feature clearly tells users what the AI can and can't do. It offers an easy opt-out or fallback path, provides helpful explanations or confidence hints, and lets users report issues quickly.
- Security & safety checks are green: We have tested for malicious prompts, accidental exposure of sensitive information, and unsafe or misleading outputs. Guardrails like input limits, output filters, and kill switches are implemented and verified.
- Governance is documented and current: A short system card explains what the feature does, its data sources, and any known limits. Changes are logged. Risks and mitigations are mapped to the internal controls. If you operate in the EU, you have assessed the transparency requirements under the EU AI Act timeline.

To the point
Developing AI-enhanced features requires a cross-functional, end-to-end approach, integrating new key roles like data and security engineers to manage the probabilistic, data-dependent, and user-sensitive nature of AI.

15.7 GenAI-Assisted Development of GenAI Agents

15.7.1 Scope and New Role

If you recall our detailed introductions of the concept of an AI agent in Sect. 11.4.4, Chap. 13, and Sect. 14.6, then you know that agents take a small amount of initiative to complete a task under explicit policies (what it may do, with which data, and when it must ask for approval). It differs from a plain GenAI feature—which answers a prompt or transforms content in a single step—by planning a few steps, calling tools or APIs, managing basic decision-making and error recovery, and handing control back to a human when needed.

It also differs in terms of development. In our book we call the development of agents *Agent Engineering* and the process the *Agent Development Life Cycle* as a special form of the Software Development Life Cycle (SDLC). We explicitly exclude multi-agent systems here (see 15.8); the focus is on single agents embedded in a product or workflow (see Fig. 15.20).

There are a few terms that you come across when it comes to Agent Engineering. One we have used before in 15.6.2: the system card. Other terms are used here for the first time:

- Golden sets (DAC.digital, 2025)
- Runbooks (Digital Workforce, 2024)

- Agent Experience (AX) Design (AINativeDev, 2025)

You find short descriptions of all these terms also in the glossary. However, we want to go into detail with the Agent Experience Design.

Since an agent can plan steps, use tools, and act with some limited independence, designers need to clearly define what the agent can do, what it cannot do, and how users can stay in control. Agent Experience (AX) emphasizes *transparency*, *user permissions*, *recovery* options, and *accountability*, so that even small, controlled amounts of autonomy remain safe and easy for users to understand.

UX Design remains important for Agent Engineering, but AX Design requires additional attention. A seasoned UX designer can cover AX with a short upskilling—no new profession required. The key is practicing a few agent-specific patterns:

- Safety & consent patterns: permission prompts, scoped access, sensitive-action confirmations.
- Autonomy patterns: plan previews, next-step prompts, stop/pause/undo.
- Explainability patterns: concise rationales, confidence ranges, links to evidence.
- Failure & recovery patterns: retries, alternative sources, human escalation, and clear fallbacks.
- Operational literacy: basic grasp of logs/metrics used in reviews (task success, cost, intervention rate).

Later in this section, we largely set aside UX Design to focus on the differences between Agent Engineering and other forms of digital product development.

> **To the point**
> Agent engineering is the process of creating AI agents that can plan, call tools, and act with limited autonomy within a product or workflow, requiring a specific focus on design, safety, and accountability.

Figure. 15.21 shows the task mindmap for an AX Designer.

And here are the descriptions including GenAI support suggestions and tool recommendations:

Expose capabilities
Users must know what the agent can do, what it will attempt next, and what it cannot do. Clear communication prevents unrealistic expectations and builds trust.

GenAI can generate plain-language capability statements, simulate user questions to test if descriptions are understandable, and draft preview flows of upcoming steps.

Tool Recommendations: Figma (FigJam AI), Notion AI

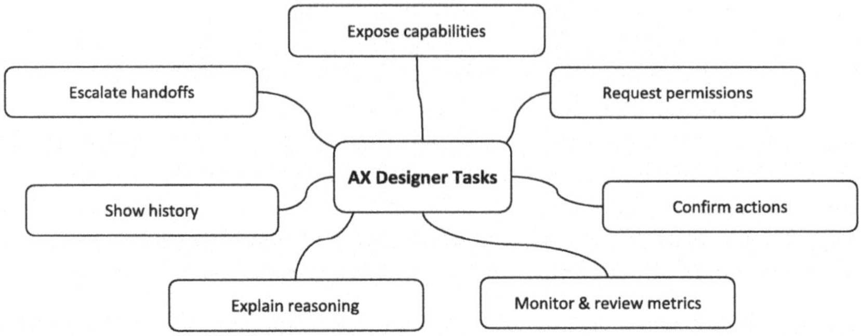

Fig. 15.21 Tasks of an AX Designer

Request permissions

Agents often need access to tools or data. Users should be asked for consent in a transparent, contextual way, with clear scope and duration.

GenAI drafts permission dialogues in natural language, tailor explanations for different user groups, and simulate potential misuse scenarios to improve clarity.

Tool Recommendations: Pactum, MS Power Platform

Confirm actions

Sensitive or irreversible steps must be confirmed, with options to undo or take a safe fallback path. This protects users and ensures accountability.

GenAI suggests confirmation wording, creates variations of fallback prompts, and generates test cases where confirmations are bypassed or misinterpreted.

Tool Recommendations: Grammarly Business, Figma Plugins

Explain reasoning

Users should understand why the agent made a decision, including confidence levels and evidence.

GenAI generates concise rationales, confidence ranges, and links to supporting evidence.

Tool Recommendations: Perplexity Sonar API, Vectara

Monitor & Review Metrics

Designers should understand operational metrics like task success, cost, and intervention rates to improve AX over time.

GenAI summarizes logs into dashboards, highlights anomalies, and suggests design improvements based on performance data.

Tool Recommendations: Power BI, Amplitude

Show history
Agents need to leave a human-readable trace of what they tried, why they acted, and what the outcome was. This provides transparency and supports troubleshooting.

GenAI generates action logs in user-friendly summaries, clusters sequences into digestible steps, and drafts explanatory tooltips or "why did the agent do this?" answers.

Tool Recommendations: Amplitude, Logsec AI

Escalate hand-offs
When agents cannot complete a task, they must gracefully return control to humans, providing enough context for a smooth handover.

GenAI generates concise escalation messages, proposes templates for handing over logs or evidence, and simulates edge cases where escalation is triggered.

Tool Recommendations: Atlassian Jira (Atlassian AI), ServiceNow Now Assist

What is missing is the list of artifacts that an AX designer is going to create. Summarized we call them the AX kit. Here are the components of the AX kit:

- Agent Flow (with permission/approval steps and fallbacks).
- Action History View (human-readable trace).
- Sensitive-Action Checklist (what needs confirm/undo).
- Microcopy Kit (disclosure, confidence, escalation, and apology texts).
- Explainability Templates (rationale, confidence, evidence links).
- Escalation Templates (hand-off messages and context bundles).
- Metrics Dashboard Wireframe (logs, success rates, intervention stats).

15.7.2 When to Use an Agent vs. an AI-Enhanced Feature

Use an agent only when it buys you something you cannot get from a standard GenAI feature or from process automation. Here's a compact "Agent or Simple Automation?" checklist:

Agent signals:

☐ The task spans multiple actions or tools (e.g., search → draft → validate → file).
☐ It needs conditional choices (if/else branches, tool selection based on input).
☐ It requires retries and recovery paths when things fail.
☐ Certain outcomes need human approval (human-in-the-loop checkpoints).
☐ You must enforce permissions and keep an audit trail of what was done and why.
☐ It's asynchronous and long-running (minutes/hours).

Simple automation signals:

- ☐ It's a single, deterministic step (same input → same output).
- ☐ Success is easy to verify with a binary check.
- ☐ It touches one stable tool/API with low risk.
- ☐ It just needs scheduling (e.g., daily/weekly) and alerting on failure.

If you tick 2 or more agent signals, build a lightweight agent. Design for least-privilege access, clear user confirmations, human-in-the-loop checkpoints, safe fallbacks, and measurable success so the autonomy you grant remains controlled and accountable. If you tick mostly simple automation signals, use a script/workflow + scheduler (optionally call an LLM inside for generation) for single-turn experiences like summarizing, classifying, recommending, or generating.

When in doubt, start simple and promote to an agent only if exceptions (branching, approvals, recovery) accumulate.

15.7.3 Roles & Responsibilities

In Table 15.3 we suggest the team setup and their responsibilities.

Three gates should be defined in Agent Engineering:

Table 15.3 Roles & Responsibilities

Role	Responsibility
Requirements engineer/product owner	Accountable for outcomes and scope; owns the agent brief and system card; makes go/no-go decisions at gates.
AX designer	Designs transparency, confirmations/undo, error recovery, and human hand-offs; reviews logs for UX issues.
Developer	Builds and maintains the agent package; integrates tools; implements guardrails (approvals, budgets, retries); sets up observability and rollouts.
Data engineer	Curates and versions evaluation datasets ("golden sets"); maintains input/output pipelines; monitors data quality and drift.
Security engineer	Defines permissions/policies (least privilege, scopes, budgets); leads adversarial testing; reviews inputs/outputs for safety.
Quality engineer	Turns scenarios into tests (incl. Fallbacks); runs pre-release checks; monitors failures/flakiness after launch.

Based on this table, we can create a RACI matrix for the core artifacts created during agent engineering.

Table 15.4 RACI matrix in Agent Engineering

Artifact\Role	RE	AX	Dev	Data Eng	Sec Eng	QE
Agent brief	A/R	R	C	C	C	C
Agent package	I	C	A/R	C	C	C
AX kit	C	A/R	C	C	C	C
Tool & permission spec	C	C	R	I	A/R	I
Evaluation Plan & Golden set	C	I	C	A/R	I	R
Runbook	I	C	A/R	C	C	R
System card	A/R	R	I	R	C	I

Legend: A = Accountable, R = Responsible, C = Consulted, I = Informed.

- Gate A (Discovery exit): RE (A); AX/Data/Sec/QE/Dev consulted.
- Gate B (Pre-release): QE (A) for quality, Security Engineer (A) for safety, AX Designer (A) for verification of AX patterns against AX kit; RE confirms scope fit.
- Gate C (Pilot scale/rollout): RE (A); QE and Security confirm production stability, AX Designer monitors AX metrics and safety; Dev owns rollout.

15.7.4 Complexity Drivers: Code and Agent Type

The project team setup can vary in size and is dependent on the overall complexity of the agent. This complexity is influenced by two main factors: the amount of code required (no-code, low-code, or full-code; see also 14.6.3) and the type of agent being built (e.g., a simple Q&A agent versus a multi-step workflow agent). The roles and artifacts depend on these dimensions:

- *No-code:* Requirements and prompt engineer, AX designer, quality engineer, security engineer (reviews scopes once).

  Artifacts: Agent brief, agent package (config, export from platform), AX kit, small golden set, basic runbook.

  Note: Workflow agents may require additional design effort and more extensive testing compared to Q&A agents.
- *Low-code:* Additionally developer and data engineer.

  Artifacts: Agent brief, agent package (config + lightweight glue code and webhooks), AX kit, Tool & Permission Spec, versioned golden sets in CI, System Card with data sources and limits.

  Note: Workflow agents often need more orchestration logic and integration points, increasing complexity beyond code alone.
- *Full-code:* Same as low-code, plus deeper developer and security engineer involvement, possibly legal.

Artifacts: Everything above (with agent package containing full source module, policy files, and SDK integrations), telemetry dashboards, incident playbook, and stricter gates.

Note: For workflow agents, expect additional roles for process design and more rigorous governance.

15.8 GenAI-Assisted Development of Agentic Systems

15.8.1 Scope & What's Extra beyond a Single Agent

Developing a single agent already requires clear goals, guardrails, and cross-functional responsibilities. Moving from a single agent to an agentic system (Fig. 15.22) multiplies the challenge: instead of one autonomous unit, you now design, coordinate, and monitor networks of agents that collaborate or specialize. This shift introduces new layers of complexity—defining how agents interact, how they resolve conflicts, and how the overall system remains safe, cost-effective, and observable. The project approach must expand accordingly: more emphasis on system architecture, orchestration, and evaluation at the network level, while still re-using many practices from single-agent development. A key question is whether new roles are needed or whether existing ones simply take on broader responsibilities. GenAI itself can support these additional steps by helping design coordination strategies, simulate multi-agent interactions, and generate richer evaluation scenarios.

What's extra comes in five areas.

- Coordination & roles: define specializations (e.g., planner, worker, reviewer) and the rules for hand-offs, second opinions, and tie-breaks.
- Shared state & memory: choose how agents exchange facts (blackboard/task graph/message bus), how long state persists, and how to keep it consistent.

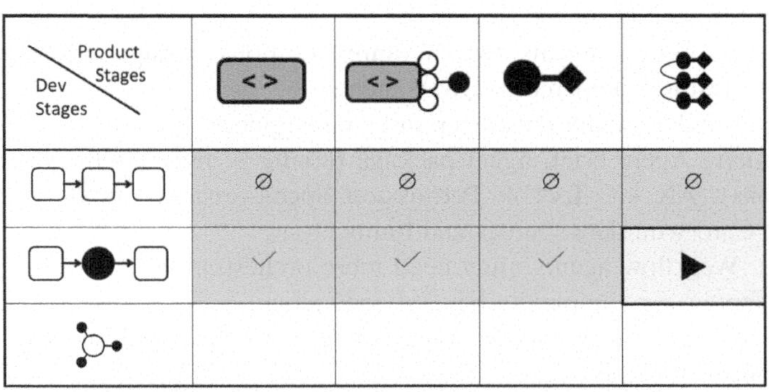

Fig. 15.22 Section Locator (4) for the Product x Process Matrix

- Conflict resolution: decide how disagreements are detected and arbitrated (confidence thresholds, majority vote, human checkpoint), and when to fall back to a simpler single-agent path.
- Global safety & budgets: set system-wide limits for time, cost, data scope, and permissions; add pause/stop and escalation controls that act across all agents.
- System-level evaluation: move from per-agent accuracy to **end-to-end task success**, robustness under contention, and the rate of human interventions.

Your core artifacts evolve accordingly.

- The *System-Level Card* documents the overall purpose, the agent roles, their coordination pattern, inter-agent data flows, and global constraints (budgets, safety, escalation paths).
- Testing shifts to *Scenario Suites*—versioned, end-to-end workflows that include typical paths, edge cases, contention scenarios, and recovery loops—with clear success thresholds for quality, latency, cost, and safety.
- Operations rely on a *System Runbook* that covers monitoring and incident handling at the coordination layer (e.g., pausing all agents, resetting shared memory, stepping down to a single-agent fallback).

GenAI can assist with these extras by

- drafting coordination strategies (candidate role splits and task graphs)
  Tool recommendation: LangGraph (LangChain), AutoGen.
- simulating multi-agent runs to surface deadlocks or conflicts before you build them
  Tool recommendation: LangGraph Studio/notebooks, CrewAI.
- generating adversarial scenarios to enrich your Scenario Suites.
  Tool recommendation: Promptfoo, garak.

GenAI also helps keep the System-Level Card and System Runbook current:

- summarizing telemetry into human-readable updates and proposing refinements to budgets, hand-offs, and checkpoints as the system learns.
  Tool recommendation: Langfuse, Weights & Biases, Datadog.

15.8.2 When to Use an Agentic System vs. a Single Agent

Not every problem needs more than one agent—most teams are better served by starting with the simplest thing that can work, and only "promoting" to an agentic system when the work itself creates clear benefits from coordination, specialization, or parallelism.

You're likely looking at an agentic system when the following signals appear, because each points to values that a single agent struggles to deliver:

☐ Specialization helps quality: the agent's task decomposes naturally into roles—planner, researcher, drafter, reviewer, and actor—and distinct agent skill profiles tend to catch each other's mistakes and raise the final standard.
☐ Parallelism matters: you must process many items at once or consult multiple sources in parallel, where concurrency improves throughput or latency beyond what a single workflow can achieve.
☐ Independent verification is required: there's a need for a second opinion or cross-check before acting (e.g., safety, compliance, financial impact), so a reviewer agent reduces risk without blocking the whole pipeline.
☐ Heterogeneous tools and data are involved: different steps require different credentials, systems, or domain knowledge, and specialized agents can keep access narrower and reasoning cleaner.
☐ System-level constraints apply: you need global time and cost budgets, fairness or priority rules, or shared memory that coordinates multiple efforts—mechanisms that sit above any single agent's scope.

By contrast, a single agent is often the better choice when the work is simpler and the overhead of coordination would add cost without payoff:

☐ The task is sequential and narrow: one toolchain, predictable steps, and success can be verified straightforwardly, so adding roles brings complexity with no real gain.
☐ Coordination cost exceeds benefit: splitting the problem into multiple agents introduces orchestration and monitoring burdens that don't translate into better quality, speed, or safety.
☐ The stakes and volume are low: a single agent with a human checkpoint provides adequate assurance without the need for a system-wide design.

To the point
Begin with a single agent plus a human checkpoint; move to an agentic system only when specialization, parallelism, or independent verification deliver measurable gains.

Finally, a few *anti-patterns* are worth naming because they look attractive but rarely pay off:

- Believing more agents automatically means more intelligence, when unclear roles and weak arbitration just amplify noise.
- Splitting work to mirror your org chart rather than the task structure, which adds interfaces without improving outcomes.
- Running multiple agents with no global budget or safety rules, which invites inconsistent behavior or overspend.

- Relying on a hidden single-point specialist with no fallback, which undermines the supposed resilience of the system.

15.8.3 Roles & Responsibilities

Moving from a single agent to an agentic system doesn't require a new department; it asks the same people to own outcomes at system level. Responsibilities broaden from "make this one agent safe and useful" to "keep a coordinated network of agents effective, observable, and governable."

For the Requirements Engineer (in collaboration with the Product owner), the job expands from feature goals to system-level intent and guardrails, because multiple agents need a shared definition of success and limits to avoid drift or overspend.

- Own the *system* goal and success metrics (quality, latency, cost, safety), set global budgets and stop conditions, and decide when independent review is required before actions.
- Prioritize coordination patterns (e.g., "drafter → reviewer → actor") when they measurably improve outcomes, and remove them when they do not.
- Approve the System-Level Card and changes to it, so scope and constraints remain clear to everyone.

For the AX Designer, the canvas shifts from a single conversation to multi-agent transparency and control, because users must understand what the agentic system is doing.

- Design system-wide visibility: what each agent can do, what will happen next, and how results were combined (the "across-agents" action history).
- Place permissions and confirmations at the right points (tool scopes, data use, sensitive actions) and make fallbacks and hand-offs obvious when the system can't proceed.
- Maintain the AX Kit (system view)—flows, history spec, sensitive-action checklist, and microcopy—so patterns stay consistent as agents change.

For the Developer, the work moves from building one agent to building the coordination fabric, because reliability now depends on the glue as much as the agents.

- Implement the orchestrator, registry, routing, and shared memory, with clear time and cost budgets and backoff policies.
- Instrument global telemetry (task success, intervention rate, latency, cost) and expose an audit trail that's human-readable for reviews and post-incident analysis.

- Treat each Agent Package as code (prompts/policies/tools), versioned and tested against Scenario Suites before rollout.

For the Data Engineer, the focus widens from inputs for one agent to shared data quality and evaluation across workflows, because coordination amplifies the effect of bad data.

- Curate Scenario Suites—versioned, end-to-end evaluation workflows with typical paths, contention cases, and recovery loops—and track thresholds for success.
- Maintain lineage and freshness for inter-agent data flows; monitor drift and trigger re-tests when real-world inputs shift.
- Ensure logs and datasets respect privacy (minimize, mask, retain appropriately) while staying informative enough to improve the system.

For the Security Engineer, protections move from single-prompt checks to system-wide safety and permissions, because multiple agents compound risk if scopes are unclear.

- Define least-privilege tool scopes per role, approvals for sensitive operations, and system-level kill switches and pauses.
- Lead adversarial testing at *coordination* level (conflicting results, prompt manipulation across agents, budget abuse) and verify global guardrails before scale-up.
- Review inputs/outputs and shared memory policies to prevent unintended disclosure or unsafe actions.

For the Quality Engineer, assurance shifts from unit-style checks to end-to-end evaluation, because quality now depends on how agents interact.

- Build and run system-level evaluations using Scenario Suites; measure task success, human-intervention rate, flake/loop patterns, latency, and cost.
- Add contention and failure-injection tests (e.g., source outage, agent disagreement) to verify that recovery paths and fallbacks actually work.
- Gate releases on evidence, not anecdotes: if metrics regress, stop and adjust coordination, budgets, or roles.

Where complexity warrants it, introduce an *Agent Orchestrator* hat, because someone should keep arbitration rules, shared memory, and budgets coherent over time. On small projects, this hat typically sits with the Developer; on larger or regulated ones, it may sit with a Systems Architect or Product Owner/Requirements Engineer.

Finally, align responsibilities with three lightweight gates so decisions happen with evidence rather than opinion, because orchestration choices affect cost, safety, and user trust:

- At Gate A (discovery exit), PO/RE confirm the System-Level Card draft and the proposed role split; AX presents the system view of the flow; Data/QE show initial Scenario Suites; Security validates planned scopes and approvals.
- At Gate B (pre-release), Developer demonstrates passing Scenario Suites; QE reviews end-to-end metrics; Security signs off global guardrails; AX verifies that history/permissions/fallbacks match the AX Kit.
- At Gate C (pilot/scale), PO/RE decides to widen exposure only if production metrics (quality, intervention rate, latency, cost, safety) stay within thresholds; Developer owns rollout and telemetry; QE and Security monitor production stability and safety; and can pause or step down to a single-agent fallback if needed.

15.9 Agentic Digital Product Development for Products without AI Features

15.9.1 Scope of this Section

While AI is expected to become an integral part of how teams build software, many digital products may still ship without AI-driven features for some time. Although we anticipate that the share of products without AI will decline significantly by the 2030s, today more than half of all digital products still fall into this category.

In 15.5 we showed how such products can already be delivered faster with chatbots, single agents, or AI features inside supporting tools; this section takes the next step by applying agentic development systems to the same class of products (see Fig. 15.23). Building on the general notion of agentic systems from 11.4.4—and the merged role we introduced there as the *Digital Content Creator*—we'll adopt the software-specific title *Digital Product Creator* (DPC) to denote the human who steers and supervises the agentic workflow. In this context, an agentic development system coordinates planning, requirements documentation, UI/UX and architectural design, code generation, review, testing, documentation, and release across your existing toolchain—speeding up routine work while preserving human judgment, governance, and quality gates.

This evolution is particularly significant because the emergence of agentic development systems marks a turning point in how software is conceived and delivered. It's no surprise that this is the battleground where tool vendors are fiercely competing for market share. Whoever defines the dominant standards and ecosystems in this space will shape the future of software development.

After a literature review the subsections that follow go into detail on this.

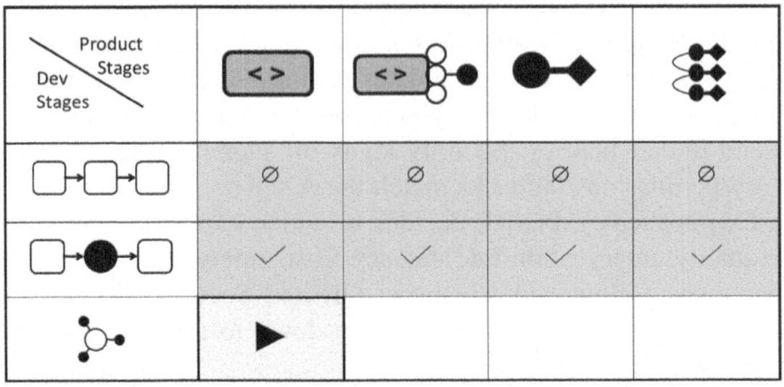

Fig. 15.23 Section Locator (5) for the Product x Process Matrix

15.9.2 Mini Literature Review: Agentic Development Systems

We reviewed recent 2025 studies and reports on agentic development workflows to understand how they are coordinated, what benefits they deliver, and where risks and open questions remain.

What we know:

- Coordination patterns are stabilizing: Recent work evaluates *coordination topologies* (chain, star, graph) for multi-agent collaboration, while protocols like A2A (see 11.4.4) address interoperability and messaging; the former concerns *how* agents are organized to work together, the latter *how* they communicate across systems (Zhu et al., 2025).
- Adaptive orchestration improves efficiency: Research introducing a "puppeteer" (central controller) shows that dynamically reallocating work among agents can reduce wasted effort versus static role charts (Dang et al., 2025).
- Evaluation is expanding beyond one-shot answers: Surveys argue that measuring success now requires end-to-end task completion, tool use, memory handling, and robustness across domains—not just single outputs (Yehudai et al., 2025).

What's unsettled

- Reproducibility is still hard: New multi-agent benchmarks highlight how the same setup can produce different outcomes across runs, posing a challenge for teams that need predictable behavior (Zhu et al., 2025).
- Complexity doesn't guarantee reliability: Empirical work cautions that adding more agents or intricate structures can reduce robustness if coordination overhead outpaces the benefits (Lee et al., 2025).

- Adoption is outpacing consensus: Industry reporting shows rapid investment and deployment of agentic workflows inside software teams, while evaluation standards are still catching up (Loucks et al., 2025).

Implications for practice

- Start small, then scale with evidence: Begin with a single agent and move to multi-agent systems only when specialization, parallelism, or independent review demonstrably improve results (Lee et al., 2025).
- Treat coordination and evaluation as first-class artifacts: Define and version your coordination strategy and test scenario suites so changes can be assessed on end-to-end success, latency, cost, and safety (Yehudai et al., 2025).
- Balance fast adoption with guardrails: Given rising enterprise use, invest early in basic governance (system-level goals, budgets, and escalation paths) to avoid brittle or costly rollouts (Loucks et al., 2025).

15.9.3 The Emerging Role of the Digital Product Creator

Over the next few years we expect a steady convergence of responsibilities across requirements, design, coding, testing, and operations. Instead of hand-offs between separate disciplines, AI lets one or a few accountable persons orchestrate the flow end-to-end: capture intent, shape a prototype, generate baseline code and tests, gate changes through policy, and decide when to ship. In other words, AI shifts effort from "throwing work over the wall" to coordinating a single, traceable loop.

Why one orchestrator role now? Modern tools can translate plain-language requirements into working artifacts within minutes. A product idea expressed as user goals or a whole requirements backlog can become a clickable UI prototype almost immediately (e.g., v0, Google Stitch, Uizard, see 15.9.4). Quality engineers already lean on AI to generate and evolve tests from acceptance criteria, while operations feedback—performance, errors, user behavior—flows back through AI summaries into design and backlog decisions. These feedback loops reduce the need for rigid role boundaries and make continuous, evidence-based iteration possible.

In this setting the Digital Product Creator (DPC)—derived from the Digital Content Creator from Fig. 11.10 —sits at the center. So you do not need to flip back, we show the figure again with the DPC as the actor in Fig. 15.24.

The DPC unifies ownership across the SDLC: curating requirements, steering code generation and review, ensuring tests reflect risk, and making deployment choices in concert with guardrails. The DPC doesn't replace specialists; rather, they conduct the work (done by agentic dev systems), keep quality and ethics visible, and decide when to involve deeper expertise.

After the increase of the size of the development team with increasing *agentification* of the product to be developed (see 15.6–15.8), we will now see a decrease

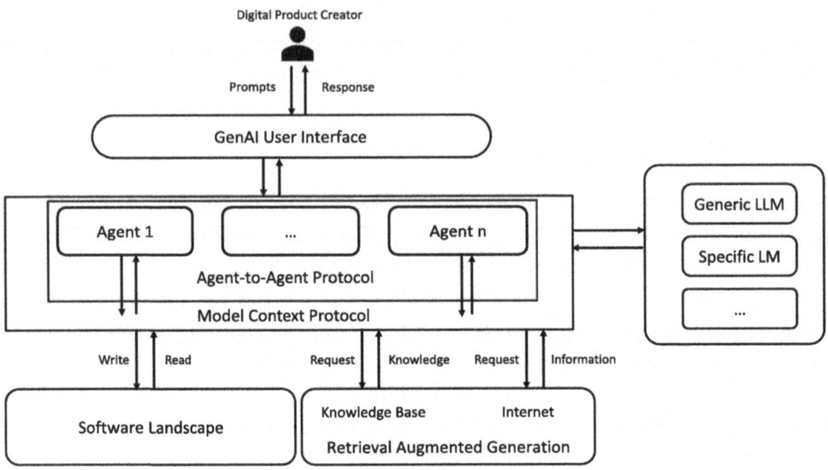

Fig. 15.24 Possible high-level Agentic Architecture diagram with DPC as orchestrator

Fig. 15.25 Increase and reduction of the development team size

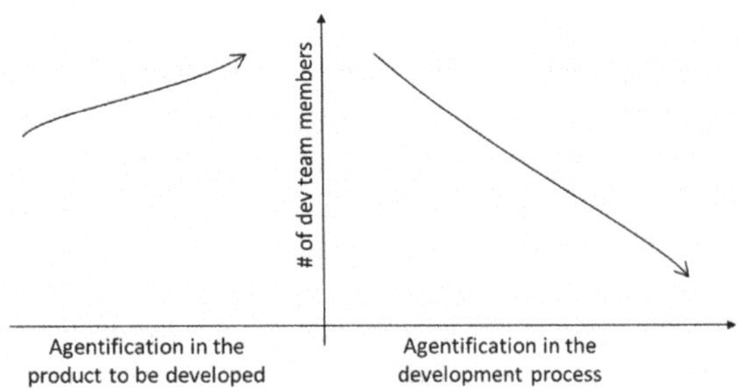

of team size. However, the transition from a full, function-siloed team to a smaller, agent-supported team will be gradual (see Fig. 15.25).

As agentification increases, more routine work is handled by agents and AI-assisted tools, and the human team narrows to the DPC. In larger projects—and depending on product maturity—you may see two complementary tracks emerge: a business-oriented DPC (closer to product strategy, outcomes, and user value) and a technical DPC (closer to architecture, code quality, and operational excellence). Both share the same core accountability: orchestrate an AI-augmented workflow that moves from intent to working software with clear metrics, guardrails, and learning loops.

15.9.4 Tooling for Agentic Development of Classic Software

The tooling landscape here is moving fast—and it's hotly contested. Vendors are racing to automate bigger slices of the SDLC, from idea → requirements →

UI → code to plan → build → test → deploy, while IDEs and platform players add agent modes and orchestration.

To the point
For the development of classic software systems, it is wise to rely on standard agentic systems rather than building them yourself.

Below is a pragmatic map with examples: first, tools that cover parts of the life cycle; then, those that claim end-to-end coverage already.

Tools covering parts of the SDLC

- Requirements/UX → UI/code generators: These tools turn prompts, sketches, or screenshots into UI designs and runnable frontend code. The results can be exported to Figma for refinement or iteratively improved in other tools. They are useful for rapid ideation and for getting from intent to a concrete prototype quickly. Example tools are.
    - Google Stitch
    - Uizard
    - Vercel v0
- Coding (agentic IDEs and code assistants). Here we consider the tools separately:
    - Cursor (Agent/Delegate mode): lets an AI agent plan tasks and modify code iteratively inside the IDE—moving beyond autocomplete toward "delegate this change."
    - JetBrains AI Assistant: multi-file edits, refactoring, test generation, and commit message help across JetBrains IDEs; useful when you want agent-like workflows inside a familiar toolchain.
    - Sourcegraph Cody: large-codebase chat and edits, with Model Context Protocol (MCP) support for external context—good for repo-wide reasoning and automated changes.
- Ops & change workflows (AI in the platform). ServiceNow Now Assist is currently—at the time of writing this—ahead: AI agents change planning and DevOps/ITSM flows (e.g., generating change plans, risk summaries). They feed operational insights back into design and backlog.

Tools that *claim end-to-end*

- GitHub Copilot Workspace: a "Copilot-native" environment to brainstorm, plan, build, test, and run code in natural language, with developers retaining control step-by-step. Early but explicitly positioned as project-level, not just autocomplete.
- Atlassian Rovo Dev Agents: public beta claims agents across the whole SDLC—planning from Jira tickets, code writing, review, and deployment—plus a Studio app to compose swarms of agents and a CLI for dev workflows.

- StackBlitz Bolt.new: an in-browser "AI web dev agent" to prompt, run, edit, and deploy full-stack apps—useful for greenfield prototypes and teaching; open-source repo shows how it wires prompt→run→deploy.
- Microsoft "Agentic DevOps" direction: Microsoft frames agents that accompany teams through the *entire* lifecycle (beyond Copilot's suggestions) as a strategic shift; details are evolving, but it signals full-SDLC ambitions.
- AWS Bedrock AgentCore: more platform than SDLC tool, but relevant infrastructure—runtime, memory, identity, gateway, and observability for production-grade agents that your dev pipeline can orchestrate.

End-to-end tools are built on agentic development systems. In Chap. 11 (see Fig. 11.9), we introduced an example of such a system focused on requirements-related use cases. Now, we extend this concept to cover the entire software development lifecycle (SDLC) within a single agentic system. Figure 15.26 illustrates this approach, highlighting the architecture at the orchestrator and coordinator levels, but only indicating the very complex skill agent level. This diagram conveys similar information as Fig. 15.24 ailed but provides a more detview of the agent architecture.

Bottom line: Most tools today are very good at one part of the development process (for example, creating screens or helping write code), while a few claim to cover everything from idea to release. Because these products change quickly, it's wise to try them on a small, real project before committing. Compare easy-to-understand results: how quickly work gets done, how many issues reviewers still find, and how smoothly handovers happen. Keep a backup plan to your current tools so you can switch back if the new approach doesn't deliver clear benefits.

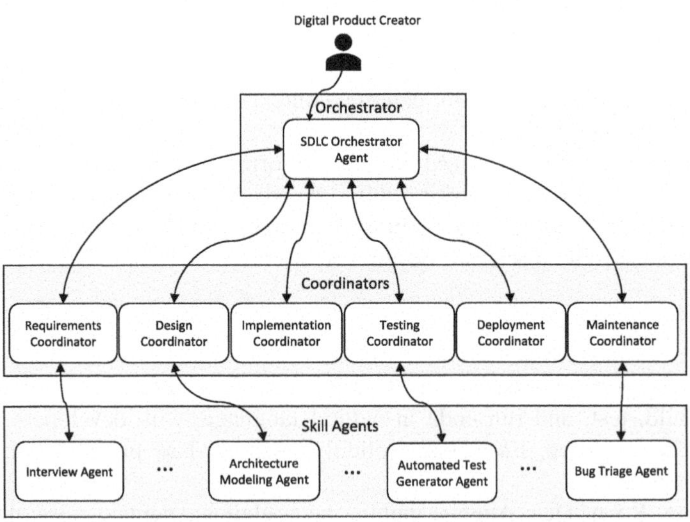

Fig. 15.26 Simplified agentic system for the Software Development Lifecycle

15.10 Agentic Digital Product Development for AI Products

We're now stepping from agentic development for classic software into its next stage: agentic digital product development for AI-native products (Fig. 15.27). Where the last wave used agents to supercharge conventional apps and pipelines, this wave treats AI products and especially agents as the product—durable systems that perceive, decide, act, and collaborate, often across clouds, devices, and organizations.

If agentic systems as products define what we're building, the next leap is how we build them—using agents as first-class co-developers. In this operating model, human engineers specify intent, guardrails, and success criteria; then orchestrated builder-agents generate designs, code, data, evals, and deployment artifacts—continuously testing and improving the very agents that power the product.

Agentic development of agentic systems means building the factory and letting the factory learn—under strict governance. Teams that install this loop early will ship AI products that not only work on day one, but get better on day two—safely, observably, and on purpose (Fang et al., 2025). Increasingly, that loop will not stop at the boundaries of the product team. It will extend all the way to the user.

In such systems, the future user is no longer a passive consumer of fixed functionality, but an active shaper of behavior. Software products will ship with an agentic development platform as part of their foundation, enabling users to add, adapt, and recombine capabilities themselves. The visible interface of this power may be deceptively simple—often little more than a prompt input line—but behind it sits a governed, evolvable system that translates intent into new workflows, agents, and automations.

This field is very early—expect patterns, standards, and even role definitions to evolve quickly. The distinction between "developer" and "user" will blur, then

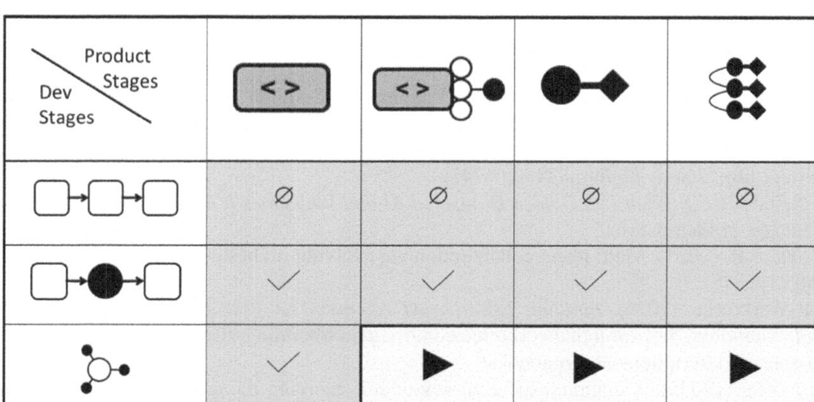

Fig. 15.27 Section Locator (6) for the Product x Process Matrix

erode, as agentic systems absorb more of the complexity traditionally handled by code. Yet by the time you read this, it may already be a hot topic as platforms harden and exemplars emerge. Or, just as likely, there may be a completely different approach altogether that has gained traction. That uncertainty is precisely why we will not go into more detail here. However, the supreme discipline might remain the agentic development of agentic systems: designing ensembles of evolving agents that decompose work, coordinate robustly, learn safely in the wild, and remain intelligible to their human owners—who now participate directly in their evolution. In this case, teams that master this will set the pace for the next decade of digital products—where the core user value isn't just a feature, but a trustworthy coalition of agents that anticipate, decide, and do (Nuñez, 2025)—while allowing their users to continuously redefine what the product is capable of.

References

AI Testing Tools. (2025). *Synthetic test data: The future of software testing without real user data.* https://www.testingtools.ai/blog/synthetic-test-data-the-future-of-software-testing-without-real-user-data

AINativeDev. (2025). *The new frontier in AI development: Why agent experience matters.* https://ainativedev.io/news/agentic-experience

Angi, A., Nedoshivina, L., Sacco, A., Braghin, S., & Purcell, M. (2025). *A perspective on LLM data generation with few-shot examples: From intent to kubernetes manifest.* https://aclanthology.org/2025.acl-industry.27.pdf

AWS. (2025). *Generative AI Lens—AWS well-architected framework.* https://docs.aws.amazon.com/wellarchitected/latest/generative-ai-lens/generative-ai-lens.html

Bandi, A., Nukala, H. S. T., Tatavarthi, B., & Boggavarapu, A. (2025). *Automated test case generation for software testing using generative AI.* Conference Paper. https://link.springer.com/chapter/10.1007/978-3-031-92178-0_7

Baqar, M., & Khanda, R. (2025). *The Future of Software Testing: AI-Powered Test Case Generation and Validation.* https://arxiv.org/pdf/2409.05808

Baqar, M., Naqvi, S., & Khanda, R. (2025). *AI-Augmented CI/CD Pipelines: From Code Commit to Production with Autonomous Decisions.* https://arxiv.org/abs/2508.11867

Bavor, C., & Taylor, B. (2024). *The Agent Development Life Cycle.* Sierra. https://sierra.ai/blog/agent-development-life-cycle.

Cerejo, L. (2025). A week in the life of an AI-augmented designer. *Smashing Magazine.*. https://www.smashingmagazine.com/2025/08/week-in-life-ai-augmented-designer

Cheng, H., et al. (2025). *Generative AI for Requirements Engineering: A Systematic Literature Review.* https://arxiv.org/html/2409.06741v1

DAC.digital (2025). *What Is a Golden Dataset in AI and Why Does It Matter?* https://dac.digital/what-is-a-golden-dataset/

Dang, Y., et al. (2025). Multi-agent collaboration via evolving orchestration. https://arxiv.org/abs/2505.19591

Digital Workforce. (2024). *Building Effective AI Agents: The Essential Role of Descriptions and Runbooks.* https://digitalworkforce.com/rpa-news/building-effective-ai-agents-the-essential-role-of-descriptions-and-runbooks/

Fang, J., et al. (2025). A comprehensive survey of self-evolving AI agents. https://arxiv.org/pdf/2508.07407.

Gancarz, R. (2025). Datadog employs LLMs for assisting with writing accident postmortems. InfoQ. https://www.infoq.com/news/2025/04/datadog-postmortem-llm-genai

Guo, X., Li, C., & Tsuchiya, T. (2025). *Boundary Value Test Input Generation Using Prompt Engineering with LLMs: Fault Detection and Coverage Analysis.* https://arxiv.org/abs/2501.14465

Hale, J., et al. (2025). *AI-Mediated Dispute Resolution.* Proceedings of the 2025 AAAI Spring Symposium Series. https://ojs.aaai.org/index.php/AAAI-SS/article/view/35558

Hallikeri, P. (2025). *Accelerating Java modernization with IBM watsonx Code Assistant.* IBM. https://www.ibm.com/new/product-blog/accelerating-java-modernization-watsonx-code-assistant

Heuel, S., (2025). *Creating architecture diagrams with C4 and AI.* https://blog.heuel.org/2025/01/creating-architecture-diagrams-with-c4-and-ai

Ilas, G. (2025). *GenAI in the Backend: Refactoring, Testing, and Automation With Confidence.* Bytex. https://bytex.net/blog/genai-in-the-backend-refactoring-testing-and-automation-with-confidence.

Jeon, J., Park, J., Park, S., Choi, J., Kim, M., & Park, N. (2025). *Possibility for Proactive Anomaly Detection.* https://arxiv.org/abs/2504.11623

Kim, M., Sinha, S., & Orso, A. (2025). LlamaRestTest: Effective REST API Testing with Small Language Models. https://arxiv.org/pdf/2501.08598

Krpan, L.,Vidović, D. I., & Talajić, M. (2025). *Artificial Intelligence and ONA: Transforming Project Management Practices.* European Project Management Journal, Volume 15, Issue 1, May 2025. https://epmj.org/wp-content/uploads/2025/05/EPMJ-25-1-Krpan-Ivandic-Vidovic-Talajic.pdf

Kumar, A., Haiduc, S., Das, P. P, Chakrabarti, P. P. (2025). *LLMs as Evaluators: A Novel Approach to Evaluate Bug Report Summarization.* https://arxiv.org/abs/2409.00630

Lange, K., & Parra-Moyano, J. (2025). Research: How AI helped executives improve communication. *Harvard Business Review..* https://hbr.org/2025/02/research-how-ai-helped-executives-improve-communication

Laskowski, M., & Michalak, T. (2025). *Using generative AI as an architect buddy for creating architecture decision records.* https://handsonarchitects.com/blog/2025/using-generative-ai-as-architect-buddy-for-adrs

Lee, X., et al. (2025). *Reliable Decision-Making for Multi-Agent LLM Systems.* https://multiagents.org/2025_artifacts/reliable_decision_making_for_multi_agent_llm_systems.pdf

Lin, X., et al. (2025). *IRCopilot: Automated Incident Response with Large Language Models.* https://arxiv.org/abs/2505.20945

Linders, B. (2025). *Using Artificial Intelligence for Analysis of Automated Testing Results.* InfoQ. https://www.infoq.com/news/2025/03/AI-analysis-automated-test

Loucks, J., et al. (2025). Autonomous generative AI agents: Under development. Deloitte. https://www.deloitte.com/us/en/insights/industry/technology/technology-media-and-telecom-predictions/2025/autonomous-generative-ai-agents-still-under-development.html

Marri, S. P. (2025). *AI-Driven Approaches to Enhance Budgeting and Forecasting: Transforming Financial Planning in Organizations.* European Journal of Computer Science and Information Technology. https://eajournals.org/ejcsit/wp-content/uploads/sites/21/2025/05/AI-Driven-Approaches.pdf

McGowan, B., et al. (2025). *When trust in AI matters, system cards keep score.* KPMG. https://kpmg.com/kpmg-us/content/dam/kpmg/pdf/2025/system-cards-keep-score.pdf

Microsoft. (2025). Get AI architecture guidance for Azure platform services (PaaS) for AI. https://learn.microsoft.com/en-us/azure/cloud-adoption-framework/scenarios/ai/platform/architectures

Nuñez, M. (2025). Microsoft announces over 50 AI tools to build the 'agentic web' at build 2025. VentureBeat. https://venturebeat.com/ai/microsoft-announces-over-50-ai-tools-to-build-the-agentic-web-at-build-2025.

Poth, A., Rrjolli, O., Wang, H., Schmid, K. *Baseline Evaluation of LLM-Facilitated UI Test-Case Generation from Gherkin Specifications.* https://link.springer.com/chapter/10.1007/978-3-032-04288-0_3

Project Management Institute. (2025). *Leading AI Transformation: Organizational Strategies for Project Professionals.* https://www.pmi.org/standards/leading-ai-transformation-organizational-strategies-for-project-professionals.

QED42. (2025). *The future of Front-End development | how GenAI is revolutionizing workflows and efficiency.* https://www.qed42.com/insights/the-future-of-front-end-development-how-generative-ai-is-revolutionizing-workflows-and-efficiency

Revilla, E., & Saenz, M. J. (2025). How AI is reshaping supplier negotiations. *Harvard Business Review.* https://hbr.org/2025/07/how-ai-is-reshaping-supplier-negotiations

Shamim, M., et al. (2025). *Advancement of Artificial Intelligence in Cost Estimation for Project Management Success.* MDPI. https://www.mdpi.com/2673-3951/6/2/35

Szandała, T. (2025). *AIOps for Reliability: Evaluating Large Language Models for Automated Root Cause Analysis in Chaos Engineering.* https://www.iccs-meeting.org/archive/iccs2025/papers/159090307.pdf

Wavhal, A. (2025). *The Impact of Generative AI on Frontend Development. Incerro.* https://www.incerro.ai/insights/the-impact-of-generative-ai-on-frontend-development

Yehudai, A., et al. (2025). Survey on evaluation of LLM-based agents. https://arxiv.org/pdf/2503.16416

Yu, Z., et al. (2025)*Triangle: Empowering Incident Triage with Multi-LLM-Agents.* Microsoft. https://www.microsoft.com/en-us/research/wp-content/uploads/2025/02/TRIANGLE_FSE25.pdf

Zhu, K., et al. (2025). MultiAgentBench: Evaluating the collaboration and competition of LLM agents. https://arxiv.org/abs/2503.01935.

Final LLM Thoughts

Fittingly, a book on GenAI should end with GenAI: these final thoughts were generated by a language model—GPT-5.

This book has moved from the discipline of requirements engineering to the frontier of generative and agentic systems. Part I focused on the craft: establishing clarity of intent, shared language, and verifiable outcomes. Part II widened the lens to strategy, governance, and the operating models needed to turn capability into value. Taken together, the throughline is simple: sound requirements practice is not made obsolete by AI—it becomes more essential as systems grow more adaptive, probabilistic, and autonomous.

Clarity still wins. In an AI-driven lifecycle, the artifacts may change—prompts, policies, guardrails, evaluators, agents—but the questions remain familiar: Who is this for? What does "good" look like? How will we observe, test, and improve behavior over time? Treat prompts and agent behaviors as first-class requirements. Make them traceable to stakeholder needs, measurable by outcomes, and testable under real conditions. When ambiguity is expensive, rigor is a kindness.

Trust is designed, not assumed. Governance, risk, and compliance are not a brake on innovation; they are the rails that let teams move fast without leaving the track. Align use cases to business value and organizational principles; instrument for safety, security, and fairness; and close the loop with monitoring and evaluation. Models will drift, contexts will shift, and regulations will evolve—so build for change, not for a moment.

Adoption is a socio-technical journey. Tools matter, but teams, roles, and incentives determine whether value shows up in practice. Create small, well-bounded slices where AI augments real work, measure the outcomes, and scale what proves itself. Pair domain expertise with product thinking and AI engineering. Make learning visible; let patterns spread.

As systems grow more agentic, product boundaries will blur. We are moving from "adding AI to products" toward "designing products around AI"—services that perceive, decide, and act with people in the loop. New roles will emerge at this intersection—people who can translate intent into behavior across data,

J. Kawelke and T. Niebisch, *AI-Driven Transformation - Practical Frameworks for Real-World Impact*, Future of Business and Finance,
https://doi.org/10.1007/978-3-662-72549-8

models, and experience. Whatever we call them, the mandate is the same: turn responsibility into capability, and capability into outcomes customers can feel.

The future won't be delivered to us; it will be specified, designed, and iterated by us. If the work in these pages has a single message, it is that human judgment—expressed through clear intent, careful design, and continuous learning—remains the cornerstone of progress. May you take these practices, adapt them to your context, and build systems that are not only powerful, but worthy of the trust we place in them.

The next release is ours to ship.

Glossary

Acceptance Criterion A feature or condition that must be met for stakeholders to accept the implementation of a requirement.

Activity Diagram UML diagram type for representing processes.

Agent See AI Agent

Agent Development Life Cycle A structured methodology for building, testing, releasing, and maintaining AI agents, particularly those powered by large language models (LLMs), first formalized by Sierra.

Agent Engineering Extends prompt engineering by designing autonomous agents with memory, planning, and tool use.

Agent Experience The overall quality and effectiveness of interactions between a user and an AI agent, encompassing usability, responsiveness, personalization, and trustworthiness.

Agentic AI AI systems that plan, reason, and act autonomously toward goals (goes beyond single-prompt responses).

Agentic System A system of one or more AI agents that can pursue goals with limited supervision by planning, calling tools, taking actions, and learning from feedback.

Agentic Web Refers to an emerging vision of the internet where autonomous AI agents can interact, transact, and collaborate on behalf of users or organizations across websites, services, and platforms without constant human intervention.

Agentification The process of transforming systems, entities, or processes into agents or agentic systems by endowing them with autonomy, decision-making capabilities, and goal-directed behavior within their environment.

Agent-to-Agent Protocol (A2A) A standard for communication and cooperation among AI agents.

Agile Manifesto Created in 2001 by 17 software developers, it defines four core values and twelve principles that guide successful agile practices.

AI Agent A software entity powered by AI models that can perceive information, make decisions, and act autonomously toward goals. Often built on GenAI, AI agents can plan tasks, interact with tools, and collaborate with humans or other

J. Kawelke and T. Niebisch, *AI-Driven Transformation - Practical Frameworks for Real-World Impact*, Future of Business and Finance,
https://doi.org/10.1007/978-3-662-72549-8

systems, making them useful for automation, assistance, and adaptive problem-solving.

Artifact Any document, model, or work product that records requirements for the future IT solution. Figuratively, it acts as a container holding one or more requirements.

Artificial Intelligence (AI) A field of computer science focused on enabling machines to perform tasks that typically require human intelligence.

Asynchronous Communication Communication that occurs at different times, where delayed responses do not halt or terminate the process.

Boundary condition One of the five requirement categories that groups conditions to be considered during solution development.

Business Process Model and Notation (BPMN) Standard of the OMG for process modeling.

Chain-of-Thought Prompting (CoT) Explicitly asking the model to reason step by step.

Chatbot A computer program designed to simulate human-like conversations with users, typically powered by Large Language Models or other AI-based systems.

Class Diagram A UML diagram type that represents classes or concepts, their attributes, and the relationships between them.

Classical AI A term commonly used to describe traditional AI approaches based on symbolic reasoning, logic, and rule-based systems, as opposed to modern machine learning methods.

Compliance The adherence to externally imposed laws and regulations, as well as self-imposed company policies, behaviors, and norms.

Context The surrounding conditions, relationships, and environmental factors that influence the system's development and operation.

Conversational AI AI systems designed to understand natural language and engage in coherent, meaningful dialogues, focusing on language processing and maintaining context in conversation.

Decision Matrix A tool for evaluating multiple alternatives by assigning and comparing utility values to support informed decision-making.

Decision Table A structured way to represent a set of rules or conditions and their corresponding actions, often used to define decision logic in complex processes.

Deep Learning A subset of machine learning that uses multi-layered artificial neural networks to model complex patterns and representations.

Definition of Done (DoD) An agile development checklist of criteria that must be met for an increment or artifact to be considered complete and accepted.

Definition of Ready (DoR) An agile development checklist of criteria that a backlog item must meet before it is considered ready for implementation.

Design System A structured collection of reusable components, patterns, and guidelines that ensure consistent, efficient, and scalable user experiences across products and platforms.

Design Thinking An iterative, human-centered approach to problem-solving that fosters creativity and innovation through five phases: Empathize, Define, Ideate, Prototype, and Test.

Developer Message See System Prompt

Digital Product Development Lifecycle (DPDL) An extension of the Software Development Lifecycle (SDLC) that covers the creation of three artifact types: traditional software, agents, and agentic systems. In broader usage, it integrates technical execution with product strategy and lifecycle management.

Digital Product Creator A hybrid role in software development that integrates requirements, design, coding, testing, and deployment, often leveraging AI to streamline and accelerate delivery.

Few-Shot Prompting See Shot Prompting.

Foundational Models Large-scale, general-purpose AI models pre-trained on vast datasets and adaptable to a wide range of downstream tasks through fine-tuning.

Functional Requirement A requirement category that specifies what the system should do by defining its expected behaviors and functions.

GenAI Transformation Organizational change to adopt and scale generative AI, covering leadership, workforce, and governance.

Generative AI (GenAI) A branch of AI that learns patterns from data and generates new content, such as natural language, code, images, or other domain-specific outputs.

Gherkin A domain-specific language that uses structured syntax and predefined keywords to describe scenarios, commonly applied in defining acceptance criteria for user stories.

Golden Set A small, high-quality dataset used to rigorously test an AI system on specific, difficult, or important examples. It's often manually curated to include critical edge cases and challenges. This helps ensure the model is reliable and catches failures that a standard dataset might miss.

Graphics Processing Unit Originally designed for rendering graphics, GPUs excel at parallel data processing and complex matrix operations, making them highly suitable for training and running neural networks.

Green AI Practices to reduce the environmental impact of AI (e.g., optimizing model size, energy use).

ICIO Framework (Instruction, Context, Input, Output Indicator), a structured way to build prompts.

Item A requirement or task represented as a backlog entry in Scrum, managed within the Product Backlog or Sprint Backlog.

Kano Model A framework for classifying product features based on their impact on customer satisfaction, used to prioritize and evaluate requirements.

Key Performance Indicator (KPI) A measurable metric that defines a target performance value and enables comparison between actual and expected performance.

Large Language Model (LLM) An AI model trained on massive text datasets to generate human-like language by predicting the most probable next word.

Legal Obligation A requirement clause specifying whether implementation is mandatory, optional, or deferred to future product versions.

Machine Learning A subfield of AI focused on algorithms and statistical models that enable systems to learn from data and improve performance without explicit programming.

Method A systematic approach for solving problems using defined strategies, processes, or models, such as collection, analysis, modeling, or quality assurance methods.

Model An abstraction representing essential features of a real-world entity while omitting irrelevant details, tailored to a specific purpose or audience.

Model Context Protocol (MCP) A protocol that enables agents to securely interact with external tools and resources.

Neural Networks A machine learning model composed of interconnected layers (input, hidden, output) that autonomously detect complex patterns and relationships in large datasets.

Notation A structured way of representing requirements, which can be graphical, textual, or UI-based, depending on the context.

Object Management Group (OMG) An international organization that develops and maintains IT standards, including UML and BPMN.

One-Shot Prompting See Shot Prompting.

Operational Requirement A requirement category that defines conditions necessary for the stable and reliable operation of a software solution.

Persona A fictional profile representing a user group with shared characteristics, goals, or behaviors, commonly used in design and development.

Process Brief Clear and structured presentation of the essential points of a process. It is the preliminary stage to a process modeling.

Product Backlog An ordered list of product requirements in agile development, prioritized for incremental implementation.

Product Owner (PO) A Scrum role responsible for managing the Product Backlog and prioritizing its items to maximize product value.

Prompt Chains A sequence of interconnected prompts designed to solve complex tasks step by step.

Prompt Engineering The practice of designing and refining prompts to optimize the performance and output of language models.

Prompt Injection A security vulnerability where malicious input manipulates an AI model to ignore original instructions or perform unintended actions.

Quality Assurance (QA) A process that verifies stakeholder requirements are met, ensuring the quality and correctness of deliverables.

Quality Requirement A requirement category specifying quality attributes that a product must meet, such as performance, security, or usability.

RACE Framework A lightweight prompt design framework based on four elements: Role, Action, Context, and Expectation.

Request for Information (RfI) An initial step in the tendering process, requesting providers to supply details about their products or services.

Requirement A stakeholder's expressed expectation regarding the properties or functions of an IT system.

Requirement Category A classification system that groups requirements by defined criteria, such as functional, quality, constraint, operational, and solution design requirements.

Requirement Defect An error, omission, or absence of a requirement that could cause issues during solution development.

Retrieval-Augmented Generation (RAG) A technique that combines LLMs with external knowledge retrieval to enhance accuracy and contextual relevance.

Return on Investment (ROI) A business metric expressing the ratio of profit gained to capital invested.

Rule Set A collection of rules governing business processes, often documented in formats such as decision tables.

Runbook In generative AI, a structured set of instructions guiding an agent's behavior, intent, and steps to achieve a desired outcome.

Scrum An agile project management framework that organizes work into iterative cycles called sprints.

Self-Reflecting Reasoning A technique where models iteratively review and refine their own outputs to improve accuracy and coherence.

Sentence template A structured natural language pattern that prescribes sentence structure for requirements, aiming to reduce defects and improve clarity.

Service Level Agreement (SLA) A contractual agreement between a service provider and a customer that defines the expected service standards and performance metrics.

Shot Prompting A technique in which prompts include one or more examples to guide the model's output. This approach helps the model understand the desired format, tone, or reasoning process by providing concrete illustrations.

Solution Design A requirement category that groups requirements related to the design of a solution, such as its structure, components, and interactions.

Sprint Backlog A list of requirements or tasks in agile development that are planned to be implemented during a single sprint.

Stable requirement A requirement with a low probability of change. In contrast, a **volatile requirement** has a high probability of change.

Stakeholder A person or group that has an interest in, or provides requirements for, an IT solution. Stakeholders can be classified as **active** (directly involved) or **passive** (indirectly affected).

State Diagram A type of UML diagram used to represent the possible states of an object and the transitions between them. It is commonly applied to model status values and state changes of individual objects, such as a process ticket.

Story Points A unit of measure used by a Scrum team to estimate the relative effort and complexity of backlog items in agile development. Teams often use the Fibonacci sequence (1, 2, 3, 5, 8, 13, …) for assigning story points.

Surrounding system An external IT system that interacts with our system and requires corresponding interfaces. Surrounding systems form part of the overall system context.

Synchronous communication A communication method where both parties must be available at the same time to complete the exchange. If a response is missing, the process is blocked or terminated until the communication is completed.

System A combination of related IT applications, processes, actors, interfaces, and organizational elements that together form a coherent whole and can be distinguished from their environment (see **Context**).

System Card A transparency document for an AI system, similar to a nutrition label. It provides a comprehensive overview of the system's purpose, limitations, and risks. This tool is crucial for promoting accountability and informed use within the AI community.

System Prompt High-priority, persistent instructions that guide an AI system's behavior across interactions.

Traceability The ability to establish and maintain relationships and dependencies between requirements and related artifacts throughout the development lifecycle.

Transformers A neural network architecture designed for processing sequential data, widely used in natural language processing (NLP) and generative AI. Transformers leverage self-attention mechanisms to capture contextual relationships in data, enabling state-of-the-art performance in tasks such as translation, text generation, and more.

Trustworthy AI Artificial intelligence designed to operate ethically, transparently, and in alignment with human values. Trustworthy AI emphasizes principles such as fairness, accountability, explainability, privacy, and safety.

UI/UX-Design A collective term for techniques, methods, and notations aimed at creating a positive user experience and a clear, intuitive user interface, including the necessary design aspects of applications.

Unified Modeling Language (UML) A standardized graphical notation for modeling software systems, consisting of various diagram types such as class diagrams, sequence diagrams, and activity diagrams. UML is maintained by the Object Management Group (OMG).

Use Case A description of how a user (or another actor) interacts with a system to achieve a specific goal. Use cases capture functional requirements and typically include the main scenario, alternative flows, and exceptions.

Use Case Diagram A type of UML diagram used to represent use cases, actors, surrounding systems, and their relationships. It provides a high-level view of system functionality and interactions.

User Story A short, natural language description of a requirement from the perspective of a stakeholder, focusing on the value or goal for the user. In agile development, a user story can also refer to a backlog item planned for implementation in a sprint.

Utility Analysis An analysis method used to evaluate and compare alternatives based on defined criteria and their assigned weights, resulting in a calculated utility value for each option.

Vibe Coding An intuitive, fast-paced style of programming that emphasizes exploration, prototyping, and flow over strict planning or optimization. Closely linked to GenAI tools, vibe coding often involves leveraging AI-generated code and suggestions to accelerate creativity and experimentation.

Virtual Machine (VM) A software-based emulation of a physical computer that runs an operating system and applications. Virtual machines are managed by a hypervisor and are commonly used for testing, development, and running multiple isolated systems on a single physical device.

Walkthrough A quality assurance method in which stakeholders review a product or artifact to identify defects, ambiguities, or improvement opportunities. Walkthroughs are commonly used in agile development to ensure shared understanding and quality.

Way of Working (WoW) A defined approach to collaboration within an agile team or project, including agreed practices, processes, and tools. The term also refers to the document that describes these guidelines.

Web 2.0 A stage of the internet characterized by centralized platforms and services that collect and control user data in the cloud. It enables users to create and share content globally, for example through social media platforms.

Web 3.0 A decentralized, blockchain-based evolution of the web that emphasizes security, transparency, and user control over data. Web 3.0 often incorporates artificial intelligence and semantic technologies to enable smarter, more personalized interactions. Examples include the Decentralized Web and the Semantic Web.

The manufacturer's authorised representative in the EU is Springer Nature Customer Service Centre GmbH, Europaplatz 3, 69115 Heidelberg, Germany. If you have any concerns regarding our products, please contact ProductSafety@springernature.com

Printed and bound by CPI Group (UK) Ltd, Croydon, CR0 4YY
21/09/2026
02219989-0017